HAMLET AND THE PHILOSOPHY OF LITERARY CRITICISM

HAMLET AND THE PHILOSOPHY OF LITERARY CRITICISM

Morris Weitz

Meridian Books
THE WORLD PUBLISHING COMPANY
CLEVELAND AND NEW YORK

A Meridian Book
Published by The World Publishing Company
2231 West 110th Street, Cleveland, Ohio 44102

Published simultaneously in Canada by Nelson, Foster & Scott Ltd.

First Meridian Printing 1966

Reprinted by arrangement with The University of Chicago Press

Library of Congress Catalog Card Number: 64-22245

Printed in the United States of America

FOR MARGARET

Hamlet is also the cross-roads of Shakespearian criticism, at which all the highways and every conceivable lane and field-path seem to converge.

J. DOVER WILSON

INTRODUCTION

Criticism is a form of studied discourse about works of art. It is a use of language primarily designed to facilitate and enrich the understanding of art. Involved in its practice are highly developed sets of vocabularies, various sorts of procedures and arguments, broad assumptions, and a vast diversity of specific goals and purposes.

These assumptions, procedures, terms, and goals are perennially scrutinized by critics and by those philosophers who are interested in criticism as one area of aesthetic inquiry. Certain problems have come to be recognized as basic in the philosophy of criticism. Among them are: the meaning and legitimacy of the fundamental terms of criticism; the validation of critical utterance; the nature of critical disagreement; the nature of critical argument; and the primary function of criticism. Is criticism objective or subjective? Is it verifiable or mere expression of feeling? Are there absolute standards of evaluation? Is criticism important or trivial in the understanding of art? These are but some of the specific questions raised by critics or philosophers in the traditional philosophy of criticism. In criticism itself, whole schools have arisen and still arise giving large-scale answers to these particular questions and to the central question of the exact nature of criticism. Critics call themselves—but more often call their opponents—"impressionistic," "historical," "psychological," "biographical," "stylistic," and even "new," thinking that these labels characterize and distinguish their answers to the question: What is criticism?

Although philosophers may probe more deeply than critics these questions of objectivity, meaning, argument, and validation, however vague philosophers realize these questions are, they concur for the most part with the critics in this omnibus approach to the philosophy of criticism. What is criticism? is, for them, as central and clear a question as it is for the critics themselves.

I agree with the critics and philosophers that these traditional questions about the objectivity, meaning, justification, and function of critical utterance are important in the philosophy of criticism. But I cannot accept the persistent logical motivation of traditional philosophy of criticism that a definitive and univocal answer is forthcoming to the question, What is criticism? For, if we actually "look and see" (to borrow a phrase from Wittgenstein), i.e., if we examine what critics do in their essays of criticism instead of what they *say* they do in their philosophical moments or what philosophers sometimes say critics do or must do, we will uncover answers to what criticism is that are radically different from the traditional ones in the philosophy of criticism. Indeed, thinking about this discrepancy between what critics do when they criticize and what they or others say they do has led me to the writing of this book.

Hamlet is not very old as world literature goes. Nevertheless, in its three hundred and fifty year history, it has probably occasioned more critical writing than any other work of art. And the quality of this criticism is as excellent as its quantity is great; as the work of critics like Voltaire, Dryden, Pope, Johnson, Goethe, the Schlegels, Coleridge, Tolstoy, Bradley, T. S. Eliot, Dover Wilson, and many others, shows. Indeed, the whole corpus of *Hamlet* criticism includes some of the finest critical writing in Western thought. The range of this criticism is vast, for almost every viable critical approach or method or school has its major representative in the history of *Hamlet* criticism. Thus, the criticism of *Hamlet,* more than any other single instance, can serve as a test case of what criticism is, of its many procedures and problems.

My aim, then, is to investigate the traditional question, What is criticism? by focusing that question on the criticism of *Hamlet.* I am convinced that the major philosophical problems of criticism are fully present in this one corpus. The nature, meaning, and functions of the terms of criticism, the relation between criticism and poetics or aesthetics, the problem of the justification of aesthetic judgment, the nature of critical disagreement, the role of description, interpretation, explanation, evaluation, and poetics in criticism, the conflict between "schools" or "methods" of criticism, the problem of standards or criteria of evaluation of works of art, and the nature of critical argument—among others—are all present in their richest variety in the history of *Hamlet* criticism.

Some of this investigation of *Hamlet* criticism has already been done by critics and their historians. But these studies have not centered on the basic issues of that criticism, which are logical and, therefore, cannot be handled without the most meticulous and stringent of philosophical techniques. It is not my primary aim to present another running survey of, and commentary on, *Hamlet* criticism. Instead I shall concentrate upon the elucidation of the conceptual issues involved in the practices, doctrines, assumptions, and disagreements of the major critics of *Hamlet.*

Two illustrations perhaps will clarify my objective. Critics of *Hamlet* ask, for example: Is Hamlet mad? Is Gertrude an adulteress? or Does Hamlet vacillate? They then go on to ask, Why is Hamlet tragic? or Is Claudius tragic? They discuss and debate these questions, sometimes vehemently disagreeing with each other over the correct answers. Examination of the nature of these questions—from the point of view of their logic—discloses a crucial assumption that these critics make, around which much of their dispute and disagreement revolves. They assume with no indication of doubt whatever that these questions are of the same type, namely, factual ones that can be answered by references to data in the play. This assumption, I believe, rests upon an erroneous view of language according to which *all* questions are of the same type, namely, questions to which true (or false) answers can be given.

Elucidation of the logical status of these questions, as they function in *Hamlet* criticism, reveals great differences among them and, consequently, among the types of answers they may yield. Is Hamlet mad? Is Gertrude an adulteress? or Does Hamlet vacillate? is not like Is Claudius tragic? or Why is Hamlet tragic? The concept of the tragic is not like the concepts of madness, vacillation, or adultery. When the critics ask, Does Hamlet vacillate? in effect they are asking if the recognized, accepted criteria of vacillation apply to Hamlet. But when they ask, Is Claudius tragic? or Why is Hamlet tragic? their questions involve a debate on the very criteria of tragedy themselves, and not merely on whether any established set of criteria is applicable to Hamlet or Claudius. Thus, much critical dispute and disagreement are not only about the application of established criteria for concepts but involve fundamental debates over the criteria themselves. Hence, much critical talk is not factual; rather it attempts to redefine certain basic concepts, such as the tragic.

Consider another question that constantly arises in *Hamlet* criticism (indeed in all criticism), a question that brings us to the borders of poetics. What is central in *Hamlet:* character, plot, imagery, language, theme, etc.? Here, too, we do not have a question that can be answered by any simple reference to the data of the play. For what datum in *Hamlet* reveals itself as central in the way, say, that Hamlet's melancholy as a datum is revealed? The whole concept of centrality or of what is most important in any work of art is not factual; it is a concept that serves to explain, not to describe. Hence, there is no true (or false) answer to What is central in *Hamlet* (or any work of art)? It is simply a mistake to construe all questions in criticism as questions to which true or false answers can be given.

By philosophy of criticism, then, I mean the clarification of the conceptual apparatus of criticism. The truly big issues of criticism are in the logic of its concepts. Beneath the many procedures, doctrines, and disagreements of criticism are varying strands of logical tissues that must be delineated and separated before criticism can be understood and its problems resolved.

Some of this work of untangling the logical problems of critical discourse has already been done by philosophers. In recent philosophy, A. Isenberg, M. Macdonald, and especially C. L. Stevenson, have offered clarifications of certain aspects of criticism. Their work is a solid contribution to any further analysis. My objection to it, however, is that it is not concrete enough. Their discussions of critical terms, arguments, disagreements, and evaluation, finely wrought as they are, do not relate sufficiently to a living body of critical discussion. What is needed is a probing of these philosophical problems in the large empirical context of a whole corpus of criticism. Instead of beginning with problems of evaluation, disagreement, etc., then, I want to put these problems in a living context wherein their logical functioning can be concretely discerned. If I may paraphrase the title of one of Dover Wilson's books on *Hamlet*, my aim boils down to an investigation of what happens—logically, conceptually—in *Hamlet* criticism.

My goal, thus, is to elucidate the nature of criticism, to sort out the important logical differences among critical utterances, to clarify and, if I can, to solve the real issues involved in critical dispute, with the major corpus of *Hamlet* criticism as my touchstone. This elucidation is important to both philosophy and criticism. Its special significance, however, is interdisciplinary in that it attempts to bridge the contemporary gap between philosophy and the humanities.

Pursuant of my aim, I divide this study into two related parts. Part One consists of eleven chapters in which I try, through concise, systematic expositions of the doctrines of the major critics of *Hamlet*, to arrive at a correct statement of the main issues of *Hamlet* criticism. Part Two comprises seven chapters in which I attempt to clarify, through elucidations of certain key concepts, these issues. In Part One I quote the critics at length; to do so is absolutely necessary to render concrete some of the problems of criticism and philosophy of criticism. I hope that the reader is compensated for his patience with these many quotations by my efforts at precise and systematic analyses of the essays that contain them. Not to allow the critics to speak in their own full voice, I believe, is to prejudice my whole case. The discerning reader will also notice that my role in Part One is not merely metacritical, since I indulge in critical remarks of my own about *Hamlet*. Although I make clear in Part Two (chap. xiii) that these remarks function only to further a particular critic's argument and not at all to compete with him on the answer to a particular question about *Hamlet*, perhaps it is well to point out here that all my own observations on *Hamlet* are prompted solely by the desire to sharpen or to enlarge upon an argument of an individual critic. Consequently, when I cannot find other critics who reject specific doctrines or arguments of a particular critic, and when I feel that an objection may clarify an important issue, I venture objections of my own. But these are objections to certain views about *Hamlet*, not counterviews of my own about *Hamlet*.

Quotations from *Hamlet* are from the various editions referred to or employed by the individual critics in their essays on the play. Here again it seems more consistent with the ideal of the integrity of exposition of their views to incorporate their preferred editions than to substitute a different edition in order to achieve uniformity. However, wherever I could choose, I use Dover Wilson's edition, "The New Shakespeare" *Hamlet*, second edition, 1957 reprinting.

I wish to express my gratitude to the following for their aid in the writing of this book: the John Simon Guggenheim Memorial Foundation, for a Fellowship (1959–60), during which period of tenure I was able to revise and complete the manuscript; The Ohio State University, especially its Graduate School and its Committee on Research, for various grants; a host of friends, who not only read part or the whole of the manuscript in mimeographed form, but who gave unselfishly of their time and energy to bestow on this book whatever felicity it may have: Robert Elliott, Marvin Fox, Carl Ginet, Franklin Ludden, E. J. Nelson, Roy Harvey Pearce, Edward Penn, Alvin Scodel, Richard Severens, Andrew Wright, and my wife, to whom this book is dedicated.

Finally, I wish to state that the following kindly gave me permission to quote passages from their publications:

Cambridge University Press: *Shakespeare's Tragic Heroes*, by Lily B. Campbell; *The Manuscript of Shakespeare's Hamlet*, "The New Shakespeare" *Hamlet*, and *What Happens in Hamlet*, by John Dover Wilson.

The Clarendon Press: *Hamlet: Father and Son*, by Peter Alexander; *Essays of John Dryden*, 2 vols., edited by W. P. Ker; and *Johnson on Shakespeare*, edited by W. Raleigh.

J. M. Dent & Sons Ltd. and E. P. Dutton & Co., Inc.: *Coleridge's Shakespearean Criticism*, 2 vols., edited by T. M. Raysor.

George G. Harrap & Co. Ltd.: *Character Problems in Shakespeare's Plays*, by Levin Schücking.

The Macmillan Company, New York: *Shakespeare and the Nature of Man*, by Theodore Spencer, copyright 1942, 1949.

Macmillan & Co. Ltd., St. Martin's Press, Inc., New York, and The Macmillan Company of Canada Limited: *Shakespearean Tragedy*, by A. C. Bradley.

Methuen & Co. Ltd.: *The Wheel of Fire*, by G. Wilson Knight.

Methuen & Co. Ltd. and Harvard University Press: *The Development of Shakespeare's Imagery*, by W. H. Clemen.

W. W. Norton & Company, Inc., New York and Katherine Jones, M.A.: *Hamlet and Oedipus*, by Ernest Jones, M.D., F.R.C.P., copyright 1949.

Oxford University Press: *Leo Tolstoy: Recollections and Essays*, edited by A. Maude.

Sidgwick & Jackson and the Trustees of the late Harley and Helen Granville-Barker Estates: *Preface to Hamlet*, by Harley Granville-Barker.

M. W.

CONTENTS

PART ONE

PART TWO

PART ONE

I A. C. BRADLEY

A. C. BRADLEY'S discussion of *Hamlet*, in his *Shakespearean Tragedy* (1904), is an excellent starting point for this study in the philosophy of criticism.[1] For Bradley, the most important problem in the criticism of *Hamlet* is to provide an adequate explanation of the character of Hamlet in the play. He distinguishes, without analysis or argument, between character and plot, and proceeds to his major task, the delineation of Hamlet's character which he says is basic to any understanding of the plot and the play.

Bradley's distinction between character and plot is not his only assumption. He takes for granted other things—all very important—that have inspired much later criticism of *Hamlet*. Among them are that Hamlet's behavior is central in the play; that the concept of being artistically central is unambiguous; and that the Shakespearean text of *Hamlet*, from which the critic can derive the characterization of Hamlet, is relatively intact. As we shall see, each of these assumptions—all accepted by Bradley with such confidence that he never discusses them—is fundamentally challenged by later critics.

A correct explanation of Hamlet's character, Bradley says, begins inevitably with Hamlet's delay in avenging his father's murder. Here,

[1] A. C. Bradley, *Shakespearean Tragedy* (London, 1904; 2d ed., 1924). All references are to the second edition.

too, Bradley assumes, without question, that Hamlet's delay is an undeniable datum of the play. (This has been challenged also, most radically by G. B. Harrison: "In the play which Shakespeare wrote there was no delay."[2]) Bradley's initial critical problem then becomes that of giving an adequate explanation of the delay. His procedure is to state, test, and adjudicate various contending views regarding this problem.

There have been many "theories" (Bradley's term) of Hamlet's delay. Each purports to explain the relevant data of the play. Bradley dismisses all of them for the same reason: that none covers these data without distorting some of them. For example, according to one theory, Hamlet delays because of certain *external* difficulties—among them, the King's being protected by his guards or Hamlet's desire to bring the King to public justice. Bradley refutes this theory by appealing to the facts that Hamlet never states such a difficulty, he always assumes he can obey the Ghost, he never talks of public justice, and Laertes—less popular with the people than Hamlet—raises the people against Claudius with ease.

Other theories center on certain *internal* difficulties. One is that Hamlet delays because of his moral scruples. This, too, cannot be supported by the drama since, throughout it, Hamlet assumes that he ought to revenge his father and never mentions any moral scruple as a cause of his neglect. A more sophisticated version of this theory—that Hamlet has a deep moral repulsion to his task—cannot be reconciled with the dramatic data either, especially with the crucial scene of the King at prayer (III, 3); in this scene it is Hamlet's desire to see the King in hell and not Hamlet's moral scruples that saves the King. A third version of this theory is that Hamlet delays because he is, as Goethe conceives him, "a lovely, pure and most moral nature, *without the strength of nerve which forms a hero. . . .*"[3] Graceful, sweet, sensitive, and delicate, Hamlet is incapable of avenging anyone. Bradley accepts these qualities as Hamlet's but insists on the other qualities of cruelty, heroism, callousness, and cynicism—Hamlet's non-sentimental side. The Goethe theory fails, then, because it is based

[2] G. B. Harrison, *Shakespeare's Tragedies* (London, 1951), p. 109.

[3] Quoted by Bradley, *op. cit.*, p. 101 (Bradley's italics).

on an inadequate conception of the whole character of Hamlet as he is presented in the drama. Finally, there is the theory of Coleridge and Schlegel, that Hamlet delays because of his excessive reflectiveness: Hamlet is "thought-sick." As Coleridge expresses it, there is in Hamlet "an almost enormous intellectual activity and a proportionate aversion to real action consequent upon it. . . ."[4] Bradley concedes that much of the play supports this hypothesis, especially the soliloquies, the contrast between Hamlet and Laertes or Fortinbras, and Hamlet's state of mind in which "the energy of resolve is dissipated in an endless brooding on the deed required" (Coleridge).[5] Nevertheless, Bradley argues, the theory fails, because it rests on the assumption that Hamlet's irresolution is caused by his excessive intellectual activity; which in turn presupposes that excessive intellectual activity leads to irresolution and that Hamlet is excessively intellectual. Bradley denies these presuppositions and, with them, the particular hypothesis that Hamlet delays because of his thought-sickness. The theory "misconceives the cause of that irresolution which, on the whole, it truly describes. . . . The direct cause was a state of mind quite abnormal and induced by special circumstances,—a state of profound melancholy."[6] Thus, according to Bradley, the Coleridge-Schlegel theory is mistaken because it implies what is false, that Hamlet's procrastination is the normal response of an over-speculative person who is confronted by a difficult, practical problem.

This brings us to Bradley's own theory: that Hamlet delays because he is melancholy. Bradley formulates and confirms this hypothesis by clarifying and expanding upon Hamlet's melancholy, his delay, and the relation of the melancholy to various aspects of the plot. Consider, to begin with, Hamlet's personality before the play opens, i.e., his character before his mother's remarriage and his encounter with the Ghost. We know from the play that Hamlet, before his father's death, was not one-sidedly reflective. He was athletic, joyful, happy, fearless, idealistic, and open—even to the end of the play; he was intellectually alert and perceptive; and he was full of adoration for his father and mother. (Indeed, it will be important later to remember Bradley's

[4] Quoted by Bradley, *ibid.*, p. 105.
[5] Quoted by Bradley, *ibid.*, p. 106.
[6] *Ibid.*, pp. 107–8.

words about Hamlet's love for his father: "Where else in Shakespeare is there anything like Hamlet's adoration of his father? The words melt into music whenever he speaks of him.")[7] But Hamlet was also by temperament

> inclined to nervous instability, to rapid and perhaps extreme changes of feeling and mood, and . . . was disposed to be, for the time, absorbed in the feeling or mood that possessed him, whether it were joyous or depressed. This temperament the Elizabethans would have called melancholic.
>
> He [Shakespeare] gives to Hamlet a temperament which would not develop into melancholy unless under some exceptional strain, but which still involved a danger. In the play we see the danger realised, and find a melancholy quite unlike any that Shakespeare had as yet depicted, because the temperament of Hamlet is quite different.[8]

Now, Bradley argues, these traits and tendencies involve some danger but, in an ordinary life, not much, certainly not enough to produce a state of irresolution. Hamlet, however, was vulnerable; a great shock could turn his extraordinary gifts into vices. This shock was his mother's hasty marriage. "It was the moral shock of the sudden ghastly disclosure of his mother's true nature, falling on him when his heart was aching with love, and his body doubtless was weakened by sorrow."[9] His mother's sensuality—"rank and gross"—filled him with horror, loathing, and despair. If Hamlet had had a blunter moral nature, the shock would have been assimilated. But Hamlet's moral sensitivity and perceptiveness, provoked by his mother's behavior, drove him to the laceration of his soul. Hard upon his reaction to his mother's marriage come the revelation of the Ghost and the burst of the energy of revenge. But the melancholy has already taken over and Hamlet cannot act.

Thus, for Bradley, the only hypothesis that can adequately explain Hamlet's delay is Hamlet's melancholy—that he had a temperament given to brooding, instability, and obsession with the mood of the moment; and that this disposition or tendency is fully activated by the shock of his mother's marriage. The result is the delay: he is unable to

[7] *Ibid.*, p. 111. [8] *Ibid.*, p. 110. [9] *Ibid.*, p. 118.

execute the task laid upon him by the Ghost. Bradley, it should be noted, gives a dispositional rather than a causal or motive explanation of Hamlet's delay. That is, he does not mean that Hamlet's melancholy caused his delay—although he sometimes talks this way—but that Hamlet is the sort of person who, under certain circumstances, including one of shock, would act as he does.

That Hamlet is melancholic accounts for much in the play, especially his inaction, the "main fact." His tendency toward melancholy has become a state of mind. Hence, as the play opens, Hamlet's feeling is "one of disgust at life and everything in it, himself included. . . . Such a state of feeling is inevitably adverse to *any* kind of decided action."[10]

The melancholy also explains the incessant dissection of the assigned task, all the intellectual brooding emphasized by the Coleridge-Schlegel theory, as "symptoms of melancholy which only increased it by deepening self-contempt."[11] It also accounts for Hamlet's energy; his quickly decided actions; his savage irritability; and his callousness—these, too, are symptoms of melancholy. Finally, it explains Hamlet's lethargy, i.e., Hamlet's forgetting of his duty, as well as his inability to understand why he delays. "Why do I linger?" Hamlet asks at the sight of Fortinbras' army, or in response to the Player's emotion in Act II. "These are the questions of a man stimulated for the moment to shake off the weight of his melancholy, and, because for the moment he is free from it, unable to understand the paralysing pressure which it exerts at other times."[12]

Now, in accordance with his dictum that "the only way, if there is any way, in which a conception of Hamlet's character could be proved true, would be to show that it, and it alone, explains all the relevant facts presented by the text of the drama,"[13] Bradley offers further confirmation of his hypothesis by relating Hamlet's melancholy to the action of the plot. There are certain recognized crucial parts of the action that the "melancholy theory" (or any theory, for that matter) must explain. One of these is Hamlet's doubt regarding the genuineness of the Ghost at the end of the second soliloquy. For Bradley, this

[10] *Ibid.*, p. 122 (italics in original).
[11] *Ibid.*, p. 123.
[12] *Ibid.*, p. 127.
[13] *Ibid.*, p. 129.

is no genuine doubt but "an unconscious fiction," an excuse for Hamlet's delay and its continuance. Another is the "To be or not to be" soliloquy, which Bradley asserts is explicable only as Hamlet's expression of weariness at life, hence as part of his melancholy. The play scene is a further manifestation of Hamlet's melancholy, this time in the form of energetic action. "How characteristic it is that he appears quite as anxious that his speech should not be ranted as that Horatio should observe its effect upon the King!"[14] Even Hamlet's sparing of the King at prayer Bradley explains as an effect of Hamlet's melancholy; this, too, is an unconscious excuse for delay since the "Now might I do it pat" (III, 3, 73–74), Bradley contends, implies that Hamlet has no effective desire to kill the King. Moreover, this scene is the turning point of the tragedy because, after it, all the disasters, including Hamlet's own, follow ineluctably. Hamlet never reactivates himself, not even after his return from the pirate ship adventure. "The Hamlet of the Fifth Act shows a kind of sad or indifferent self-abandonment, as if he secretly despaired of forcing himself to action, and were ready to leave his duty to some other power than his own."[15] In the whole of the last act, Bradley concludes, Hamlet seems to behave in the manner that he describes to Laertes: " 'It is no matter:' *nothing* matters."[16]

So much for Bradley's theory. Primarily, he tries to answer the question, Why does Hamlet delay? as well as its correlatives: Why does he doubt the Ghost? Why does he spare the King at prayer? Why does he lacerate himself?—Why does Hamlet behave as he does? All are requests for explanations, and Bradley proceeds as we normally do in explaining human behavior. He formulates a hypothesis that can be precisely stated and tested, and which makes Hamlet clearer to readers than he would otherwise be. Here, then, for Bradley, criticism functions as explanation, where the explanation purports to be true and testable.

Readers of Bradley may ask at this juncture, Is his account true? Does Bradley explain the important data of the play? More particularly, Does Hamlet act as he does because he is, as a melancholic,

[14] *Ibid.*, p. 133.
[15] *Ibid.*, p. 145.
[16] *Ibid.*, p. 146 (italics in original).

disposed to excuses and rationalizations? Two difficulties notoriously call into question Bradley's whole hypothesis: (1) the doubting of the Ghost in the second soliloquy and (2) Hamlet's sparing of the King at prayer. Among the many critics who point up these difficulties in order to dispute Bradley, I choose A. J. A. Waldock. In his *Hamlet: A Study in Critical Method* (1931), Waldock argues that Hamlet's doubting of the Ghost, genuine doubt or not, is at least based on a legitimate ground, namely, the Elizabethan complexity of attitudes toward ghosts; and that Hamlet's sparing of the King at prayer or, more particularly, his "Now might I do it pat" does not at all show that Hamlet has no effective desire to kill Claudius. Bradley's reading, Waldock claims, is the very ecstasy of sophistication since what Hamlet says in effect is: "Here is the very opportunity I have been looking for, here and now is my chance."[17] For Waldock, then, the melancholy theory fails because it distorts two crucial data in *Hamlet* that cannot be explained as mere rationalizations.

Bradley turns from Why does Hamlet delay? and related explanatory questions to other aspects of criticism. To begin with, there is a series of succinct and penetrating descriptions of the various leading characters of *Hamlet*. Two such descriptions are given of Hamlet himself (in addition, of course, to the description of those qualities already mentioned, e.g., Hamlet's idealism, brutality, openness). First, there is Hamlet's habit of repeating words. "O, God! God!," "Thrift, thrift, Horatio," "Indeed, indeed, sirs," "Wormwood, wormwood," "Very like, very like," "Words, words, words," "Except my life, except my life, except my life," "Well, well, well." Bradley makes little of these repetitions except to ask: "Is there anything that Hamlet says or does in the whole play more unmistakably individual than these replies?"[18] Second, Bradley observes that Hamlet is extremely fond of quibbles and conceits, which Bradley interprets as tokens of a nimbleness and flexibility of mind and an imaginative humor that are characteristic of Hamlet. Bradley also does little with

[17] A. J. A. Waldock, *Hamlet: A Study in Critical Method* (Cambridge, 1931), p. 40. See also pp. 39, 46.

[18] Bradley, *op. cit.*, p. 149.

this observation; later Caroline Spurgeon and especially W. H. Clemen return to these quibbles, and construe them as among the basic clues for an adequate understanding of Hamlet.

Ophelia, Bradley describes as "simple, unselfish affection,"[19] and argues, against her detractors, that she behaves nobly, kindly, strongly, and not weakly at all, in her dealings with Hamlet. Gertrude, for Bradley, "had a soft animal nature, and was very dull and very shallow. She loved to be happy, like a sheep in the sun; and, to do her justice, it pleased her to see others happy, like more sheep in the sun."[20] Two other things are true of her, Bradley says: she was unfaithful to her first husband while he lived; and she was not privy to his murder. Claudius, Bradley describes as quick-witted, adroit, courteous, dignified, efficient, and not cruel or malevolent, but essentially a little man, having "the inclination of natures physically weak and morally small towards intrigue and crooked dealing."[21]

Finally, there is the Ghost, whose basic quality is his great majesty. He is no apparition, Bradley says, but

> the representative of that hidden ultimate power, the messenger of divine justice set upon the expiation of offences which it appeared impossible for a man to discover and avenge, a reminder or a symbol of the connexion of the limited world of ordinary experience with the vaster life of which it is but a partial appearance.[22]

Thus, the second kind of question Bradley raises as a critic of *Hamlet* is the purely factual one to which a true answer seems forthcoming: Is Hamlet mad or melancholic? Is Gertrude an adulteress? Is Ophelia honest? or, more generally, What are the salient features of the characters of *Hamlet?* Some of Bradley's most illuminating writing has to do with descriptions of these features.

Bradley's description and interpretation of the Ghost in *Hamlet* lead naturally to another dominant theme in his criticism of the play: *Hamlet* as a tragedy. His initial claim about the tragic in *Hamlet* is that its hero is the only tragic figure. "All the persons in *Hamlet* except the hero are minor characters, who fail to rise to the tragic

[19] *Ibid.*, p. 161. [20] *Ibid.*, p. 167. [21] *Ibid.*, p. 169.
[22] *Ibid.*, p. 174.

level."[23] Hamlet's melancholy is the center of the tragedy. But his melancholy is not equivalent to the tragic which, for Bradley, is the mystery inherent in human nature:

> Wherever this mystery touches us, wherever we are forced to feel the wonder and awe of man's godlike "apprehension" and his "thoughts that wander through eternity," and at the same time are forced to see him powerless in his petty sphere of action, and powerless (it would appear) from the very divinity of his thought, we remember Hamlet. . . . *Hamlet* most brings home to us at once the sense of the soul's infinity, and the sense of the doom which not only circumscribes that infinity but appears to be its offspring.[24]

The questions, Why is Hamlet tragic? and Why is he the only tragic figure in *Hamlet?* Bradley discusses in his powerful first lecture in *Shakespearean Tragedy.* Here Bradley deals with *Hamlet, Othello, King Lear,* and *Macbeth* in an attempt to relate their common properties to the fundamental nature of tragedy itself. He begins by asking, What is the tragic aspect of life as represented by Shakespeare, at least in these four tragedies? and ends by asking and answering, What is tragic at all?

Shakespearean tragedy has many characteristics: It is primarily concerned with one person, the hero, and his story and death. "It is, in fact, essentially, a tale of suffering and calamity conducting to death."[25] The suffering and calamity are exceptional, befalling a conspicuous person; they are unexpected, and they contrast with a previous glory and happiness. Hence, Shakespearean tragedy includes the medieval notion of the tragic as a total reversal of fortune, but it goes beyond this notion in that the hero's fall affects the welfare of the whole state.

> And when he falls suddenly from the height of earthly greatness to the dust, his fall produces a sense of contrast, of the powerlessness of man, and of the omnipotence—perhaps the caprice—of Fortune or Fate, which no tale of private life can possibly rival.[26]

[23] *Ibid.*, p. 159. [24] *Ibid.*, pp. 127–28. [25] *Ibid.*, p. 7.
[26] *Ibid.*, p. 10.

Further, Shakespearean tragedy does not simply happen but proceeds mainly from the actions of men. "The centre of the tragedy, therefore, may be said with equal truth to lie in action issuing from character, or in character issuing in action."[27] It also includes abnormal conditions of mind, the supernatural, and chance; but these are always subordinate to deeds that issue from character.

The heroes are all exceptional:

> Desire, passion, or will attains in them a terrible force. In almost all we observe a marked one-sidedness, a predisposition in some particular direction; a total incapacity, in certain circumstances, of resisting the force which draws in this direction; a fatal tendency to identify the whole being with one interest, object, passion, or habit of mind. This, it would seem, is, for Shakespeare, the fundamental tragic trait.[28]

The hero, although he need not be good, has "so much of greatness that in his error and fall we may be vividly conscious of the possibilities of human nature."[29] This greatness is connected with an impression of waste. And with this waste we are at the very center of the tragic:

> "What a piece of work is man," we cry; "so much more beautiful and so much more terrible than we knew! Why should he be so if this beauty and greatness only tortures itself and throws itself away?" We seem to have before us a type of the mystery of the whole world, the tragic fact which extends far beyond the limits of tragedy. Everywhere, from the crushed rocks beneath our feet to the soul of man, we see power, intelligence, life, and glory, which astound us and seem to call for our worship. And everywhere we see them perishing, devouring one another and destroying themselves, often with dreadful pain, as though they came into being for no other end. Tragedy is the typical form of this mystery, because that greatness of soul which it exhibits oppressed, conflicting and destroyed, is the highest existence in our view. It forces the mystery upon us, and it makes us realise so

[27] *Ibid.*, p. 12. [28] *Ibid.*, p. 20. [29] *Ibid.*, p. 22.

> vividly the worth of that which is wasted that we cannot possibly seek comfort in the reflection that all is vanity.[30]

In Shakespeare's universe, Bradley concludes, there is an ultimate power that sometimes converges on this tragic fact. This power is piteous, fearful, and mysterious, yet does not, in its dramatic representation, leave us crushed, rebellious, or desperate. Consequently, the universe of the tragedies is not a moral order, just and benevolent, nor is it dominated by fate. Nevertheless, almost all accounts of Shakespeare's tragic view of the world, Bradley points out, find tragedy in such a moral order or fate. Neither fatalism, nor rigid determinism, nor "poetic justice," Bradley counters, characterizes Shakespeare's universe. Rather the ultimate power is one that "shows itself akin to good and alien from evil,"[31] where "good" means "human excellence" and "evil" its opposite. In Shakespeare the source of tragedy is in every case evil. It is evil that violently disturbs the order of the world; and "this order cannot be friendly to evil or indifferent between evil and good, any more than a body which is convulsed by poison is friendly to it or indifferent to the distinction between poison and food."[32] But the essence of tragedy is that in the convulsion of evil, good suffers and is wasted: "There is no tragedy in its expulsion of evil: the tragedy is that this involves the waste of good."[33] Thus, the tragic fact in Shakespeare's dramatic universe is this mystery of good expelling evil and being destroyed in the very process.

> We remain confronted with the inexplicable fact, or the no less inexplicable appearance, of a world travailing for perfection, but bringing to birth, together with glorious good, an evil which it is able to overcome only by self-torture and self-waste. And this fact or appearance is tragedy.[34]

Bradley's third class of question in his criticism of *Hamlet*, then, is: Why is Hamlet a tragic figure? along with its correlatives, Why is Hamlet the only tragic figure in the play? What is the tragic fact in *Hamlet?* and What is tragedy? I believe it is correct to say that

[30] *Ibid.*, p. 23.
[31] *Ibid.*, p. 33.
[32] *Ibid.*, p. 34.
[33] *Ibid.*, p. 37.
[34] *Ibid.*, p. 39.

Bradley offers as answers to these questions what he considers to be true statements about the nature of certain facts in *Hamlet* and ultimately about the tragic fact in the world. His procedure is to present his purportedly true analysis of tragedy or the tragic fact in the world, then locate the dramatic representation of this fact in Shakespeare's dramas, enlarge upon the other features that Shakespeare includes in this representation and, finally, apply the properties of tragedy and its representation to *Hamlet* and its hero. Bradley's procedure here is a clear case of criticism merging with poetics: Why is Hamlet tragic? Bradley explains by his answer to What is the tragic? Tragedy is the mystery of the irretrievable, ultimate self-waste of spirit in the struggle between good and evil; Hamlet exemplifies (he is the only one in the play to do so) this mystery.

Bradley's account of the tragic in *Hamlet* also is challengeable. Many critics dispute his definition of tragedy, his conception of Shakespearean tragedy and the tragic fact in *Hamlet*. They reject his views on the ground that these views are false and offer counter-doctrines of their own that they claim to be true. These disagreements between Bradley and his critics on the issues of tragedy and *Hamlet* as tragic, especially as they involve problems of "true definitions," are important and crucial enough to deserve extensive discussion, which I reserve for a later chapter.[35] It will perhaps suffice here simply to point out that nowhere in this whole dispute does there seem to be any indication whatever that some of the issues may not yield a true or false answer.

In order to state further what Bradley does as a critic of *Hamlet*, I must now introduce and clarify briefly some familiar terms. Criticism, whatever else it is, is always talk about works of art. It may be talk about one work or many. As such, criticism may describe, analyze, relate, explain, or evaluate. The critic, even as he engages in any one of these modes, may go on to seek clarification or definition of his basic terms. Some of this search leads to poetics, some to aesthetics. The attempt to clarify or define his most general terms is a part of

[35] See chap. xvii.

aesthetics: What is art? What do works of art have in common? What is artistic greatness? How can we best analyze or talk about any work of art? These are some of the problems in aesthetics that critics sometimes raise and try to solve even in their critical essays on particular works of art. Further, each of the arts has its own basic problems; attempts to solve some of these have been called, since Aristotle, "poetics": What is drama? What is poetry? What is music? What is the tragic? What is metaphor? How can one best analyze or talk about the drama? These are a few of the problems of poetics. And these, too, are sometimes raised and purportedly solved by critics in their essays on particular works of art. Bradley is certainly one of many critics who include as integral parts of their critical essays fundamental excursions into poetics and aesthetics.

More particularly, Bradley, as a critic of *Hamlet*, engages in poetics when, as we have just seen, he offers a definition of tragedy. He also practices poetics in his attempt to answer the question, How can criticism best analyze *Hamlet* as a drama? *Hamlet*, he claims, can be best analyzed as substance, i.e., characters and plot, and form, i.e., construction and versification. Of course, he insists that the substance and form are organically related; the aesthetic implications of which he develops fully in his classic, "Poetry for Poetry's Sake."[36] But he also claims that what is most important in *Hamlet* is its substance, especially the character of the hero, around which everything else revolves.

Bradley's poetics of the drama, especially his view of the primacy of character and plot, have also been questioned. Some of his critics deny that *Hamlet* or any drama can be best analyzed into plot and character as the basic elements; others go further to suggest that Bradley's view of the centrality of Hamlet in the play constitutes a distortion of the play and of Shakespearean drama altogether. G. Wilson Knight and Francis Fergusson, as we shall see later, reject this feature of Bradley's poetics, i.e., his answer to How can criticism best analyze or talk about *Hamlet* as a drama? Knight and Fergusson do not challenge his distinction between plot and character, although they

[36] A. C. Bradley, "Poetry for Poetry's Sake," *Oxford Lectures on Poetry* (London, 1909).

refuse to separate them as sharply as Bradley; rather they subsume them under metaphor or ritual, which they claim illuminate the play as poetic drama better than the traditional plot and character.

Other problems in the philosophy of criticism are suggested by Bradley's poetics. First, what sort of question is What is the best set of methods or categories with which to discuss drama or any work of art? Is there a poetics or an aesthetics that guarantees the truth of such a set and consequent analyses of works of art? Second, Bradley raises the very important problem of the relation between criticism and poetic-aesthetic theory. For many critics, including Bradley, state or imply that no criticism is possible without a theory of art, or at least of the particular genre of art in question; without a doctrine of the defining properties of art or an art, that can function in critical analysis and evaluation, there can be no criticism. Even as a critic of *Hamlet*, when Bradley insists upon the primacy of character and plot in the play, he raises one great question in our inquiry into the philosophy of criticism: Does criticism need a poetics and an aesthetics? Bradley, for one, answers affirmatively.

There remains a final point about Bradley as a critic of *Hamlet*. It concerns what for many is central in criticism, namely, evaluation. Now, Bradley, like any other critic, does not discuss everything in the play. Instead, he makes a choice, which is to write about *Hamlet* (and the other major Shakespearean tragedies) in order "to increase our understanding and enjoyment of these works as dramas."[37] This choice precludes lengthy discussions of Shakespeare's life, the sources of the plays, plays other than the major tragedies, and even the qualities of style, diction, and versification of the four tragedies under review. Bradley's whole criticism of *Hamlet*, then, is avowedly incomplete. Which is to say that his criticism is determined, as it must be, and perhaps should be, by a *decision* to concentrate upon a few things in a work of art or works of art, although he realizes that there remains much, perhaps an inexhaustible amount, to be discussed.

Does Bradley, in choosing to analyze *Hamlet* as character and plot rather than, say, as versification or imagery, commit himself to an

[37] Bradley, *Shakespearean Tragedy*, p. 1.

evaluation of the play? Many critics and philosophers say yes, arguing that every critic, by virtue of his choice of what aspect or aspects of a work of art he is to talk about, thereby implies the worth of the object of his choice. Thus, the critic, even if he does not *say* of a work that it is aesthetically good or bad, nevertheless implies an evaluation of it in his very act of choosing to talk about it at all; from which it follows that all criticism is evaluative, if only on this level of implying that some aspect is more worthy of critical talk than some other aspect of the work in question.

The contention that criticism entails evaluation is a simple confusion that we shall do well to expose right at the beginning of our inquiry. To discuss X rather than Y or Z in any work of art, of course, is to imply that X is worth talking about. But it does not at all follow from its being worth talking about that it is aesthetically good. Evaluation of a work of art is saying that it is aesthetically good (or bad or indifferent), and it is in this sense that evaluation *can* play a role in criticism, but hardly a necessary one, as the traditional argument claims. The critic commits himself to *an* evaluation when he chooses to talk about something, just as the scientist does when he chooses his object of investigation. And just as the scientist's choice exists quite independently of his evaluation of what he is talking about, so does the critic's; neither need offer any evaluation of the particular object of his choice.

Now, in Bradley, there is a remarkable paucity of evaluation. His only explicit aesthetic assessments are of some of the elements in Shakespeare's plots which he judges to be defective. Nowhere in his criticism of *Hamlet* is the question that many would take to be basic—Is *Hamlet* a great work of art?—raised, let alone discussed. Of course, it goes without saying that he thought the answer to be an undeniable affirmative, which is probably why he did not spend time debating the merits of *Hamlet*. He takes for granted that *Hamlet* is a great drama and does not bother to give reasons for his assumption, choosing instead to answer other and, for him, more pressing problems in *Hamlet* criticism.

So much for our first example of criticism at work. I have tried to set forth, by means of a précis, the main ideas and procedures of one of the great critics of *Hamlet,* mostly in the critic's own language and categories. In my judgment, the most important point that emerges from this presentation is how multifarious criticism is. With Bradley on *Hamlet* as an example, we can now see that criticism includes at least description, explanation, and poetic-aesthetic theory and its application. Each of these activities, and more, too, seems to have its secure place in any total view of the nature of criticism. Questions as different as Why does Hamlet delay? Is Ophelia honest? Is Claudius tragic? What is Shakespearean tragedy? What is tragedy? What is the best way to talk about *Hamlet* as a dramatic work of art? How does *Hamlet* differ from *Othello?* and Is *Hamlet* a great work of art? also seem to stand as legitimate questions in critical inquiry.

II ERNEST JONES

I TURN next to Ernest Jones's *Hamlet and Oedipus* (1949).[1] His criticism of *Hamlet,* as he himself affirms, follows naturally from Bradley's, and is also primarily concerned with a correct explanation of Hamlet's behavior, especially with his vacillation in the play. Indeed, in Jones's essay, Hamlet's delay becomes practically the only problem, the importance of which is such that its explanation is a necessary condition of any assessment of the artistic greatness of Hamlet as a drama.

In his analysis of *Hamlet,* Jones makes two assumptions, both well-stated and argued for, and neither of which strikes us as initially implausible. The first is that all drama (and *Hamlet* in particular) is a representation of the actions of people in real life; and, consequently, that the motives and patterns of dramatized human behavior are subject to the same psychological laws as those of real-life behavior. As he expresses it:

> Characters are created whose impersonating representatives act and move on the stage, and we are asked to believe that they are living persons; indeed, the dramatist's success is largely measured by this criterion. . . .[2]

[1] Ernest Jones, *Hamlet and Oedipus* (New York, 1949). All page references are to this edition.

[2] *Ibid.*, p. 17.

> In so far and in the same sense as a character in a play is taken as being a living person, to that extent must he have had a life before the action in the play began, since no one starts life as an adult.[3]
>
> No dramatic criticism of the personae in a play is possible except under the pretence that they are living people, and surely one is well aware of this pretence.[4]

Jones's second stated assumption is that *Hamlet*, like any work of art, is the expression of deep-seated mental processes in the artist's unconscious; and, consequently, that his work can be related to these processes: "the source of Shakespeare's inspiration in the creation of Hamlet lay in the deepest, i.e., the oldest, part of his being. . . ."[5]

Jones's procedure, like Bradley's, is to state and test a number of reigning hypotheses about Hamlet's character. He recognizes three basic hypotheses, along with their subgroups:

> The first of these sees the difficulty about the performance of the task in Hamlet's character, which is not fitted for effective action of any kind; the second sees it in the nature of the task, which is such as to be almost impossible of performance by any one; and the third in some special feature of the task that renders it peculiarly difficult or repugnant to someone of Hamlet's particular temperament.[6]

Jones, relying mostly on Bradley's arguments, rejects the first two hypotheses and decides on one version of the third, the psychoanalytical. According to this hypothesis, Hamlet delays because the task reactivates certain mental and emotional processes that he has long repressed and which are too horrible for him to bear: "So far as I can see, there is no escape from the conclusion that the cause of Hamlet's hesitancy lies in some unconscious source of repugnance to his task."[7]

For Hamlet, to kill Claudius is to kill what he wished to destroy before—his father, as the rival for his mother's love. It is his infantile desire or incest with his mother as well as his desire to see his father dead, both long repressed by Hamlet, that are reactivated in him by his uncle's crime and incestuous marriage:

[3] *Ibid.*, pp. 18–19.
[4] *Ibid.*, p. 18.
[5] *Ibid.*, p. 120.
[6] *Ibid.*, p. 26.
[7] *Ibid.*, p. 127.

> The call of duty to kill his stepfather cannot be obeyed because it links itself with the unconscious call of his nature to kill his mother's husband, whether this is the first or second; the absolute "repression" of the former impulse involves the inner prohibition of the latter also.[8]
>
> Killing his mother's husband would be equivalent to committing the original sin himself, which would if anything be even more guilty.[9]

Jones's hypothesis about Hamlet's vacillation is, of course, derived from Freudian psychoanalytic doctrine; hence its plausibility depends at least in part on the adequacy of the general Freudian theory of psychoanalysis. Jones does not defend or detail the whole theory in his essay on *Hamlet;* instead, he sums up that portion of the theory that applies to Hamlet and his counterparts in real life. Thus, he begins, psychoneurosis is

> a state of mind where the person is unduly, and often painfully, driven or thwarted by the "unconscious" part of his mind, that buried part that was once the infant's mind and still lives on side by side with the adult mentality that has developed out of it and should have taken its place.[10]

In each of us, but especially in those who suffer from this state of mind, there are certain mental processes that are less accessible than others to consciousness. These processes are repressed yet work as dynamic forces always ready to become reactivated and, possibly, to produce internal mental conflict. Hamlet, Jones contends, is a clear case of this sort of mental conflict:

> How if, in fact, Hamlet had in years gone by, as a child, bitterly resented having had to share his mother's affection even with his own father, had regarded him as a rival, and had secretly wished him out of the way so that he might enjoy undisputed and undisturbed the monopoly of that affection? If such thoughts had been

[8] *Ibid.*, p. 90.

[9] *Ibid.*, p. 91. Harry Levin, with his usual felicity, sums up the Jonesian hypothesis: "It motivates Hamlet's delay by identifying him with Claudius, through whom he has vicariously accomplished the Oedipal feat of murdering his father and marrying his mother." *The Question of Hamlet* (New York, 1959), p. 65.

[10] Jones, *op. cit.*, p. 69.

> present in his mind in childhood days they evidently would have been "repressed," and all traces of them obliterated, by filial piety and other educative influences. The actual realization of his early wish in the death of his father at the hands of a jealous rival would then have stimulated into activity these "repressed" memories, which would have produced, in the form of depression and other suffering, an obscure aftermath of his childhood's conflict. This is at all events the mechanism that is actually found in the real Hamlets who are investigated psychologically.[11]

Thus, for Jones, Hamlet acts in the way that real-life Hamlets act under the strains of their oedipal complexes. Shakespeare leaves Hamlet's behavior as puzzling as it is and in need of an explanation, Jones adds, because Shakespeare was himself unconscious of what he projected in *Hamlet* of his own reactivated and formerly repressed oedipal processes.[12]

Jones employs his hypothesis that Hamlet is suffering from a specific neurosis to explain a number of relevant data of the play. His hypothesis makes clear, he claims, all of Hamlet's behavior: his inaction, taunts, lethargy, distractions, depressions, bad dreams, weariness, near-madness (which Jones diagnoses as a form of hysteria) and, most important, Hamlet's tortured conscience, the "hidden ground for shirking his task, a ground which he dare not or cannot avow to himself."[13]

It clarifies also the complexities of Hamlet's relations with both his mother and Ophelia, as well as his gradual rejection of women altogether: "The intensity of Hamlet's repulsion against woman in general, and Ophelia in particular, is a measure of the powerful 'repression' to which his sexual feelings are being subjected."[14]

And, Jones concludes, his hypothesis of course explains the main relation, in all its complexity, of Hamlet and Claudius. For Claudius has committed two crimes, incest and murder, which are intermingled in Hamlet's mind and loathsome to him, although it is the incest that he hates most. Hence, it is true that Hamlet detests Claudius,

> but it is the jealous detestation of one evil-doer towards his successful fellow. Much as he hates him, he can never denounce

[11] *Ibid.*, p. 70. [12] *Ibid.*, chap. vi. [13] *Ibid.*, p. 57.
[14] *Ibid.*, p. 86.

> him with the ardent indignation that boils straight from his blood when he reproaches his mother, for the more vigorously he denounces his uncle the more powerfully does he stimulate to activity his own unconscious and "repressed" complexes.[15]

Jones's criticism of *Hamlet,* thus, is almost entirely an attempt at an explanation of the hero in relation to the other characters and the action of the plot. For Jones everything is clear and, as he suggests, the riddle of the sphinx of modern literature is solved.

Is it? There is one serious doubt, that has to do with Jones's *absolute* silence about one datum of the play, namely, Hamlet's relation to his father and his father's spirit after the play opens, when, that is, he is an adult. How does Jones, on his hypothesis, explain Hamlet's expressions of love and adulation for his father? Remember Bradley's words: "Where else in Shakespeare is there anything like Hamlet's adoration of his father? The words melt into music whenever he speaks of him."[16]

I find it incredible that Jones does not even *mention* this fact of the text, i.e., Hamlet's own words concerning his father. (It is equally amazing that no critic of Jones, at least none that I have been able to find, comments on this silence.) Surely Hamlet's expressions of love for his father are sufficiently important in the text to be accounted for or explained by any theory that purports to make the whole play clear. Why, then, is Jones silent on this issue?

One answer that suggests itself and is, I think, consistent with Freudian theory and Jones's assumption of the drama as a representation of life, is that Hamlet's expressions of love and adulation for his father are some sort of *cover-up,* unknown to him, for his infantile, repressed hatred of his father as the successful rival for his mother's affection. "The real Hamlets who are investigated psychologically"—to use a phrase of Jones's—seem to act in this way; that is, young men with unresolved oedipal complexes do have a tendency to cover up their guilts about their hatred of their fathers by talking as eloquently as Hamlet does about his father. Indeed, Hamlet, as Jones's patient, would no doubt prove excellent material for psychoanalysis, and Jones's presumption would prevail that Hamlet must really hate his

[15] *Ibid.,* p. 88.

[16] Bradley, *Shakespearean Tragedy,* p. 111.

father and his father's memory very deeply to need to talk so exaggeratedly about his father's virtues.

I am very far from expert on the exact explanation (and treatment) of a real Hamlet who talks the way the stage Hamlet does about his father, but I think I am right in saying that the similar words of a real Hamlet would be quite suspect and interpretable as indicative of some deeper feeling, associated not with love but with hate or perhaps a mixture of both.

Now, if my extension, or any sounder extension along Freudian lines, is correct, what are we to reply? Does it explain Hamlet's love for his father? Or does it deny his love altogether by explaining it away? These questions are important, I believe, because they raise a basic issue in critical method: Can we accept an interpretation of *Hamlet*, or of any play, that—with no textual evidence in the play to warrant it, and with much textual evidence in the play not to warrant it—asks the reader to controvert, or to change into its very opposite, some given part of the text and its obvious ostensible meaning? No

Consider, for example, Iago's relations with Othello. Iago expresses his love for Othello; yet we know that he is lying, that he really hates Othello. But we do not know this or infer it from a theory of people like Iago; we know it simply from other passages in *Othello*, other textual evidence. That Iago hates Othello is a given fact in the play that no theory of *Othello* can explain away by resolving the hatred into something else.

In *Hamlet* there is no textual evidence that Hamlet is lying or even deceiving himself, consciously or unconsciously, about his love for his father. Hence there is no reason to say that Hamlet in the play does not love his father exactly as he says he does. His love stands as an incontrovertible datum that requires no explanation for it raises no problem. Does Hamlet love his father? is not a problem for criticism in the way that Does Hamlet love Ophelia throughout the course of the play? is and remains a problem. In *Hamlet* (or any play), there are certain obvious, given, textual data. There is Hamlet's love for Horatio, his hatred for Claudius, his love, at least at times, for Ophelia, his mixed feelings for Gertrude. No reading of the play can legitimately ask us to reject these data or distort them by means of particular explanations. In real-life situations, I suppose, we are prepared to accept explanations of emotions that convert them into something else, even into their very opposites; no real-life Hamlet, let us grant, could love his father and yet act and feel toward a real-life Gertrude or Claudius as the stage Hamlet does in the play. But in Shakespeare's *Hamlet* we must accept what may in real life appear strange and implausible. We have no alternative except to open up the possibility of reading any datum of any text in any way that we like. And, clearly, that way lies chaos, not criticism. Jones, I conclude, fails in his theory or critical job of explaining *Hamlet* because he does not, and, so far as I can see, cannot, account for the inexpugnable textual fact that Hamlet loves his father, without reducing that love to a travesty. Whatever Hamlet protests too much about, he does not about his father.

Although Jones's main concern as a critic of *Hamlet* is to provide a scientific, true explanation of one aspect of the play, his criticism also includes some elements of poetic theory. He, too, offers an answer to the question, What is the best way to analyze *Hamlet* (or any drama)? Our categories of analysis, according to Jones, must be derived from our understanding of parallel life situations. Indeed, in Jones's whole criticism of *Hamlet* this doctrine of drama as a representation of life is basic, for it is with the aid of this doctrine that he affirms that drama, including *Hamlet,* is analyzable best as a representation of real-life situations.

J. Dover Wilson most fundamentally challenges Jones on this approach to *Hamlet* and drama. Wilson does not disagree with Jones's explanation of Hamlet-like people in real life or with psychoanalytic theory, only with Jones's poetics of the drama as a representation of life. "A fundamental misconception," Wilson writes, "vitiates this and most previous attempts of the kind: that of treating Hamlet as if he were a living man or a historical character, instead of being a single figure, if the central figure, in a dramatic composition."[17] To which, Wilson adds:

[17] J. Dover Wilson, "The New Shakespeare" *Hamlet* (2d ed.; Cambridge, 1957), pp. xliv–xlv.

> Apart from the play, apart from his actions, from what he tells us about himself and what other characters tell us about him, there is no Hamlet. . . . Critics who speculate upon what Hamlet was like before the play opens . . . or attribute his conduct to a mother-complex acquired in infancy, are merely cutting the figure out of the canvas and sticking it in a doll's-house of their own invention.[18]

Jones and Wilson, then, suggest another fundamental issue in criticism: Is drama a representation of life and to be comprehended and analyzed as such? Jones answers affirmatively; Wilson, negatively. Is either critic correct? Or are there other alternatives? I shall return to this issue in due course.

[18] *Ibid.*, pp. xlv–xlvi. In *What Happens in "Hamlet"* (Cambridge, 1951), p. vii, Wilson again attacks Jones's poetics: "To abstract one figure from an elaborate dramatic composition and study it as a case in the psychoanalytical clinic is to attempt something at once wrong in method and futile in aim."

III G. WILSON KNIGHT

G. WILSON KNIGHT, our third example, writes about *Hamlet* in his book, *The Wheel of Fire* (1930).[1] His criticism differs in method and scope from that of Bradley and Jones. Instead of beginning with the application of certain categories for the understanding of drama, such as character or plot, as Bradley and Jones do in order to proceed to their major task of the explanation of *Hamlet*, Knight starts with a lengthy exposition and justification of a particular poetics of Shakespearean drama which he then applies to *Hamlet*.

His problem, as he sets it, is to give a correct reading of the play. He prefers to call this task "interpretation" rather than "criticism," restricting the latter to comparison and evaluation. But this usage seems unnecessary, as he himself admits,[2] and I prefer to construe what he calls "interpretation" simply as one part of the critical enterprise, with evaluation and comparison among the other parts. This will be less confusing than his redefinitions and will not in any way, I believe, distort his aims. Thus, for Knight, the primary task of the critic of *Hamlet* is to give an interpretation of it. This is equivalent to understanding the play.

[1] G. Wilson Knight, *The Wheel of Fire* (London, 1930; 5th ed. revised, New York, 1957). All references are to the fifth revised edition.

[2] *Ibid.*, p. 16.

For Knight, the interpretation of *Hamlet* rests upon a correct theory of the nature of Shakespearean drama. Without such a poetics, interpretation or understanding of *Hamlet* is impossible. The best introduction to Knight's poetics of Shakespearean drama, I think, is contained in his lecture, "Tolstoy's Attack on Shakespeare" (1934), reprinted in *The Wheel of Fire*. Knight writes:

> We have not understood Shakespeare. And our error has been this: a concentration on "character" and realistic appearances generally, things which do not constitute Shakespeare's primary glory; and a corresponding and dangerous, indeed a devastating, neglect of Shakespeare's poetic symbolism.[3]

Character and plot are not ultimate in Shakespeare's dramas, but aspects of something larger, what Knight identifies as the space-time reality of the play. In each of the plays, he says in his first chapter, "On the Principles of Shakespeare Interpretation," there is

> a set of correspondences which relate to each other independently of the time-sequence which is the story: [e.g.,] . . . the death-theme in *Hamlet*. . . . This I have sometimes called the play's "atmosphere."[4]

The characters and plot are fused with this set of correspondences. Characters, thus, obey spatial as well as temporal necessities; the recognition of these spatial aspects does much to minimize the finding of "faults" in character development. "In Shakespeare there is this close fusion of the temporal, that is, the plot-chain of event following event, with the spatial, that is, the omnipresent and mysterious reality brooding motionless over and within the play's movement. . . ."[5] Beneath the surface of character and plot (the temporal) is "that burning core of mental or spiritual reality [the spatial] from which each play derives its nature and meaning."[6] In its basic spatial character, each Shakespearean play is "an expanded metaphor, by means of which the original vision has been projected into forms roughly correspondent with actuality. . . ."[7] These forms can be

[3] *Ibid.*, pp. 271–72.
[4] *Ibid.*, p. 3.
[5] *Ibid.*, pp. 4–5.
[6] *Ibid.*, p. 14.
[7] *Ibid.*, p. 15.

conceived as themes, for example, the hate-theme or death-theme, which are the inner core or essence of the play.

Thus, for Knight, each Shakespearean drama has an ultimate nature consisting of the spiritual, symbolic, or thematic element—the spatial—in which the characters and plot—the temporal—are fused. The basic, defining character of each drama is its static, pervasively thematic element. According to Knight, this definition of Shakespearean drama is the true analysis of its nature or essence and, by implication, a correct statement of what, for example, *Hamlet* essentially is as a drama.

Criticism as interpretation is then defined by Knight in terms of his definition of drama: Interpretation is the mode of understanding drama in which one grasps its spatial-temporal reality. It tries to arrive at "the true focus" of the play, at "the very essence of the play concerned."[8] Interpretation is an attempt to reconstruct the poet's vision, not by understanding the poet but his creation; by trying "to understand its subject in the light of its own nature, employing external reference, if at all, only as a preliminary to understanding."[9] It sees "the whole play laid out, so to speak, as an area, being simultaneously aware of these thickly-scattered correspondences in a single view of the whole. . . ."[10] It is metaphysical, aiming at a comprehension of the organic reality of the work of art before it.

Negatively, interpretation involves the rejection of inquiries into the intentions of the poet in his composition of the work, into the sources of the play, and into the ethical aspects of the characters and their motives in the play, on the same ground that these inquiries "impose on the vivid reality of art a logic totally alien to its nature."[11]

Interpretation, to sum up, is the attempt on the part of the critic to elucidate the basic, controlling, thematic pattern of a play; if it expresses the reality of the play, then the concrete elucidation can be said to be the *true* interpretation or reading of the play.

Hamlet can now be interpreted; its spiritual core, that which defines it as a drama, can be grasped, and meaning can be given to the

[8] *Ibid.*, p. 2. [9] *Ibid.*, p. 1. [10] *Ibid.*, p. 3.
[11] *Ibid.*, p. 7.

whole play only by the interpreting mind. Knight thus offers his interpretation, and this he claims is the true reading of the play. The central reality of the play, according to Knight, is the conflict between good and evil, health and disease, life and death.[12] But with Hamlet as its hero, the theme of death is primary and determines all the correspondences of the play as well as the characters and plot: "Death is indeed the theme of this play, for Hamlet's disease is mental and spiritual death."[13] The play, in effect, represents the triumph of mortality over life.

> Except for the original murder of Hamlet's father, the *Hamlet* universe is one of healthy and robust life, good-nature, humour, romantic strength, and welfare: against this background is the figure of Hamlet pale with the consciousness of death. He is the ambassador of death walking amid life.[14]
>
> In the universe of the play—whatever may have happened in the past—he is the only discordant element, the only hindrance to happiness, health, and prosperity: a living death in the midst of life.[15]

Claudius and the court, on the other hand, symbolize life and health. "They are of the world—with their crimes, their follies, their shallownesses, their pomp and glitter; they are of humanity, with all its failings, it is true, but yet of humanity."[16] It is Denmark and the world that are well, as human well-being goes, and it is only Hamlet who is sick. Such is Knight's "fundamental apprehension" originating, as he says, "from a centre of consciousness near that of the creative instinct of the poet."[17] Claudius "is not drawn as wholly evil—far from it."[18] His government works smoothly. He shows great tact to his courtiers, a genuine concern for his wife, and even kindness, at least at the beginning, to Hamlet. "He is—strange as it may seem—a good and gentle king, enmeshed by the chain of causality linking him with his crime. And this chain he might, perhaps, have broken except for

[12] Knight discusses the "life-themes" in his essay, "The Rose of May," *The Imperial Theme* (London, 1931). His interpretation in this essay supplements but does not contradict anything on *Hamlet* in *The Wheel of Fire.*

[13] Knight, *The Wheel of Fire*, p. 28. [14] *Ibid.*, p. 32.

[15] *Ibid.*, p. 40. [16] *Ibid.*, p. 34. [17] *Ibid.*, p. 33. [18] *Ibid.*

Hamlet, and all would have been well."[19] He even rises to greatness, Knight says, after the play scene in his prayer: "the fine flower of a human soul in anguish," perhaps closer to heaven in that scene than the murder-seeking Hamlet.[20]

In contrast to Claudius and the others, except the Ghost, Hamlet is inhuman.

> He is a superman among men. And he is a superman because he has walked and held converse with death, and his consciousness works in terms of death and the negation of cynicism. He has seen the truth, not alone of Denmark, but of humanity, of the universe: and the truth is evil. Thus Hamlet is an element of evil in the state of Denmark.[21]

Hamlet is dominated by "the poison of negation, nothingness, threatening a world of positive assertion."[22]

Death, thus, is the theme of *Hamlet* and the shadow of death looms over the play from the beginning to the end. Hamlet, ultimately, reflects the theme. In order to pluck out the heart of his mystery, therefore, we must focus on the sickness of his soul. All the problems and difficulties about Hamlet's character, Knight claims, can be explained in the context of Hamlet's symbolization of death. When we first meet him, he has already lost all sense of purpose and is spiritually atrophied. His father's death and his mother's second marriage, as his first soliloquy reveals, provoke his state of despondency. "His hope of recovery to the normal state of healthy mental life depended largely on his ability to forget his father, to forgive his mother. Claudius advised him well."[23] Then Hamlet encounters the Ghost who asks for revenge, not forgetfulness or forgiveness. But

[19] *Ibid.*, p. 35.

[20] *Ibid.*, p. 36. Cf. Bradley: "When he [Claudius] is praying for pardon, he is all the while perfectly determined to keep his crown; and he knows it. More —it is one of the grimmest things in Shakespeare, but he puts such things so quietly that we are apt to miss them—when the King is praying for pardon for his first murder he has just made his final arrangements for a second, the murder of Hamlet. But he does not allude to that fact in his prayer. If Hamlet had really wished to kill him at a moment that had no relish of salvation in it, he had no need to wait." (*Shakespearean Tragedy*, p. 171 and n. 1.).

[21] Knight, *The Wheel of Fire*, p. 38.

[22] *Ibid.*, p. 41.

[23] *Ibid.*, p. 19.

Hamlet is already condemned. He cannot act and is left a sick soul, commanded to heal. Ophelia, his last hope from neurotic despair, fails him, and Hamlet is finished. Bitterness, cynicism, detestation of life, and hate become his trappings. "He does not avenge his father's death . . . because his 'wit's diseased' (III, 2, 341); his will is snapped and useless, like a broken leg. Nothing is worth while."[24] Hamlet remains until almost the end in "a continual process of self-murder. . . ."[25] From cruelty, wanton torture, and insult, he becomes more and more the symbol of death. He vacillates, but only in the revenge and not in the prosecution of his father's final bequest,

> Adieu, Adieu, Hamlet, remember me [I, 5, 91].

Hamlet "obeys it, not wisely but only too well."[26] He does nothing except remember his father's ghost. Hamlet says:

> The Spirit that I have seen
> May be the Devil. . . . [II, 2, 635]

> It was.
>
> It was the devil of the knowledge of death, which possesses Hamlet and drives him from misery and pain to increasing bitterness, cynicism, murder, and madness.[27]

In the dramatic universe of the play, then, Hamlet symbolizes the principle of the negation of life pitted against the world of affirmation.

Knight's criticism of *Hamlet,* thus, is a combination of a poetics, a theory of interpretation, and a particular reading of the play. What, now, shall we say of this criticism? At least one thing must be said immediately: His entire criticism, both in theory and practice, is not true. Consider, to begin with, his particular interpretation of *Hamlet.* Is it the true one? Does what he says about the fundamental thematic core of *Hamlet* correspond to the core of the play, assuming, for the moment, that *Hamlet* has a core that determines everything else in the play? There are very serious doubts. First, Knight's conception of the *Hamlet* universe as one of health, strength, and humanity, with Hamlet the only sick individual in it, seems utterly perverse and about as far from "the poet's centre of consciousness" as one could get. If

[24] *Ibid.,* p. 23. [25] *Ibid.,* p. 26. [26] *Ibid.,* p. 30. [27] *Ibid.,* p. 39.

anything, as Francis Fergusson, among others, points out, it is the other way round. The *Hamlet* universe, which includes the court, is corrupt, unhealthy, rotten, founded on murder and incest, and Hamlet is the healthy one seeking, not decisively to be sure, to uncover and scourge the hidden imposthume. Now, I am not claiming that this latter view is correct, only that whatever the core or spiritual reality of *Hamlet* may be—if it has one—Knight makes a moral mockery of it by his reversal of sickness and health. After all, it is Claudius, not Hamlet, who is the usurper in the *Hamlet* universe.

Second, Knight's conception of Hamlet as the principle of negation, the symbol of death, of anti-life, is too narrow. Hamlet is surely more than that, however one interprets the rest of him. Bradley seems much closer to the truth—if there is *the* truth about Hamlet's spiritual reality in the play—when he interprets Hamlet as a symbol, not of negation but of the vastness and mystery of our spiritual world, a world in which such greatness of soul as Hamlet's can destroy itself in its struggle against evil. Again, I am not contending against Knight that Hamlet *is* a symbol of vastness, but only that, if Hamlet can be said to symbolize anything, a different interpretation is possible. How one decides or can decide which is the true interpretation, or whether one can so decide, I shall discuss later. All I wish to maintain at this stage is that one can certainly decide when a particular interpretation is woefully inadequate, namely, when it distorts or omits some of the obvious facts of the play and, in this particular case, Hamlet's *non*-negative attitudes toward life and the world.

Thus, third, Knight does not grasp the sets of correspondences that he himself seeks in *Hamlet*. On his own theory of interpretation, there is more to be understood than he perceives. He reduces the reality of the play to certain "spatial" themes: good versus evil; health versus disease; life versus death. But the play clearly offers a richer prospect than these polarities. If a spiritual atmosphere be required, why not one that encompasses the infinite vastness and the infinitesimal comprehensibility of our human experience, which are dramatized in the play—an infinite vastness and an infinitesimal comprehensibility that seem to defy the possibility of their reduction to a single formula? Surely, in considering what is fundamental in *Hamlet*, this fact of the glorious range of human experience is part of the fascination of the play and can be located in it.

For these three reasons, Knight's particular interpretation of *Hamlet* seems to me to be not true. It omits areas of the play that demand interpretation and it distorts, at times to the point of travesty, the areas that it surveys.

What about his theory of interpretation? First, it is important to point out that although Knight joins his theory with a particular interpretation of the play they are logically distinct. That is, one can accept or reject his theory of interpretation without necessarily accepting or rejecting his particular reading of the play. For example, one could agree that interpretation in criticism aims at the core of the play and then deny that Knight gets at this core. I have already shown, I think, that Knight does not grasp the possibilities of the scope of *Hamlet*. I wish now to raise questions about interpretation altogether.

Knight's definition of interpretation as the apprehension of the spiritual reality of the play implies that this reality is in the play, *there* to be grasped by the interpreter in the "light of its own nature." But what can this mean? Once more, we are up against the question of what is central in a work of art. Is this a factual question, to be settled by looking and apprehending? There are questions about *Hamlet* that can be decided in this way, for example, about some of Hamlet's physiological or psychological traits. But, What is the core, or central or spiritual reality, in *Hamlet?* cannot be decided in this way. We do not find, it seems to me, the spiritual reality of a play by any mode of apprehension. Instead, what we do, when we interpret a play, is formulate a hypothesis about what is central and then use this hypothesis to clarify everything else. A play has characters, dialogue, plot, moods, perhaps stated themes, but nothing that is its true essence, which we can discover in the light of its own nature. It is the critic who projects this centrality or essence onto the data so that these data are thereby unified by means of *his* hypothesis about the play.

Knight's theory of interpretation, I am contending, is not correct, for he claims that interpretation is a mode of understanding drama that is autonomous: it depends on nothing except seeing the play "in the light of its own nature." But interpretation is not autonomous, since it is defined in the light of a theory of Shakespearean drama (e.g., Knight's) that is employed to explain all of *Hamlet*. What Knight means by interpretation, then, is a mode of explanation by which the critic seeks an explanation of the *whole* play and not, say, merely of one of the characters in it. Interpretation, hence, is not a theory but a maxim: To criticize a drama of Shakespeare's, always seek a hypothesis which will clarify and relate all the various constituents in it. This problem of the independent status of interpretation as against explanation raises another basic issue in criticism. I shall return to it in chap. xv.

Finally, let us examine Knight's poetics of Shakespearean drama. Knight's theory of interpretation is based upon his theory of Shakespearean drama. Or, to put it in the language I suggest above, his mode of explaining Shakespearean plays by their spiritual realities is derived from the assumption that these plays have these realities and that these are their defining property. Knight's poetics of Shakespearean drama, then, is that each of the dramas has a spiritual (thematic) reality, and that this reality is more important than characters or plot or anything else.

Here again, we must raise fundamental questions: (1) Are his defining terms of poetic drama clear? What does he mean by "atmosphere," "spiritual," "burning core of mental and spiritual reality," and "spatial?" Are these more than vague, metaphorical terms? (2) Is his definition true? How could one prove that themes are basic in Shakespeare's dramas? (3) Is his claim true that the spiritual, the spatial, or the sets of correspondences are more important than character and plot? Rather, does not his definition of Shakespearean drama function not as a true statement of the essence of this drama but as a *recommendation* to look at Shakespearean drama in a certain way: to see theme in it as more important than character and plot? My own opinion is that Knight has not given a real definition, i.e., a true statement of the necessary and sufficient properties of this drama, but that, in the disguise of a definition, he has proffered a strong recommendation to attend to the themes of Shakespearean dramas rather than to anything else for the formulation of basic hypotheses about the meaning of the individual plays.

IV T. S. ELIOT

FOR T. S. ELIOT, in his short but remarkable essay, "Hamlet" (1919),[1] the primary concern of the critic of *Hamlet* should be to study the whole play, compare it with others, and evaluate it. In his insistence upon evaluation rather than interpretation, and in his preoccupation with *Hamlet* the play instead of Hamlet the hero, he harks back to the seventeenth and early eighteenth century critics of *Hamlet* and Shakespeare.

As Eliot engages in it, evaluation of *Hamlet* comprises making a judgment of the artistic merits of the play, giving reasons for his judgment, and providing an explanation of the play's failure. For Eliot begins his assessment of *Hamlet:* "So far from being Shakespeare's masterpiece, the play is most certainly an artistic failure."[2] Indeed, it is the "Mona Lisa" of literature, more an interesting than a great work of art.

Eliot offers three reasons for his negative judgment. First, the play is not consistent in its versification. Second, it contains "unexplained scenes—the Polonius-Laertes and the Polonius-Reynaldo scenes—for which there is little excuse."[3] Third, and most important, much of the

[1] T. S. Eliot, "Hamlet," *Selected Essays* (London, 1932). This essay was first published under the title, "Hamlet and His Problems," *The Athenaeum*, No. 4665 (1919). All references are to the revision in *Selected Essays*.

[2] Eliot, *Selected Essays*, p. 143. [3] *Ibid.*

action of the play is in excess of its essential emotion. This is the only reason Eliot enlarges upon. In the play that Shakespeare wrote, the essential emotion "is the feeling of a son towards a guilty mother."[4] But Hamlet "is dominated by an emotion which is inexpressible, because it is in *excess* of the facts as they appear."[5] What has gone wrong, Eliot says, is that Shakespeare has not found an "objective correlative" for this emotion, i.e.,

> a set of objects, a situation, a chain of events which shall be the formula of that *particular* emotion; such that when the external facts, which must terminate in sensory experience, are given, the emotion is immediately evoked.[6]

Macbeth, for example, does contain this exact equivalence. Lady Macbeth's state of mind as she walks in her sleep, for example, is rendered

> by a skilful accumulation of imagined sensory impressions. . . . The artistic "inevitability" lies in this complete adequacy of the external to the emotion; and this is precisely what is deficient in *Hamlet*.[7]

Thus, *Hamlet* fails in part because much in it is not linked, as it should be, to its essential emotion and the objectification of this emotion in Hamlet's relations with his mother.

Eliot rejects interpretation or explanation as a proper critical function.[8] The only interpretation of *Hamlet* he allows "is the presentation of relevant historical facts which the reader is not assumed to know."[9] But Eliot seems to contradict this disclaimer in the third reason for his evaluation of *Hamlet*. For part of that reason consists in an explanation or interpretation of *Hamlet*, viz., "the essential emotion of the play is the feeling of a son towards a guilty mother." Now, if Eliot can be shown to be wrong in his explanation, it may be that his reason collapses and his particular assessment is thereby weakened, if not entirely defeated.

[4] *Ibid.*, p. 144. [5] *Ibid.*, p. 145 (italics in original).

[6] *Ibid.* (italics in original). [7] *Ibid.*

[8] Eliot later repudiated his rejection of interpretation; see his Introduction to Knight's *The Wheel of Fire*.

[9] Eliot, *Selected Essays*, p. 142.

Eliot next explains why Shakespeare fails in *Hamlet,* by means of a presentation of "the relevant historical facts." He borrows from J. M. Robertson and E. E. Stoll in his argument that *Hamlet* is a stratification of older plays in which Shakespeare's conception of Hamlet's essential emotion is superimposed upon, but not integrated with, this older material. Kyd's *Spanish Tragedy,* Kyd's (lost) *Hamlet,* the tale of Belleforest, and the German version of *Hamlet* allow us to infer some of these older materials and an older play in which

> the motive was a revenge motive simply; . . . the action or delay is caused . . . solely by the difficulty of assassinating a monarch surrounded by guards; and . . . the "madness" of Hamlet was feigned in order to escape suspicion, and successfully.[10]

In Shakespeare, the delay is not explained by external difficulties; madness arouses suspicions; and Hamlet seems motivated by much more than revenge, where the "much more" is never expressed clearly or objectively in action. Shakespeare's *Hamlet* fails, then, because Shakespeare was unable to derive Hamlet's essential emotion from the intractable material of the old play. Eliot concludes: "We must simply admit that here Shakespeare tackled a problem which proved too much for him."[11]

Even in this brief essay, it can be seen, Eliot engages in a number of different tasks. He describes some aspects of Hamlet, for example, his madness—"less than madness and more than feigned";[12] he explains the play; he explains why it fails; and he evaluates it. Since his major task is evaluation, let us examine it first. *Hamlet,* Eliot claims, is an artistic failure. His argument for this judgment is, I think, as follows:

Premise One (P1): One criterion of a great work of art is that it must contain an objective correlative of its basic emotion.

Premise Two (P2): *Hamlet* does not have this objective correlative.

[10] *Ibid.* [11] *Ibid.*, p. 146. [12] *Ibid.*

Conclusion (C): Therefore *Hamlet* is not a great work of art (i.e., is an artistic failure).

Now, there are many possible replies here. One is to attack P2. This amounts to asserting that *Hamlet* does satisfy Eliot's criterion since the facts are not in excess of Hamlet's emotion but indeed equivalent to it. Eliot fails as critic, then, because he does not grasp this basic emotion in *Hamlet*, which does externalize itself in the action. This reply is tantamount to saying that Eliot does not understand the play because he simply fails to explain Hamlet. J. Dover Wilson takes this line, contending that Hamlet's emotion is not in excess of the facts of the play, because his emotion is not merely toward a guilty but also an incestuous mother:

> The hideous thought of incest . . . is the monster present in Hamlet's mind throughout the First Soliloquy. It is that, far more than the indecent haste of the wedding, which makes "all the uses of this world" seem "weary, stale, flat and unprofitable," sullies his very flesh, causes him to long for death and prompts the bitter cry "Frailty, thy name is woman!" Is the passion of that speech in excess of the facts? This is the test question by which Mr. Eliot's thesis stands or falls; for if the First Soliloquy be accepted as dramatically appropriate all the rest follows.[13]

Is it possible, then, as Wilson suggests, that it is Eliot and not Shakespeare who has tackled a problem that proves too much for him?

Another possible reply to Eliot's negative assessment of *Hamlet* is to secure an objective correlative in the drama not in one emotion, which is thought to be basic, but, say, in some pervasive theme. This possibility is suggested by the criticism of G. Wilson Knight, in his concept of a set of correspondences in *Hamlet*, and by Francis Fergusson in his interpretation.[14] Why, they imply, must the action of *Hamlet* embody merely a basic emotion—why cannot a theme or a contrast of themes or a myth and ritual pattern serve as the objective correlative?

[13] Wilson, "Mr. Eliot's Theory of Hamlet," *What Happens in "Hamlet,"* Appendix D, p. 307.

[14] See chap. vii.

A further possible reply to Eliot skips P2 and turns to P1, the major premise of Eliot's argument. This reply raises serious questions about the objective correlative altogether. Eliot claims that the realization of an objective correlative is one criterion of great art. It is clear from his discussion, that this is for him a necessary although not a sufficient condition for artistic greatness. Now, in his essay, he gives no argument to support this claim. Consequently, one question that naturally can arise concerns the status of this claim or doctrine. Is it self-evident? Is it empirically true? Or, perhaps, is it merely Eliot's aesthetic postulate?

Another more immediate question is, of course, What does "objective correlative" mean? Eliot does not define the concept; he gives examples, and one is left wondering just what he means by it and why he restricts it to emotion in art. Certainly, "artistic inevitability" is not always of this emotional sort. Eliot owes us either a definition or a clarification of this key concept.[15]

There are other, even more basic, questions about Eliot's or any theory of evaluation in criticism. I shall discuss these in detail in chap. xvi but it will serve us well at least to enumerate some of them here since they arise out of this one essay in criticism. Eliot's main objective is to give a reasoned assessment of the play. He seems to assume that evaluation is intrinsic to criticism. Is evaluation a necessary part of "the study of any work of art?" Can criticism dispense with evaluation? Further, Eliot makes a judgment on the play. Is his judgment true or false? If it is, in what sense? If it is not, what sort of utterance is it? Finally, Eliot presents reasons for his judgment. Three questions can be asked here: What is the relation between judgment and reasons? Is Eliot's argument for the artistic failure of *Hamlet* deductive, as he seems to suggest, or is it inductive? Is there another possibility?

The second concern of Eliot's essay, his protests notwithstanding, is explanation. As J. Dover Wilson remarks, "What is wrong with Hamlet?" becomes for Eliot, "What is wrong with *Hamlet*?" Eliot,

[15] For a penetrating criticism of Eliot's "objective correlative," see Eliseo Vivas, "The Objective Correlative of T. S. Eliot," *Creation and Discovery* (New York, 1955), pp. 175–206.

following Robertson and Stoll, states that the critic can utilize certain historical facts (i.e., descriptions and explanations of data outside the play) to frame a hypothesis that will clarify what is puzzling in the play. This claim introduces us to one statement of a powerful "method" in criticism, the so-called "historical," about which I shall have much to say in the next two chapters. Suffice it to say here that Eliot accepts the relevancy of historical facts in the formulation of his hypothesis and consequent explanation of why *Hamlet* fails. Once again, it is J. Dover Wilson who leads the attack on this specific application of "historical method" to *Hamlet*. He writes:

> Shakespeare, they [Eliot, Robertson, Stoll] inform us, threw the cloak of his inimitable poetry over the primitive construction of Kyd's drama, but he was quite unable to bring it dramatically to life. . . . They appear to have no aesthetic, or at least dramatic, principles whatever, but seek to explain and appraise everything in Shakespeare by reference to historical causes. Thus, when they come upon passages, scenes or characters which perplex them, instead of asking themselves what Shakespeare's purpose might have been or what artistic function such passages, scenes or characters might conceivably possess in a play written for the Elizabethan stage and for an Elizabethan audience, they label them "relics of an old play" and talk of the stubbornness of Shakespeare's material or the crudity of Elizabethan drama.[16]

Wilson concedes that some of the difficulties in *Hamlet* can be explained "historically," i.e., as discrepancies arising out of revisions; for example, Hamlet's age. But most cannot. "I doubt," he says, "whether any of these are to be set down to the intractability of the inherited plot, and I am certain that they vanish one and all in the illusion of the theatre."[17]

But Wilson's main objection to the "historical" critics of *Hamlet* is directed against their neglect of the many difficulties in the play that require historical knowledge for their solution: "The main trouble with the 'historical' critics is their ignorance of history and their lack of historical curiosity."[18] We need to know a great deal about Elizabethan

[16] Wilson, "The New Shakespeare" *Hamlet*, pp. xlvi–xlvii.
[17] *Ibid.*, p. xlvii. [18] *Ibid.*, p. l.

demonology, political theory, psychology, political events, and linguistic usage, Wilson insists, if we are to comprehend at all certain important data of the play. Wilson, then, does not deny the relevancy of history to the criticism of *Hamlet;* instead, he emphasizes its proper use, as a propaedeutic to the aesthetic analysis of the play.

V SOME HISTORICAL CRITICS

THE USE of historical data in the criticism of Shakespeare is as old as Dryden. Pope and Dr. Johnson also relate certain aspects of Shakespeare's dramas to his age and audience. So the historical approach, if interpreted widely, is not new. But there is a particular version of it that, at least so far as *Hamlet* criticism is concerned, is relatively new, and avowedly so since its many proponents proclaim it revolutionary. These include critics as different as J. M. Robertson, E. E. Stoll, L. L. Schücking, Theodore Spencer, and Lily Campbell, whom I mention because I wish to discuss their work as acknowledged examples of the major forms this particular version of the historical approach to *Hamlet* has taken. What distinguishes them from other critics of *Hamlet*, whether anti-historical, such as G. Wilson Knight, unhistorical, such as A. C. Bradley, or historical, such as J. Dover Wilson (who, as we shall soon see, uses history to elucidate *Hamlet* aesthetically), is their basic commitment to the doctrine that *Hamlet* can be correctly understood only in Elizabethan terms, where by "terms" they mean Elizabethan theatrical conditions, stage and dramatic conventions, or philosophical, psychological, and political ideas and ideals. It is from this doctrine of an "Elizabethan *Hamlet*" that their theory of criticism is derived: The primary aim and job of the critic of *Hamlet* is to explain the play by relating it to its conditions in the Elizabethan age. The critic may, if he wishes, go on to evaluate the play or to interpret it for our time, but his central task remains an explanation of the play in *its* contemporary terms.

I

J. M. Robertson is our first example of this version of the historical criticism of *Hamlet*. In *The Problem of "Hamlet"* (1919), Robertson argues that the fundamental problem of *Hamlet* criticism is to explain the difficulties of the play as these converge on Hamlet's delay.[1] These difficulties cannot be reconciled by any aesthetic theory of an inner consistency in the play or in Hamlet's character. Only a scientific, genetic account of the play, a relating of the play to its immediate sources, can clarify *Hamlet*. "The history of the play," Robertson writes, "is thus vital to the comprehension of it."[2]

Shakespeare's *Hamlet* is an adaptation of an older play or, more accurately, a double-play, by Thomas Kyd, the author of *The Spanish Tragedy*. In this play—the pre-Shakespearean *Hamlet* or the "Ur-*Hamlet*," as it is now called which was alluded to by Nashe in his preface to Greene's *Menaphon* (1589) and noted in Henslowe's *Diary* (1594), Kyd laid down the main action of the drama. Because of its popularity with audiences, Shakespeare could not transform this action in his adaptation. Kyd took the old Belleforest story (derived from Saxo) and introduced a Senecan ghost (who reveals the murder), the play within the play, and the dumb-show, and kept the feigned madness that was no longer needed to provide Hamlet with a safety device, since the murder of the old King Hamlet now became a secret only between him and his son. Kyd also introduced the irrelevant and superfluous scenes: those of Polonius and Reynaldo; the ambassadors before and after the visit to Norway; Hamlet's expedition to England; and the campaign of Fortinbras.

Robertson supports this part of his thesis, that *Hamlet*, as Shakespeare wrote it, derives from an earlier *Hamlet*, now lost, by Thomas Kyd, by citing verbal parallels between *The Spanish Tragedy* and the

[1] J. M. Robertson, *The Problem of "Hamlet"* (London, 1919). See also *"Hamlet" Once More* (London, 1923).

[2] Robertson, *The Problem of "Hamlet,"* p. 30.

First Quarto of *Hamlet* (1603), Shakespeare's first draft, and by comparing this First Quarto with the German version of *Hamlet*, *Der bestrafte Brudermord* (1710).

Recently, however, Robertson's argument, especially his insistence on the verbal parallels between *The Spanish Tragedy* and the First Quarto of *Hamlet*, which for him are "a proof of the survival of portions of Kyd's original text in *Hamlet*,"[3] has been challenged by G. I. Duthie in *The "Bad" Quarto of Hamlet* (1941).[4] According to Duthie (I quote from Clifford Leech's succinct summary of Duthie's view): The First Quarto is

> a memorial reconstruction of the full text, made for provincial performance by the actor who played Marcellus and perhaps Lucianus. . . : When the actor's memory failed, he wrote blank verse of his own made up of echoes from the full text and from other plays: occasionally he drew on the phraseology and other characteristics of the Ur-*Hamlet*, deriving from that source the names Corambis and Montano. *Der bestrafte Brudermord* . . . was derived from a further memorial reconstruction made for a continental tour by a company that included one or two who had acted the *Hamlet*-text used for the First Quarto: the reporters in this instance made some fresh use of the Ur-*Hamlet*.[5]

Leech's own observation on Duthie's views also is worth quoting:

> These views are, of course, speculative, but Duthie has in many instances provided plausible demonstrations of the First Quarto reporter's patch-work. In any event, his theories have yet to be seriously challenged.[6]

In effect, then, Robertson's explanation of Shakespeare's *Hamlet* as a derivative from Kyd has been challenged and, if Duthie is correct, refuted. But what is important from our point of view is not so much who, if either, is right; rather that two critics disagree on a historical, genetic account of Shakespeare's *Hamlet*. Of course, if Duthie *is*

[3] *Ibid.*, p. 41.

[4] G. I. Duthie, *The "Bad" Quarto of Hamlet* (Cambridge, 1941).

[5] Clifford Leech, "Studies in *Hamlet*, 1901–1955," *Shakespeare Survey*, IX, (1956), 6. I have found this article invaluable in my own attempt at a survey of *Hamlet* criticism.

[6] *Ibid.*

correct in his theory of the origins of the First Quarto, it follows that Robertson, as a critic dedicated to an explanation of *Hamlet* in terms of its sources, fails in his task.

The second part of Robertson's explanation of Shakespeare's *Hamlet* is that in the Second Quarto (1604–5) and in the final version, Shakespeare added entirely new elements to the older material given by Kyd. These include the infusion of pessimism and the transfiguration of the characters:

> Utter sickness of heart, revealing itself in pessimism, is again and again dramatically obtruded as if to set us feeling that for a heart so crushed [Hamlet's] revenge *is no remedy*. And this implicit pessimism is Shakespeare's personal contribution: his verdict on the situation set out by the play.[7]

As for the transfiguration of the characters, what Shakespeare

> did remains a miracle of dramatic imagination. In the place of one of the early and crude creations of Kyd, vigorous without verisimilitude, outside of refined sympathy, he has projected a personality which from the first line sets all our sympathies in a quick vibration, and so holds our minds and hearts that even the hero's cruelties cannot alienate them. The triumph is achieved by sheer intensity of presentment, absolute lifelikeness of utterance, a thrilling and convincing rightness of phrase, and of feeling where wrong feeling is not part of the irremovable material.[8]

Hamlet has made good; this is enough. "But the critical intellect too has its rights: *its* concern is simply conceptual truth,"[9] and the undeniable conceptual truth, Robertson concludes, is that Shakespeare could not do what no man could do: render Kyd's archaic plot consistent with his own transfiguration of the characters.

> And the ultimate fact is that Shakespeare *could not* make a psychologically or otherwise consistent play out of a plot which retained a strictly barbaric action while the hero was transformed into a supersubtle Elizabethan.[10]

[7] Robertson, *The Problem of "Hamlet,"* pp. 73–74 (italics in original).
[8] *Ibid.*, p. 75.
[9] *Ibid.*, p. 87 (italics in original).
[10] *Ibid.*, p. 74 (italics in original).

For Robertson, then, to criticize *Hamlet* is primarily to explain it. To explain it is to give up the attempt to render the play aesthetically consistent and to see it instead as an adaptation of older materials that is effective on the stage even though it fails in the study.

2

E. E. Stoll has written voluminously on Shakespeare. His three important writings on *Hamlet* are *Hamlet: An Historical and Comparative Study* (1919); *Art and Artifice in Shakespeare: A Study in Dramatic Contrast and Illusion* (1933), chap. v; and *Hamlet the Man* (1935).[11]

As a critic of *Hamlet,* Stoll also is dedicated primarily to an explanation of the play in Elizabethan terms, and specifically in the way that Shakespeare intended and his audience comprehended it. The most important result of this explanation for Stoll is the complete repudiation of the Romantic conception of *Hamlet* that has dominated *Hamlet* criticism since the late eighteenth century. "The right and proper critical method"[12] in dealing with the play is to seek Shakespeare's *intention* in writing it: to compare his techniques, constructions, situations, characters, and sentiments with other plays contemporary with *Hamlet.* Then we can begin to understand the play.

Stoll's hypothesis, the result of his (and others'[13]) research into the sources of *Hamlet* and the influences upon Shakespeare, is that *Hamlet* is in the tradition of revenge tragedy or heroic romance, a drama of intrigue, blood, and fate—a tradition, derived from Seneca and sponsored in the Renaissance especially by Kyd, in which the hero remains ideal (with no defect) throughout the play and attains his appointed revenge. Hamlet

> dies young, dies in the moment of his triumph, dies, as it must seem to others, with all this blood on his head. This is his triple

[11] E. E. Stoll, *Hamlet: An Historical and Comparative Study* ("Research Publications of the University of Minnesota," Vol. VIII, No. 5, September, 1919); *Art and Artifice in Shakespeare: A Study in Dramatic Contrast and Illusion* (Cambridge, 1933); and *Hamlet the Man,* The English Association, Pamphlet No. 91, 1935.

[12] Stoll, *Hamlet,* p. 74.

[13] Stoll acknowledges his debt especially to C. M. Lewis, *The Genesis of Hamlet* (New York, 1907).

tragedy, as Shakespeare, I think, intended it,—a simpler and nobler, possibly less interesting and piquant, conception than the usual one, though one not less appealing. To some it may even be more interesting because it seems to be more nearly what Shakespeare intended—more like him and his age.[14]

In writing *Hamlet,* Shakespeare rewrote or, rather, rewrote twice, in the First Quarto version, mutilated in the pirated reporting of it, and in the Second Quarto, an old play, the now lost Ur-*Hamlet* by Kyd, a play that was similar to Kyd's *Spanish Tragedy.* Always ready to meet the needs of his company of players, The Lord Chamberlain's Servants, and the desires of his audience, Shakespeare composed his *Hamlet* to complete with the rival Henslowe company, The Children of the Blackfriars, in the popular market of revenge tragedy.

Shakespeare knew that in writing his *Hamlet* he could not tamper with the plot of the old Ur-*Hamlet;* he could change only the form—the words and sentiments. So, perforce, he retained the Kyd plot with the inherent weakness of the delay, his major transmutation being that of a slurring over of the delay. He was forced to do this so as not to reflect on his hero because,

> even if Shakespeare had desired it, he could scarcely, on the contemporary stage, have introduced so fundamental an innovation as, in the place of a popular heroic revenger, a procrastinator, lost in thought and weak of will.[15]

Stoll sums up Shakespeare's modification of Kyd's *Hamlet:*

> When Shakespeare rewrote for his company Thomas Kyd's Senecan melodrama, now lost, he was, as usual, interested in the tragedy as a whole, not in a psychology; . . . he strengthened the structure, sharpened the suspense, and in particular pitted against the hero a King that was more nearly and worthily a match for him. The difficulty was the hero's delay, which was unavoidable. The dramatist could not (if he would) change the popular old story; the capital deed must, as there and in all other great revenge tragedies, ancient or modern, come at the end.[16]

[14] Stoll, *Hamlet,* p. 69.
[15] Stoll, *Art and Artifice,* p. 94.
[16] Stoll, *Hamlet the Man,* p. 3.

Stoll supports his contention that Shakespeare's *Hamlet* is a revenge tragedy (or heroic romance) by an appeal to both external and internal evidence. His external evidence is that the play was regarded as a typical revenge tragedy from its origins to the late eighteenth century. Readers and spectators during this early period complained of the defects of the play, but no one of any psychological deficiencies in the hero. The author of *Some Remarks on the Tragedy of Hamlet* (1736) is typical: "The Poet therefore was obliged to delay his Hero's Revenge; but then he should have contrived some good Reason for it."[17] The Romantic interpretation of Hamlet as a weak, vacillating person has no support whatever in the allusions to *Hamlet* until the late eighteenth century. The Prince is referred to in heroic terms or as Avenger and Malcontent but never as ineffectual.

> Before Mackenzie's day, then, there was, so far as we can discover from popular and literary opinion concerning Hamlet, nothing wrong with him. He was a gallant, romantic figure, instrument and (at last) victim of fate.[18]

The internal evidence is the textual. Stoll's claim is that every relevant datum in the text supports his hypothesis. Indeed, his three major writings on *Hamlet* are mostly directed to his confirmation of the thesis that *Hamlet* is a revenge tragedy or heroic romance and not at all a psychological study.

There is, in the first place, the delay. Stoll does not deny that Hamlet delays. What he denies is that this signifies psychological inadequacy in Hamlet. The delay functions in *Hamlet* as it had from the Greeks on, as part of the epical tradition; it does not reflect upon the defects of the hero, but makes the deed momentous when it comes at the end of the play. The tradition required the delay and so did the Kyd Ur-*Hamlet*. Shakespeare simply resorted to established devices to bridge it over. Two of these devices, woefully misconstrued by later critics, are the hero's self-reproaches and exhortations, which Shakespeare employed not to ground them in Hamlet's character but to remind

[17] *Some Remarks on the Tragedy of Hamlet*, p. 33; this work is commonly attributed to Sir Thomas Hanmer.

[18] Stoll, *Hamlet*, p. 11.

> the audience that the main business in hand, though retarded, is not lost to view. They motive it by showing the audience that the hero, even in his delay, is a conscious and responsible and (so far) consistent being. In short, they give a reason for the delay. . . . They provide an epical motive, if I may so call it, rather than a dramatic one.[19]

Hamlet reproaches himself twice: in the second soliloquy ("O, what a rogue") and in the fourth ("How all occasions do inform against me"). Neither, Stoll argues, bespeaks a sense of infirmity. They contain execrations, interrogations, even lacerations, but these serve dramatically as exhortations and, finally, as exculpation, since in both soliloquies the self-reproaches "are so contrived as to end each in a definite resolve, and that a resolve which is kept."[20]

As for the Ghost's

> Do not forget, this visitation
> Is but to whet thy almost blunted purpose—[III, 4, 110–11],

in answer to Hamlet's

> Do you not come your tardy son to chide,
> That, lapst in time and passion, lets go by
> The important acting of your dread command? [III,4, 96–98],

this, too, is exhortation. For the Ghost's reply to Hamlet is no judgment of Hamlet's character "but a reflection on his conduct in this particular matter, with a practical end in view."[21]

Hamlet's highly emotional scenes, the cellarage, the nunnery, the play, and the graveyard, are not pathological either. They are all natural enough in the dramatic circumstances, and, again, they function to enhance the emotional pitch, not to reduce the stature of Hamlet. They are part of the action—art as artifice not as psychology. Like the cannon shot, heard intermittently throughout the play, Hamlet's seemingly hysterical behavior serves to heighten the total effect: a "*fortissimo tutti*," Stoll calls it.[22]

[19] *Ibid.*, p. 17.

[20] *Ibid.*, p. 25; see also Stoll, *Hamlet the Man*, pp. 16 ff; and *Art and Artifice*, pp. 96 ff.

[21] Stoll, *Hamlet*, p. 16.

[22] Stoll, *Art and Artifice*, p. 128.

Then there are Hamlet's cruelty, melancholy, third ("To be or not to be") soliloquy, feigned madness, and chastisement of his mother, each of which has been distorted by Romantic critics. Stoll's view is that the cruelty is simply part of the role of the Avenger; to make Hamlet's cruelty tolerable to his audience, Shakespeare retained the feigned madness as a pretense not as a *malaise* and added a few touches of melancholy. The "To be or not to be" soliloquy, like the first, "O that this too, too solid flesh would melt," is meditation, not weakness of will. And the scene with his mother, after the play, is Hamlet as Malcontent, not as Neurotic, engaged in a malcontentism that is "bent for burrowing under the surface of things,"[23] whether in matters of sex or in matters of death.

The doubting of the Ghost (II, 2) and the sparing of the King at prayer (III, 3) are not moments of weakness either; these are Hamlet as a typical Elizabethan, knowing that the Ghost could be the devil rather than his father's spirit, and as Avenger, sparing the King out of a hardness of heart, an eye for an eye, and not out of kindness or weakness.

Even the trip to England is dramatic, not a piece of psychology.

> The trip to England, like the doubt of the Ghost and the sparing of the King at prayer, is, though for the Elizabethan stage adequately motived, a deliberate prolongation of the situation, an artful postponement of the catastrophe. . . .[24]

Finally, that Hamlet was meant by Shakespeare to be a heroic figure can be inferred from the fact that no one in the play, except himself and the Ghost, reproaches him. More importantly, at the end of the play—"one of the surest indexes of your dramatist's thought"[25]—there is nothing but praise for Hamlet and not even a hint of dereliction of duty from Horatio, who should know the truth.

Hamlet, Stoll sums up, is meant to be heroic, not faltering. He fuses the Avenger and the Malcontent. Shakespeare never intended him to be an unbalanced neurotic or even an exemplar of the humor of melancholy.

[23] Stoll, *Hamlet the Man*, p. 24.
[24] Stoll, *Art and Artifice*, p. 103.
[25] Stoll, *Hamlet*, p. 63.

> Shakespeare's romantic tragedy, like all other great popular tragedy, presents human nature, not a doctrine of human nature; heroes, not weaklings, or psychopathic cases . . .[26]

Hamlet has no defect, hence, is without the "tragic flaw" or fault, without the weakness of will so central to traditional conceptions of his tragic stature. His whole conception, Stoll concludes,

> has the advantage over the morbid one of being stage-fit and fairly intelligible, which the psychologists have never made him; and of being in keeping with the text, the times, and the dramatic tradition and theatrical favour of two centuries; and that outweighs, I take it, the critical tradition of a century and a half. Such a Hamlet, above all, is in keeping with the whole play of which he is only an inseparable component, and with the nature of drama. . . . He is a dramatic figure, not a psychological study.[27]

Stoll's criticism of *Hamlet*, provocative as it is, has quite understandably been disputed by his colleagues. Lily Campbell, as we shall soon see, vigorously challenges Stoll's conception of Hamlet as an ideal hero. Jones, Bradley, and Dover Wilson, among many, differ with Stoll on his reduction of Hamlet to an Avenger-Malcontent with no trace of inner conflict. Stoll's reduction of the play is also open to question by critics who find in *Hamlet* a transcendence of the tradition of revenge tragedy. Dürer, for example, in his "Melencolia I," successfully transcended and transformed the entire traditional pictorial treatment of melancholy. Why, one can ask, cannot this apply also to Shakespeare, equally great in his art, in his treatment of the tradition of revenge tragedy?[28] Finally, Duthie and J. I. M. Stewart, independently of each other, attack Stoll's view that Shake-

[26] Stoll, *Hamlet the Man*, p. 10.

[27] Stoll, *Art and Artifice*, p. 121.

[28] See Erwin Panofsky's discussion of Dürer's "Melencolia I." Panofsky's criticism of this engraving can serve as an object lesson in our understanding of the problem of tradition and transformation, of how the artist can sometimes soar above his tradition. Panofsky's discussion is in *The Life and Art of Albrecht Dürer* (1 vol. ed.; Princeton, 1955), pp. 156–71.

speare in *Hamlet* forsakes the "truth-to-life" in his characterization and his depiction of motivation and behavior.[29]

Thus, there are basic issues between Stoll and *his* critics: Is *Hamlet* a revenge tragedy? Is Hamlet an ideal hero? Is he sorely distracted or merely feigning in his madness and antic disposition? Is Hamlet true to life as a character?

Probably the most debated issue is the traditional one of the delay. For many, the truth of Stoll's entire explanation of *Hamlet* rests upon the truth or falsehood of his account of the delay. Once again it is Dover Wilson who best brings into focus this area of disagreement. Wilson rejects Stoll's thesis that the self-reproaches are exculpations. He writes:

> That [Stoll's] thesis is moonshine any unprejudiced reader of the soliloquy in 4.4. may see for himself. Not that the evidence of the soliloquies by any means stands alone. Hamlet's sense of frustration, of infirmity of purpose, of character inhibited from meeting the demands of destiny, of the futility of life in general and action in particular, finds utterance in nearly every word he says. His melancholy and his procrastination are all of a piece, and cannot be disentangled. Moreover, his feelings are shared and expressed by other characters also. The note of "heart-sickness" is struck by the sentry Francisco nine lines from the beginning of the play. . . . In short, that
>
> the native hue of resolution
> Is sicklied o'er with the pale cast of thought,
>
> is not merely the constant burden of Hamlet's meditation but the key-note of the whole dramatic symphony.[30]

Hamlet delays: Does his delay imply a psychological weakness or not? This, too, is one issue that arises from Stoll's criticism of *Hamlet*.[31]

[29] See G. I. Duthie, *Shakespeare* (London, 1951), chap. i; and J. I. M. Stewart, *Character and Motive in Shakespeare* (London, 1949), chap. v.

[30] Wilson, "The New Shakespeare" *Hamlet*, pp. lx–lxi.

[31] See Helen Gardner, *The Business of Criticism* (Oxford, 1959), esp. pp. 45 ff., for a recent attempt at a reconciliation of Stoll and Wilson about the delay.

3

Levin Schücking also has written extensively on Shakespeare and the Elizabethans from the historical point of view we are now sketching. His writings on *Hamlet* include: *Character Problems in Shakespeare's Plays* (1922); *The Meaning of "Hamlet"* (1937); *The Baroque Character of the Elizabethan Tragic Hero* (1938); and the (as yet) untranslated *Shakespeare und der Tragödienstil seiner Zeit* (1947).[32]

Like Stoll, but at first quite independently of him—Schücking's master being the German scholar Rümelin—Schücking takes as the primary problem in *Hamlet* criticism the correct explanation of the play in Elizabethan terms. These basic terms for him comprise the devices and conventions that Shakespeare found and used in the composition of all his plays, where these devices and conventions were the usual ones of the popular drama of the Elizabethan age. Further, like Stoll, his two major critical desiderata are (negatively) to stem the "subjective tide" in Shakespearean criticism and (positively) to secure the interpretation "which is most probably true"[33] of *Hamlet* and the whole of Shakespeare by relating Shakespeare to his age.

If we are to explain *Hamlet,* Schücking says, we must place it in the context of Elizabethan dramaturgy. But we cannot even begin to do this until we locate the basic difficulty in Shakespeare's art. And his initial challenging thesis, in his most original work, *Character Problems in Shakespeare's Plays,* is that this difficulty is *ours,* not Shakespeare's or his age's. It is we who are mistaken by turning what was once simple, primitive, and clear into something that we consider, out of our ignorance of Elizabethan dramatic conditions, subtle and sophisticated. What is fundamental in the understanding of Shakespeare and *Hamlet* is an immediate transparency of his work which

[32] Levin Ludwig Schücking, *Die Charakterprobleme bei Shakespeare* (Leipzig, 1919), trans. as *Character Problems in Shakespeare's Plays* (London, 1922); *Der Sinn des Hamlet* (Leipzig, 1935), trans. as *The Meaning of "Hamlet"* (Oxford, 1937); *The Baroque Character of the Elizabethan Tragic Hero,* Annual Shakespeare Lecture of the British Academy (London, 1938); and *Shakespeare und der Tragödienstil seiner Zeit* (Bern, 1947).

[33] Schücking, *Character Problems,* p. 8.

was shared by his audience, composed as it was of the various segments of Elizabethan society. Shakespeare's was a popular art, an art that appealed to a demanding, mostly ignorant public. It was not an esoteric or individualistic art. Nor was any Elizabethan drama that attained contemporary success; Jonson, for example, failed miserably when he wrote tragedies that violated the taste of his audience. Shakespeare's theatrical environment embodied certain conditions that neither he nor any one else overcame, whether he wished to or not. He wrote in an age in which the choices among plots or stories were determined by the strong competition between the rival companies. The contrary notion that Shakespeare wrote as he liked contradicts all that we know about the Elizabethan theater. Further, authorship, although it was not wholly a matter of anonymity, was far from the important thing it became. As in the early cinema, it was the popular story and not the author of the script that counted. Again, public opinion, especially on morals and religion, was a conditioning factor that restricted the author's individuality. In this connection, Schücking cites the ending of *Doctor Faustus,* where Marlowe conceded to an opinion he did not share, simply because of the demands of the public (and not those of his play). Finally, certain anachronisms, such as references to contemporary events (e.g., Hamlet's talk of the war of the Theaters), gruesome atrocities, epical amassing of armies on the stage, and especially the clown, "coarse and primitive and calculated to destroy all illusion,"[34] strengthen Schücking's assumption, he claims, of the popular nature of Shakespeare's art.

Of course, Schücking concedes, Shakespeare wavered in his response to the demands of the audience but, on the whole, he reconciled himself to its primitive conceptions. This is why he succeeded with his traditional, direct, primitive, and almost childish devices. And we shall persevere in our modern misunderstanding of him until we take Shakespeare "much more literally than we have been wont to do, his art as more naïve, his methods as frequently far more primitive."[35]

Shakespeare's drama, Schücking contends, is a mixture of the primitive and the highly sophisticated. But these are rarely fused

[34] *Ibid.*, p. 23. [35] *Ibid.*, p. 27.

organically because of the controlling factor of the primitive. In *Character Problems*, Schücking concentrates on what he considers to be central among the primitive elements of Shakespeare's art, his handling of character. Schücking's aim is

> to open out new methods for an historically correct conception of his characters by indicating the limits of realism and primitive art in Shakespeare's technique.[36]

Schücking's first discovery in the analysis of Shakespeare's characterization is that frequently his characters speak of themselves with an objectivity that is psychologically unnatural. Schücking infers from this that the objectivity must be construed as a device which serves dramatically to inform the audience of some of the traits of the characters. He calls this device "direct self-explanation." Shakespeare employed it in soliloquy and, more important, in dialogue. It was sponsored by the intimacy of audience and actor in the Elizabethan playhouse, and it enabled the author to address his audience directly through his actor's or character's explanation of himself. One crude version of this device is the "Mark me now!" of the actor. Shakespeare retained this primitive device in one form or another throughout his career. It is a mistake, therefore, to regard this device as a subtle instrument of introspection. Rather it enables the characters to "supply the audience with the most important information about themselves and reveal the innermost secrets of their nature."[37]

Hamlet is a good example of the use of this simple device, especially the hero's soliloquies and dialogue. In Hamlet, there is a harmony between what he is and what he says: "self-expression in harmony with the character," Schücking calls it. "A fundamental feature of Hamlet's character is a fanatical sense of truth."[38] In some of his talk (e.g., "I know not 'seems' "), this is obvious. But, at other times, when he berates himself, speaks of his "weakness and melancholy," his ambition, his pride, his lack of pity, and so on, it is not so obvious and yet these, too, are direct self-explanation and, in Hamlet's case, a striving "for truth at any cost."[39]

There is also ambiguous self-explanation: characters who tell us,

[36] *Ibid.* [37] *Ibid.*, p. 30. [38] *Ibid.*, p. 31.
[39] *Ibid.*, p. 32.

for example, of their villainy not out of a subtle form of villainy invented by Shakespeare but only as a device of presenting themselves to the audience, as it were, from *all* sides. When Iago proclaims his evil intent, this is simply making sure that everyone grasps it; consequently, it is a critical fantasy to embark on a wild chase into seemingly motiveless villainy. Shakespeare departed from reality here out of respect for the limited mental capacity of his audience.

Related to self-explanation are characters who afford testimony for others than themselves. Here, too, Shakespeare sometimes departed from the psychologically natural when, for example, he allowed a villain to speak well of his victim and to solidify his talk by speaking badly of himself. When characters do this, they also offer true pointers about whom they speak. Shakespeare used this device—"the objective appropriateness of dramatic testimony"[40]—to achieve simplicity and clarity, not to create insoluble psychological complexities.

Schücking relates this last device to Laertes' conversation with Ophelia concerning Hamlet's love for her (I, 3), when Laertes tells us about the real nature of the Hamlet-Ophelia relation. Laertes, in this scene, warns his sister about Hamlet's feelings for her. Critics censure Laertes for this admonition; but in so doing they distort Shakespeare's technique, which is to facilitate understanding by allowing Laertes to speak correctly, as the rest of the play shows. For Hamlet never loved Ophelia nor did Ophelia love him. The early *Hamlets* (of Saxo and Belleforest) bear this out as does Shakespeare's *Hamlet*. The one difficulty, Hamlet's bravado at Ophelia's grave, is no expression of love but a mere expression of Hamlet's melancholy where the "victim is infuriated by the idea that anyone else wants to be more unhappy than himself."[41] Thus, Laertes was right at the very beginning. From this Schücking generalizes:

> This confirms the view which is of the utmost importance, *that the first mention in the drama of things which are important for the action or the characterization of the central figure must never be allowed in the interest of the characterization of secondary figures to distort the representation of the facts.*[42]

[40] *Ibid.*, p. 66. [41] *Ibid.*, p. 71.
[42] *Ibid.* (Italics in original).

Also related to these devices of self-explanation is Shakespeare's use of explicitly stated motives for action. In general, Schücking contends, Shakespeare intended that the motives as stated by the characters are correct and sufficient; hence, it is a futile though happy hunting ground to go beyond these to the existence of implied motives, waiting to be probed by astute critics. The sparing of the King at prayer is a substantial example of this clarity and unambiguity of stated motivation. Hamlet's "That would be scann'd" (III, 3, 75), when he finds the King at prayer, is not a rationalization by Hamlet. "These lines give, circumstantial and clear, the reasons for his inaction."[43] The Elizabethan audience would raise no question about Hamlet's reasons. On the contrary, it would share with Hamlet his convictions that the most horrible aspect of the murder of his father was that he had had no time for repentance and that, in sparing the King, he was only waiting for a cruel revenge, as his speech reveals. We do Shakespeare wrong when we complicate his simple machinery for moving his characters and plots. As Schücking states it toward the end of *Character Problems:*

> *The less complicated and the more natural . . . the solution of the difficulties we attempt, the more we endeavour to make the given ideas suffice for the explanation, the fewer the unexpressed ideas we introduce, the greater is the probability that we shall hit upon the correct meaning—that is to say, the meaning intended by Shakespeare himself.*[44]

Schücking next turns to character and expression. Some characters are developed in harmony with their speech, Shylock, for instance. But some lack this harmony, and Shakespeare sometimes allowed his characters to forsake their unity in order to promote a particular scene or other. The scene becomes all-important; the character suffers in his delineation by being made to speak "out of character." This device of reducing character unity to what Schücking calls "episodic intensification,"[45] that is, the playing-up of the emotional effect of a particular scene regardless of its relation to the whole play, is also employed effectively in *Hamlet,* especially in the case of Polonius.

[43] *Ibid.,* p. 214.
[44] *Ibid.,* p. 235 (italics in original).
[45] *Ibid.,* p. 114.

The purpose of Polonius in the play is to help create the atmosphere of the Court. He gives it its background and dignity. He is genuinely obsequious and devoted to the Court. He says he is and so do the King and Queen. Thus, as Shakespeare presents him, he is not contemptible or void of moral principles. Shakespeare delineates him well and consistently, with the exception of his role in I, 3, where he talks to his son. Polonius' "And these few precepts . . . ," in their precision, clarity, and strength, are completely out of keeping with Polonius' verbosity and obtuseness. Shakespeare wanted *that* speech in *that* scene, so he sacrificed Polonius' character in order to insert it, thereby destroying the harmony between the character and the language of Polonius.

Schücking's claim about the lack of unity in Polonius as this (as well as many other disunities of character and expression) was dictated by a dramaturgy of episodic intensification, brings us to the heart of his thesis: that Shakespeare's primitive devices, antithetical to ordinary realism, were employed by him to produce a drama of juxtaposition rather than of continuity. Shakespeare disturbed not only the harmony of character and speech but also of character and action. Intensity of individual scenes, not internal coherence, was Shakespeare's basic principle of drama, to which all else was adjusted.

Hamlet's completely irrelevant remarks on the war of the Theaters (II, 2) constitute another case for Schücking of episodic intensification. Shakespeare—and not only in *Hamlet*—varied his characters from scene to scene, introduced episodes irrelevant to the main action, and allowed great improbabilities (e.g., Horatio's recollections of King Hamlet, which gives Horatio a good memory from his cradle!). Of course Shakespeare did not always destroy coherence but always there was lurking "what we may call a *tendency to episodic intensification.* If this peculiarity is not properly kept in mind one is always in danger of misunderstanding and misinterpreting him."[46]

It is in this general context of character and action that Schücking presents his main analysis of *Hamlet*. He calls his explanation "the filling in of the given outline of the action,"[47] and his main theme is

[46] *Ibid.* (italics in original).

[47] *Ibid.*, p. 146.

that Shakespeare simply added new elements to the sacrosanct plot handed down by Kyd in the Ur-*Hamlet*. These new elements also derive from Kyd, in Kyd's creation of Hieronimo, in *The Spanish Tragedy*. Shakespeare's novelty consisted in his fusion of the plot of one Kyd play with the hero of another:

> In this new treatment of the subject [the story of Hamlet] and partial revision of the old play Shakespeare worked out the character in accordance with a plan which in a simpler form . . . was in all likelihood already contained in the play, viz., the *idea of melancholy*.[48]

The "melancholy type," in both its "forsaken lover" and "humor" forms, was already fashionable when Shakespeare wrote *Hamlet*. Shakespeare took advantage of the popularity of the melancholy type and revenge tragedy to combine these in his own way. The clue to "the meaning of Hamlet" is in this combination. Once we recognize the device of self-explanation, Hamlet's nature is evident from the very first act:

> If, then, we are asked to define the first principle of Hamlet's nature we must reply, disregarding entirely the apparent violence of his passion, that it is *weakness and irritability*.[49]

Thus, Schücking, in major disagreement with Stoll, holds that Hamlet is a neurotic, morbid, melancholy type, lonely and censorious, and not an ideal hero with no defect. "The point of departure for the explanation of Hamlet . . . lies in the morbid weakness of will of the melancholy character."[50] Shakespeare did not attempt to integrate all the elements of the play; he chose instead to fill in the traditional story with an equally popular melancholy type on which he could lay "some especially effective colours."[51]

In his lecture, *The Baroque Character of the Elizabethan Tragic Hero* (1938), Schücking enlarges upon the historical explanation of *Hamlet* to include certain principles of Elizabethan literary taste as a category of explanation. More particularly, his thesis is that Shake-

[48] *Ibid.*, p. 153 (italics in original).

[49] *Ibid.*, p. 160 (italics in original). See also Schücking, *The Meaning of "Hamlet,"* pp. 26 ff.

[50] Schücking, *Character Problems*, p. 167.

[51] *Ibid.*

speare and his fellow dramatists, and their audience, were part of a *Stilwille* that was more "Baroque" than it was "Renaissance." Consequently, if we wish to further our understanding of *Hamlet* (or of any of Shakespeare's or other Elizabethans' tragedies), we must relate it to this prevailing style and see it, as they did, as expressive of this style. Among the defining characteristics of the Elizabethan Baroque are a

> wonderful striving for increased energy, extraordinary motion, emphasis, plenitude of power, variety, exuberance on the one hand and the tendency to sharp contrast on the other hand. . . .[52]

The Elizabethans, Schücking says, reiterating Voltaire's comment, tolerated everything but the tedious, and they demanded, at any rate in their tragedies, an arousal of violent emotions rather than an Aristotelian purgation of pity and fear. Spelled out in the action and plot, this requirement called for a certain sensationalism in tragic drama, especially in the role of the tragic hero. "It is certainly this love of sensation that best explains a phenomenon of the first importance with regard to him, viz. the rareness of the representation of an ideal character."[53] Thus, the heroes are mixtures of the sensational and great: they had to be *impressive* in order to meet the wishes of the audience. Consequently, playwrights went beyond the mirroring of nature and of people in real life.

> This "outdoing the life" is, to put it roughly, achieved by heightening the figure of the hero beyond life-size, mostly through an extraordinary intensification of emotional stress. This is why above all the extremely *passionate* individual is chosen for representation, the exhibition of unrestrained passion being the climax of Elizabethan tragedy.[54]

Passion, thus, is primary in Elizabethan tragedy. And Schücking (along with Lily Campbell, whom we shall discuss soon) disagrees with Stoll (and others) that Elizabethan tragic heroes are ideal and noble. To see Hamlet, for example, as an ideal hero, as Stoll does, is, for Schücking, to sin against the whole spirit of the Elizabethan epoch.[55]

[52] Schücking, *The Baroque Character of the Elizabethan Tragic Hero*, p. 4.
[53] *Ibid.*, p. 7.
[54] *Ibid.*, p. 8 (italics in original).
[55] *Ibid.*, p. 22.

The Elizabethan tragic heroes have other characteristics: they are, in their "livelier-than-life" status, not only intensely emotional, but bizarre, i.e., eccentric and extravagant, self-exalting, although not overbearing. Macbeth, Othello, Lear, and Hamlet are best conceived as Shakespeare's transformation of these qualities. Indeed, Shakespeare's secret is that

> he, too, presents the required exalted and passionate character to the spectator, and shows him in the grip of the mental tempests the audience expects; but in Shakespeare's case this passionate character is complex, the composition of his qualities being such as to evoke tragic pity, and his actions remain in accordance with his psychological structure.[56]

About *Hamlet* in particular Schücking says little in this lecture. For the most part he repeats his early description of Hamlet as a melancholy type and then relates this type to the general traits of the Elizabethan tragic hero: Hamlet's bizarre, emotionally intense, and self-exalting yet dignified qualities. The Elizabethan audience would have had no difficulty in comprehending his peculiarities, that is, his disdain for the world, his treatment of Ophelia and Gertrude, and his reflections on death, as typical, albeit crazy, characteristics of the melancholy type.

Schücking's criticism of *Hamlet* also has given rise to much controversy. One dispute, already mentioned, between him and Stoll about whether *Hamlet* is a revenge play with an ideal, noble hero, is especially interesting because both disputants share a basic commitment to *Hamlet* criticism as explanation. Given their assumption that a *correct* explanation of *Hamlet* is forthcoming, the issue they raise should, on their assumption, yield a clean-cut decision.

Another dispute, also mentioned in connection with Stoll, concerns Dover Wilson's general indictment of any historical or other approach which, without detailed scrutiny, condemns *Hamlet* as a mixture of

[56] *Ibid.*, pp. 18–19. In his *Shakespeare und der Tragödienstil seiner Zeit*, Schücking elaborates on the family likenesses among Marlowe, Chapman, Webster, Jonson, Kyd, Marston, Tourneur, and Shakespeare. Shakespeare, he says, differs from his contemporaries not in the fantastic, spectacular, or sensational, but only in his greater poetic power. See also *The Meaning of "Hamlet,"* chap. i, about *Hamlet* as an early Baroque drama.

relics and fine poetry. His disagreement with Schücking on this point boils down to the issue whether *Hamlet* is an organic, coherent work of art or merely a series of episodic intensifications. J. I. M. Stewart reinforces Wilson's objection by pointing out that at least some of Schücking's examples of non-coherence will not stand up under close reading. Hamlet's talk of the war of the Theaters, for example, is not a crude, anachronistic device for holding the audience's attention, as Schücking claims, but Shakespeare's subtle and dramatically economical means of exhibiting Hamlet's catholicity of interests as an important facet of his character as a Renaissance gentleman.[57] Stewart also raises issues about the relation between old, simple devices and Shakespeare's transformations of them which, in many cases, become genuine innovations. It is Schücking, not Shakespeare, who is crude, in his simple critical device of *reducing* the play and its constituent elements to the non-Shakespearean elements they resemble. Indeed, Stewart probes so deeply into Schücking's criteria of "correct explanation" that he questions the validity of the whole historical approach to *Hamlet*. Can we get the correct explanation of *Hamlet?* Can we even secure the Elizabethan conception of the play? Since we lack any good evidence, such as a single extended critical notice of the play by an Elizabethan, Stewart thinks we cannot. He concludes:

> It is only too probable that what he [the historical critic] would have us accept as a criterion is simply what he conjectures was felt, expected, taken for granted, understood, approved by a synthetic or generic Elizabethan of his own fabrication. And thus, at the best, he will stop short just where the dramatist himself must be supposed to begin. Surely such a historical method is like Bottom's dream: it hath no bottom.[58]

[57] Stewart, *op. cit.*, p. 63.
[58] *Ibid.*, p. 42.

VI SOME HISTORICAL CRITICS (*Continued*)

I

In *Hamlet* evil appears full-fledged, and we have a very different kind of tragedy from anything that Shakespeare had previously written. For with *Hamlet* we feel as if Shakespeare had had a new vision of what a play could contain, and in this play, as in the other tragedies that follow it, the characters and events become larger than the characters of the 1590's; they make more reverberations in our minds; they take on a symbolic and universal meaning.

To describe how this is accomplished is one of the central problems in Shakespearean criticism.[1]

SO BEGINS the criticism of *Hamlet* by Theodore Spencer in *Shakespeare and the Nature of Man* (1942). Spencer writes on *Hamlet* and Shakespeare primarily from the point of view of the history of ideas. His methodology and major themes derive from Arthur Lovejoy's classic, *The Great Chain of Being* (1936); his criticism of *Hamlet* and Shakespeare is one among

[1] Theodore Spencer, *Shakespeare and the Nature of Man* (2d ed.; New York, 1949), pp. 93–94.

a number of important essays on the intellectual background of Shakespeare.[2]

I hesitate placing Spencer's criticism of *Hamlet* in my present classification of historical criticism because, in his total aim and criticism, he goes beyond the historical, as I am limiting it here, to relate *Hamlet* to the purported nature of man and certain fundamental truths about man that are dramatized in Shakespeare's work. This humanistic conception of criticism is, of course, larger than the historical, so perhaps it is incorrect to tie Spencer's version of criticism as the history of ideas to a form of criticism that unites him with Robertson, Stoll, Schücking, Miss Campbell, and many others. I do so, justifiably, I think, because he, like these others, takes as his *fundamental* critical task the explanation of the play in Elizabethan terms, where the terms are specified as certain doctrines about reality and the dramatic treatment of them. As he expresses it:

> Our aim is to describe the point of view that underlies all these things [the sources of Shakespeare's plots, the texture of his poetry, literary fashions, dramatic devices, and so forth], the framework that gave Shakespeare his terms and his values.[3]

How can we best understand *Hamlet?* This, I believe, is Spencer's basic question in his criticism of *Hamlet*. His answer is this:

> I suggest that we can understand it best by realizing that in *Hamlet* Shakespeare for the first time used to the full the conflict between the two views of man's nature which was so deeply felt in his age.[4]

These two views Spencer calls the "optimistic" and the "pessimistic." They function in his criticism of Shakespeare as the defining characteristics of the Elizabethan Weltanschauung. A comprehension of them is essential to the understanding of *Hamlet*. In the first part

[2] Four others are: E. M. W. Tillyard, *The Elizabethan World Picture* (London, 1943); Hardin Craig, *The Enchanted Glass: The Elizabethan Mind in Literature* (New York, 1936); D. G. James, *The Dream of Learning: An Essay on the Advancement of Learning, Hamlet and King Lear* (Oxford, 1951); and Virgil K. Whitaker, *Shakespeare's Use of Learning: An Inquiry into the Growth of his Mind and Art* (San Marino, 1953).

[3] Spencer, *op. cit.*, p. vii.

[4] *Ibid.*, p. 94.

of his book, Spencer expounds these views and the Elizabethan conflict between them.

Elizabethan optimism was one aspect of a complete metaphysical, theological, and moral picture of the world, shared by all contemporary popular writers alike regardless of their minor differences, according to which man is the predesigned center of a created universe made by God and sustained by him as part of an eternal, pervasive order. God, in his goodness, has given man two "Books," the Bible and Nature, so that man shall be able to read and master his message. To know God is to know his works; to know his works is to know man's nature, as part of God's works; to know man's nature is to know his end: which is to know God. Thus, the circle is complete and man's great vocation in this life is to discover and adhere to this order which God had wrought for man so that he could fulfil his assigned, noble destiny.

Spencer quotes a number of writers, either English or translated into English during the sixteenth century, to substantiate his exposition of this part of the "Elizabethan World Picture." All of these, widely read by the Elizabethans, agreed on this major tenet of optimism, that man is "a piece of the order of things," created by a benevolent God.

This optimism pertained to more than themselves; it was an integral part of an optimism about everything since man is part of a larger order, an order of Nature. And man must try to comprehend this order as it includes him and as he reflects it. This larger optimism is part of the classical conception of the universe as a chain of being—a conception formulated by Plato, especially in the *Timaeus*, the summative doctrine of which is that the universe in its full perfection is a hierarchy, plenitude, and continuum of related entities. According to Spencer, the Elizabethan version stressed the role of Nature as "God's Deputy" in ruling over God's created unity of hierarchical entities. Nature, that is to say, rules over *three* domains, each reflecting the others as an aspect of the same unity: the universe, the created objects on earth, and man in society. These three domains, the cosmological, the natural, and the human, have their own individual hierarchies and relations among the elements in the separate hierarchies, as well as their parallels or sets of correspondences among the ranks of the different hierarchies.

The first domain over which Nature rules and in which order prevails is that of the created universe. This is an enormous sphere that contains the heavens with the earth as its center. The universe is divided into two unequal parts: one, "sublunary," is fixed and stationary in the middle of the sphere, and is composed of the four elements (earth, water, air, and fire) and their mixtures in the forms of minerals, plants, animals, and men, all in an ascending hierarchy; the other, "celestial," comprises the eight concentric spheres above the element of fire (the moon, Mercury, Venus, the sun, Mars, Jupiter, Saturn, and the fixed stars), which revolve around the sublunary and, in their different speeds of motion, rub against each other to produce the "music of the spheres." [5] Each of these spheres is governed by an angelic intelligence. There is thus an affinity between man and these spheres in that both are ruled by their superior part: soul or intelligence. One reason why man should study the celestial region is to learn of this affinity.

Beyond the sublunary and celestial is the "Primum Mobile," and beyond that is the realm of the "Empyrean," outside of Nature altogether. This is God's abode and, after the Last Judgment, the dwelling place of the blessed.

The second domain of Nature's rule and order, also arranged hierarchically and corresponding to the different levels of the first domain, is that of created objects on earth. Objects have been created, in an ascending scale of reality and value, from things like stones, which have no soul or life, to plants and their rudimentary souls capable of growth, then to animals with their capacities of growth and feeling, to man and his capacities of growth, feeling, and reason. Beyond man are angels,[6] as pure intellect, and, finally, of course, God, who is pure actuality. So the chain here is from God to matter in a descending scale of importance.

[5] Tillyard emphasizes this "music" more than Spencer, interpreting it as part of the "cosmic dance," where the latter is coessential with the universe "as a chain" and as a "set of correspondences" in the total Elizabethan world picture; see Tillyard, *op. cit.*, chap. viii.

[6] See Tillyard, *op. cit.*, chap. v, on the gradations among the angels.

Man is central in Nature's second domain. He has a definite place in the universe, nature, and society; thus, his relations to God, the rest of creation, and his fellowmen are duly appointed by God. And because he, and he alone, has free will, he can choose to descend to the beasts or ascend, through pure apprehension, to the angels. In man, God has reflected his macrocosm; therefore, man epitomizes the whole universe. His designed place in God's eternal natural order is to contemplate the world, himself in it, and to govern himself accordingly.

It is this governance that constitutes Nature's third domain. Here, too, is a divinely ordained hierarchy: of laws, from the natural to national to civil; and of members of society, from the king to his agents to his subjects.

Throughout, in this total scheme of Nature's domains, analogies are established: the cosmos, for example, is explained by the body, the body by the state; and the king, as center of his realm, parallels the sun, center of the heavens which, in turn, parallels the heart, the center of man.

Elizabethan optimism, then, was a basic belief in the divine unity of the three interrelated hierarchies of the cosmic, the natural, and the human, all of them embodying and reflecting each other's eternal order, an order in which man is the perfection and end of all the creatures of the world.[7]

Elizabethan pessimism was a series of devastating doctrines that led to the denigration of man. The mildest doctrine, indeed the other side of the coin of optimism, was the orthodox Christian attack on the worth of man since his fall in Adam's sin. Man, it was said, is wretched because he had disrupted Nature's order through his sin of disobedience. But, Spencer observes,

> man's wretched condition did not at all decrease his immense importance to the universe. He was, in fact, so necessary that

[7] Ulysses' speech on order in Shakespeare's *Troilus and Cressida* is a superb example of Shakespeare's use of the unity of the three interrelated hierarchies: Ulysses draws parallels between the heavens, civil law, the four elements, natural law, moral law, and psychological law, in his explanation of the defeat of the Greeks in their war with Troy. The order of the state is reflected in the order of the heavens and in the order of the faculties of man; see Spencer, *op. cit.*, p. 21.

> God himself, after man's fall, had taken on man's shape in order to set things right again. . . .
>
> The basic conflict . . . could—by the doctrines of grace and redemption—theoretically be solved.[8]

There were, however, three independently launched campaigns against Elizabethan optimism by revolutionary thinkers that were not mild, which together destroyed the belief in the cosmological, natural, and political orders of the age. Copernicus, the first of these thinkers, rejected the Ptolemaic system of cosmology, especially its notion of the earth as the center of the universe. The impact of the Copernican revolution came too late, Spencer points out, to influence Shakespeare. But John Donne, in 1611, already articulated the implications of this revolution for the other orders: "'Tis all in pieces, all coherence gone."

Montaigne, on the natural order, and Machiavelli, on the political, bequeathed their destructive forces before 1600. There can be no doubt that their views influenced Shakespeare profoundly. Montaigne, in his famous "Apology for Raymond Sebond," went beyond mere Christian reiteration of the misery of man to challenge the traditional concept of a human being. He attacked the arrogance and vanity of man by repudiating the accepted distinction between man and the animals. Man, Montaigne argued, is only another animal, with no prerogative or pre-eminence except in his own fiction about his superiority. In effect, "he thereby knocked man out of his crucial position in the natural hierarchy."[9] Because of the corollary of the orthodox doctrine of the three interrelated hierarchies that the downfall of one of them can cause the downfall of the others,

> Montaigne, by destroying the psychological order, destroys everything else; a human being who is indistinguishable from animals is not a human being who can comprehend the order of the universe or discover any Laws of Nature in society.[10]

Machiavelli, because of the practical implications of his views, was the most influential of the three, especially in his attack on the traditional political conception of order. In *The Prince* and the

[8] Spencer, *op. cit.*, p. 29. [9] *Ibid.*, p. 38. [10] *Ibid.*, p. 40.

Discourses on Livy, Machiavelli rejected the traditional Ciceronian doctrines of political virtue and rule. Man is not virtuous; he is by nature evil, therefore he must be governed by fear and force. Notions of universal justice, natural or national law, and divinely ordained rule are all unrealistic. Machiavelli expressed it thus:

> Whoever desires to found a state and give it laws . . . must start with assuming that all men are bad and ever ready to display their vicious nature, whenever they may find occasion for it.[11]

It is no wonder, Spencer observes, that Machiavelli became the embodiment of villainy in Elizabethan drama.

Now, besides these attacks, Spencer points out, there were certain political, economic, and religious events that fostered a growing pessimism during Elizabeth's reign, especially toward the end, when Shakespeare was writing *Hamlet*.

There are two conditions that are necessary for the writing of great dramatic tragedy, Spencer claims:

> first, a conventional pattern of belief and behavior, and second, an acute consciousness of how that conventional pattern can be violated. . . . It was because Shakespeare, as he developed his art, was able to see individual experience in relation to the all-inclusive conflict produced by this violation, that his great tragedies have such wide reverberations and give us so profound a picture of the nature of man.[12]

Shakespeare was not only influenced by the views and conflict of his age. He also dramatized them and in doing so employed dramatic forms that were current. Spencer, therefore, traces next the development of English drama from the medieval cycle and morality plays, in which order and disorder are dramatized abstractly in characters called "Everyman" or "Vice" or "Innocence," and so forth, to the first English tragedy, *Gorboduc* (1561), in which the characters

[11] Quoted from Machiavelli's *Discourses* by Spencer, *op. cit.*, p. 43.

[12] Spencer, *ibid.*, p. 50. Duthie sums up the Elizabethan world picture, given by Spencer and Tillyard, as the "order-disorder synthesis." "It is everywhere in Shakespeare: the reader *must* know something about it: and no book about Shakespeare can be of much help without some account of it. . . . It is basic." (*Shakespeare*, p. 56; italics in original).

(although wooden) are conceived of as individual human beings set in relation to a universal truth. Marlowe, in *Tamburlaine* and *Doctor Faustus,* developed further this important technique of individualizing heroes in a general, universal setting that enlarges their actions. Faustus, for example,

> is no abstract figure, but a concrete human being, and we have the moral conflict presented not merely externally, by the good and bad angels, but internally through the conflict in Faustus' soul.[13]
>
> The individual hero, no longer a mere abstraction, is seen against the background of the cosmos, and the dramatic conflict, no longer a mere battle of virtues and vices, takes place inside a man's soul.[14]

This placing of individual action against the background of universal beliefs became a basic dramatic form for Shakespeare. From his early plays on, Shakespeare created credible characters who are placed in an ordered universe, which is shaken by violation but eventually restored.

The great change came in the 1590's when Shakespeare put the conflict between order and violation

> *inside* the consciousness of his heroes and heroines, and the split between appearance and reality, between man as tradition said he should be and what experience proved he was, is no longer an external matter . . . ; it is something which can tear a soul apart in pieces as it tears the souls of Hamlet and of Lear.[15]

In *Hamlet,* Spencer argues, in his all-too-brief analysis of the play rather than of its ideological and dramatic background, Shakespeare used to the full the Elizabethan conflict between optimism and pessimism. In his previous plays the conflict functioned only as background; in *Hamlet* Shakespeare made it central by putting it inside the hero's consciousness.

Hamlet, we learn from Ophelia and others, had been a confirmed optimist, unbounded in his faith in the established orders. But soon after the play opens, Gertrude's hasty marriage and, later, the discovery of Claudius' crime shatter entirely his faith. Suddenly

[13] Spencer, *op. cit.*, p. 67. [14] *Ibid.*, p. 69.

[15] *Ibid.*, p. 92 (italics in original).

everything is corrupt: his mother's lust mirrors the disorder in nature and (later) the rottenness of the state under a murderer.

Hamlet is central in the play. It is he who senses fully and agonizingly the reality of evil under the mere appearance of good. Evil becomes full-fledged in the cosmic, natural, and human world, and Shakespeare, through Hamlet, dramatizes this defeat of order by its violation. In the play, Hamlet proceeds from optimism to pessimism until at the very end, Spencer says, Hamlet attains a new sense of order in his acceptance of Stoicism.

Spencer also explains two of Hamlet's traits in terms of the Elizabethan tradition: Hamlet's preoccupation with the difference between appearance and reality; and his tendency to generalize. Throughout the play Hamlet penetrates beyond things as they appear to things as they are: "I know not 'seems' " is pervasive with him. His soliloquies especially reveal his generalizing mind. From the "I" of the first two major ones to the "we" of the "To be or not to be" soliloquy, Hamlet places at first himself, then everyone, in the general context of the world.

Of course, there is also much affirmation of traditional optimism in *Hamlet*. Rosencrantz and Guildenstern on the sanctity of kingship, Hamlet on the sovereignty, nobility, and "god-like" character of reason, and the constant reiteration of parallels between heaven and man, and macrocosm and microcosm are all examples of typical Elizabethan optimism.

Spencer's final point in his criticism of *Hamlet* concerns the truth in the play. *Hamlet* dramatizes the Elizabethan conflict between optimism and pessimism. But, because this conflict reflects the perennial struggle between good and evil, Shakespeare transcends the Elizabethan age and speaks for all time on the nature of man:

> Shakespeare was in touch with something more than his age. . . . We must see [his work] as a reflection of deeper truths than any that can be described by a local and temporary picture of the cosmos, of psychology, or of the state.[16]

These deeper truths, found by Spencer in Shakespeare, especially in *Hamlet*, are those which he refers to as truths about the *basic* nature

[16] *Ibid.*, p. 222.

of man: about his cycle of birth, maturation, and death. All great literature, Spencer claims, revolves around this theme. In *Hamlet*, the theme is rendered explicit in the Elizabethan conflict and is proclaimed dramatically by Shakespeare as the ultimate truth about man, that he, too, comes into being, lives, and passes away.

Spencer's criticism of *Hamlet* also raises important issues. For one thing, much of his criticism seems to be pure history of ideas and dramatic practices. Even though he applies his historical research to an interpretation of *Hamlet*, one can ask, as many have, Is this history really criticism or only history that is included in a book that for the most part is criticism of Shakespeare's dramas? A similar question is forthcoming about biographical scholarship that becomes a part of books on criticism. What, then, is the relevance of scholarship, historical and biographical, to actual criticism?

Directly related to this issue is one raised by critics who question the major assumption of Spencer's historical approach, namely, Is there such a thing as the Elizabethan World Picture? Helen Gardner, for one, has recently challenged Spencer and others on this assumption:

> The fundamental danger of the approach to a writer through the study of his age is that it encourages us to attempt to interpret the concrete by the abstract, the particular by the general, even more the exceptional by the average. We are rightly sceptical when we read statements about modern man and the modern mind and dismiss both as figments of journalism. We ought to be at least as sceptical about statements about the "Elizabethan mind." The "Elizabethan World Picture" tidily presented to us as a system of thought cannot tell us how much of that picture had truth and meaning for any single Elizabethan.[17]

Miss Gardner does not ask, Is Spencer's account of the Elizabethan World Picture correct? which is a possible move here, but, Is Spencer's assumption that there was such a picture correct? If Miss Gardner's skepticism is warranted, Spencer cannot explain *Hamlet* satisfactorily in terms of something that never existed.

[17] Gardner, *op. cit.*, p. 34.

Second, Spencer offers his explanation of *Hamlet* as the best one. Other critics disagree. Indeed, each of the historical critics already discussed disagrees: Stoll claims that the best explanation of *Hamlet* is as a revenge tragedy with an ideal hero; Schücking says that it consists in *Hamlet's* being understood as a revenge tragedy with a fashionable melancholy hero; and so on. Clearly, now, if there is the best explanation of *Hamlet,* not *all* of these competing ones can be it. So Spencer also raises the issue, What is the best explanation of *Hamlet?*

Third, Spencer raises crucial issues in his discussion of the truth in *Hamlet.* One of these issues is directly related to his whole historical approach to *Hamlet.* Of course, the major issue is how drama can contain truth, which Spencer leaves woefully unclarified. But I skip over this as well as whether or not Spencer grasps the particular truth in *Hamlet,* if there is one, and turn to the historical issue. We require historical knowledge, Spencer eloquently argues, if we are to understand *Hamlet* as a dramatization of the conflict between the two sets of Elizabethan doctrines. Part of what is involved in this historical understanding is the recognition of the falsehood of at least some of these doctrines. For example, we know today (or we should know) that there is no chain of being and that man is not inherently evil. The value of Spencer's historical approach is that it enables us, provided we waive the truth or falsehood of these doctrines, to come to aesthetic terms with *Hamlet* as a work of art. Our comprehension of *Hamlet* is not dependent upon our acceptance of the truth of its doctrines, any more than our aesthetic response to Dante's *Divine Comedy* is dependent upon our adherence to Thomist doctrines.

But Spencer also claims that we can understand *Hamlet* best if we grasp its truth about the basic nature of man, a truth that does not depend upon particular knowledge of the Elizabethan conflict. Here we need metaphysical, not historical, insight.

Now, it seems to me, Spencer offers us a real dilemma in his total criticism of *Hamlet:* Either we should seek the truth of *Hamlet,* in which case we do not need historical understanding of it, or we should seek its historically correct meaning, in which case the truth of *Hamlet* is either doubtful or irrelevant. (I am assuming, but only for the sake of clarifying what I take to be Spencer's views, that there are propositions in *Hamlet* that are true or false.)

In sum, Spencer himself calls into question the whole relevancy of the historical approach to *Hamlet* in his claim that the meaning of *Hamlet* and the comprehension of that meaning are quite independent of any detailed knowledge of Elizabethan ideas. Consequently, one may seriously ask at the conclusion of his book, Why should the reader of *Hamlet* bother his head over a mass of outmoded ideas in the attempt to understand the play if its heart can be sounded by anyone who has his finger on the rhythmic pulse of life itself?

2

In her book, *Shakespeare's Tragic Heroes: Slaves of Passion* (1930), Lily Campbell offers an historical critique of the four major tragedies, *Hamlet, Othello, King Lear,* and *Macbeth.*[18] Her basic contention is that these dramas can be understood only if they are placed against the background of the English Renaissance. Thus, for her, too, the primary aim and task of the critic of *Hamlet* (and of the other tragedies of Shakespeare) is to explain the play in terms that an Elizabethan would have accepted. She differs from the other historical critics already considered mainly in her choice of explanatory terms: Elizabethan theory of the nature and function of tragedy, its conception of the role of passion, and the Elizabethan relation between passion, medicine, and moral philosophy are for her the controlling conditions of Shakespearean tragedy.

Throughout her book, her avowed motive is not so much to stem the tide of subjectivism or romanticism in Shakespearean criticism as to crush Bradley's doctrine that Shakespearean tragedy is essentially one of action, of a great hero who goes down to defeat in his struggle with inner and external spiritual forces. For her it is passion and its justifiable punishment rather than action that constitute the essence of Shakespearean tragedy.

She begins her essay on *Hamlet:*

[18] Lily B. Campbell, *Shakespeare's Tragic Heroes: Slaves of Passion* (Cambridge, 1930). All page references are to the 1952 reprint, published by Barnes and Noble, New York.

If *Hamlet* is read against a background of contemporary philosophy, it will come to life as a study in passion, rather obviously constructed to show the profound truth of its dominant idea:

What to ourselves in passion we propose,
The passion ending, doth the purpose lose,
The violence of either grief or joy
Their own enactures with themselves destroy.
Where joy must revels, grief doth most lament;
Grief joys, joy grieves, on slender accident. [III, 2, 204–9][19]

These words, spoken by the Player-King, in "The Murder of Gonzago," she glosses as the dominant idea of the play, paraphrasing and specifying it, I think, later in her essay as the idea "of one impelled by passion to revenge and yet through excess of passion having the cause of his passion blurred in his memory. . . ."[20]

Passion is central in Shakespearean tragedy; in each of the tragedies, the hero is dominated by one passion, which is also central in the play; Shakespeare analyzes it, as the play progresses, in accordance with the medical and philosophical doctrines of his age.

Her justification of the thesis that *Hamlet* is a study in passion is in two parts: (1) the clarification of the general hypothesis regarding passion in the sixteenth century, and (2) the specific confirmation of this hypothesis in *Hamlet*.

Passion, as thematic material in Shakespeare, is systematically related to Elizabethan theories of human nature and tragedy, especially dramatic tragedy. With this as her claim, she begins her confirmation with an exposition of these theories.

The problem of tragedy has always been one aspect of the problem of evil. Tragedy exists in literature to present and explain evil. Hence, to discover the meaning of Shakespearean tragedy is to remind ourselves of how Elizabethans thought about the problem of evil. And since Elizabethan thought is an outgrowth of medieval thought, she starts her account with three late medieval writers, Chaucer, Lydgate, and Boccaccio. These three are in agreement on the doctrine that tragedies function as *exempla* for man to warn him, through the

[19] *Ibid.*, p. 109.

[20] *Ibid.*, p. 132.

fall of princes and the uncertainty of prosperity, of the fickleness of fortune and, through the cause of the fall in vice, of divine justice in the world. In their recognition of the perennial tragic fact as the change from happiness to misery, these writers of stories of the fall of illustrious men—summarized in *The Mirror for Magistrates* (1559) —also present and explain evil.

Directly tied to this conception of tragedies as *exempla* is an extensive literature of consolation that offers philosophical understanding and acceptance of the uncertainty of fortune and the workings of divine justice on all, the good as well as the wicked. From Boethius and Plutarch, through other writers, evolved the Renaissance view that tragedy is part of God's punishment of the wicked through eternal revenge and the strengthening of the good through human suffering.

Gradually, however, writers on tragedy turn from the presentation and explanation of the fall of princes to a particular justification of evil, as the retribution of God against all who bring evil upon themselves in their exercise of passion. In the Renaissance, tragedies are interpreted as *exempla* of moral philosophy which admonish men to attend to the lessons of evil in order to avoid ruin and misery. Theorists of dramatic tragedy enrich and reinforce this notion of tragedies as *exempla* by combining the Aristotelian notion of drama as imitation with the medieval notion of tragedy. We learn naturally from imitation; we delight in the works of imitation; therefore, we are instructed delightfully in tragedy. And, because poetry is the liveliest form of imitation, dramatic tragedy teaches us delightfully in the liveliest manner. All the apologists for dramatic tragedy, Miss Campbell points out, defend it on the ground that it teaches morals by examples to a willing and receptive audience. Tragedies on the stage, thus, serve as mirrors of our vices and passions and as reminders of our need to repent.

The great difference between medieval and Renaissance tragedies is the Renaissance substitution of a just and computative God for a fickle fortune; and of the corresponding substitution of the cause of our fall in our passions that lead to sin and folly for the medieval cause in the caprices of fortune. But both medieval and Renaissance writers are one in their view of tragedy as presentation and explanation of evil. Miss Campbell sums up this aspect of Shakespeare's background:

> Tragedies teach by *exempla* how to avoid ruin and misery by avoiding the loose and ungoverned passions which lead thereto. And dramatic tragedies teach by their *exempla* so much the more effectively in that they are imitation, and imitation pleases and convinces. Dramatic tragedies are, therefore, the most effective method of teaching by *exempla* the lessons of moral philosophy.[21]

To understand *Hamlet,* then, is, first, to grasp its significance as an Elizabethan tragedy, i.e., as an example of how to avoid ruin, misery, and destruction by not sinning against God. But to understand *Hamlet* we must also come to terms with the Elizabethan conception of passion and the relation of passion to medicine and moral philosophy. Passion, as the Elizabethans thought of it, is one aspect of the whole of human nature. Hence, to understand passion, its significance for the Elizabethans, and its role in Shakespearean tragedy, we must see it in its context of the Elizabethan theory of man. "Know thyself," Miss Campbell reminds us, is as important for the sixteenth century as it is for the Greeks. Man is compared to the cosmos; and a whole science of microcosmography flourishes. Man is also anatomized, in soul and in body; and many theories of the parts of the soul, their functions, and their causal relations are formulated. The Elizabethans especially take seriously the quest for systematic knowledge of the nature of man.

According to Elizabethan microcosmography, man is a little world, a microcosm, who partakes of the four elements and their qualities of the larger world, the macrocosm: the hot and dry qualities of fire; the hot and moist qualities of air; the cold and moist qualities of water; and the cold and dry qualities of earth. Man is also thought of in

[21] *Ibid.,* p. 38. Miss Campbell points out that Dryden, in *The Grounds of Criticism in Tragedy,* also fuses the Aristotelian doctrine of *catharsis* with the Renaissance theory of tragedies as *exempla.* Dryden goes from the medieval assumption that tragedy teaches by example the uncertainty of prosperity to the Renaissance doctrines that sins must be avoided in order to escape God's revenge and that men could see in tragedy the vices and passions that lead to their destruction.

terms of the traditional four humors in the blood: blood, choler, phlegm, and melancholy; with blood like air in their common qualities, choler like fire, phlegm like water, and melancholy like earth. Besides his humors (vital moisture), man has natural heats and spirits. A healthy body is one in which the four humors, natural heat, and spirits are in equilibrium.

Different temperaments also are recognized. The only conflict during the Renaissance is over their determination, one group claiming that the sanguine (blood), choleric, phlegmatic, and melancholic temperaments are determined by the humors, the other group classifying the different temperaments in terms of the hot, cold, moist, and dry qualities in the elements themselves.

The sanguine (blood)—that "pure, cleare, delecate, lovely, and amyable Juyce"[22]—is considered to be the ideal humor and temperament. But most interest in the sixteenth and seventeenth centuries is in the melancholy temperament. Here Miss Campbell makes what she claims to be a fundamental distinction that we shall expand upon in her analysis of *Hamlet*. Two sorts of melancholy men are recognized: one is the man in whom the natural melancholy humor is dominant, the other is the melancholic or choleric whose humor has been burnt out. The second is the "melancholy adust."

As for the soul and its anatomy, the Elizabethans distinguish within the soul its vegetative, sensible, and rational parts. The vegetative engenders, nourishes, waxes, and grows. The sensible knows and desires. It knows either externally through the five senses that send messages to the brain or internally through its common sense, imagination, and memory. It desires through its two faculties or powers, the concupiscible and the irascible. The irascible serves to spur on its possessor to satisfy his desire. The whole sensible soul is the moving power of the soul and, together with the animal spirits, determines the human purposes of the soul. The rational part also has two powers, the understanding and the will. The will is the intellectual appetite and is contrasted with the sensible appetite that resides in the desiring part of the sensible soul. Basic in this theory of the

[22] The expression is Thomas Newton's, quoted by Campbell, *op. cit.*, p. 58.

anatomy of the soul is the doctrine of the conflict between the desiring part of the soul and the rational. "Hence the fundamental moral concern of the period is with the passions and the reason."[23]

Passions are designated as the concupiscible (love and hatred, desire and aversion, joy or pleasure, and sadness or grief) and the irascible (hope and despair, courage and fear, and anger). There are two prevailing attitudes toward the passions. Elizabethans who follow the Stoic tradition consider them inherently evil. Those who follow the Aristotelians and acknowledge the passions of Christ and God regard passions as evil only if they are not governed by reason.

But there is unanimity on the nature of the passions. They are related to the humors. The body is nourished by the liver, the heart is the seat of the passions, and the brain is the instrument of sense and motion. The passions, consequently, can affect the body and the mind in two ways. Some Elizabethans assert that the passions, akin to the four elements and located in the heart, can affect the spirits and heat in the heart and thereby can disturb the balance of the humors. And the humors, through the same channel of spirits and heat, can move the passions. Any *excess* of humor can affect the passions in a harmful way by disturbing the equilibrium. Other Elizabethans affirm that, because a healthy body and mind depend on the balance between the humors, the spirits, and natural heat, an unnatural humor can result once the humors are excessively heated. This unnatural humor differs from the natural and the unnatural excesses of the natural humors. It is called "melancholy adust." "Melancholy adust, then, was the unnatural humour that resulted from any one of the humours putrifying or being burnt through excessive heat."[24] It is "melancholy adust" and not natural melancholy that concerns Bright and Burton, Miss Campbell points out:

> Of most concern were the sorts of melancholy adust that came from the adustion of the melancholic and the choleric humours. And it is significant that these are the two humours that are also represented as passions (for choler and anger seem to be used as synonyms). It therefore behoves all who would understand

[23] Campbell, *ibid.*, p. 68.

[24] *Ibid.*, p. 75.

the writers of the sixteenth and seventeenth centuries to tread warily.[25]

Thus, for Elizabethans, the humors could move the passions and the passions could cause the distemperature of the humors. Inordinate passions could blind the understanding, pervert the will, alter the humors, and create physical and mental diseases:

> Whether, then, the passions be regarded as perverting the workings of the mind in the brain, or whether they be regarded as impelling to action the end of which is unjudged, the result is the same: the passions are the potential enemy of the rational soul.[26]

Renaissance moral philosophy is based on this interactionist theory of mind and body and the implicit conflict between the sensible appetite and reason. Philosophers and especially physicians are also deeply concerned with abnormal conditions of disease caused by this struggle, among them drunkenness, melancholy, fever, madness, and frenzy. Burton, for example, diagnoses these diseases as states of the predominance of passion over reason. The effects of passion function as materials for tragedy as well:

> [It was] because passion wrought and was wrought upon in these states of unreason that a tragedy of passion is necessarily a tragedy in which drunkenness, fevers, melancholy, and madness appear in turn upon the stage as they do in the great tragedies of Shakespeare.[27]

Passion is related also to the Christian concept of sin. The will is in the rational soul and is the rational appetite; the passions are in the sensible soul and are the sensible appetite.

> The passions, then, make, so to speak, representations to the understanding, which when judged, are referred to the will for action, and are by the will passed on again to the passions. The will may be misdirected through ignorance or through error. And . . . the passions may, according to the Renaissance authorities, blind the understanding or pervert the will as well as cause alteration of humours and bring about maladies and diseases. Sin, therefore, as the result of passion may arise through

[25] *Ibid.*, p. 77. [26] *Ibid.*, p. 78. [27] *Ibid.*, p. 83.

> either cause, blindness of understanding, or perversion of the will.[28]

Venial sin is passion clouding the understanding or directing the will, or passion becoming so excessive as to unbalance the humors; in either case, moral judgment becomes impossible. Mortal sin is passion perverting the will or reason in such a way that a malicious will reigns supreme.

This distinction between the venial and mortal sins is important in our understanding of Shakespeare's tragic heroes as against his villains.

> The tragic hero sins under the influence of passion, his reason failing to check his passion. His passion may lead him to madness, but as long as his passion is in conflict with reason, he has not committed mortal sin. When, however, passion has taken possession of his will, has perverted his will, when in perfect accord with passion his reason directs evil through the will, then we have a villain, one who is dyed in sin, and one whose sin is mortal.[29]

Hamlet, Miss Campbell states, is a study in the passion of grief. As a dramatic tragedy it, too, is an *exemplar* of moral philosophy that delightfully and in a lively manner teaches us how to avoid sin and consequent ruin. Like the other tragedies of Shakespeare, it shows people of different temperaments reacting to the same passion so that the audience can see this passion in its various manifestations. *Hamlet* is a story of three sons, each called upon to mourn his father and to revenge a wrong suffered by his father.

> Grief in each for the loss of his father is succeeded by the desire for revenge. But each must act according to the dictates of his own temperament and his own humour.[30]

Shakespeare's fundamental problem in *Hamlet* is how men accept sorrow when it comes to them. His solution consists in the dramatization of the grief of Fortinbras, where it is dominated by reason, and the griefs of Hamlet and Laertes, where grief leads to their destruction.

[28] *Ibid.*, p. 99. [29] *Ibid.*, p. 101. [30] *Ibid.*, p. 109.

The response of all three to grief is determined by their different temperaments: Fortinbras, a northerner, is phlegmatic or sanguine; Laertes, a lover of France, is choleric and hot-complexioned; and Hamlet, also a northerner, is, at least before the play opens, sanguine or phlegmatic. His development during the play is from the sanguine which is changed by excessive grief to the sanguine adust or, as it was called, the "melancholy adust," i.e., unnatural melancholy induced by excessive grief.

Hamlet is never the natural melancholic. If he were, he would be splenitive (which he denies in V, I, 284), and he would not be "solid" or "fat, and scant of breath" (which he is, as both he and the Queen say of him).[31] Indeed, Hamlet compares in all particulars with Walkington's picture of the sanguine temperament in *The Optick Glasse of Humors* (1607).

Shakespeare does more than diversify the passion of grief in *Hamlet*, he ties it to the medical and moral thought of his age that relates especially to grief. The main problem is that of consolation in grief. Shakespeare contrasts in *Hamlet* a grief that seeks consolation with a grief that remains inconsolable and thereby results either in dullness and loss of memory (the sin of sloth) or in hasty anger and rashness (the sin of ire). Fortinbras exemplifies grief consoled by reason; Laertes, inconsolable grief that results in anger and the sin of ire; and Hamlet, inconsolable grief that culminates in his dullness and sin of sloth. Both Claudius and Gertrude, in their first interview with Hamlet, state "the real significance of the play in the challenge of philosophy to passion, of consolation to grief."[32] They try to console him, but Hamlet responds only with a grief that will not be consoled. He is already the victim of his passion; in refusing to allow reason to console him in his grief, Hamlet perseveres in the sin of sloth, a sin that ultimately leads to his destruction under a punishing but just God. Thus, if we see Hamlet as the Elizabethans saw him, we shall see him as a *type* of grief: one that results in a melancholy which dries

[31] Miss Campbell says nothing of Dover Wilson's "sullied" for "solid" or "sweaty" as the Elizabethan meaning of "fat."

[32] Campbell, *op. cit.*, p. 115.

and cools the brain so excessively that the memory and mind become fogged, hence, as a grief

> of one moved to revenge by heaven and hell and yet stayed by excess of grief from action, of one impelled by passion to revenge and yet through excess of passion having the cause of his passion blurred in his memory. . . .[33]

Hamlet, then, is a case study of a man who will not yield to the consolations of philosophy and the claims of reason in the moderation of his passion of grief. Even though Shakespeare presents in Hamlet a man who retains our sympathy, Hamlet is nevertheless shown as justly punished, as "passion's slave."

Ophelia is also part of the pattern of grief. In her is exemplified grief in its intemperate form, a grief that leads to madness and destruction.

The King and Queen represent mortal sin, not the venial sins of Hamlet and Laertes. Passion has perverted their wills: in Claudius and Gertrude the objects of their passion are objects of a will that has perverted reason. Hence both are alienated from God and pay supremely for this alienation.

Thus, if we take the whole play as a study in passion, the King and Queen represent the mortal sin of passion warping reason; they are damned. Hamlet, Laertes, and Ophelia represent the venial sin of passion undirected by reason; they are destroyed but not damned. Fortinbras and Horatio represent reason in control of passion, with Fortinbras shown as a victor over passion in the achievement of his revenge, and Horatio presented, in Hamlet's words about him, as one in whom "blood and judgement are so well commingled," as one who is no slave of passion, no pipe of fortune to play upon.

> And this is but to say again that those who balance passion by reason are not Fortune's puppets. And such is the lesson of tragedy.[34]

Miss Campbell's criticism of *Hamlet* also has provoked many objections. Among them are important ones that further our survey

[33] *Ibid.*, p. 132.

[34] *Ibid.*, p. 147.

of issues in *Hamlet* criticism. I shall enumerate only these objections along with one of my own that I have not seen elsewhere.

Stoll and Spencer question her account of Shakespearean tragedies, specifically *Hamlet,* as *exempla.* Spencer accepts her general account of the Elizabethan theory of the passions but rejects "her description of how Shakespeare used the passions for drama, since it seems to me likely that he was interested in doing more than the writing of case-histories."[35] Stoll goes further:

> Shakespeare's romantic tragedy, like all other great popular tragedy, presents human nature, not a doctrine of human nature; heroes, not weaklings, or psychopathic cases; and, above all, men as we know them, not curiosities of the contemporary or even the Elizabethan psychology or physiology. In himself Hamlet is no more a prey to melancholy than he is (as thought by other recent scholars) to the deadly sin of sloth. . . . How unexhilarating, unprofitable the conception! . . . Audiences at a tragedy . . . were not . . . expecting to sit in at a clinic.[36]

Stoll, thus, rejects Miss Campbell's conception of Elizabethan tragedies as *exempla,* of *Hamlet* as a study in passion, and of Hamlet as a slave of passion. Indeed, on historical grounds, he dismisses her entire explanation and criticism of *Hamlet.* Between them the issues are rife: both agree that criticism of *Hamlet* should aim at a correct explanation of the play in Elizabethan terms, yet they disagree completely with each other's explanation. In accordance with their theories of criticism, both cannot be correct. Which explanation, if either, is correct? How can it be shown to be correct? Only one thing seems clear: according to their theory of criticism of *Hamlet* as explanation, the questions, Are Elizabethan tragedies *exempla?* Is *Hamlet* a study in the passion of grief? and, Is Hamlet a slave of passion? should allow for unequivocal yes or no answers. Do they; if they do, why the enormous disagreement?

Peter Alexander also raises some important issues in his rejection of Miss Campbell's views about *Hamlet,* Elizabethan tragedy, and the nature of tragedy altogether. In *Hamlet: Father and Son* (1955),[37]

[35] Spencer, *op. cit.,* p. 25 n.
[36] Stoll, *Hamlet the Man,* p. 10.
[37] Peter Alexander, *Hamlet: Father and Son* (Oxford, 1955).

Alexander, in a vigorous defense of Bradley's emphasis on action in tragedy, examines the Aristotelian concepts of *catharsis* and *hamartia* and goes on to argue that *catharsis* (which he unites with *arete* or virtue) rather than *hamartia* or fault is the essence of tragedy. We shall return to his important analysis when we discuss the issue of tragedy in relation to *Hamlet* (in chap. xvii). At present I shall state only his specific objections to Miss Campbell's criticism of *Hamlet.* He writes of her historical method and its general results:

> If the essence of Shakespeare's work lay in these outmoded speculations of the psychologists it would have lost its interest long ago. To attempt to establish the meaning or significance of Shakespeare's work by the line of argument used by Professor Campbell . . . is to mistake the true historical approach to the work of art. Such interpretations preclude any historical understanding of Shakespeare's career as an artist and of his struggle to formulate in his work what he himself had learnt from his study of man and the actions of man.[38]

On her doctrine of Elizabethan tragedies as *exempla* he comments:

> Those great explorers of the human soul the tragic artists have shrunk to preachers whose business it is to recommend a safe standard of conduct by means of cautionary tales.[39]

But his basic challenge, which applies to more critics than Miss Campbell, has to do with the "tragic flaw" interpretation of the famous "dram of eale" speech of Hamlet to Horatio (I, 4, 14–37). Miss Campbell says of it:

> Here in a "dram of eale" is figured the whole theory of venial and mortal sin, of the sin that though not mortal sin yet brings the whole man into corruption.[40]

Alexander replies to Miss Campbell (and others) that such an interpretation distorts Hamlet's speech. In the actual speech, in its full context of I, 4, Hamlet is not commenting on a tragic flaw but on the King's drunkenness and its implications:

> Hamlet, provoked by the drunkenness of the King, is commenting on a fault in his countrymen that draws on them the censure

[38] *Ibid.*, pp. 130–31. [39] *Ibid.*, p. 57. [40] Campbell, *op. cit.*, p. 120.

> of the world, and so soils their reputation that their virtues lose all colour and commendation.[41]

Hamlet makes his "dram of eale" speech *before* he talks with the Ghost, so he cannot be reflecting on any neglected duty of his. Moreover, the speech is perfectly natural in the tense situation of awaiting the possible arrival of the Ghost:

> It is natural for men in such a situation as that in which Hamlet and his companions find themselves to fasten on some topic apparently unconnected with the business that holds them in suspense. . . . Shakespeare here achieves one of those studies in darkness and light with which painters and poets so often quicken our imagination.[42]

Hamlet's speech may also be interpreted dramatically, as Hamlet reinforcing for the audience the King's self-indulgence and thereby effecting for the whole drama an economy of character delineation. Finally, if "dram of eale" is read as a version of *hamartia*, then, Alexander points out, *any* blemish can be a tragic flaw, from "nature's livery" to "fortune's star." From which it follows that a man may be doomed not merely by sin and folly but also by the mole on his cheek; which implication Shakespeare could not have intended, so patently absurd is it.

My own objection to Miss Campbell's interpretation of *Hamlet* is that she distorts the nature of Hamlet's grief. For her, Hamlet's grief is the mainspring of the play. I waive the question whether it is or is not. But it seems to me that in either case she does not grasp the full nature of that grief. She ties Hamlet to Fortinbras and Laertes, all in grief over a father lost. But surely, if Hamlet's state is one of grief, he is grieving for more than a father lost or even a father wronged. Recollect Hamlet's first soliloquy, especially his reflection on his mother's bestial act of hasty remarriage:

> O most wicked speed . . . to post
> With such dexterity to incestuous sheets!
> It is not, nor it cannot come to good,

[41] Alexander, *op. cit.*, p. 40. See also Bertram Joseph, *Conscience and the King: A Study of Hamlet* (London, 1953), pp. 14–16.

[42] Alexander, *op. cit.*, p. 43.

But break my heart, for I must hold my tongue. [I, 2, 156–59]

Do not these lines express a grief that goes beyond a father's death to include a mother's incest and, also, if Spencer is right, a total loss of faith in the traditional orders? Hamlet's salient trait may be his grief, but, if it is, it calls for more than consolation for a father lost or wronged. Hence, my question to Miss Campbell is this: Is it a clear case of the sin of sloth to remain inconsolable in one's grief over a father murdered and a mother whored? What would the moral philosophers she continually cites have said about *this* sort of grief? Miss Campbell, thus, it seems to me, fails as a critic of *Hamlet* even in her central point that *Hamlet* is a study in grief because she does not at all discern the full and horrible nature of Hamlet's sorrow as he reveals it to us.

SUMMARY AND CONCLUSION

There are other important representatives of the historical approach to *Hamlet*, all in agreement with those already discussed in their basic thesis that criticism of *Hamlet* is primarily explanation of the play in Elizabethan terms.[43] Discussion of these, however, is not necessary for my purpose since they add nothing to the basic issues sponsored by the historical approach to *Hamlet*. I take it that the five I have detailed constitute a fair sample. By way of summary, then, I shall systematize the major issues produced by this form of criticism.

Many of the issues are those or similar to those already encountered in the previous survey: Is Hamlet melancholic, ideal, mad, true to life? Is *Hamlet* a revenge tragedy, a psychological study, a study in the passion of grief, a study in the conflict of ideas? Is *Hamlet* incoherent or an aesthetic unity? Does Hamlet delay? Is his delay occasioned by his character or by external circumstances? What kind of tragedy is *Hamlet*? As an Elizabethan tragedy, what is its distinctive

[43] Some examples are: Joseph, *op. cit.*; J. W. Draper, *The Hamlet of Shakespeare's Audience* (Durham, 1938); Ruth L. Anderson, *Elizabethan Psychology and Shakespeare's Plays* (Iowa City, 1927); J. V. Cunningham, *Woe or Wonder: The Emotional Effect of Shakespearean Tragedy* (Denver, 1951); and G. R. Elliott, *Scourge and Minister: A Study of Hamlet* (Durham, 1951).

tragic quality? These questions and the answers given to them and the disagreements over these answers among the historical critics themselves, as well as between them and critics who repudiate the historical approach, embody clearly stated issues.

Is *Hamlet* an adaptation of an older play? Is the relation between Kyd and Shakespeare in regard to *Hamlet* correctly stated by Robertson or Stoll or Schücking? Does Schücking describe Elizabethan dramatic devices and Shakespeare's use of them accurately? Is Stoll or Miss Campbell right on the Elizabethan response to *Hamlet* and tragedy? Is Spencer correct in his analysis of the Elizabethan ideological conflict? Are Elizabethan psychology and moral philosophy what Miss Campbell claims they are? These, too, are questions about which there is and can be much dispute, both among the historical critics and between them and their individual opponents.

There is also a third class of issues provoked by historical critics that converges on the very assumptions of the historical approach itself. These issues are indigenous to the historical group, hence, new in our survey, and important on that account.

Historical criticism of *Hamlet,* as I have described it here, is a fourfold claim: (1) there was the Elizabethan conception of *Hamlet;* (2) there is the correct conception of *Hamlet;* (3) the correct conception of *Hamlet* is the Elizabethan; and (4) the fundamental aim and job of the critic of *Hamlet* is to state this one and only one correct Elizabethan conception of *Hamlet.* Each of the five historical critics I have considered subscribes to this fourfold claim as his basic tenet of *Hamlet* criticism.

From these four doctrines there is a fifth that is implied by historical critics: (5) there is the real *Hamlet,* which is the one intended by Shakespeare when he wrote it and shared by his Elizabethan audiences as they saw it. It is this *Hamlet* that the critic should describe so that we can come to comprehend the play and not some non-Elizabethan distortion of it.

Now, each of these five doctrines is vigorously challenged by critics who, in rejecting the historical approach to *Hamlet,* raise certain fundamental issues for the philosophy of criticism.

(1) Was there *the*—one and only one—Elizabethan conception of

Hamlet? To begin with, the historical critics are of little help here since they disagree among themselves on this Elizabethan conception. But since nothing follows about the truth or falsity of such a conception from these disagreements, historical critics can continue to affirm the existence of an Elizabethan conception of *Hamlet* which scholarship, at least theoretically, can someday determine. After all, it may be said, there is a difference between the questions, Was there the Elizabethan conception of *Hamlet?* and Do we actually know what it was?

As we have seen, Stewart, in his reply to Schücking, characterizes the historical quest for the Elizabethan conception of *Hamlet* as "Bottom's Dream," suggesting that the evidence being what it is, we shall probably never know what that conception was or if there was one. Miss Gardner, in her reply to Tillyard and Spencer, goes further and raises a serious question about an implicit and (to her) unwarranted premise in the argument that there was the Elizabethan conception of *Hamlet.* She challenges, on what she considers to be a more accurate understanding of history than that which she finds in the historical critics, the basic notion that there was anything so neat and compact as the Elizabethan conception. Such a notion, she says, "substitutes for historical reality a kind of Golden Age of the Mind. . . ."[44] The Elizabethans were individuals, not a collective consciousness and, among them, there were great divergences of belief—"everybody did not think alike"[45]—that were brought by audiences to Shakespeare's *Hamlet.* It is more likely, she suggests, that there were many conceptions of *Hamlet* in Shakespeare's time than that there was just one, which the historian can try to ascertain. It is still possible that all Elizabethans shared with Shakespeare one conception of *Hamlet,* she allows us to infer from her argument, but the possibility seems very improbable once we recognize the complexity of the age of Elizabeth or, for that matter, of any other age.

Together, then, Stewart and Miss Gardner raise the issue whether the Elizabethan conception of *Hamlet* is a fiction, hence, an infeasible goal of criticism.

[44] Gardner, *op. cit.,* p. 135. [45] *Ibid.*

(2) Is there the correct conception of *Hamlet?* Historical critics, of course, assert that there is and that it is of the *Hamlet* that Shakespeare wrote and the Elizabethan response to it. Many non-historical critics, for example, Bradley, Jones, and Knight, agree that there is the correct conception of *Hamlet* but they base their answers on more than historical data—psychoanalysis for instance in the case of Jones. So, on this issue of a correct conception of *Hamlet*, the split is not between historical and non-historical critics but between the historical plus some non-historical critics and those critics who deny that there is anything like the correct conception of *Hamlet* or of any work of art. Stewart, in his repudiation of the historical approach, suggests that *Hamlet* exists only as it is re-created in the individual mind of any period; from his suggestion one can go on to ask just what *the* or *a* correct conception (or explanation or reading or analysis) of *Hamlet* means. And this question involves a big issue: What is *the* or *a* correct conception of any work of art?[46]

(3) Is the Elizabethan conception of *Hamlet* the correct one? On this question the range of debate is already discernible from answers given to (1) and (2). It is obvious that a critic can deny (3) by rejecting the application of either of the key terms, "Elizabethan conception" or "correct conception," to *Hamlet:* if there is no Elizabethan conception of *Hamlet* or no correct one, there can be no Elizabethan conception of *Hamlet* that is the correct one.

(4) Is criticism of *Hamlet* primarily explanation of it? Here, too, there is much disagreement. For example, many critics claim that the major task of the critic is to evaluate the play. To cite but one of these, Helen Gardner writes: "The critic's function . . . is to assist his readers to find the value which he believes the work to have."[47] The critic should elucidate the significance, beauty, and meaning of a work of art in terms that are valid for the readers. In her and similar views, where elucidation and evaluation are stressed, historical criticism is reduced to the gathering of historical information which can provide a

[46] See also Lascelles Abercrombie, "A Plea for the Liberty of Interpreting," British Academy Lecture, 1930; reprinted in *Aspects of Shakespeare* (Oxford, 1933).

[47] Gardner, *op. cit.*, p. 7.

relevant context for a work of art and can remove certain obstacles to its evaluation:

> The ultimate end of scholarship and literary history and biographical study for me is the assistance it will give to the elucidation of a work of art.[48]

Is evaluation or explanation in historical terms the primary task of criticism? Does criticism have a primary task? These are at least two major issues raised by this fourth question of historical criticism.

(5) Is the real *Hamlet* the Elizabethan *Hamlet,* which the critic should try to render comprehensible to us? It is Lionel Trilling, I think, who most radically challenges the historical critic on this question. In his essay, "The Sense of the Past,"[49] he rejects both parts of the question. Ironically, the context of his rejection is not the historical critics but his attack on the "New Criticism" for its anti-historical bias. It is an illusion, he claims, to suppose that we of the twentieth century can think, for example, like men of the sixteenth or seventeenth centuries. Hence, it must be an illusion to suppose, as contemporary historical critics do, that they can reproduce the Elizabethan conception of *Hamlet,* even if it existed. Second, the assumption that the real *Hamlet* is the Elizabethan *Hamlet* is also an illusion. The real *Hamlet,* Trilling proclaims, is a combination of what Shakespeare intended, what his first audiences saw, his first readers read, and what we now perceive: in sum, the real *Hamlet* is *Hamlet*

> as it has existed in history, as it has lived its life from Then to Now, as it is a thing which submits itself to one kind of perception in one age and another kind of perception in another age, as it exerts in each age a different kind of power.[50]

Thus, for Trilling, part of the real *Hamlet* or of any literary work of art, is its "historicity"—its pastness—which is as organic to the work as any other element.

Trilling uses this notion of historicity in his own formulation of an

[48] *Ibid.,* p. 23.
[49] Lionel Trilling, "The Sense of the Past," *The Liberal Imagination* (New York, 1950).
[50] *Ibid.,* p. 186.

adequate historical approach to literature. Discussion of his conception of the historical criticism of literature is out of place here but there is an immediate relevance of his views to question (5) that induces another much disputed issue: What is the real *Hamlet?* Critics and philosophers alike refer to this as the "ontological problem" of a work of art.[51]

But the basic issue raised by these historical critics is the central one of criticism itself, the issue that I have already touched upon and must eventually discuss fully once we have before us an adequate survey of the criticism of *Hamlet:* What is the logical status of all the questions raised by the historical critics as well as by their opponents? Is their assumption warranted that all their questions, disagreements, and issues are of the same type, namely, factual ones, to which true solutions are forthcoming?

[51] See especially René Wellek and Austin Warren, *Theory of Literature* (New York, 1942), chap. xii.

VII FRANCIS FERGUSSON

IN HIS book, *The Idea of a Theater* (1949), Francis Fergusson enriches this survey by his interpretation of *Hamlet* as a "myth and ritual" drama.[1] Starting with Eliot's negative judgment of the play, part of what he essays is a reassessment of *Hamlet*, along traditional laudatory lines, that is based upon a new interpretation of the play, involving a repudiation of Eliot's own reading of it.

His criticism, certainly his interpretation, is eclectic, a synthesis of many contemporary strands: Ernest Jones, Dover Wilson, T. S. Eliot, Caroline Spurgeon, and the Cambridge School of Classical Anthropology, especially Jane Harrison and Gilbert Murray. Much of their work is brought together into a complex hypothesis that Fergusson then employs to interpret the entire play. Each of these critics from whom he borrows he calls a "reflector," that is, one who perceives a single aspect of the play but not others. Any adequate reading must bring these reflectors into a single focus that can illuminate the whole play.

The basic obligation of the critic of *Hamlet* is to make clear, through description and interpretation, all the *données* of the play. These include: Hamlet, as the dispossessed prince as well as son,

[1] Francis Fergusson, *The Idea of a Theater* (Princeton, 1949). All page references are to this edition.

lover, and revenger; all the other characters; their various relationships; the parallel stories; the language, especially the metaphors and similes (stressed by Caroline Spurgeon); the rottenness of Denmark; and the rituals and improvisations in the play—the music, drums, cannons, pageantry, rites, playlet, gags, and puns. No interpretation can be correct that does not explain all of these as constituents of the play.

But a correct interpretation also must explain something else, something deeper and more difficult to comprehend than the *données*, namely, the myth and ritual role that *Hamlet* played in Elizabethan culture, i.e., the place that *Hamlet* and Shakespearean tragedy occupied in Elizabethan life, a life in which the theater still retained its old ritual function.

Fergusson's fundamental thesis about *Hamlet* is that the main action, "the basic situation," of the play is the attempt to find and destroy the "hidden imposthume" of Denmark. It is this quest that ties *Hamlet* inextricably with Greek tragedy and ancient ritual. For it is the welfare of Denmark and not the hero's plight that is central. The whole action is based on the time's being out of joint. Everything reflects this main action; consequently, *Hamlet* must be seen as a series of shifting perspectives on this analogue of the basic situation. Moreover, since everyone in the play has a share in the main action, the welfare of Denmark, there is nothing irrelevant in it; hence Eliot is simply myopic in his perception of superfluous scenes in the play.

Hamlet is thus a multiple plot, paralleling, at least in its form, *The Odyssey* rather than Greek or French classical tragedy. *The Odyssey* also is a series of analogues on one major theme: the attempt to return home. Like Homer, Shakespeare composed by analogy, not by emotional or conceptual progression. And the anagoge (the ultimate meaning) of the play, which is Denmark as it mirrors the world, is present in all the relations within the play: the tragic and the comic as ironic parallels; the father-son relationships; the women and their relations to their men; and the various stories. All of these relationships embody the total concern of everyone for the welfare of the state.

Fergusson divides the main action of the play into a prologue (I, 1, 2, 3), in which the malady of Denmark is brought out; the agons or conflicts and contrasts (I, 4, 5; II; III, 1), in which there is the attempt to identify and destroy the malady; the climax, peripety, and recognition (III, 2, 3, 4), in which the hidden imposthume is opened; the pathos and/or sparagmos (IV), in which there occurs all the suffering that ensues from the opening; and the epiphany or collective revelation (V), in which the illness of Denmark is perceived by all.

To grasp the total meaning of *Hamlet* we must recognize also in *Hamlet* the many examples of ritual and improvisation as part of the basic myth and ritual pattern of human expression. "Both the ritual and the improvisational elements in *Hamlet* are essential—as essential as the stories—in the structure of the whole."[2] *Hamlet* is more than its interwoven plots and Hamlet's motives. It has its peculiar rhythms, effects and tensions. The rituals and improvisations in the play offer means of imitating the main action which the plot cannot assimilate.

There are in the play religious, cultural, and moral values, aspects of a tradition that reaches back to the origins of Western drama itself. "*Hamlet* was formed in a Theater which was close to the root of drama itself. . . ."[3] It "can take myth and ritual as still alive."[4] Shakespeare employed this idea of theater as myth and ritual. It was accepted also by his audience. Indeed, *Hamlet* escapes us if we think of it "in abstraction from the theater in which it was formed."[5]

Now, in order to understand Fergusson's thesis, we must try to clarify his notions of myth, ritual, and improvisation. "Improvisation" he does not define but explains by some examples from *Hamlet:* Hamlet's sermon on drunkenness (I, 4); his wisecracks to Polonius, Rosencrantz, Guildenstern, and the players (II, 2); his charge to the players (III, 2); and some features of the play scene which becomes the center of improvisation and ritual combined since it "is both rite and entertainment, and shows the Prince as at once clown and ritual head of the state."[6]

"Myth" and "ritual" Fergusson discusses in his chapter on *Oedipus*

[2] *Ibid.*, p. 113. [3] *Ibid.*, p. 98. [4] *Ibid.*
[5] *Ibid.*, p. 112. [6] *Ibid.*, p. 115.

Rex. Both terms derive from the Cambridge School of Classical Anthropology. Greek tragedy, according to Gilbert Murray and Jane Harrison, two members of this school, follows the form of the ancient ritual of the seasonal god. Sophocles' *Oedipus Rex,* for example, is the dramatization of the myth that is to be found in the ancient ritual.

> Which came first, the myth or the ritual? Is the ancient ceremony merely an enactment of the Ur-Myth of the year-god—Attis, or Adonis, or Osiris, or the "Fisher-King"—in any case that Hero-King-Father-High-Priest who fights with his rival, is slain and dismembered, then rises anew with the spring season? Or did the innumerable myths of this kind arise to "explain" a ritual which was perhaps mimed or danced or sung to celebrate the annual change of season?[7]

The ancient ritual celebrated the rebirth of the seasonal god. It had its sacred combat, the tearing asunder of the royal victim, and the ensuing lamentation and rejoicing: in other words, it had the same rhythm as that of Greek tragedy. Both ritual and tragedy were celebrations of the mystery of human life.

> The figure of Oedipus himself fulfills all the requirements of the scapegoat, the dismembered king or god-figure. The situation in which Thebes is presented at the beginning of the play—in peril of its life; its crops, its herds, its women mysteriously infertile, signs of a mortal disease of the City, and the disfavor of the gods—is like the withering which winter brings, and calls, in the same way, for struggle, dismemberment, death, and renewal. And this tragic sequence is the substance of the play. It is enough to know that myth and ritual are close together in their genesis, two direct imitations of the perennial experience of the race.[8]

Next, in order to further his hypothesis that *Hamlet* is in the myth-ritual pattern, Fergusson attempts to show

> that the Elizabethan theater had, in fact, this ritual aspect: that Shakespeare's audience, like that of Sophocles, was prepared to

[7] *Ibid.*, pp. 26–27.

[8] *Ibid.*, p. 27.

accept his play not only as an exciting story but as the "celebration of the mystery" of human life.[9]

His evidence that *Hamlet* is a species of ritual drama is, first, the fact that "a great deal of the religious culture of the Middle Ages was still alive in Shakespeare's time."[10] As Tillyard and others have shown, Hamlet's speech on man, for example, is an expression of the medieval conception of man. Second,

> the Elizabethan stage itself, that central mirror of the life of its times, was a symbolic representation of this traditional cosmos: it was thus taken both as the physical and as the metaphysical "scene" of man's life. . . .
>
> The symbolic character of this stage seems to imply a conception of the theater akin to that of ritual: the celebration of the mystery of human life.[11]

Third, the role of the Tudor monarch as the symbol

> and the visible center of the traditional world order. . . . The role of the monarch in Shakespeare's time (and in his plays) was thus very close to that of Sophocles' Oedipus or Creon: he was at once ruler, high priest, and father of the community.[12]

Of course, Fergusson admits, neither Shakespeare nor his audience

> could have expounded this genealogy and these parallels. If the tradition was alive in Shakespeare's time, it was as a "habit of thought and feeling" rather than as an explicit and integrated philosophy. But Shakespeare seems to have felt the essential elements of this great "theater" as alive still; to have assumed that his audience would respond to them, and to have based his dramaturgy upon them.[13]

Hamlet, therefore, is in many ways a parallel to *Oedipus Rex.* In both, the royal one is associated with pollution; there are invocations for well-being; and there is the interweaving of the individual and society. The main difference between them is that one comes at the beginning and the other at the end of the tradition of theater as ritual.

[9] *Ibid.*, p. 114. [10] *Ibid.* [11] *Ibid.*, p. 116.
[12] *Ibid.*, p. 117. [13] *Ibid.*

Hamlet celebrates the mystery of human life. It is in the ritual pattern. In the play, all the rituals show forth the main action. They are "lamps lighting the rottenness of Denmark (the basic situation of the play). . . ."[14] From the beginning—the changing of the guards—to the end—Hamlet being borne like a soldier by four captains—there are rituals that function to focus attention on the body politic and ceremoniously to invoke well-being.

The play scene is at the center of ritual and improvisation. "It has a ritual aspect, it is Hamlet's most ambitious improvisation, and it is the climax and peripety of the whole complex plot-scheme."[15] If we grasp the significance of this scene, we shall be close to understanding Shakespeare's sense of the theater. For this scene "reveals the malady of the regime in all its ambiguity, mystery, and spreading ramifications. . . . It catches more than the conscience of the King."[16] It represents the hidden crime, the incestuous theft, the usurpation. Altogether it functions as an anagoge of human weakness in *Hamlet* itself. The Player-King

> presents very pithily the basic vision of human action in the play, at a level so deep that it applies to all the characters: the guilty, the free, the principals, the bystanders, those in power and the dispossessed.[17]

What, now, of Hamlet in the play? He is "both chief 'agonist' and central 'reflector.' "[18] For three acts he is "a puzzled and, as it were, unconvinced hero and prince."[19] Because of a father murdered and a mother stained he has become ambivalent toward the traditional values. He cannot do with or without the ancient order: "he sees too deeply and skeptically into that cosmic setting of human life which Shakespeare's theater symbolically represented."[20]

Hamlet is the traditional scapegoat hero, the appointed victim to cleanse the scourge of a sick society.

> Hamlet is apparently thought of as undergoing a similar [to that of Oedipus] transformation, from hero to scapegoat, from

[14] *Ibid.*, p. 120. [15] *Ibid.* [16] *Ibid.*, p. 122. [17] *Ibid.*, p. 126.
[18] *Ibid.*, p. 127. [19] *Ibid.*, p. 128. [20] *Ibid.*

> "the expectancy and rose of the fair state" to the distracted, suffering witness and victim of Act V.[21]

But as the play closes,

> we are certainly intended to feel that Hamlet, however darkly and uncertainly he worked, had discerned the way to be obedient to his deepest values, and accomplished some sort of purgatorial progress for himself and Denmark.[22]

Fergusson also places the other characters in the ritualistic scheme he finds in the play. His most important observation is on Fortinbras and his role in the entire ritual. Fortinbras is referred to early in the play, as one threat to a (corrupt) regime, appears briefly in IV, 4, and turns up at the very end of the play, to become the future recognized legitimate monarch. His role must be accounted for: "In the scheme of the whole the role of Fortinbras, though it is very economically developed, is of major importance."[23] Fergusson explains his role, especially his appearance at the end of the play, as a symbol of spiritual rebirth after the cleansing of the scourge. Consequently, he, too, functions as part of the ancient myth and ritual pattern of drama, the celebration of the mystery cycle of human life:

> Fortinbras does not destroy, he "places" the action of the play by suddenly revealing a new analogue of this action. The effect, once more, is not to provide us with an intellectual key, an explicit philosophy, but to release us from the contemplation of the limited mystery of Denmark by returning us to the wider mystery of life in the world at large.[24]

Fergusson's criticism of *Hamlet* is fundamentally criticism as explanation. Unlike, for example, G. Wilson Knight, Fergusson does not begin with or develop a poetics of the drama. Instead he employs certain aspects of a dramaturgy that are stated by him without any debate or argument. In effect, he places his poetics historically by relating the notion of drama as myth and ritual to Elizabethan times and then utilizes this poetics as a category of explanation of *Hamlet*.

[21] *Ibid.*, pp. 127–28. [22] *Ibid.*, pp. 132–33. [23] *Ibid.*, p. 139.
[24] *Ibid.*, p. 140.

Before we examine Fergusson's particular interpretation of *Hamlet,* comment on his theory of interpretation is in order. Fergusson says of other critics of *Hamlet*:

> It is not necessary to rule out the Eliot-Robertson, or the Joycean interpretation, merely because one accepts Mr. Dover Wilson's: on the contrary, the various critics should be taken as Jamesian "reflectors," each lighting a facet of the whole from his own peculiar angle.[25]

I find this remark puzzling. It seems to imply that each of the interpretations of *Hamlet* is true; yet Fergusson rejects each of them. Perhaps what he means is that each clarifies *something* in the play, although none explains everything in the play; hence each is false if it purports to explain everything. Thus, Jones may be said to clarify one aspect of the play, namely, the oedipal relation, and Eliot may be said to explain another aspect, and so on. But all go astray when they enlarge their limited claims about some aspects into general ones about the whole play. Unless Fergusson does mean or imply what I am suggesting he does, his own lengthy, careful analysis of the play loses its driving point, that his interpretation *is* the correct one. It follows from his implied claim that his is the correct interpretation that at least one piece of criticism of *Hamlet,* his own, is more than a reflector. And I think that this is exactly what he is contending, that his own eclectic hypothesis about the whole play is true whereas the other hypotheses are not, although they can be made true by restricting their reference to something less than the whole play and its ultimate meaning.

Of course "criticism as a reflector" might also be construed as the view that critical interpretations are neither true nor false, but invitations on the part of the critic to see the play or some aspect of it in the way the critic proposes in his particular interpretation. Perhaps Fergusson subscribes to this view of interpretation, and, indeed, as we shall see later (chap. xv), it may be the only satisfactory attitude to take toward the different interpretations of *Hamlet.* However, if interpretation is construed as invitation, Fergusson's particular interpretation of the play is also a "reflector," one spotlighting of *Hamlet*

[25] *Ibid.*, p. 101.

rather than a true or false explanation of it. I doubt that Fergusson subscribes to the view that his interpretation of *Hamlet* is merely one among many invitations. Consequently, I assume that he offers us his reading of the play as the correct one.

Is it correct?

Insofar as his interpretation or reading of the play involves the categories of myth and ritual, it is not clear or convincing. First, the notions of myth and ritual, especially in Fergusson's handling of them, are vague, and one could ask for greater precision than he provides for two such basic terms. Second, and more important, his argument that *Hamlet* is a species of ritual drama which celebrates the mystery of human life and not merely a drama with some ordinary rites in it is far from cogent. For his evidence in support of his claims that *Hamlet* reiterated the doctrine of the universe as a chain of being, that the Elizabethan stage symbolized the cosmos, and that the Tudor monarch was sacred, is incomplete. Indeed, there is considerable evidence for the opposite view that *Hamlet* represented a break from traditional values; rather than a celebration of the mystery of human life it celebrated an exciting entertainment on one's afternoon off. Moreover, in *Hamlet* the cracks in the chain are already beginning to show (as Spencer, for example, brings out), the stage is referred to in secular not ritual terms, and the monarch is as much challenged as he is revered.

Let me make my objection more specific: Fergusson's reading of the play is forced throughout. What he says about *Hamlet* as a multiple plot and the main action may be true enough, but his reduction of these and of *Hamlet* as a whole to an analogue of *Oedipus Rex* seems to suffer from the defects of all the univocal readings I have considered and Fergusson himself rejects. To be sure, there are parallels between *Oedipus Rex* and *Hamlet* and even between the two heroes. But the differences between them, as plays or as heroes, are certainly as great as the similarities. For even if one grants Fergusson his reading of *Oedipus Rex*, Hamlet is no mere scapegoat hero; whatever else he is, he is much more than "a witness and a sufferer for the hidden truth of the human condition."[26] To reduce Hamlet to

[26] *Ibid.*, p. 127.

Oedipus, or *Hamlet* to *Oedipus Rex*, is to dismiss the variety and complexity of *Hamlet* that make it a Renaissance play and not a version of an ancient ritual drama. In the way that Jones reduces *Hamlet* to the oedipal complex, to which Fergusson himself objects, does not Fergusson reduce *Hamlet* to his own complex, the *Oedipus Rex* one?

The *Hamlet-Oedipus Rex* parallel distorts by leaving out certain elements of *Hamlet*. But it also distorts some of the elements that Fergusson does not leave out. One crucial example is his reading of Laertes' admonition to Ophelia in I, 3. Fergusson writes: "Laertes . . . instinctively thinks of Hamlet as the source of infection, much as Claudius does, though for less specific reasons."[27] But when we look at the text we find that Laertes does no such thing. His admonition to Ophelia is founded not on his fear that Hamlet is a source of infection to anyone but, quite rightly, on his fear that Hamlet cannot make good his professed love because of his princely station. The passage does not yield Fergusson's dark rendering of it; one feels here as well as elsewhere that Fergusson has already committed himself to the view that the entire play is the search for and the destruction of the hidden imposthume, of which the first act, including the scene of Laertes and Ophelia, is the *setting forth* of the malady.

Another misreading of the same sort is that *all* the characters in the play seek the identification and destruction of the potential malady. One cannot but react against this "hide and seek" conception of the play. Claudius, for one, does not seek to identify and destroy the potential or actual malady. He tries to keep it hidden since, after all, he is responsible for it.

I conclude that Fergusson's interpretation of *Hamlet* explains some but not all of the play. If I may borrow a cue from him about other critics, what he does, and successfully, is to set forth some of the various sets of relationships and some of the neglected elements of the play. This exploration of the basic *données* of *Hamlet* is descriptive

[27] *Ibid.*, p. 106.

criticism. And Fergusson certainly shows by example just how important this criticism can be. If we separate his descriptions from his explanation of the whole play, there is much to be said for the actual truth of his remarks, even though, I think, it must also be said that his interpretation of *Hamlet* remains inadequate.

VIII J. DOVER WILSON

IN HIS trilogy, *The Manuscript of Shakespeare's "Hamlet"* (1934), "The New Shakespeare" edition of *Hamlet* (1934), and *What Happens in "Hamlet"* (1935), J. Dover Wilson has produced a combination of scholarship, editorship, and dramatic interpretation which, because of its power, elegance, audacity, and illumination, makes him as worthy of study as any critic in the corpus of *Hamlet* criticism.[1] His total contribution to the understanding of *Hamlet* and Shakespeare, it seems to me, is in the tradition of greatness established by Johnson, Coleridge, and Bradley.

Unlike these three, however, his primary concern is not with evaluation, poetics of drama, or even analysis of character, although he discusses these in his context of the determination of an accurate text and reading of *Hamlet*.

Wilson proffers no grand theories of art, drama, or tragedy. He seems to work comfortably with certain established Aristotelian notions of tragedy and well-constructed dramas.[2] In his criticism of

[1] John Dover Wilson, *The Manuscript of Shakespeare's "Hamlet"* (2 vols.; Cambridge, 1934); (ed.), *Hamlet* (Cambridge, 1934); and *What Happens in "Hamlet"* (Cambridge, 1935).

[2] See esp. *What Happens in "Hamlet":* "Shakespeare asks every spectator, every reader, to *sympathise* with his hero, to feel with him, to place himself in

Hamlet there is no attempt to reduce the play to a basic meaning or interpretation that is derived from a theory of symbolism, art, or life. As a critic, his main objective is to ascertain just what happens in the play, a task which, he claims, had never been pursued adequately before him and yet is a *sine qua non* for any large-scale interpretive criticism.

Hamlet is an Elizabethan drama. Consequently, if we are to understand it, we are obliged to see it in its own terms of Elizabethan dramatic art and not, as too many critics have done, in terms foreign to Shakespeare's and dramatic art altogether. First, we must not treat any of the characters, especially

> Hamlet as if he were a living man or a historical character, instead of being a single figure, if the central figure, in a dramatic composition. . . . Apart from the play, apart from his actions, from what he tells us about himself and what other characters tell us about him, there is no Hamlet.[3]
>
> It is entirely misleading to attempt to describe Hamlet's state of mind in terms of modern psychology . . . because . . . Hamlet is a character in a play, not in history.[4]

Nor must we

> try to fit Shakespeare's creatures and his conceptions of human nature into the procrustean bed of Elizabethan psychology; his vision altogether transcended such limitations.[5]

Second, we cannot understand *Hamlet* by a reduction of it to its sources. Critics who so reduce it

---

his shoes, to understand his situation, and to attempt, in imagination, a solution. That is, in part, the meaning of tragic drama . . ." (p. 44; italics in original).

"Rob us of our respect for the hero and *Hamlet* ceases to be a tragedy . . ." (p. 102).

"Hamlet struggles against his weakness, and the struggle is in great measure the ground-work of his tragedy." (p. 218).

"In poetic tragedy we contemplate beings greater than ourselves, greater than it is possible for man to be, enduring and brought to a calamitous end by sorrow or affliction or weakness of character which we should find unendurable; and we contemplate all this with unquestioning assent and with astonishment that deepens to awe." (pp. 219–20).

[3] Wilson, *Hamlet*, p. xlv.

[4] Wilson, *What Happens in "Hamlet,"* p. 218.

[5] *Ibid.*, p. 116.

> appear to have no aesthetic, or at least dramatic, principles whatever, but seek to explain and appraise everything in Shakespeare by reference to historical causes. Thus, when they come upon passages, scenes or characters which perplex them, instead of asking themselves what Shakespeare's purpose might have been or what artistic function such passages, scenes or characters might conceivably possess in a play written for the Elizabethan stage and for an Elizabethan audience, they label them "relics of an old play" and talk of the stubbornness of Shakespeare's material or the crudity of Elizabethan drama.[6]

These critics

> sin against a primary canon of criticism [which is that] we must first understand, or do our best to understand, exactly what Shakespeare's dramatic purposes are, before we even begin to explore how the play came to be constructed.[7]

Third, the critic must not, even as Bradley does, indulge in "the fallacy of regarding separate episodes of the play, especially episodes early in the play, in the light of his knowledge of the whole."[8]

Wilson, thus, is not especially concerned with aesthetics or poetics, or the conversion of drama into psychology or history. His major interest as a critic of *Hamlet* is embodied in the title of his book, *What Happens in "Hamlet,"* that is, in the correct elucidation of the plot of *Hamlet*.

But this is no easy business. In his gracious "epistle dedicatory" to W. W. Greg, one of the great contemporary Elizabethan scholars, Wilson relates how difficult this job was for him and others who were struggling along the same lines. In 1917, Greg raised fundamental problems about Claudius and the dumb-show that precedes "The Murder of Gonzago."[9] Greg proposed that the Ghost and his tale are products of Hamlet's diseased imagination and offered as evidence for his hypothesis the important fact that Claudius does not blench at the depiction of the crime in the dumb-show. Greg's was so unorthodox an

[6] Wilson, *Hamlet*, pp. xlvi–xlvii.

[7] Wilson, *What Happens in "Hamlet,"* p. 15.

[8] *Ibid.*, p. 94.

[9] W. W. Greg, "Hamlet's Hallucination," *The Modern Language Review*, XII (October, 1917), 393–421.

interpretation that Wilson was led to a refutation of it which, because of what the refutation involved, took some seventeen years to complete.

> Did Claudius see the dumb-show? and if not, why not? It is just because I think the posing of that problem a turning-point in the history of Shakespearian criticism that I have written this book.[10]

Guided and abetted by historians, bibliographers, handwriting experts, and dictionary editors, Wilson moved from the dumb-show and the play scene to studies of Elizabethan spiritualism and politics; thence, inevitably to the shatteringly important fact that basic research on the textual foundations of the play was an absolute beginning of the criticism of *Hamlet*. The dumb-show became but one of the puzzles. Others, equally important, presented themselves, demanding their dramatic solutions, especially since nothing short of Shakespeare's reputation as an artist was at stake.

Criticism of *Hamlet,* Wilson contends, revolves around three different, yet related, sets of problems:

> There are, in fact, three groups of *Hamlet* problems: textual, exegetic, and dramatic. They are distinct, and require different instruments for their manipulation. Yet no group can be satisfactorily handled apart from the others. It is impossible, for example, to be certain that we have justly estimated Hamlet's character, until we know the meaning of everything that he says and that other characters say about him, while it is equally impossible to be certain what the speakers say until we have made up our minds exactly what Shakespeare intended to write. The textual problems are therefore fundamental. Yet they cannot be solved in isolation or without regard to exegetic and dramatic considerations.[11]

For Wilson, then, the criticism of *Hamlet* starts with the determination of the Shakespearean text and proceeds to the interpretation of the dialogue and the narration of the plot; only then can it engage in character analysis and large-scale readings of the play.

[10] Wilson, *What Happens in "Hamlet,"* p. 23.

[11] Wilson, *The Manuscript of Shakespeare's "Hamlet,"* I, xi–xii; see also *What Happens in "Hamlet,"* pp. 12–13 and *Hamlet*, p. x.

What are the textual problems? The basic one is to ascertain exactly what was Shakespeare's text of *Hamlet*. What complicates this problem is that we simply do not know what kind of manuscript lay behind the two main texts of Shakespeare's *Hamlet:* the Second Quarto of 1604–5 and the First Folio of 1623. (The First Quarto of 1603, discovered in 1823, is now universally regarded as a pirated edition, based on a memorial reconstruction of performances of *Hamlet* in 1601–2.) What is the relation between the Second Quarto and the Folio? Who was responsible for their transmission? Which text is closer to Shakespeare's own manuscript?

Wilson has tried to answer these questions as well as others suggested by them. Since his full discussion occupies the two volumes of *The Manuscript of Shakespeare's "Hamlet,"* I can do no more here than to summarize his results and relate them to one example which can then serve as a paradigm of textual issues in criticism. In the Introduction to his edition of *Hamlet,* Wilson writes:

> In *The Manuscript of Shakespeare's "Hamlet"* I have been able to prove—or so at least I hope—that the copy for *Hamlet* used by the printers of the First Folio, though ultimately derived from the author's autograph, reached them in a very corrupt condition. It was in short a transcript of a transcript: a transcript made in 1622 or 1623 for the publication of the Folio; made from the Globe prompt-book which, though itself in all probability taken direct from Shakespeare's manuscript, had been edited in a more or less high-handed fashion by the bookholder of the theatre; and made by a slovenly playhouse scribe, who to save himself the trouble of keeping his eye constantly on the prompt-book before him frequently trusted to a treacherous memory of the play as he had seen it performed. On the other hand, there is good reason for believing that the *Hamlet* of 1605 was printed, if badly printed, from Shakespeare's autograph, which the company sold to the publisher, the bookholder having no further use for it once he had prepared his prompt-copy for the actors.[12]

The Second Quarto (1604–5), thus, is the authoritative text for Wilson. Unfortunately, however, it contains many printing errors:

[12] Wilson, *Hamlet,* p. xxvii.

misprints and omissions of words, phrases, lines, and sometimes even whole passages. These errors, Wilson surmises, are the products of an inexperienced printer and a slovenly proofreader. But if one edits cautiously, with the Folio or even the First Quarto as aids to the rectification of the errors, an adequate text of Shakespeare's *Hamlet* is forthcoming.

As an editor concerned with textual criticism, one fundamental change Wilson advocates is "too too sullied flesh" for "too too sallied flesh" (Second Quarto), "too much grieu'd and sallied flesh" (First Quarto), and "too too solid Flesh" (First Folio), in the first line of Hamlet's first soliloquy. His argument for this change must suffice as our paradigm of Wilson as a textual critic.

There are graphical, linguistic, literary, and dramatic issues involved in this crux. Wilson's main discussion of them is in his *Manuscript*, II, 307–15.

The Second Quarto reads "too too sallied flesh." "A," Wilson claims, is a misprint for "u:"

> A:u misreadings are very common in Shakespeare, and especially common in *Hamlet* Q2. . . . Q2's collection comprises "Gertrad" for "Gertrude" (*passim*), "course" for "coarse" (=corse), "quietas" for "quietus," "raine" for "ruin," "heaue, a" for "heaven," "waters" for "winters," and on two occasions "deale" for "deule," which was evidently Shakespeare's spelling of "devil," and is so printed at 3. 2. 137. . . . This double misreading of "deule" . . . is paralleled by "sallied" itself. For my second point is that the word "sully" is misprinted "sally" in Q2 not only at 1. 2. 129 but also at 2. 1. 39 ("laying these slight sallies on my sonne" is the context); and not only in *Hamlet* but also in *Love's Labour's Lost*. . .[13]

Can "sallied" mean "assaulted," as some have suggested? Wilson says no since this usage has no support from the *New English Dictionary;* nor is this usage applicable to other instances of "sally": "Polonius cannot mean Reynaldo to 'lay assaults' upon Laertes, however 'slight'. . . . 'Sallied' simply will not do."[14] "Solid" will not

[13] Wilson, *The Manuscript of Shakespeare's "Hamlet,"* II, 307–8.
[14] *Ibid.*, p. 308.

do either: Richard Burbadge, the original Hamlet, already stout in 1601, could hardly have uttered the line, "O that this too too solid Flesh would melt!" Even the First Quarto lends support to "sullied." "Grieu'd and sallied flesh" is intelligible enough, Wilson says, and it shows that the reporter-pirate at least grasped the meaning of the phrase when he wrote it down from his memory of the performance. "Sullied," thus, was in the text from the beginning. It was perverted later into "solid" by one of the slovenly scribes who prepared the Globe promptbook for the press. "Sullied," furthermore, is right from the literary point of view:

> I am bold enough to think that the case for "sullied" is strong enough to stand by itself on literary grounds without requiring any critical canons to buttress it. . . . "Melt—thaw—dew"; the image behind those words is unquestionable. Hamlet is thinking of snow begrimed with soot and dirt, as it often is in melting, and wishing that his "sullied flesh" might melt as snow melts in time of thaw. Without the word "sullied" there would be no clue at all to this, and the picture of melting, thawing, and dissolving into dewdrops would remain pointless—with "solid flesh," I venture to think, a little ridiculous. . . .
>
> There is a good deal more behind this epithet than an image of purity defiled. It stands as the most important word in the opening line of the First Soliloquy, and it strikes the keynote of Hamlet's dream-like meditation . . . [and is] one of the principal motifs of the whole play.[15]

Wilson also relates "sullied" to Hamlet's strange conduct toward Ophelia, specifically, to his talk of himself to her: "Virtue cannot so inoculate our old stock, but we shall relish of it" (III, 1, 117–18); and "I could accuse me of such things, that it were better my mother had not borne me" (III, 1, 123–24). Both remarks, Wilson claims, reveal Hamlet's fear of involvement in his mother's lust.[16]

The second set of problems, the exegetic, concerns the correct

[15] *Ibid.*, pp. 312–14; see also *Hamlet*, Notes, pp. 151–52; and *What Happens in "Hamlet,"* pp. 39 ff. Cf. *Hamlet*, Additional Notes, p. 294.

[16] For Wilson on the relation between textual criticism and stage directions, speech headings, punctuation, etc., see esp. *Hamlet*, p. xxxi; and *What Happens in "Hamlet,"* pp. 40–41.

assignments of meanings to words and phrases in *Hamlet.* "Commentary," resulting in a "glossary," are Wilson's terms for this branch of criticism. In *Hamlet,* the specific exegetical problems have to do with the vocabulary in general, "which seems richer here than ever before or after . . .":[17] Hamlet's riddling habit of speech; the tremendous variety of the scenes as they relate to Elizabethan life; and all the topical allusions. In his Introduction Wilson lists "some thirty of the more important passages upon which I think I have been able to throw fresh light."[18] But this claim seems unduly modest since one can add more passages if one includes his glosses in *What Happens in "Hamlet."* Here, to begin with, is a simple example of his work as a commentator. In I, 1, 166–67, Horatio says:

> But look, the morn in russet mantle clad
> Walks o'er the dew of yon high eastward hill.

Wilson *comments:*

> The word "russet," used to describe the indeterminate reddish-brown or grey of the sky at daybreak, recalls the coarse home-spun cloth, which is its original sense, and so gives birth to the image of Dawn as a labourer mounting the hill to his work of the day, his mantle thrown across his shoulder.[19]

Another example: In I, 5, 81, the Ghost says to Hamlet,

> If thou hast nature in thee bear it not,

about which Wilson comments: "What could be more palpable or straightforward? Yet the discovery that the simple-looking word 'nature' may mean 'natural feeling,' and consequently 'filial affection,' illuminates not only this line but four other passages in the play. . . ."[20]

The *New English Dictionary,* Wilson reminds us, is indispensable for any adequate commentary and glossary. Take, for example, Hamlet's reference to "mortal coil" (III, 1, 67). "Coil v^3" is defined in the *N.E.D.* as "to wind or lay it up round or in a ring." Hence, Wilson says, "We need not hesitate, therefore, to credit Shakespeare with the quibble upon 'coil, a winding of rope,' or Hamlet with the

[17] Wilson, *Hamlet,* p. viii.
[18] *Ibid.,* p. xxxii.
[19] *Ibid.,* p. xxxvi.
[20] *Ibid.,* p. xxxiii.

notion of the body as a troublesome entanglement which the soul 'shuffles off' at death."[21]

A final example: In I, 2, 63–66, we have the first dialogue between Hamlet and Claudius:

> KING: But now my cousin Hamlet, and my son—
> HAMLET (*aside*): A little more than kin, and less than kind.
> KING: How is it that the clouds still hang on you?
> HAMLET: Not so, my lord, I am too much in the "son."

Hamlet's last reply, Wilson comments,

> is another quibble, but this time direct, defiant and (to Elizabethan ears) unambiguous. I say to Elizabethan ears, because unfortunately until recently the point has been missed by modern readers. Hamlet was known, by comparison with similar quibbles in *King Lear* and other books of the period, to be alluding to the now obsolete proverbial expression "Out of heaven's blessing to the warm sun"; but it was only discovered four years ago [in 1931, by P. L. Carver] that the true interpretation of this expression was "From an exalted, or honourable, state or occupation to a low or ignoble one," an interpretation, to quote the words of the discoverer himself, which "seems to favour the belief that one cause, among others, of Hamlet's bitterness was his exclusion from the throne."[22]

Wilson's third set of critical problems, the dramatic, has to do with what happens in the play. There are many of these problems. Some of the important ones are: (1) Does Claudius see the dumb-show? (2) Why does Hamlet behave as he does in the cellarage scene? (3) Why does Hamlet insult Ophelia in the nunnery scene? (4) Does Hamlet really doubt the Ghost after he has seen and talked with him? (5) Why do Rosencrantz and Guildenstern talk to Hamlet of ambition? (6) Does Hamlet regard Claudius as a usurper? These problems, Wilson contends, can be solved, provided we make one assumption:

> that Shakespeare knew his own business as a dramatist better than his critics. . . . I shall draw attention to a large number of difficulties, of which many have hitherto passed unnoticed and

[21] *Ibid.*, p. xxxiv.
[22] Wilson, *What Happens in "Hamlet,"* pp. 32–33.

most have never been explained, and I shall seek a *dramatic* reason for them all. . . . In brief, I shall try to show that parts of the plot have fallen into disuse through "bestial oblivion." Fortunately, there is nothing, I think, lost beyond recovery, nothing that care cannot restore to its pristine beauty and its original function.[23]

"Bestial oblivion," here comprises ignorance of Shakespeare's text, an accurate glossary, Elizabethan thought, and Shakespearean stagecraft. Once these are recovered and understood in their proper settings, the plot and the whole play will be seen to work.[24]

Hamlet, Wilson begins, is primarily a tragedy, "the tragedy of a genius caught fast in the toils of circumstance and unable to fling free."[25] The first act of the play is the presentation of Hamlet's burden; the second and third acts, "the testing of the Ghost's story, or to put it in other words, Hamlet's attempt to probe the secret guilt of Claudius";[26] and the fourth and fifth acts, Hamlet's eclipse, victory, and death.

But Wilson is more concerned with the particular workings of the plot, especially the obscure parts, than he is with the general pattern of *Hamlet* as a tragedy. First, he analyzes Hamlet's burden which, for him, has three elements: Hamlet's loss of his throne, Gertrude's incest, and the Ghost's revelation and complex assignment. Wilson elucidates each of these, bringing in relevant textual, exegetical, and historical data in order to make it clear.

From Shakespeare to Dr. Johnson, Wilson points out, Claudius was regarded as a usurper and Hamlet as the rightful heir to the throne. "It is extraordinary how blind modern commentators have been to this fact and to all that it involves. Yet it is implicit throughout the play and even twice explicit [III, 4, 99; V, 2, 66]."[27] Wilson concedes

[23] *Ibid.*, pp. 15–16 (italics in original).

[24] See esp. Wilson, *Hamlet:* "Before we can decide whether a plot works effectively we ought at least to enquire whether all the parts of the plot are in working order. It is my contention that important elements of the plot of *Hamlet* have been lost or overlaid, and that the real 'problem' is to recover these elements" (pp. xlix–l).

[25] Wilson, *What Happens in "Hamlet,"* p. 39.

[26] *Ibid.*, p. 88.

[27] *Ibid.*, p. 30.

that Shakespeare does not make the references to usurpation explicit until late in the play, but only because "he knew his audience would assume the situation from the outset."[28] The constitution of the state of Denmark in *Hamlet* is English, not Danish; for English institutions are always implicit in the dramas of Shakespeare, whatever the dramatized locale. Furthermore, the stage directions of I, 2, distorted in the Folio but not in the Second Quarto, show that the second scene "is intended to represent a meeting of the Privy Council. *Enter Claudius, King of Denmarke, Gertrud the Queene, Councillors, Polonius, and his Sonne Laertes, Hamlet, Cum Alijs.* . . ."[29] Textual criticism, therefore, proves that this second scene is no court gala but "The King in Council" transacting official business. Hamlet's attitude toward Claudius also supports the usurpation motive, for Hamlet's "A little more than kin, and less than kind," especially "less than kind," refers to Hamlet's disappointed hopes of the succession, and is echoed by Hamlet's "I am too much in the 'son'," where the latter is glossed as "From an exalted position to an ignoble one."

"The usurpation is one of the main factors in the plot of *Hamlet*."[30] Both Hamlet and Claudius are aware of it. It becomes central in the dialogue between Hamlet and Rosencrantz and Guildenstern, and it clarifies one crucial aspect of the play scene. "In a word, suppress the usurpation-motive and we miss half the meaning of what happens in acts 2 and 3. As an aid to the operation of the plot it is second only in importance to a true understanding of the Ghost. And this in itself is strong evidence in its favour."[31]

The usurpation motive, however, is not as important as Gertrude's sin of incest. Here, too, we must understand her second marriage in Elizabethan terms, as an infringement upon prevalent ecclesiastical law. Hamlet's first soliloquy, especially in its Second Quarto wording and punctuation, presents the full force of Gertrude's share in Hamlet's tragic burden. "Sullied" carries the weight of the soliloquy, and betokens much of what is to come in the whole play; "sullied" is, "as it were, a window through which we view the rest of the drama."[32] An understanding of its meaning and implications shows, for example,

[28] *Ibid.*, p. 31.
[29] *Ibid.*, pp. 28–29.
[30] *Ibid.*, p. 34.
[31] *Ibid.*
[32] *Ibid.*, p. 43.

just how wrong Goethe was in his claim that Hamlet's tragedy is "a great deed imposed upon a soul unequal to the performance of it." Rather Hamlet's tragedy reveals how "a great and noble spirit [is] subjected to a moral shock so overwhelming that it shatters all zest for life and all belief in it."[33]

The third part of Hamlet's tragic burden is the task laid upon him "to avenge his father without in any way injuring the woman who shared the murderer's crown and his incestuous bed."[34]

The last part of his burden is his doubt about the honesty of the Ghost, a doubt that is born during the cellarage scene at the end of the first act. This is important, yet it "has been almost entirely overlooked hitherto [and] involves an enquiry into the nature of Elizabethan spiritualism. . . ."[35]

Wilson sums up the first act:

> At the end of the first act, the back upon which the tragic load rests begins to show signs of breaking . . . simply because of the sheer weight of the load. So great is Hamlet's moral stature, so tough is his nerve, that the back does *not* break. But he is crippled, and the arm which should perform the Ghost's command is paralysed. Thus he continues to support the burden, but is unable to discharge it. That, in a sentence, is "the tragical history of Hamlet, Prince of Denmark."[36]

Next, we must consider Wilson's elucidation of the Ghost in *Hamlet*. "The Ghost is the linchpin of *Hamlet;* remove it and the play falls to pieces."[37] The Ghost also must be conceived in Elizabethan terms because "the majesty of buried Denmark is an English spirit, English of the late sixteenth and early seventeenth centuries, and the story of *Hamlet* turns upon this fact."[38]

There are a number of questions about the Ghost that must be answered if we are to make him intelligible in the play:

> (i) Where does the Ghost come from: Heaven, Hell or Purgatory? and if from the last, why does Hamlet constantly associate it in his speech with Hell, and even suggest at one point that it may be a devil?

[33] *Ibid.* [34] *Ibid.*, p. 46. [35] *Ibid.*, p. 49.
[36] *Ibid.*, p. 50 (italics in original). [37] *Ibid.*, p. 52. [38] *Ibid.*, p. 53.

(ii) How comes it that Hamlet, after talking with the spirit of his father, refers in a later scene to the next world as

> The undiscovered country, from whose bourn
> No traveller returns?

(iii) What is really happening in the cellarage scene?
(iv) Why does Hamlet find it necessary to test the truth of the Ghost's story by having the Gonzago interlude played before his uncle?
(v) Why does the Ghost appear in the bedroom scene? and why can Gertrude neither hear nor see him?[39]

In answering these questions, Wilson begins by observing that Shakespeare's Ghost was a revolutionary innovation in that Shakespeare transformed the traditional Senecan jack-in-the-box-spook into a humanized ghost who is dramatically convincing. But Wilson's basic point about the Ghost in *Hamlet* is that his reality is never in doubt, only his nature or provenance. The four witnesses of the Ghost reflect the prevalent different attitudes of the Elizabethans: the Catholic, which held that "ghosts might be spirits of the departed, allowed to return from Purgatory for some special purpose, which it was the duty of the pious to further if possible, in order that the wandering soul might find rest";[40] the Protestant, which could no longer accept Purgatory, hence held that, although ghosts could be angels, they were more likely to be "devils, who 'assumed'—such was the technical word—the form of departed friends or relatives, in order to work bodily or spiritual harm upon those to whom they appeared";[41] and the Skeptic, according to which ghosts either were not real or could not assume a material form. Marcellus and Barnardo share in the first attitude, Hamlet accepts the second, and Horatio, until he sees the Ghost, represents the skeptical attitude. The basic problem for Hamlet as well as for his audience, consequently, was: Is the Ghost that Hamlet has seen and conversed with his father's spirit, a devil—as he seems to be in the cellarage scene—or an angel? Until we understand that this was a crucial problem for Hamlet and his audience, much of the drama, especially Hamlet's expressed motive for the play (II, 2, 592–609), remains unintelligible.

[39] *Ibid.*, pp. 53–54. [40] *Ibid.*, p. 62. [41] *Ibid.*

Historical information about Elizabethan spiritualism also clarifies the give and take of the cellarage scene, where "father and son seem to be playing into each other's hands in order to hoodwink an inconvenient witness [Marcellus]."[42] The strange language and the threefold oath fall into their dramatic place because the Ghost behaves exactly like an Elizabethan underground demon. Thus, it is no wonder that Hamlet (and his audience) are left in real doubt about the nature of the Ghost.

Wilson also elucidates the Hamlet-Ophelia problem and offers a solution of it. Critics have been unanimous in their perplexity at Hamlet's treatment of Ophelia. Bradley even gave up on any satisfactory explanation of it. Ernest Jones explains Hamlet's behavior as part of his unresolved oedipal complex. Schücking and others construe it as a relic of the old story in which Ophelia was a female decoy. None of these views, Wilson says, is adequate. Here is his own:

> Hamlet's outrageous language to her . . . can indeed only be excused if he had good grounds for supposing her to be that which he appears to assume. Something is lost, some clue. . . . And what is lost is a very simple thing—a single stage-direction, giving Hamlet an entry (on the inner Elizabethan stage) nine lines before his entry on the other stage at 2. 2. 167, an entry which enables him accidentally and unseen to overhear the eavesdropping plot hatched between Polonius and Claudius, and so implicates Ophelia beyond possibility of doubt in his ears as one of his uncle's minions. The stage-direction is found in neither of the good texts; but the double-entry in Shakespeare's manuscript would naturally puzzle compositor and copyist; while omission, especially of stage-directions, is so common a feature of both texts that the absence of this one need not seriously disturb us, when weighed against the evidence of the surrounding dialogue. . . .[43]

Polonius' "I'll loose my daughter to him," which is overheard by Hamlet, brings down on Polonius Hamlet's epithets, "fishmonger" (panderer) and "carrion" (flesh), and on Ophelia, the insults of the

[42] *Ibid.*, p. 81.

[43] Wilson, *Hamlet*, pp. lvi–lvii.

nunnery scene. The lost stage direction also explains some of the events of the second and third acts, especially the play scene, where Hamlet is aware of the plot that has been hatched against him.

The play scene is the dramatic center of *Hamlet* for Wilson. "It is the climax and crisis of the whole drama. Yet it remains almost wholly unintelligible to the modern reader and playgoer."[44] The corresponding center of Wilson's dramatic criticism of *Hamlet* is to narrate exactly what happens in this one scene. To understand or to play correctly this scene presupposes answers to at least these questions:

> How is it that the players bring with them to Elsinore a drama which reproduces in minute detail all the circumstances of the King's crime? What is the dramatic purpose of the long conversation between Hamlet and the First Player immediately before the play begins? Why is the play preceded by a dumb-show? Why does not Claudius show any signs of discomfiture at this dumb-show, which is a more complete representation of the circumstances of the murder than the play which follows it? What is Hamlet's object in making the murderer the nephew and not the brother of the King? Why should the courtiers, who know nothing of the real poisoning, assume later that Hamlet has behaved outrageously to his uncle and even threatened him with death?[45]

We can answer these questions, Wilson claims, by recovering what has been lost. Consider, first, the "technical" problems, the main one being that of the parallelism between the play and Claudius' crime:

> Now it is surely clear that this coincidence is deliberate and purely structural; the two inner plots, so strangely alike, are two main pillars of the play, which run up into a great arch and meet in the play scene; remove them, or disturb their balance by alterations, and the whole drama would come toppling down.[46]

The dumb-show is "the key-stone of the Ghost-Gonzago arch. . . . Remove it and . . . the play scene is ruined."[47]

The play, "The Murder of Gonzago," is a mousetrap that must

[44] Wilson, *What Happens in "Hamlet,"* p. 138.
[45] *Ibid.*, p. 139.
[46] *Ibid.*, pp. 140–41.
[47] *Ibid.*, p. 145.

catch the king. Shakespeare uses the dumb-show to let his audience know that the play to follow is such a mousetrap. Consequently, the dumb-show is as essential to the play scene as the latter is to the whole of *Hamlet.* Ophelia says,

> Belike this show imports the argument of the play [III, 2, 137–38];

this is Shakespeare's cue—to let the audience know what is to come.

What of Claudius? Does he see the dumb show? Here we reach the crux of the play scene and of Wilson's investigations, "the turning-point in the history of Shakespearian criticism."

Greg had suggested that Claudius sees the dumb-show and is unmoved by it. Others have held that he sees it, is moved, but says nothing; this is the "second-tooth" theory according to which Hamlet deliberately tests the King twice. Wilson rejects Greg's theory because it implies that Hamlet never saw the Ghost and the "second-tooth" theory because "Hamlet cannot have planned the dumb-show, inasmuch as he disliked dumb-shows in general, is as completely taken aback by this one as we are ourselves, and is withal exceedingly annoyed at it."[48] As Hamlet's discourse on the drama to the Players shows, he is completely opposed to dumb-shows; consequently, the dumb-show is the work of the First-Player, who stupidly betrays Hamlet with it as he does later in the "Murder of Gonzago" with his gapings and mouthings. "Miching mallecho" (which means "sneaking mischief") is the clue: these words do not refer to Claudius, "but to the *skulking iniquity* of the players, who have introduced this unauthorised and ridiculous dumb-show, and so have almost ruined the whole plot."[49] Hamlet's fury and anxiety over the dumb-show are simply incompatible with the "second-tooth" theory. Hamlet, therefore, does not plan to test the King twice.

Claudius does not see the dumb-show—this is Wilson's theory. Consider again the dialogue of the play scene: Claudius repeats Ophelia's remark about the argument of the play in his query,

> Have you heard the argument? is there no offence in't [III, 2, 231–32]

[48] *Ibid.*, p. 153.

[49] *Ibid.*, p. 157 (italics in original).

This question "makes it certain that the King cannot have seen the dumb-show, which *is* the argument of the play, as every member of the audience is now aware."[50]

What, then, is Claudius doing during the dumb show? He is talking to Polonius about Hamlet. Just before the dumb show begins, Hamlet says to Ophelia,

> What should a
> man do but be merry, for look you how
> cheerfully my mother looks, and my father
> died within's two hours [III, 2, 123–25].

Hamlet's "look you," Wilson says, "is a direction, not merely to Ophelia and the court, but also to the audience in the theatre. . . . It is essential to Shakespeare that his audience should be fully aware of what Claudius is doing at this critical moment, *because it is the moment before the dumb-show appears.*"[51] Claudius and Polonius are concerned only with Hamlet's madness at that moment.

The King, of course, sees the play, or part of it; when he realizes that Hamlet knows all, he runs: "King Mouse has become a shambling, blinking paddock."[52] The play has caught the conscience of the King.

So much for the play scene and Wilson as a critic engaged in restoration. One more item of his criticism of *Hamlet* should be noted, his own attempt at an interpretation of the hero. For Wilson, it is Hamlet's behavior, more than his much-discussed character, that is important: how he acts, what he says, what others say of him, and not what sort of person he is. In the first place, there is Hamlet's "antic disposition." Is it madness, near-madness, or feigned madness?

> Shakespeare wishes us to feel that Hamlet assumes madness because he cannot help it. The tragic burden has done its work, and he is conscious that he no longer retains perfect control over himself. What more natural than that he should conceal his nervous breakdown behind a mask which would enable him to let himself go when the fit is upon him?[53]

[50] *Ibid.*, p. 159 (italics in original).
[51] *Ibid.*, p. 183 (italics in original).
[52] *Ibid.*, p. 195. [53] *Ibid.*, p. 92.

Hamlet assumes his madness after the cellarage scene "obviously prompted by his hysteria at the moment; and it would be accepted as a convenient disguise while he was maturing his plans."[54]

But Hamlet is also "sorely distracted." He is hysterical at least seven times in the play; these are moments of "emotional instability." They comprise his behavior in the cellarage, his interview with Ophelia in her closet, his self-reproach in the second soliloquy (II, 2), the "nunnery" speech to Ophelia, the latter half of the bedroom scene with his mother, the graveyard episode with Laertes, and the play scene after the King leaves. Is this emotional instability equivalent to madness? Wilson, following Robert Bridges'

> the artful balance whereby
> Shakespeare so gingerly put his sanity in doubt
> Without the while confounding his Reason,

rejects the equivalence in favor of the view that "the fulcrum of the balance, the chief device by means of which Shakespeare prevents us seeing where sanity ends and madness begins is, as Bridges hints, the 'antic disposition.' "[55]

Hamlet also procrastinates; Wilson thus agrees with those critics who insist on the delay as an important fact of the play. But Wilson places the delay later in the play than most critics: "Hamlet's procrastination does not become really glaring until after the Gonzago-play."[56] The delay, to be sure, is related to Hamlet's emotional instability; even so, we cannot pluck out the heart of his mystery.

> That it has heart is an illusion; the mystery itself is an illusion; Hamlet is an illusion. The secret that lies behind it all is not Hamlet's, but Shakespeare's: the technical devices he employed to create this supreme illusion of a great and mysterious character, who is at once mad and the sanest of geniuses, at once a procrastinator and a vigorous man of action, at once a miserable failure and the most adorable of heroes. The character of Hamlet, like the appearance of his successive impersonators on the stage, is a matter of "make-up."[57]

[54] *Ibid.*, p. 95.
[55] *Ibid.*, p. 223.
[56] *Ibid.*, p. 202.
[57] *Ibid.*, p. 229.

To sum up Dover Wilson as a critic of *Hamlet:* From a negative point of view, he does not aim at an aesthetics or a poetics. He propounds no theories; he offers no definitions of art, drama, or even tragedy. Instead he works with certain established criteria, without debating or defending them; his notions of the tragic hero and the fictional aspect of dramatic characters are cases in point. So is his criterion of evaluation: the effective working of the plot. He does not argue for this criterion, but assumes its adequacy and employs it in order to reassess Shakespeare's craft in *Hamlet* and to answer critics of the plot of the play. Wilson has no theory of plot either, in spite of the fact that "plot" is the basic category in his dramatic criticism of *Hamlet.* I find in his writings no analysis of the concept of plot or even of the Aristotelian dictum that plot is more important than character in drama. As a critic, Wilson simply does not enter upon these matters.

On the positive side, Wilson's primary objective as a critic of *Hamlet* is to give an elucidation of the plot, with all that this entails textually, exegetically, and dramatically. By elucidation he means the narration, clarification, and explanation of the various elements in *Hamlet* as these elements unfold dramatically. His book, *What Happens in "Hamlet,"* one might say is an explanation of *Hamlet.* Yet how very different it is from other explanations that derive from one big hypothesis which is then employed to interpret everything in the play. For Wilson, explanation, in his sense of correct retelling of the plot, depends, at least in great part, on previously established knowledge of facts outside of *Hamlet:* Elizabethan stagecraft or spiritualism, for example. Wilson's "historical method," therefore, is not directed toward the explanation of the play in Elizabethan terms but toward the use of historical materials in order to provide an aesthetic analysis of the play.

Wilson's criticism of *Hamlet,* original and provocative as it is, has naturally given rise to much argument and disagreement among his fellow-critics.

First, on the textual criticism, everyone recognizes the pioneer quality of his work, however he assesses Wilson's methods and results.

W. W. Greg, in his famous "Principles of Emendation in Shakespeare,"[58] pays tribute to Wilson's achievements in the establishment of the textual foundations of *Hamlet* and remarks specifically on the one example we surveyed, "sullied flesh":

> The folio's "solid" is a guess we must reject: the "sallied" of the quartos is unintelligible. But "sallies" occurs elsewhere in the second quarto as a misprint for "sullies," showing that the words could be easily confused in Shakespeare's hand. Thus, when he intended "sullied" flesh, it was twice misread as "sallied" and finally misemended to "solid." Of this explanation I have little doubt.[59]

Fredson Bowers, a distinguished American bibliographer, in *On Editing Shakespeare and the Elizabethan Dramatists* (1955),[60] agrees with Greg on Wilson's emendation, "sullied," although he rejects vehemently Wilson's "impressionistic" argument for "sullied" because the argument rests in part on the erroneous assumption that Q2 was printed by an inexperienced, incompetent compositor. Bibliographical study, especially compositor identification and analysis, Bowers states, establishes that Q2 was printed by two equally competent and experienced compositors. It also establishes that "sullied" is authoritative but on evidence that is not Wilson's.[61] Wilson, Bowers points out, was simply lucky in his correct emendation, not scientifically rigorous. Nevertheless, Bowers' assessment of Wilson's work in textual criticism is generous:

> It is fair to say, I think, that in the history of *Hamlet's* editors from Rowe to Sisson only one man, Dover Wilson, saw the need thoroughly to analyze the documents in which variant forms of

[58] W. W. Greg, "Principles of Emendation in Shakespeare," Shakespeare Lecture of the British Academy (1928); reprinted in A. Bradby (ed.), *Shakespearean Criticism 1919–1935* (Oxford, 1936), pp. 78–108.

[59] Greg, "Principles of Emendation in Shakespeare," p. 106.

[60] Fredson Bowers, *On Editing Shakespeare and the Elizabethan Dramatists* (Philadelphia, 1955).

[61] Bowers, *op. cit.*, p. 119; see also pp. 39, 41–42, and 111. Bowers discusses this famous crux also in "Hamlet's 'Sullied' or 'Solid' Flesh: A Bibliographical Case-history," *Shakespeare Survey*, IX, 44–47. Cf. F. W. Bateson, "Modern Bibliography and the Literary Artifact," *English Studies Today* (2d ser.; Bern, 1961), pp. 67–77, for a criticism of both Bowers and Dover Wilson on "sullied."

the text are preserved, and to arrive at a coherent theory about their origins and relations, before undertaking to edit the text according to principles consistent with an overall hypothesis dependent upon this analysis. It is apparent now that Wilson did not investigate the documents with enough rigor to secure all the available evidence, and that he seriously misinterpreted in some important respects the evidence he did secure; thus his hypothesis and the resulting text are affected by various wrong conceptions not only about the printing of the important *Hamlet* second quarto but also about the relations of the first quarto and of the Folio to this quarto. Nevertheless he was right in principle even though—unfortunately—wrong in practice.[62]

Of Wilson's exegetical criticism, there is one issue—the dispute between Wilson and G. Wilson Knight over Hamlet's speech on man—that is worth discussing because it, too, furthers our inquiry into the nature of critical disagreement. Wilson writes:

> A single emendation or choice of variants, even at times the position of a comma or semicolon, may involve first-class issues of poetic criticism or dramatic interpretation.[63]

The punctuation or pointing of Hamlet's speech, the meanings of the key words, and the meaning of the whole speech, are debated by Wilson and Knight.

Q2 reads:

> What a peece of worke is a man, how noble in reason, how infinit in faculties, in forme and moouing, how expresse and admirable in action, how like an Angell in apprehension, how like a God: the beautie of the world; the paragon of Annimales; and yet to me, what is this Quintessence of dust:

F1 reads:

> What a piece of worke is a man! how Noble in Reason! how infinite in faculty! in forme and mouing how expresse and admirable! in Action, how like an Angel! in apprehension, how like a God! the beauty of the world, the Parragon of Animals; and yet to me, what is this Quintessence of Dust?

[62] Bowers, *On Editing Shakespeare and the Elizabethan Dramatists,* pp. 4–5.
[63] Wilson, *The Manuscript of Shakespeare's "Hamlet,"* p. xii.

Wilson argues for the Second Quarto pointing; Knight, for the Folio. The Folio reading, Wilson says, is a declamation entirely out of keeping with Hamlet's brooding and meditation, but these qualities are preserved in the light pointing of the Second Quarto. Furthermore, Q2 has the right rhythm and sense: "infinit in faculties, in forme and moouing" is a comprehensive summary of the physical nature of man, where his "faculties" denote sense qualities; "forme," facial expression and gesture; and "moouing" ("motion"), activity of the body; and "how expresse and admirable" denote purpose. On the Folio reading ("in forme and mouing how expresse and admirable"), "expresse" must be given a nonce-use, namely, "well-formed." Further, "how like an Angell in apprehension" relates to "wings as swift As meditation" (I, 5, 29–30) and, besides being a lovely image, it is consistent with the Elizabethan conception of angels as predominantly discarnate intellects who are limited to apprehension or thought. Finally, "how like a God" is in the very spirit of the Renaissance.[64]

Knight rejects Wilson's reading of Hamlet's speech and argues for the Folio punctuation or pointing.[65] First, "infinite" (Knight modernizes the spelling in his exposition) cannot apply to the singular "form" and "moving," whereas it fits "faculty" perfectly. Second, "express" is unlikely with "action," whereas it is likely with "form," as is "admirable" with "moving." Third, angels in Shakespeare—Elizabethan scholasticism aside—are conceived of as definitely active beings (*The Merchant of Venice*, II, 7, 51–55; *Romeo and Juliet*, II, 2, 18–25; *I Henry IV*, IV, 1, 98–104; *Macbeth*, I, 7, 11–18; and *Hamlet*, III, 4, 48–55). "How like an angel in apprehension" (Q2), therefore, robs angels of active significance and attributes apprehension to them, which Shakespeare's angels simply do not possess. In his most extended references to angels, Knight points out, Shakespeare visualizes them as athletic and, at times, even as riding (from the Greek, "angelos" or "messenger"). They blow trumpets, ride aerial steeds, and inspire emotion. Shakespeare depicts them as beauteous

[64] Wilson's argument for Q2 is in *The Manuscript of Shakespeare's "Hamlet,"* II, 211 ff.

[65] Knight's argument for F1 is in *The Wheel of Fire*, Appendix, Note B, pp. 332–43.

creatures of fine action and graceful poise—almost as courtiers. They combine masculine strength with feminine grace, thereby epitomizing a bisexual excellence. Shakespeare's angels do many things but there is no instance of one of them thinking. Wilson is wrong, Knight concludes, in his identification of Shakespeare's angels with discarnate spirits. Consequently, Hamlet says: "in action how like an angel" and not (as Wilson reads it) "how like an angel in apprehension." Fourth, "in apprehension how like a god" (Folio) is also correct because "apprehension" for Shakespeare is a godlike quality, not an angelic one; to apprehend is to have the ability to grasp the mysterious, to extend consciousness beyond space and time. Shakespeare, consequently, sees man as godlike *only* in his faculty of apprehension, hence, the Q2 "how like a god" is suspect. Finally, if we keep the whole speech before us, we shall see that

> Hamlet, in surveying man's various attributes, characterizes, by his comparison of man to an angel, all those excellences of outward beauty, grace, poise, artistry and valour that are elsewhere his concern; but, by his comparison of man's "apprehension" to a god, advances to a more inward consideration. . . , characterizing here rather his own potentialities at their best; while his tragedy lies in his inability to harmonize his own godlike faculties with the angelic world of fine action and gracious behaviour. . . .[66]

H. Granville-Barker, in his "Preface to *Hamlet*" (1937),[67] a classic in its own right, is the best foil for Wilson as a dramatic critic. In his thorough analysis of the play he debates many of Wilson's interpretations of the various sequences of the plot. He accepts, for example, Wilson's views about the divergences of opinion on spirits which are dramatized in the first act, although he cavils with Wilson on the staging of the Ghost-Hamlet interview and the nuances of the cellarage scene. He also accepts "sullied" but, as he says, Wilson "finds a more extended dramatic value in it than I fear I can."[68]

[66] Knight, *op. cit.*, p. 342.

[67] Harley Granville-Barker, "Preface to *Hamlet*," *Prefaces to Shakespeare* (3d ser.; London, 1937).

[68] Barker, *op. cit.*, p. 43 n.

His main objections, however, are to Wilson's insistence on the lost stage direction that gives Hamlet an entry on the inner stage in II, 2, 158, enabling him to overhear Polonius and Claudius plotting the eavesdropping; and, of course, to Wilson's conception of the play scene. Of the first Granville-Barker writes:

> I did not like the spoiling of that entrance "reading upon a book," nor the commonplace symmetry of letting Hamlet stand there overhearing a plot by which the plotters were to stand there a little later overhearing him. Besides which—and far more important!—Dover Wilson's argument leads him fatally to having Hamlet regard Ophelia as a decoy the minute he (later on) sets eyes on her, and to knowing from the beginning of their scene together that the King and Polonius are listening. None of this can I admit for a moment. For the result will be to rob Hamlet's part in the scene of all the ebb and flow of tenderness and regret, inexplicable suffering and passion, to reduce it to a dead level of resentment, to make him, indeed, something of a self-righteous scold.[69]

Of the play scene and its dumb-show, Granville-Barker says by way of repudiation of Wilson:

> One editorial answer is that the King is at the moment [of the dumb-show] talking to the Queen or Polonius, and does not see it. That can hardly be. Shakespeare does not leave such crucial matters in the air. Failing plain indication to the contrary, we must assume, I think, that whatever there is to be seen the King sees.[70]

More tenable than Wilson's view, Granville-Barker insists, is that the King sees the dumb-show but does not suppose it to "import the argument," since dumb-shows are mostly inexplicable and this particular one could have been a mime of the traditional ballet or *Commedia dell'Arte* sort. The King sees the dumb-show and at once becomes alert; it may be coincidence, it may not be, but he must wait and see.

> The Dumb Show falls quite pertinently into Hamlet's—and Shakespeare's—scheme. The mimic play as a whole is a calcu-

[69] *Ibid.*, p. 201 n.

[70] *Ibid.*, p. 90.

> lated insult both to King and Queen. The "one scene" which "comes near the circumstance" of the old King's death, and into which Hamlet has inserted his "dozen or sixteen lines," is to be the finishing stroke merely. Were it a single one, Claudius might outface it. It is the prolonged preliminary ordeal which is to wear him down. . . . What Shakespeare means, surely, is to make this simply the culmination of a long, tense, deliberate struggle to break down the King's composure, on his part to maintain it. Treat it thus and the confusion, when at last it comes, makes its true effect.[71]

Granville-Barker adds that according to Wilson's reading, the play scene,

> faces, so to speak, two ways. There is the effect of the play upon the King and Queen . . . and there will be the effect upon Hamlet of the jeopardy of his plan . . . no actor of Hamlet could convey to an audience all this extra and very different kind of anxiety. . . . [Shakespeare] would never dissipate the force of such a scene by so dividing its interest, or handicap Hamlet at this juncture with a quite extraneous difficulty. Besides, there is literally nothing in the play which is not, in some way or another, germane to its story or illustrative of Hamlet's character, or a consequence, direct or indirect, of what he does or leaves undone. Such an irrelevancy as this betrayal of his plan by the players, springing from nothing, leading nowhere, would be a rift in the fabric, and dramatically meaningless.[72]

Dover Wilson as a critic of *Hamlet* raises three sets of questions whose detailed answers are disputed by other eminent critics. It is not within my province to try to settle these issues. My aim, rather, is to elucidate the nature of the questions and disputes. What is most important in such an elucidation is to see that all three sets of questions, from a logical point of view, are exactly the same in that

[71] *Ibid.*, pp. 92–93.

[72] *Ibid.*, pp. 97–98 n. But Harold Child offers evidence of successful performances of Wilson's reading; see his letter on some recent productions of *Hamlet,* printed in Wilson's *What Happens in "Hamlet,"* pp. xvi–xx. See also S. L. Bethell, *Shakespeare and the Popular Dramatic Tradition* (London, 1944), pp. 151 ff.

they are about matters of fact to which true (or false) answers can be given.

Did Shakespeare write in Hamlet's first soliloquy, "too too sullied flesh"? Does Hamlet overhear Claudius and Polonius plotting at II, 2, 158? What is the correct pointing of the first soliloquy? These are examples of textual questions.

Does Shakespeare mean that man is like an angel in action or in apprehension? What does "nature," "coil," or "kind" mean in *Hamlet?* These are examples of exegetical questions.

Does Claudius see the dumb-show? Does Hamlet really doubt the Ghost or only its provenance? Is Claudius a usurper? Does Hamlet feign madness in Ophelia's closet? These are examples of dramatic questions.

For Wilson, as well as for many other critics, these are all factual questions that could be definitely answered if we could only secure the evidence; and they could be answered in such a way that at most one answer would be correct and the others false.

But Wilson raises other questions the logical status of which is not clear. Is Hamlet mad? Does he vacillate? Is he emotionally unstable? These, I think, he also construes as factual questions that could be answered definitely through adequate knowledge of the text.

What about the other questions raised by Wilson and disputed by his critics? Is Hamlet or *Hamlet* only fictional? That is, is it illegitimate to explain the character or the play by comparing either to the real world and human life? What is the issue, say, between Ernest Jones and Dover Wilson since they are in complete opposition on the relation between fictional characters in drama and their real life counterparts? Only one thing seems clear: that this is not a factual but, at the very least, a normative issue, because it involves an aesthetic decision about how one ought to construe characters and situations in drama. Perhaps a true (or false) answer is forthcoming to such a question but there are serious doubts: Is Hamlet only fictional? may be more like Is Hamlet tragic? than it is like Does Hamlet vacillate?

Similar observations are suggested by Wilson's claims that Hamlet is a mystery and that there is no heart to his mystery. Here, too, dispute is possible; and many critics, perhaps too many, have tried to pluck out this mystery, that is to explain Hamlet. What is the correct explanation of Hamlet's behavior and character? This remains a burning issue in *Hamlet* criticism. Once again, I would suggest that the solution is not forthcoming until we become clear about the question itself. Is the question, Is there a heart to Hamlet's mystery? a factual one to which a yes or no reply could be given?

Then there are problems about the relations between the textual, exegetical, and dramatic parts of Wilson's criticism of *Hamlet*. For Wilson, each of these is or may be a legitimate part of the whole of criticism. One criticizes *Hamlet*, for example, if one ascertains and sets forth the words or stage directions of the play as Shakespeare wrote it; or states the meanings of the words of the play; or relates the various elements of the plot of the play. Although these are distinct, they are related hierarchically: the textual is basic to the exegetical, and these two are basic to the dramatic. This conception of criticism seems to imply that there can be no dramatic criticism (or no overall interpretive criticism) which is not founded on accurate textual and exegetical work. Further, it seems to imply that no dramatic criticism, at least of *Hamlet*, is possible without much accurate historical knowledge.

Now, it seems to me, as it does to others, that Wilson presents a brilliant case for his thesis about the range and requisites of criticism. But the implications of his thesis leave us with fundamental and disturbing problems, the most important of which, I believe, is this: Is scholarship (knowledge of the textual foundations and the meanings of certain words and of the ideas of the Elizabethan age) essential to dramatic or any other sort of interpretive criticism? What, for example, is the status of readings of *Hamlet* that are not based upon and secured by accurate historical and textual knowledge? Is, for instance, Coleridge's criticism of *Hamlet* irrelevant, inadequate, or illegitimate because he worked with a text that, let us grant, was not the authoritative one? Can there be no cogent criticism of *Hamlet* (or of other works of art) without an adequate scholarly foundation of this criticism?

A final point: Let us grant that textual and exegetical criticism are important for dramatic or interpretive criticism; what, then, is their relation? Are the textual and exegetical claims part of criticism or only necessary conditions of criticism? Is, for example, the statement, " 'O, that this too too sullied flesh would melt' is the correct first line in Hamlet's first soliloquy," a statement *of* criticism or is it perhaps a statement that is *propaedeutic to* criticism? Ultimately, of course, this question turns on the question, What is criticism?—the major concern of this book. I shall return to it in due course. Here I conclude merely by asking again: Is scholarship a part of criticism or at most a necessary condition of it?

IX IMAGERY AND OTHER APPROACHES

THERE are other important contemporary essays on *Hamlet*. Since most of these, at least in aim and content, are similar to the body of criticism already discussed, especially in their reduction of the play to a univocal meaning or of Shakespearean drama to a particular poetics, I can forego detailed exposition of them. Later, when I turn to a systematic analysis of the issues of *Hamlet* criticism, some of these essays will be brought into the discussion.[1]

[1] Among these essays are: (*a*) on "the meaning of *Hamlet*": Alexander, *Hamlet: Father and Son*; Roy Walker, *The Time is Out of Joint* (London, 1948); Salvador de Madariaga, *On Hamlet* (London, 1948); J. Q. Adams (ed.), *Hamlet* (Boston, 1929), esp. his commentary, pp. 173–334; Levin, *The Question of Hamlet*; James, *The Dream of Learning: An Essay on the Advancement of Learning, Hamlet and King Lear*; Harrison, *Shakespeare's Tragedies*; Geoffrey Bush, *Shakespeare and the Natural Condition* (Cambridge, 1956); Alfred Harbage, *As They Liked It* (New York, 1947); Cunningham, *Woe or Wonder: The Emotional Effect of Shakespearean Tragedy*; Elliott, *Scourge and Minister: A Study of Hamlet as a Tragedy of Revengefulness and Justice*; E. M. W. Tillyard, *Shakespeare's Problem Plays* (London, 1950); D. A. Traversi, *An Approach to Shakespeare* (2d ed., revised and enlarged; New York, 1956); H. D. F. Kitto, *Form and Meaning in Drama* (London, 1956); and L. C. Knights, *An Approach to Hamlet* (Stanford, 1961). (*b*) on "the poetics of *Hamlet*": L. C. Knights, *Explorations* (London, 1946); Una Ellis-Fermor, *The Frontiers of Drama* (London, 1945); and Traversi, *op. cit.*

There is one contemporary approach, however, which furthers this survey by introducing certain new issues in criticism. This is the approach to *Hamlet* (as well as the whole of Shakespearean drama) through its imagery. We have already encountered this interest in imagery in Wilson Knight's interpretation of *Hamlet*. But others have ploughed or tilled the same soil with different results. It is with these that I am now concerned.

Caroline Spurgeon is the recognized pioneer in this field, especially in her epoch-making book, *Shakespeare's Imagery* (1935).[2] Others anticipated her in the study of imagery in Shakespeare, but it was she who first articulated the approach and systematized some of its results.[3]

For her, the center of every Shakespearean drama is its dominant imagery. To understand the plays (as well as the personality of Shakespeare, although this is not relevant to us here), we must grasp the prevalent imagery which in each play embodies its fundamental meaning.

Although imagery is basic in her whole program, Miss Spurgeon refuses to define the term, clarifying it instead by examples of metaphors and similes. It is poetic imagery, she says, that "gives quality, creates atmosphere and conveys emotion in a way no precise description, however clear and accurate, can possibly do."[4]

Imagery is central; in *Hamlet* the pervasive atmosphere is created by "the number of images of sickness, disease or blemish of the body, in the play."[5] The dominant image is that of an ulcer or tumor that expresses the sickness of Denmark itself. Miss Spurgeon enumerates these ulcer images: "blister," "sick soul," "thought-sick," "mildew'd ear," "mote," "vicous mole," "galled chilblain," "probed wound," "purgation." Rottenness, she summarizes, is the striking quality of

[2] Caroline F. E. Spurgeon, *Shakespeare's Imagery and What It Tells Us* (Cambridge, 1935); all page refrences are to the 1958 reprint, published by the Beacon Press, Boston.

[3] For a brief history of the study of imagery in Shakespeare, see W. H. Clemen, *The Development of Shakespeare's Imagery* (London, 1951), chap. ii. Walter Whiter's *A Specimen of a Commentary on Shakespeare* (1794) is now recognized as the first essay to concentrate on Shakespeare's imagery.

[4] Spurgeon, *op. cit.*, p. 9.

[5] *Ibid.*, p. 316.

these images; physical, mental, and political corruption is given in one image after another.

> To Shakespeare's pictorial imagination . . . the problem in *Hamlet* is not predominantly that of will and reason, of a mind too philosophic or a nature temperamentally unfitted to act quickly; he sees it pictorially *not as the problem of an individual at all*, but as something greater and even more mysterious, as a *condition* for which the individual himself is apparently not responsible, any more than the sick man is to blame for the infection which strikes and devours him, but which, nevertheless, in its course and development, impartially and relentlessly, annihilates him and others, innocent and guilty alike. That is the tragedy of *Hamlet*, as it is perhaps the chief tragic mystery of life.[6]

Everyone writing after Miss Spurgeon acknowledges his debt to her work. Her emphasis on imagery in Shakespearean drama has led to a great concentration upon the language and poetry in the dramas, even at times to a new poetics of the dramas according to which the poetry and not the plot or the characterization is central.[7] But there are also objections to her work. Two of these, among others, that concern us here have to do with her interpretation of *Hamlet*. Dover Wilson points out that her reading of *Hamlet* in solely imagistic terms leaves no place for Hamlet's moral responsibility;[8] and Francis Fergusson claims that her view of *Hamlet* "leaves out the substantial elements (the beings of the individual characters, the stable elements in the traditional cosmos) which underlie the associated or contrasted *qualities* of their lives, the 'atmosphere' or feeling tone of the play."[9]

It is W. H. Clemen, in *The Development of Shakespeare's Imagery* (1951), however, who has most fundamentally criticized

[6] *Ibid.*, pp. 318–19 (italics in original).

[7] See, e.g., Knights, *Explorations*, chap. i; and Traversi, *op. cit.*, chap. i.

[8] Wilson, *What Happens in "Hamlet,"* p. 262.

[9] Fergusson, *The Idea of a Theater*, p. 136 (italics in original); see also L. Hornstein, "Analysis of Imagery: A Critique of Literary Method," *P.M.L.A.*, 1942, pp. 638–53; O. J. Campbell, "Shakespeare and the New Critics," *Joseph Quincy Adams Memorial Studies* (Washington, 1948); and esp. Gardner, *The Business of Criticism*, pp. 52–75, for crucial objections to the whole imagist approach to Shakespeare.

and yet sustained her as well as his own independent work on imagery in Shakespeare.[10] In effect, Clemen reverses her thesis: *Hamlet* (or any other Shakespearean drama) should not be interpreted in terms of its imagery; the imagery should be interpreted in relation to the whole play. An adequate critical study of Shakespeare's imagery must place the imagery in its organic context, in the whole play as a dramatic structure. For Clemen this is basic. The play as poetic drama is first and foremost. Neither imagery nor plot nor character nor theme can replace the whole play as central: as the focus of critical inquiry. A Shakespearean drama comprises a number of distinguishable albeit inseparable elements that unfold temporally, sequentially, and organically; images are but one aspect of this totality. Miss Spurgeon fails as critic, then, precisely because her statistical method of collecting and classifying images and her isolation of them from their dramatic contexts do violence to the organic role they play in the total drama. Images are worthy of critical study, then, not because they disclose any necessary *ultimate pattern* beneath the plot and characters, but simply because they contribute to the play, as do the characters, plot, theme, and atmosphere.

As a critic of Shakespeare, Clemen concentrates on the imagery of the plays as one element among others equally important. His derivative aim is to trace the development of imagery in Shakespeare's dramas from the early to the late periods. He points out and delineates Shakespeare's use of images as decorative devices—"poetic" rather than "dramatic"—in the early plays. Images function in these plays on the whole "to intensify the expression of the emotions, or to present thoughts of a general nature in epigrammatic form";[11] they do not especially further the dramatic development.

But in the great tragedies of the middle period, of which *Hamlet* is an example, the images become thoroughly integrated in the whole drama.

> They become effective instruments in the hand of the dramatist. . . . [They help] him to prepare the audience for coming

[10] This book was originally written in German (1936); it was subsequently revised and written in English. All page references are to the 1951 English edition.

[11] Clemen, *op. cit.*, p. 81.

> events. But the imagery may also emphasize and accompany the dramatic action, repeating its themes; it often even resembles a second line of action running parallel to the real plot, and providing a "counterpoint" to the events on the stage.[12]

The images now function dramatically: to "forebode" and "anticipate." They also take on a decided character of ambiguity, itself an effective instrument for dramatic development.

> This double meaning of images is also of importance for the development of the dialogue in the tragedies. In interpreting the tragedies, we must continually ask whether one character has fully understood what the other said, or whether he or she understood it in a secondary or false sense. This is of great importance for the further course of the action.[13]

Furthermore, the images are no longer rhetorical or pompous but are "borne by great passion and correspond to the depth and immensity of human emotion."[14] Imagery also becomes an expression of great metaphysical forces and relations. All Nature becomes personified, almost a character in the play. "In the tragedies . . . the imagery expresses the mutual relationship of the forces at work in human nature. Ideas such as honour, judgement, conscience, will, blood, reason, etc., frequently appear in metaphorical guise."[15] Indeed, the imagery of the major tragedies functions almost as a mode of apprehension. But the consummate fact of the imagery in this middle period is that it is in complete harmony with the other elements of the dramas.

These remarks are general ones on the dramas of Shakespeare's middle period. Clemen next applies them to an analysis of *Hamlet*. His aim (to repeat) is not to give an interpretation of *Hamlet* or to interpret *Hamlet* in terms of the imagery, but to elucidate the images of *Hamlet* and to relate them to the whole dramatic structure.

What is immediately striking in the imagery of *Hamlet* is Hamlet's language. From his first line to the end of the play, Hamlet's images, unlike the images of the earlier Shakespearean heroes, are not so much similes or metaphors as they are spontaneous visions and imaginative translations of real things and persons. His images are keen, penetrat-

[12] *Ibid.*, p. 89. [13] *Ibid.*, p. 91. [14] *Ibid.*, p. 92. [15] *Ibid.*, p. 97.

ing observations of reality, referring as they do to the most ordinary features of reality: trades, callings, objects of daily use, and games. As Hamlet says, "I know not 'seems'." Indeed, he is unique in the play in the spontaneity of his images, as we can see if we compare his to the studied, conventional images of the other characters, especially Claudius. Hamlet uses images to unmask and penetrate men and things.

> They are meant to strip [men] of their fine appearances and to show them up in their true nature. Thus, by means of the simile of fortune's pipe, Hamlet shows Rosencrantz and Guildenstern that he has seen through their intent, and thus he unmasks Rosencrantz when he calls him a "sponge," "that soaks up the king's countenance" (iv. ii. 16). He splits his mother's heart "in twain," because he tells her the truth from which she shrinks and which she conceals from herself.[16]

Clemen draws one important conclusion from this feature of Hamlet's imagery: that he is not a mere abstract thinker and dreamer. "As his imagery betrays to us, he is rather a man gifted with greater powers of observation than the others."[17] When, for example, late in the play, Hamlet looks at Yorick's skull,

> he sees *more* in it than the others, for whom the skull is merely a lifeless object. And precisely because he is more deeply moved by the reality and significance of these earthly remains, his fantasy is able to follow the "noble dust of Alexander" through all its metamorphoses. The comparisons which spring from this faculty of thinking a thing to the end, as it were, derive in fact from a more intense experience of reality.[18]

In connection with Hamlet's supposed inability to act because of his over-developed intellect, Clemen examines the much-discussed image:

> And thus the native hue of resolution
> Is sicklied o'er with the pale cast of thought,
> And enterprises of great pith and moment
> With this regard their currents turn awry,
> And lose the name of action [III. i. 85–89].

[16] *Ibid.*, p. 109. [17] *Ibid.*, p. 108.
[18] *Ibid.*, p. 111 (italics in original).

The traditional interpretation of this passage, that reflection hinders action, is wrong:

> For Hamlet does not say "reflection hinders action," he simply utters this image. The fact that he does not utter that general maxim, but this image, makes all the difference. For this image is the unique and specific form of expression of the thought underlying it, it cannot be separated from it. If we say "reflection hinders action," we make a false generalization; we replace a specific formulation by an apothegm. And thereby we eradicate in this passage that quality which is peculiarly Shakespeare's or, what is more, peculiarly Hamlet's. Here the image does not serve the purpose of merely casting a decorative cloak about the thought; it is much rather an intrinsic part of the thought.[19]

The adage, "reflection hinders action," implies that action and reflection are two opposing moral principles. But in Hamlet's image, " 'native hue of resolution' suggests that Shakespeare viewed resolution as an innate human quality, not as a moral virtue to be consciously striven after."[20] Thought and action are related in Shakespeare "not as an opposition between two abstract principles between which a free choice is possible, but as an unavoidable condition of human nature."[21]

This condition of human nature, that is, of one thing slowly disabling and destroying another, is voiced many times in the play: from the beginning, in King Hamlet's description of the poisoning, to the end, in the poisoning of all the major characters.

> A real event described at the beginning of the drama has exercised a profound influence upon the whole imagery of the play. What is later metaphor, is here still reality. The picture of the leprous skin disease, which is here—in the first act—described by Hamlet's father, has buried itself deep in Hamlet's imagination and continues to lead its subterranean existence, as it were, until it reappears in metaphorical form.[22]

Thus, from the very beginning of the play, the plot determines in part the imagery of the play, especially of Hamlet's. The murder of King Hamlet and the incest of Gertrude give rise to the imagery of disease,

[19] *Ibid.* [20] *Ibid.*, p. 112. [21] *Ibid.* [22] *Ibid.*, p. 113.

infection, and corruption, so magnificently stressed by Miss Spurgeon. But once we understand that the murder and incest are essential to the plot, and that the imagery is basically that of an ulcer eating away at everything, we can then see how "imagery and action continually play into each other's hands and how the term 'dramatic imagery' gains a new significance."[23]

At times the images in *Hamlet* are developed in clusters: an image is introduced in one form early in the play and is later reinforced by a similar image. Such images have the distinctive dramatic function to presage certain events. An example is Laertes' admonition to Ophelia early in the play:

> The canker galls the infants of the spring,
> Too oft before their buttons be disclosed,
> And in the morn and liquid dew of youth
> Contagious blastments are most imminent [I. 3. 39–42].

This image of the worm in the bud, where the worm functions as an irresistible, destructive force, comes to light again, reinforced, in the last act, when Hamlet refers to Claudius as "this canker of our nature" (V. 2. 69). Another example is "strumpet Fortune" and her broken wheel which is rolled "down the hill of heaven," in the second act; this image is repeated later by Rosencrantz who speaks of the king who, like a wheel, when he falls, brings disaster to all.

Clemen also relates Hamlet's imagery to his "antic disposition." "Hamlet needs images for his 'antic disposition.' He would betray himself if he used open, direct language. Hence he must speak ambiguously and cloak his real meaning under quibbles and puns, images and parables."[24]

Hamlet's imagery relates also to his temperament. His sudden changes of language and imagery serve to express his extremes of mood. His imagery also reveals his educational background, his adaptability, his versatility, indeed, all the important aspects of his character. But the basic image or cluster of images, Clemen concludes, is that of the ulcerous, infectious disease: it is this imagery that is determined by the plot, uttered by the characters, and contributes organically to the whole that is *Hamlet*.

[23] *Ibid.*

[24] *Ibid.*, p. 110.

The concentration on the imagery of *Hamlet* contributes something new in our survey. One can divide Miss Spurgeon's work into two parts (and indeed this is what Clemen does): her discussion of the imagery as *one* element of the play; and her contention that the imagery is *fundamental* in the play. The latter claim is solidly in the major tradition of *Hamlet* criticism, which aims at an explanation of the play by way of one controlling factor. But in its first part, Miss Spurgeon suggests that imagery is at least one important item in the play and as worthy of analysis as any other if one wishes to understand the whole play. It is Clemen's achievement to have made explicit this aspect of Miss Spurgeon's work. For him, the study of the imagery of *Hamlet*, quite independently of whether the imagery is central or not, is of importance to criticism because this study aims at the elucidation of one of the organically contributing elements of the whole play.

There is a great logical difference between the claims that imagery is central in *Hamlet* and that imagery is one contributing element in *Hamlet*. Clemen recognizes this distinction, commits himself only to the latter claim, and centers his entire criticism on it. In method and aim, his criticism is similar to many independent studies of *Hamlet* in which certain strands or elements are singled out as objects of analysis, where there is no insistence upon these being central or more than a contributory element to the play. Clemen investigates the imagery of Shakespeare. Other contemporary critics study Shakespeare's plots, characters, or heroes; his theology, politics, or philosophy; his style, satire, prose, or language; there is even one essay on the drinking habits of his characters.[25] The distinguishing feature of this kind of criticism is that it concerns itself with one aspect of a whole work of art in the attempt to clarify this aspect in relation to the whole work, where there is the absolute commitment to the aesthetic principle that

[25] See, e.g., B. I. Evans, *The Language of Shakespeare's Plays* (Bloomington, 1952); Milton Crane, *Shakespeare's Prose* (Chicago, 1951), esp. "Prose is but one of the elements in the plays and must be understood in the context of the play, not *in vacuo*" (Preface); O. J. Campbell, *Shakespeare's Satire* (New York, 1943); Oliver Elton, *Style in Shakespeare*, Annual Shakespeare Lecture of the British Academy, 1936; G. Rylands, *Words and Poetry* (New York, 1928); and E. Legouis, "The Bacchic Element in Shakespeare's Plays," *Aspects of Shakespeare* (Oxford, 1933).

there are other, equally important, aspects of the work that invite critical discussion.

Clemen, thus, is important in our survey of *Hamlet* criticism because he restricts himself to an explanation of *one* part or aspect of the play: more particularly, to an elucidation of the imagery of *Hamlet* and the dramatic relations of the imagery to the plot, characters, and theme of the play; the last three elements he chooses not to analyze in any detail. Consequently, his is criticism in the mode of description and explanation. This criticism also purports to be true (or false).[26]

[26] Cf. Una Ellis-Fermor on some of the imagery in *Hamlet:* "In Gertrude's speech there are remarkably few images, and those generally colourless and drawn almost entirely from commonplace themes. They have little vigour and hardly ever call up a vivid picture: the images of a mind that has never received sharp or deep impressions, that is, in fact, incapable of any imaginative effort." (*Op. cit.*, p. 89).

X THE MAJOR TRADITION

SHAKESPEARE'S *Hamlet* is little more than three hundred and fifty years old. Yet an incredible amount has been written on it. Bradley says that its hero has been the subject of more critical treatment than any other in the history of literature. There have been critical allusions to *Hamlet* almost since its first performances. From the beginning of the seventeenth century to Bradley there has accumulated a great corpus of criticism of *Hamlet*. Among the most important contributors to it are Hanmer, Voltaire, Johnson, Richardson, Coleridge, Lamb, Hazlitt, Goethe, the Schlegels, Brandes, Werder, Swinburne, and Dowden.

The range of ideas in their work is as vast as that of the contemporary critics already detailed. Their particular theses, their disagreements and issues, and the problems they inspired are not only important in themselves but basic to a full understanding of contemporary criticism of *Hamlet*. In any complete survey of *Hamlet* criticism, an exposition of these contributors should come first.

But my aim is not to write a history of *Hamlet* criticism. To a large extent this has been done by others.[1] Moreover, many of the traditional interpretations have already been discussed in my survey

[1] See, e.g., P. S. Conklin, *A History of Hamlet Criticism, 1601–1821* (London, 1957); and A. Ralli, *A History of Shakespearean Criticism* (2 vols.; Oxford, 1932).

of major contemporary trends; indeed, one reason for starting with Bradley is that he sums up much of the tradition although, to be sure, he directs his summary mainly to the traditional issue of the delay. My aim, rather, is to survey systematically the major issues of *Hamlet* criticism, especially as they reflect some of the central problems in the whole of criticism. Consequently, insofar as the essays of the tradition up to Bradley introduce no additional significant issues, there is no point in expounding them here. Much of the tradition is concerned with issues already presented: the meaning of *Hamlet*, the character of the hero, the truth of the play, and the various difficulties of the plot. These studies can be dealt with best, from my point of view, when I come to a systematic analysis of the issues. Thus far, the concentration on contemporary criticism of *Hamlet* has been prompted by the need to secure a working corpus of criticism in which issues, past and present, have become sharp and relatively clear. It is in the context of the major aim of the first part of this inquiry, which is to present the various procedures, doctrines, disagreements, and issues in *Hamlet* criticism, that I shall now turn to the tradition for further detailed exposition.

Criticism evaluates. Some critics even contend that it *is* evaluation. Others argue for a complete separation of criticism and evaluation. Now, whatever their proper relationship may be, evaluation has been and, for many critics, remains the central activity of criticism.

In this survey Eliot's essay stands out as an example of the primacy of evaluation in criticism. But there is also evaluation in most of the critics discussed: Bradley, Jones, Knight, Robertson, Stoll, Schücking, Stewart, Fergusson, Dover Wilson, and Clemen include as parts of their critical essays certain assessments of the plot, language, characterization, truth, or craft in *Hamlet*. Nevertheless, evaluation is not primary in these essays. No doubt, each is motivated by a particular evaluation; but in none is there, as there is in Eliot's, a dominant concern for a specific assessment or judgment of the play. Their major interest seems to be description, interpretation, explanation, or the poetics of drama or tragedy. Indeed, evaluation is not present at all in much of the contemporary criticism of *Hamlet*.

It is here that the tradition can help, especially if it is enlarged to include the criticism of the whole of Shakespearean drama, for then we will have before us a solid corpus of criticism whose preoccupation is with evaluation. The conception of traditional Shakespearean criticism as primarily evaluative is not an arbitrary one. Indeed, one subordinate claim I hope to substantiate is that Shakespearean criticism from Ben Jonson to Bradley is primarily evaluative, and that, consequently, the view prevalent among historians of the subject that this criticism divides rather sharply between evaluation and interpretation in the late eighteenth century, is false. More particularly, I hope to show that there is no fundamental difference in aim between Dr. Johnson (as a representative of neoclassicism) and Coleridge (as a representative of romanticism), or even, say, between Pope and Carlyle, since all are in complete agreement in their fundamental dedication to a cogent and true assessment of Shakespeare as a dramatist.

Thus, instead of rehearsing, this time through the tradition, the many issues already discussed, I shall interpret the tradition as a series of attempts to assess the works of Shakespeare; and I shall conclude this survey with an exposition of some of the individual traditional assessments.

But which ones? I cannot discuss all of them, brilliantly wrought or historically important as they are. One is simply dazzled by the array of contributors: Rymer, Dryden, Pope, Voltaire, Kames, Johnson, Whately, Morgann, A. W. Schlegel, Coleridge, Hazlitt, Lamb, De Quincey, Carlyle, Swinburne, Emerson, Tolstoy, Bridges—and others, too—deserve examination.

I believe I can best serve the stated aim of this study by concentrating on a few of these critics, those who state or imply the largest range of crucial issues in evaluative criticism. My choice, therefore, comprises Dryden, Pope, Johnson, Coleridge, and Tolstoy. Rymer's strictures on Shakespeare's plots, characters, "thoughts," and "rhetoric," especially in *Othello*, are incorporated in the writings of Dryden, Pope, Johnson, and Coleridge, even if only to be rejected. Voltaire's series of attacks against Shakespeare's violation of the rules of drama, especially the three unities, Shakespeare's lack of decorum, and his mixtures of the comic and the tragic that Voltaire castigates as monstrous farces, and Voltaire's description of *Hamlet* as the work of a drunken savage are countered in full at least by Johnson and Coleridge. Kames's distinction between description and delineation of passion and his insistence on Shakespeare's superiority in the latter; Whately's emphasis on Shakespeare's characterization; and especially Morgann's exhibition of Shakespeare's greatness in his magical creation of historic (real-life) rather than dramatic characters, through an analysis of Falstaff's constitutional courage—all become focal points in Coleridge's assessment. The basic criteria of greatness in drama employed by Hazlitt, Lamb, De Quincey, Carlyle, Swinburne, and Emerson are those of Coleridge: Shakespeare's power of communication, range of characterization, veracity, exhibition of passion, imagination, language and versification, profundity, "seeing eye," superiority of intellect, and "prophetic vision." These are epitomized in the fragments of Coleridge. Even Lamb's powerful paradox that Shakespeare's greatness is fundamentally meditative, hence is unamenable to stage presentation, is implicit in Coleridge. Bridge's censures, especially of the inconsistency of characterization in Shakespeare, are subsumed under Tolstoy's attack.

The omission of A. W. Schlegel is the most difficult to justify. Schlegel's evaluation of Shakespeare in his celebrated Vienna lectures, published in 1809–11, is regarded by many as one of the three or four great critical studies of Shakespeare. Furthermore, many historians consider him to be more important than Coleridge on Shakespeare. They argue that Coleridge's Shakespearean criticism is derived from Schlegel. Some even say that in many places it is a plagiarism of Schlegel. The exact relation between Coleridge and Schlegel, however, is not a problem here, since I am concerned with the content and adequacy of different evaluations not with their origins. In spite of the obvious similarities between Coleridge and Schlegel in their assessments of Shakespeare, Coleridge's seems to me a more powerful and searching analysis of Shakespeare's greatness than Schlegel's. This is why I have chosen to discuss Coleridge rather than Schlegel. And with this apologia I turn now to an examination of five evaluative critics of the dramas of Shakespeare in order to enlarge this survey of issues in criticism.

I

Dryden's evaluative criticism of Shakespeare is contained in his *Essay of Dramatic Poesy* (1668), prefaces to *All for Love* (1678) and *Troilus and Cressida* (1679), and prologues to some of his own poems.[2]

Before Dryden, Shakespeare had already been variously praised, attacked, and defended—as he has been ever since. Greene, Meres, Harvey, and especially Jonson, in his glowing tribute prefixed to the Folio of 1623, had offered assessments. But Dryden's is acknowledged as the first assessment based on principles and argument.

His *Essay* is a long dialogue on the nature of poetic drama and the merits of ancient and modern dramas. It debates many issues and evaluates many authors. Dryden's (Neander's) assessment of Shakespeare comes toward the end of the dialogue, after his attack on the professed superiority of the French drama over the English. The English drama, from Shakespeare to his own time, he says, is, in many of its plays, as "regular" as the French. It has a greater variety of plot and character; in the majority of the "irregular" plays of Shakespeare "there is a more masculine fancy and greater spirit in the writing, than there is in any of the French."[3] Then Dryden, in response to Eugenius' request to give his opinion of Jonson, compares Jonson to Shakespeare and Fletcher. Dryden's famous assessment of Shakespeare follows:

> He was the man who of all modern, and perhaps ancient poets, had the largest and most comprehensive soul. All the images of Nature were still present to him, and he drew them, not laboriously, but luckily; when he describes any thing, you more than see it, you feel it too. Those who accuse him to have wanted learning, give him the greater commendation: he was naturally learn'd; he needed not the spectacles of books to read Nature; he looked inwards, and found her there. I cannot say he

[2] D. Nichol Smith, my authority for these selections, has collected them in part in his anthology, *Shakespeare Criticism* (Oxford: World Classics, 1916). All quotations are from and page references to the standard edition of Dryden's essays: W. P. Ker, *Essays of John Dryden* (2 vols.; Oxford, 1926).

[3] Ker, *op. cit.*, I, 79.

> is every where alike; were he so, I should do him injury to compare him with the greatest of mankind. He is many times flat, insipid; his comic wit degenerating into clenches, his serious swelling into bombast. But he is always great, when some great occasion is presented to him. . . .[4]

Johnson, in his essay on Dryden, calls him "the father of English criticism, . . . the writer who first taught us to determine upon principles the merit of composition."[5] He praises the whole of the *Essay*, especially Dryden's assessment of Shakespeare:

> The account of Shakespeare may stand as a perpetual model of encomiastick criticism; exact without minuteness, and lofty without exaggeration. . . . In a few lines is exhibited a character, so extensive in its comprehension, and so curious in its limitations, that nothing can be added, diminished, or reformed; nor can the editors and admirers of Shakespeare, in all their emulation of reverence, boast of much more than of having diffused and paraphrased this epitome of excellence, of having changed Dryden's gold for baser metal, of lower value though of greater bulk.[6]

This is magnificent praise. Nevertheless, it deserves our scrutiny. Read even in the full context of the *Essay*, Dryden's assessment remains extremely general: Shakespeare's is a large and comprehensive soul; he is at times flat and insipid; he is great when confronted with a great occasion; one feels as well as sees his depictions of passions. Dryden gives no examples to support these claims. In his evaluation they serve, at best, as summaries of traits in Shakespeare's dramas that are not spelled out.

Criticism that determines merit of composition on the basis of principles has generally involved at least three distinct procedures: clarification of the principles; defense or refutation of them; and confirmation or application of them. Ideally, any evaluative criticism should satisfy all three criteria: of clarification, justification, and

[4] *Ibid.*, pp. 79–80.

[5] Samuel Johnson, "Dryden," *Lives of the English Poets* (2 vols.; Oxford: World Classics, 1906), I, 287.

[6] *Ibid.*, p. 288.

application. Whether any particular evaluation of Shakespeare has ever attained this goal I shall ask later. In any event, the history of evaluative criticism of Shakespeare has revolved around one or two and sometimes all three of these activities. Dryden's evaluation, as given in the first quotation from him, though based on a clarification and defense of principles—the importance of variety, unity, truth to nature, and delight—which are presented in the early parts of the *Essay*, does not satisfy the criterion of application, except in a very general way. Dryden says, for instance, that Shakespeare is insipid. At the very least he owes us some examples.

In his "Preface, Containing the Grounds of Criticism in Tragedy," to *Troilus and Cressida*, Dryden supplements his evaluation of Shakespeare. One of Shakespeare's failings is the manner in which he sometimes expresses the passions:

> He often obscures his meaning by his words, and sometimes makes it unintelligible. I will not say of so great a poet, that he distinguished not the blown puffy style from true sublimity; but I may venture to maintain, that the fury of his fancy often transported him beyond the bounds of judgment, either in coining of new words and phrases, or racking words which were in use, into the violence of a catachresis. It is not that I would explode the use of metaphors from passion, for Longinus thinks 'em necessary to raise it: but to use 'em at every word, to say nothing without a metaphor, a simile, an image, or description, is, I doubt, to smell a little too strongly of the buskin.[7]

Here, too, Dryden gives no examples; his only reference is to the Player's Speech in *Hamlet* which he interprets as Shakespeare's caricature of bombast.

Dryden also introduces certain principles of merit. These principles have invited challenge by later critics, thereby raising important issues for our survey: Is Shakespeare often unintelligible? Are there proper limitations on the use of metaphor in poetic drama? Is Shakespeare's judgment equal to his fancy? Coleridge transposes this question into Is Shakespeare's judgment equal to his genius? and takes it as his starting point in a revaluation of Shakespeare.

[7] Ker, *op. cit.*, I, 224.

This Preface contains the one example I have found of Dryden's concrete application of a principle of merit as well as an illustration of his claim in the *Essay* that Shakespeare is great when some great occasion is presented him and when he makes us feel and see what he is depicting. The specific principle Dryden illustrates is that of the importance of a correspondence between the matter and the manner of passion in drama. Shakespeare, Dryden submits, realizes this principle superbly:

> I cannot leave this subject, before I do justice to that divine poet, by giving you one of his passionate descriptions: 'tis of Richard the Second when he was deposed, and led in triumph through the streets of London by Henry of Bullingbrook: the painting of it is so lively, and the words so moving, that I have scarce read anything comparable to it in any other language. Suppose you have seen already the fortunate usurper passing through the crowd, and followed by the shouts and acclamations of the people; and now behold King Richard entering upon the scene: consider the wretchedness of his condition, and his carriage in it; and refrain from pity, if you can—
>
> As in a theatre, the eyes of men,
> After a well-graced actor leaves the stage,
> Are idly bent on him that enters next,
> Thinking his prattle to be tedious:
> Even so, or with much more contempt, men's eyes
> Did scowl on Richard: no man cried, God save him
> No joyful tongue gave him his welcome home,
> But dust was thrown upon his sacred head,
> Which with such gentle sorrow he shook off,
> His face still combating with tears and smiles
> (The badges of his grief and patience),
> That had not God (for some strong purpose) steel'd
> The hearts of men, they must perforce have melted,
> And barbarism itself have pitied him.[8]

What is striking in this application of a principle of merit is Dryden's direct appeal to our feelings as an essential part of his confirmation. Even Dryden's language is invocational: See what I see,

[8] *Ibid.*, pp. 226–27.

feel what I feel, as you read this scene, and you will also perceive how well Shakespeare has delineated this particular passion. He offers no proof—what would such a proof be?—of his principle. Instead his evaluation serves as an invitation to partake of his response.

2

In the Preface to his edition of *The Works of Shakespear* (1725),[9] Pope says that Shakespeare is a good subject for criticism because there are many instances of beauties and faults in his works. But his main business as an editor in a preface is "to give an account of the fate of his works, and the disadvantages under which they have been transmitted to us."[10] For such an account will "extenuate many faults which are his, and clear him from the imputation of many which are not."[11] Yet Pope cannot forego an evaluation, and he begins his preface with an enumeration of the excellences in Shakespeare.

Shakespeare is "an *Original*. . . . The poetry of Shakespear was inspiration indeed; he is not so much an imitator as an instrument of Nature; and it is not so just to say that he speaks from her as that she speaks through him."[12]

This is all Pope says about this first excellence in Shakespeare. He gives no definition or clarification of "original," instead he relates it metaphorically to a process in nature. He says nothing about the difference between an imitator and an instrument of nature. He is equally silent on the relation between originality and artistic excellence or, for that matter, between any quality and artistic excellence. As a critic engaged in evaluation, Pope simply does not enter upon these problems. What, then, does he or critics like him who make similarly vague and debatable remarks claim when they say that one of Shakespeare's excellences is his originality or that he is an original? It is also important to realize, even from this one example, just how little a critic may concern himself with a key term or the justification of a major affirmation, and, as interestingly, just how happy many of

[9] Smith, *op. cit.*, reprints the relevant portions. All quotations are from and page references to the standard edition of Pope's works by W. Elwin and W. J. Courthope, *The Works of Alexander Pope* (London, 1886), X, 534–49.

[10] Elwin and Courthope, *op. cit.*, X, 534.

[11] *Ibid.*

[12] *Ibid.*, pp. 534–35 (italics in original).

Pope's readers are with his estimate as it stands. Perhaps one should ask no more from the critic.

Shakespeare's second excellence is his delineation of character: "Every single character in Shakespear is as much an individual as those in life itself; it is as impossible to find any two alike. . . . To this life and variety of character we must add the wonderful preservation of it, which is such throughout his Plays, that, had all the speeches been printed without the very names of the persons, I believe one might have applied them with certainty to every speaker."[13]

Now, this is an evaluative argument: Shakespeare is artistically good because, among other reasons, he creates characters well, that is as individuals in their variety and with a consistency that extends to their language. To be sure, Pope does not debate or defend any view about the relation between characterization and the qualities that make it successful in drama. Like most critics, he takes it for granted that good characterization in drama involves individuality, variety, and consistency, and he simply applies these qualities to Shakespeare. No one, I believe, has challenged Pope on his implied principle that good characterization is at least a criterion of good drama. But, as we shall soon see, he has been challenged on his criterion that individuality is a necessary property of successful characterization as well as on his assertion that Shakespeare's characters are individuals.

Shakespeare's third excellence is his "*power* over our *passions*," which "was never possess'd in a more eminent degree, or displayed in so different instances."[14] He moves us to both laughter and tears by his portrayal of the full range of emotion, and he moves us without labor or contrivance.

There are two principles employed here. One is the subtlety of Shakespeare's depiction of emotion, noticed already by Dryden; the second is Shakespeare's ability to stir us. Pope joins these principles and argues that Shakespeare is great because he moves us as art should, through a just and proper handling of emotion. "The heart swells, and the tears burst out, just at the proper places. We are surprised the moment we weep; and yet upon reflection find the passion so just,

[13] *Ibid.*, p. 535.

[14] *Ibid.*

that we should be surprised if we had not wept, and wept at that very moment."[15]

Shakespeare's fourth excellence Pope calls his "coolness of reflection and reasoning." He seems to mean by it Shakespeare's ability to develop arguments and motives in a convincing manner. In a writer like Shakespeare, who had no firsthand experience of much of what he describes, this ability, Pope adds, shows that Shakespeare knew the world by intuition, and that the philosopher or the man of the world, like the poet, may be born as well as made.

What this excellence comes to is that Shakespeare is great because his dramas embody accurate and true ideas about the world. This, too, is an appeal to an ancient criterion of great art, that of truth. Once again, Pope neither analyzes nor justifies this criterion but simply employs it in a summary way by attributing it to Shakespeare.

Pope next turns to Shakespeare's faults which, he says, are as great as his virtues. They are of two sorts, real ones and imputed ones. He tries to extenuate the first and to refute the second.

It is said that Shakespeare is often vulgar in his themes, extravagant in his incidents, bombastic in his language, and pompous in his verse. These are real defects. But, Pope pleads, it is Shakespeare's audience and his part-profession of a player that are to blame, not Shakespeare. "To be obliged to please the lowest of people, and to keep the worst of company . . . will appear sufficient to mislead and depress the greatest genius upon earth."[16] At the beginning of his career Shakespeare wrote as a member of a company of players, to earn a living. He "directed his endeavours solely to hit the taste and humour that then prevailed. The audience was generally composed of the meaner sort of people; and therefore the images of life were to be drawn from those of their own rank."[17] These two pressures were relaxed as his audience improved when he moved from the town to the court; only then could he come to his maturity.

Pope's attempt at an extenuation of faults constitutes a new move in this survey of critical evaluation. Like a counsel for the defense in a court of law who accepts the charge of guilty for his client and then

[15] *Ibid.*

[16] *Ibid.*, p. 539.

[17] *Ibid.*, pp. 536–37.

goes on to try to mitigate it, Pope acts as a counsel for the defense of Shakespeare in the court of critical opinion. He neither questions that vulgarity, bombast, extravagance, and pomposity are aesthetic crimes, nor does he deny that Shakespeare committed them. Instead he tries to get Shakespeare's sentence lightened.

Here, too, are important problems: First, is Shakespeare guilty of these aesthetic crimes? Many critics have thought not. Others have challenged the very crimes themselves—What, after all, is artistic vulgarity or extravagance? Second, does Pope succeed in his defense, if we grant him his claim that Shakespeare is guilty? His argument rests upon certain assertions about alleged matters of fact which are questionable; for example, that Shakespeare's audience was mean or that it dictated dramatically to Shakespeare. If his audience was more culturally heterogeneous than Pope supposes—as we have reason to believe today[18]—his extenuation collapses and Shakespeare remains inexcusably guilty.

Shakespeare's supposed faults are that he never rewrote and that he lacked learning. Pope dismisses both of these accusations by an appeal to facts. It is not true that Shakespeare never rewrote: he rewrote *The Merry Wives of Windsor*, *Henry VI*, *Henry V*, and *Hamlet*, along with others of his plays. And it is false that Shakespeare lacked learning. If we mean by learning, knowledge acquired by reading, then, of course, Shakespeare had learning. His plays reveal much learning about

> natural philosophy, mechanics, ancient and modern history, poetical learning, and mythology. . . . Whatever object of nature, or branch of science, he either speaks of or describes, it is always with competent, if not extensive knowledge: his descriptions are still exact; all his metaphors appropriated, and remarkably drawn from the true nature and inherent qualities of each subject.[19]

Pope, thus, does at least three different jobs as an evaluative critic in his Preface. He praises Shakespeare, he defends him against charges of which he is guilty, and he refutes certain charges of which he is not

[18] See, e.g., Alfred Harbage, *Shakespeare's Audience* (New York, 1942).
[19] Elwin and Courthope, *op. cit.*, X, 540.

guilty. In praising him, he formulates or defends no principles, standards, or criteria of beauty in art or drama; he offers no definitions or analyses of his key terms; he does not debate or reject any principle of criticism on the ground that it is erroneous; and he indulges in no poetics of the drama. One is not even sure that Pope would subscribe to a universalization of his four criteria as a definition of great drama. What he does, in praising Shakespeare, is to accept certain principles (standards, criteria) of beauty in art and drama and apply them in a summary way to the whole of Shakespeare's dramas. And in this application, he gives no detailed confirmation of any of the principles; that is, no instances of Shakespeare's originality, characterization, power over our passions, or coolness of reflection and reasoning. Like Dryden before him and many critics after him, Pope rests content with an evaluation of Shakespeare that is a general attribution of certain established and accepted principles of merit to him.

In defending Shakespeare Pope introduces no new principles and challenges no traditional ones. To do both is possible in evaluative criticism, but Pope limits his defense to an extenuation of Shakespeare's violation of traditional principles.

In refuting certain charges Pope appeals to facts in order to reject one evaluation and to prepare his readers to accept another. This, too, is a useful move in evaluative criticism: to dismiss an aesthetic judgment of an author by a critic by pointing out that the judgment rests, at least in part, on statements about facts that are false.

3

Dr. Johnson, our next example, wrote a number of critical pieces on Shakespeare.[20] As editor and admirer of Shakespeare, he understood

[20] The major ones are: (1) *Miscellaneous Observations on the Tragedy of Macbeth, with remarks on Sir T. H.'s* [Sir Thomas Hanmer's] *Edition of Shakespeare; To Which is affix'd, Proposals for a New Edition of Shakespeare, with a Specimen* (1745); (2) "Prologue," spoken by Mr. Garrick at the Opening of the Theatre in Drury-Lane (1747); (3) *The Rambler*, No. 156 (September, 1751); No. 168 (October, 1751); (4) Dedication to *Shakespear Illustrated* (1753); (5) *Proposals for Printing the Dramatick Works of William Shakespeare* (1756); and (6) Preface to his edition of *The Plays of William Shakespeare, in Eight Volumes with the Corrections and Illustrations of Various Commentators; to Which are Added Notes by Sam. Johnson* (1765).

by Shakespearean criticism the ascertainment of the accurate text of the plays; elucidation of the language and customs of Shakespeare's age, as they relate to the plays; explanation and remedy of corruptions and difficulties in the plays; emendations of corruptions; and evaluation of the beauties and faults of the plays. We can but pay our respects here to the importance of his total criticism of Shakespeare, including his few explanatory notes on *Hamlet*, as we restrict ourselves to Johnson as an evaluative critic of Shakespeare. For our immediate purpose, then, all we require of Johnson's work is his Preface and some of the notes to his edition of Shakespeare (1765).[21]

Johnson begins his assessment in the Preface with a distinction in the works of man between those works whose excellence is "absolute" and "definite" and those whose excellence is "gradual" and "comparative." The Pythagorean theorem is an example of the first; Homer's epics, of the second. The first is based on "demonstrative principles," the second, on "observation and experience." The test of the excellence of the first is immediate demonstration; the test of the excellence of the second is its duration of esteem. "What mankind have long possessed they have often examined and compared; and if they persist to value the possession, it is because frequent comparisons have confirmed opinion in its favour."[22]

Johnson, thus, states as a general principle for the determination of the greatness of a work of art that it has been considered and compared with other works of art frequently and for a long time, and that it has retained our esteem. Consequently, to say of a work of art that it is great implies that it has this complex quality of lasting esteem. But Johnson does not equate greatness with lasting esteem; he affirms this esteem as a test of greatness, not as its definition. And in his formulation of the test, there is no commitment to any specific doctrine of what constitutes artistic greatness. He gives us, at most, a pragmatic criterion for determining whether a work of art is great and not a criterion for determining what greatness in art is.

Shakespeare has satisfied this test. "He has long outlived his

[21] The whole of the Preface and Notes are reprinted in Walter Raleigh, *Johnson on Shakespeare* (Oxford, 1908); all quotations are from, and page references to, this edition, in its 1957 reprinting.

[22] Raleigh, *op. cit.*, pp. 9–10.

century, the term commonly fixed as the test of literary merit."[23] Whatever the reasons for his reputation during and shortly after his lifetime, he is now read only for pleasure, which is the other side of our esteem for him. Nevertheless, human judgment being as fallible as it is, our opinion of him may be little more than "prejudice or fashion," and so "it is proper to inquire, by what peculiarities of excellence *Shakespeare* has gained and kept the favour of his countrymen."[24]

Thus Johnson shifts his question from Has Shakespeare continued in our esteem? to Why has he continued in our esteem? His answer, given in the first section of the Preface, is that Shakespeare has so continued because he satisfies the basic requirement of great drama which is to present "just representations of general nature." Only these can satisfy: "Nothing can please many, and please long, but just representations of general nature."[25] The test of Shakespeare's greatness is that he has pleased many for a long time. But the reason for his greatness, why he has pleased as he has, is his just representations of general nature.

Nowhere in his Preface does Johnson discuss the status of the principle that nothing can please many, and please long, except these representations. I have found no proof or argument for its truth; instead, Johnson seems to regard it as an empirical truth about human beings that ultimately, as he puts it in another context, "the mind can only repose on the stability of truth."[26]

Johnson's main concern in his appraisal of Shakespeare is to clarify the meaning and importance of "just representations of general nature," which he does by showing precisely how Shakespeare's dramas embody them. In addition, he makes certain inferences from Shakespeare's realization of them; and he also refutes certain other critics of Shakespeare because of their narrow interpretation of "just representations of general nature."

Johnson first tells us that these representations are not of "particular manners" or of "irregular combinations of fanciful invention," since the former can be known only by the few who can judge their

[23] *Ibid.*, p. 10.
[24] *Ibid.*, p. 11.
[25] *Ibid.*
[26] *Ibid.*

truth and the latter do not satisfy our desire for truth even though they may divert us for a time.

Shakespeare's dramas are just representations of general nature for Johnson in the sense that they hold up "to his readers a faithful mirrour of manners and of life."[27] In his characters, dialogues, plots, and themes, Shakespeare, unlike other dramatists, presents these representations. Consider, first, his characters:

> His characters are not modified by the customs of particular places, unpractised by the rest of the world; by the peculiarities of studies or professions, which can operate but upon small numbers; or by the accidents of transient fashions or temporary opinions: they are the genuine progeny of common humanity, such as the world will always supply, and observation will always find. His persons act and speak by the influence of those general passions and principles by which all minds are agitated, and the whole system of life is continued in motion. In the writings of other poets a character is too often an individual; in those of *Shakespeare* it is commonly a species.[28]

Later, Johnson adds to his assessment of Shakespeare's characters that they are "distinct" in spite of their great variety. He also modifies Pope's claim

> that every speech may be assigned to the proper speaker, because many speeches there are which have nothing characteristical; but perhaps, though some may be equally adapted to every person, it will be difficult to find, any that can be properly transferred from the present possessor to another claimant. The choice is right, when there is reason for choice.[29]

Further, unlike other dramatists who exploit "hyperbolical or aggravated characters," "*Shakespeare* has no heroes; his scenes are occupied only by men, who act and speak as the reader thinks that he should himself have spoken or acted on the same occasion."[30] He "always

[27] *Ibid.* Cf. "*Shakespeare's* Excellence is not the Fiction of a Tale but the Representation of Life; and his Reputation is therefore safe, till Human Nature shall be changed" (Dedication to *Shakespear Illustrated*, reprinted in Smith, *op. cit.* p. 88).

[28] Raleigh, *op. cit.*, pp. 11–12.

[29] *Ibid.*, pp. 13–14.

[30] *Ibid.*, p. 14.

makes nature predominate over accident; and if he preserves the essential character, is not very careful of distinctions superinduced and adventitious. His story requires Romans or kings, but he thinks only on men."[31]

In dialogue, too, Shakespeare excels by his just representations of general nature:

> The dialogue of this authour is often so evidently determined by the incident which produces it, and is pursued with so much ease and simplicity, that it seems scarcely to claim the merit of fiction, but to have been gleaned by diligent selection out of common conversation, and common occurences.[32]

Shakespeare also satisfies Johnson's principle in his plots, as other dramatists do not:

> Upon every other stage the universal agent is love, by whose power all good and evil is distributed, and every action quickened or retarded. . . . For this probability is violated, life is misrepresented, and language is depraved. But love is only one of the many passions; and as it has no great influence upon the sum of life, it has little operation in the dramas of a poet, who caught his ideas from the living world, and exhibited only what he saw before him. He knew, that any other passion, as it was regular or exorbitant, was a cause of happiness or calamity.[33]

In theme, as well, Shakespeare succeeds: He exhibits "the real state of sublunary nature, which partakes of good and evil, joy and sorrow, mingled with endless variety of proportion and innumerable modes of combination. . . ."[34]

Finally, even when Shakespeare introduces the "remote" or "wonderful," he is just in his representation:

> The event which he represents will not happen, but if it were possible, its effects would probably be such as he has assigned; and it may be said, that he has not only shewn human nature as it acts in real exigencies, but as it would be found in trials, to which it cannot be exposed.[35]

[31] *Ibid.*, p. 15.
[32] *Ibid.*, p. 13.
[33] *Ibid.*
[34] *Ibid.*, p. 15.
[35] *Ibid.*, p. 14.

From this first excellence of Shakespeare Johnson infers a corollary excellence, that Shakespeare's true picture of life enables us to derive much instruction from it. His plays are full of "practical axioms" and "domestick wisdom," so much so that "it may be said of *Shakespeare*, that from his works may be collected a system of civil and oeconomical prudence."[36]

Johnson also employs his principle and its confirmation in the dramas of Shakespeare to refute critics like Dennis, Rymer, and Voltaire. Shakespeare had been attacked by them for being false to life and, especially by Rymer and Voltaire, for mixing his comic and tragic scenes. Both charges, Johnson contends, arise out of a narrow interpretation of "just representations of general nature." Voltaire, for example, objects to Shakespeare's protrayal of Claudius as a drunkard; to which Johnson replies: "He [Shakespeare] was inclined to shew an usurper and a murderer not only odious but despicable, he therefore added drunkenness to his other qualities, knowing that kings love wine like other men, and that wine exerts its natural power upon kings."[37] The second charge Johnson takes more seriously. It is true, he concedes, that Shakespeare's mixtures are contrary to the traditional rules, but they are nevertheless consonant with the more basic rule that poetry instructs by pleasing. And Shakespeare's dramas, precisely in their representations of general nature as dramatized in his mixtures of the tragic and the comic, satisfy our desire for truth and pleasure.

Johnson concludes this section of his Preface with a general evaluation of Shakespeare as a writer of comedy and tragedy:

> In his tragic scenes there is always something wanting, but his comedy often surpasses expectation or desire. His comedy pleases by the thoughts and the language, and his tragedy for the greater part by incident and action. His tragedy seems to be skill, his comedy to be instinct.[38]

Johnson's appraisal of Shakespeare raises many questions. Two sorts of them are relevant to this discussion because they further certain issues in evaluative criticism. The first concerns Johnson's

[36] *Ibid.*, p. 12. [37] *Ibid.*, p. 15. [38] *Ibid.*, p. 19.

argument for Shakespeare's greatness. What exactly is its content? It begins simply enough: Shakespeare is great because he represents justly general nature. Then Johnson brilliantly clarifies his key terms in the application of his criterion to Shakespeare. Of course, the truth or adequacy of what he says about Shakespeare's characters, plots, themes, and language is disputable; but that he states a criterion of greatness, and clarifies and applies it in an overall detail (saving the specific details for his notes on the individual plays), cannot be denied. The explication of this criterion, that is, his exhibition of just representations of general nature in Shakespeare's dramas, is, I believe, one of the happy moments in the history of criticism.

But what about the justification of the criterion? How does Johnson defend it? Does he identify dramatic greatness with just representations of general nature? Or is his criterion only one among many criteria of greatness in drama? Is every drama that satisfies his criterion great? Can a drama be great that does not satisfy his criterion? What is dramatic greatness and, more generally, artistic greatness, if it is not identical with his criterion?

These are absolutely crucial questions, especially in a searching analysis of greatness in drama, such as Johnson wishes to provide. Yet one looks almost in vain in his Preface for an answer to any of these questions. The only reply he *seems* to offer is that just representations are one criterion at least of greatness in drama; that they are one criterion because they please many, for long; and that they so please because the mind is satisfied only to repose on the stability of truth. Thus, the ultimate appeal of Shakespeare's greatness is the pleasure we get from truth. So now we must ask again if it is an empirically true proposition that human beings find truth or its representation—in Johnson's sense—ultimately satisfying? And, more importantly, even if they do find truth pleasing, what has truth or what pleases us, whether truth pleases us or not, to do with greatness in drama or art? Johnson has no answer here.

The second sort of question has to do with Johnson's comments on the characters, plots, themes, and language of Shakespeare's dramas. Critics have taken issue with him on his assertions that Shakespeare has no heroes; that his characters are more like species than individuals;

that his plots and themes are lifelike; that his language is the familiar one of real-life situations; and that his comic scenes are better than his tragic. They have also challenged the kind of truth Johnson finds in Shakespeare. Coleridge, as we shall see, agrees with Johnson that Shakespeare's greatness is due, at least in part, to his imitation of nature, but he gives a vastly different account of what is true in Shakespeare's dramas. Others, for example Hazlitt, argue that Johnson understands little or nothing of the poetry of Shakespeare and thus falsifies the language of the plays. Taken together, these critics agree with Johnson that Shakespeare is great but reject Johnson's reasons and his particular confirmation of them.

Johnson turns next to Shakespeare's faults which, like Pope, he finds "sufficient to obscure and overwhelm any other merit."[39] He lists a number of them but gives no examples from the plays, thus leaving them quite general. Each of these faults has been questioned by later critics. Johnson's list is as follows: "He sacrifices virtue to convenience, and is so much more careful to please than to instruct, that he seems to write without any moral purpose; . . . he makes no just distribution of good or evil. . . . The plots are often so loosely formed . . . and so carelessly pursued. . . ."[40] In many of his plays he neglects the later parts. He violates probability and possibility in his frequent disregard of the customs and institutions of diverse historical periods. He is gross and licentious in many of his comic scenes. He is often mean, tedious, and obscure in his tragic scenes. His narration is often unanimated, thus obstructing the action. His declamations are "commonly cold and weak."[41] He sometimes gets entangled in an unwieldy sentiment that he does not unravel. He has too many quibbles: "A quibble was to him the fatal *Cleopatra* for which he lost the world, and was content to lose it."[42]

Johnson also considers the imputed fault of Shakespeare's neglect of the unities. Here, as evaluative critic, he rejects the charge by refuting the principle from which the imputed fault is derived. It is

[39] *Ibid.*, p. 20.
[40] *Ibid.*, pp. 20–21.
[41] *Ibid.*, p. 23.
[42] *Ibid.*, p. 24.

of course true, Johnson says, that Shakespeare does not subscribe to all the unities. But what is not true is that his neglect is a fault, since there is no virtue in the adherence to all of them. The only unity Johnson accepts is that of action, which is essential to drama, and this Shakespeare possesses. Further, Shakespeare wrote histories, comedies, and tragedies. The histories are exempt from the charge. So the issue reduces to Shakespeare's violation of the unities of time and place in the comedies and tragedies. Is this violation a fault or not?

Johnson insists that it is not, that the argument that it is rests upon a false principle: "The necessity of observing the unities of time and place arises from the supposed necessity of making the drama credible."[43] To create and preserve belief in the action on the stage, strict limitations of time and place must be observed. The audience cannot be expected to retain credibility in the action if it covers years or occurs in many different places. Such, Johnson summarizes, is the fundamental argument for the doctrine of the two unities. But the argument assumes that representation is reality, "that any dramatick fable in its materiality was ever credible, or, for a single moment, was ever credited."[44] This assumption, Johnson says, is false: "The truth is, that the spectators are always in their senses, and know, from the first act to the last, that the stage is only a stage, and that the players are only players."[45] Once, therefore, we realize that it is "delusion" we indulge in, the credibility that is founded on the two unities becomes unnecessary. The drama is still credited, Johnson hastens to add, not by actual belief in the action, but "as a just picture of a real original."[46] Moreover, Johnson concludes, the two unities, although sometimes a source of aesthetic pleasure, are never as important as "the nobler beauties of variety and instruction."[47] What is an imputed fault in Shakespeare, Johnson thus converts into an attributed virtue.

Johnson ends this section on Shakespeare's beauties and faults, like Pope, with an extenuation, through historical explanations, of some of Shakespeare's faults. He also offers further praise of Shakespeare for his innovations in the drama, his softening of the English language, and his descriptions of inanimate nature. Finally, unable to resist the

[43] *Ibid.*, p. 25. [44] *Ibid.*, p. 26. [45] *Ibid.*, p. 27.
[46] *Ibid.*, p. 28. [47] *Ibid.*, p. 30.

perennial temptation of evaluation by metaphor, Johnson sums up Shakespeare's achievement:

> The composition of *Shakespeare* is a forest, in which oaks extend their branches, and pines tower in the air, interspersed sometimes with weeds and brambles, and sometimes giving shelter to myrtles and to roses; filling the eye with awful pomp, and gratifying the mind with endless diversity. Other poets display cabinets of precious rarities, minutely finished, wrought into shape, and polished unto brightness. *Shakespeare* opens a mine which contains gold and diamonds in unexhaustible plenty, though clouded by incrustations, debased by impurities, and mingled with with a mass of meaner minerals.[48]

D. Nichol Smith, an authority on Johnson's criticism of Shakespeare, sums up the Preface:

> Johnson set himself to review the common topics of Shakespeare criticism, and to give his judgement on the points at issue. There is little new matter in his Preface, except where he deals with his work as an editor. Its importance lies mainly in its being a conclusive summing up, by a strong, wise, and impartial mind, of a prolonged discussion.[49]

This assessment of Johnson seems to me correct. The evaluative critic may do many things. He may formulate new principles, with or without a defense of them, reformulate or defend traditional principles, or systematize a whole set of principles; he may apply them in great or lesser detail to an author or employ defended principles to refute other critics. Johnson, I think, chooses to reformulate and apply traditional principles as his major activity in his evaluative criticism of Shakespeare. If we can say of Pope that he stresses that aspect of evaluative criticism which is a kind of counsel for the defense, we can as justly say of Johnson that on the whole he stresses the judicial side of criticism, not in the traditionally attributed sense of the making of official verdicts that derive from absolute principles, but in the correct legal sense of the weighing of all the evidence—all the principles, precedents, and facts of the case—followed by the handing down of a balanced, seasoned verdict supported by all the available evidence. Johnson's verdict? Shakespeare has his virtues and his faults.

[48] *Ibid.*, p. 34.

[49] Smith, *op. cit.*, p. xiv.

XI THE MAJOR TRADITION

(Continued)

LIKE HIS "myriad-minded" hero, Shakespeare, Coleridge was a man of many basic interests. He composed poetry and wrote on the principles of poetry. He speculated in metaphysics and posed new directions for discriminating the various faculties of the mind. His most famous distinction was that between fancy and imagination, in which he gives an exasperatingly brief theory of the latter. He dipped into biology and delved into psychology. He wrote lengthy critiques of other authors, notably Wordsworth. Besides his theory of imagination, he formulated definitions of art, beauty, and poetry. Throughout his writings there is a steady concern for philosophy, for essences, and fundamental principles, and a pervasive conviction that philosophy, psychology, art, and criticism are interrelated. Indeed, Coleridge's most ostensible characteristic, even as a practicing critic, is this recurrent reference to fundamental principles.

There is a whole book here, already essayed by many, on the basic doctrines of Coleridge. I do not propose to add to this list, although it would be a fascinating task, even if devastating to Coleridge, I believe, to subject his doctrines to a more adequate philosophical scrutiny than he would have tolerated.

My aim is to try to clarify one aspect of Coleridge's work: his evaluative criticism of Shakespearean drama, especially of *Hamlet*, since his is the first thorough evaluation of the play.

This task is made initially difficult by the notorious problems involved in the determination of an accurate text of his Shakespearean criticism. It is ironic that Coleridge, whom many consider the greatest Shakespearean critic, should have bequeathed textual problems almost as great as did Shakespeare himself, whom Coleridge considered the greatest dramatist. Alfred Harbage sums up the editorial problem:

> Only two brief essays were ever given final form and published by Coleridge personally: "The Specific Symptoms of Poetic Power," in the *Biographia Literaria*, 1817; and "Method in Thought," in the *Encyclopaedia Metropolitana*, 1818, revised in the same year for inclusion in *The Friend*. . . . All the rest comes to us as records of conversation, marginalia, fragmentary lecture-notes, and newspaper or shorthand reports of the lectures themselves. The most important of the reports, authentic although J. P. Collier's, were unavailable in print until 1883. The marginalia and notes, revised and conflated by the poet's nephew, H. N. Coleridge, were published in 1836–39 in *Literary Remains*, to be reprinted in substantially the same form until 1930, when Professor Raysor rescued the original texts in his model edition.[1]

The edition Harbage refers to is T. M. Raysor's *Coleridge's Shakespearean Criticism*, in which Raysor prints in exact detail all the notes, marginalia, and available reports on Coleridge's lectures on Shakespeare. This edition is now universally accepted as the definitive one.[2]

I shall now try to ascertain Coleridge's contributions to the evaluative criticism of Shakespeare. Dryden had suggested that Shakespeare's judgment is not always consonant with his genius. Voltaire,

[1] Alfred Harbage, Introduction to *Coleridge's Writings on Shakespeare*, ed. Terence Hawkes (New York, 1959), p. 13.

[2] T. M. Raysor, *Coleridge's Shakespearean Criticism* (2 vols.; Cambridge, 1930). This edition, now out of print, has been reissued, with minor omissions, by J. M. Dent, London, 1960, in Everyman's Library, Nos. 162 and 183. All page references to Coleridge's criticism of Shakespeare, unless otherwise specified, are to the 1960 edition, now readily available.

Pope, and Johnson concurred, and the charge that Shakespeare, although great, is "irregular" prevailed. Coleridge—not the first, to be sure—rejects this charge, and rejects it totally. "The judgement of Shakespeare is commensurate with his genius." This, it seems to me, is the fundamental thesis and theme in his evaluation of Shakespeare, indeed, in the whole of his work on Shakespeare since, throughout it, evaluation is primary. This thesis is tantamount to his persistent claim that Shakespeare is great not in spite of his faulty judgments but because they are also on analysis excellences along with the undisputed ones. His greatness as a dramatist, then, inheres precisely in his exquisite congruence of judgment and genius. This central concern with evaluation links Coleridge inevitably with Johnson and the major tradition of Shakespearean criticism. Consequently, if Coleridge is the romantic critic par excellence and Johnson, the neoclassic, their differences cannot rest in their aims, as some historians maintain, but in their arguments.

Like Johnson, Coleridge attempts a true assessment of Shakespeare's art. This assessment consists in a clarification, justification, and confirmation in the whole of Shakespeare's dramas and in the individual plays, of the harmony of Shakespeare's judgment and genius and, hence, of his uncompromised greatness. If we may revert to our legal analogy, Coleridge, it can be said, also serves as a counsel for the defense. But instead of accepting imputed charges and pleading extenuation, he calls into question the principles and precedents of these charges, demands a hearing for a new set of principles, affirms these new principles as the true ones and, then, on the basis of this new set, converts every ascribed fault into a major excellence in Shakespeare. In effect, Coleridge takes his case to the Supreme Court.

The central passage in Coleridge's criticism of Shakespeare, I think, is the following:

> Are the plays of *Shakespeare* works of rude uncultivated genius, in which the splendor of the parts compensates, if aught can compensate, for the barbarous shapelessness and irregularity of the whole? To which not only the French critics, but even his own English admirers, say [yes]. Or is the form equally admirable with the matter, the judgement of the great poet not less de-

serving of our wonder than his genius? Or to repeat the question in other words, is Shakespeare a great dramatic poet on account only of those beauties and excellencies which he possesses in common with the ancients, but with diminished claims to our love and honor to the full extent of his difference from them? Or are these very differences additional proofs of poetic wisdom, at once results and symbols of living power as contrasted with lifeless mechanism, of free and rival originality as contradistinguished from servile imitation, or more accurately, [from] a blind copying of effects instead of a true imitation of the essential principles?[3]

As far as I have been able to determine, Coleridge offers no definitions of his key terms: "judgement" and "genius." He presents clarifications of them instead, especially in his lengthy refutation of that criticism which denies Shakespeare's commensurability. Coleridge is passionate in his denunciation of the traditional critics of Shakespeare:

> It is humiliating to reflect that, as it were, because heaven has given us the greatest poet, it has inflicted upon that poet the most incompetent critics: none of them seem to understand even his language, much less the principles upon which he wrote, and the peculiarities which distinguish him from all rivals. . . . Nearly all they can do is to express the most vulgar of all feelings, wonderment—wondering at what they term the irregularity of his genius, sometimes above all praise, and at other times, if they are to be trusted, below all contempt.[4]

Their whole criticism of Shakespeare, Coleridge contends, rests on certain false doctrines about the drama and, in particular, about the

[3] *Ibid.*, I, 197 (editor's brackets as in original). See also a newspaper report of a lecture by Coleridge in 1813 in *ibid.*, II, 211–19. In 1818, Coleridge writes: "In all the successive courses delivered by me since my first attempt at the Royal Institution, it has been and it still remains my object to prove that in all points from the most important to the most minute, the judgement of Shakespeare is commensurate with his genius—nay, that his genius reveals itself in his judgement, as in its most exalted form." (*Ibid.*, I, 114).

[4] *Ibid.*, II, 125–26; in this same report by J. P. Collier of Coleridge's lecture, Coleridge adds: "His critics among us, during the whole of the last century, have neither understood nor appreciated him; for how could they appreciate what they could not understand?"

unity of drama, its imitative nature, and its relation to aesthetic response. I must now elaborate upon this contention.

Shakespeare's judgment is at fault in his violation of the traditional unities—this is one version of the irregularity thesis. Coleridge rejects it. Like Johnson, he insists that Shakespeare's plays possess a unity of action, which he converts into the unity of "homogeneity, proportionateness, and totality of interest";[5] consequently, the charge reduces to that of his violation of the unities of time and place. Coleridge, again like Johnson (and others), admits their absence from the plays but denies their importance, thus going further than Johnson by refusing to concede any virtue whatever to the unities in question. These two unities, Coleridge insists, are not essential to the drama; the arguments that they are essential—derived from Greek drama and the need for verisimilitude and stressed by the French theorists—are inadequate. In fact, Coleridge counters, in the Greek drama the unities were mere inconveniences, necessitated by the size and construction of the theaters. Artificial devices, such as the chorus, were required to meet these conditions. It was this device that preserved the necessity for the unities:

> As the chorus was always on the stage, there was no dropping of curtains; the same men could not be at the same time at Thebes and at Rome. It therefore became necessary that the same scene should be presented to the eye, constituting the *unity of place*, and that the piece should be acted nearly within the time that the events could have occurred in. And, lastly, they had, what is common to all dramas, a *unity of interest and action.*[6]

Coleridge adds:

> The plays represented were made to include within a short space of time events which it is impossible should have occurred in that short space. This fact alone establishes, that all dramatic performances were then looked upon merely as ideal.[7]

[5] *Ibid.*, I, 4.

[6] *Ibid.*, II, 54–55 (italics in original). For the absurdities involved in the unities of the Greek dramas and a comparison of the Greek trilogies to Shakespeare's plays, see *ibid.*, II, 214–15.

[7] *Ibid.*, ii, p. 46.

Coleridge offers a complex argument against both the theory that the unities must be preserved in order to ensure verisimilitude and credibility and Johnson's rebuttal of this theory. His argument is important because it contains some of Coleridge's positive doctrines about the nature of the drama. Belief as well as disbelief, he argues, are inappropriate responses to drama, not only to Shakespearean but to the ancient Greek and the modern French. Instead, dramatic response should be and as a matter of fact is, when correct, a kind of poetic illusion: "that willing suspension of disbelief for the moment which constitutes poetic faith."[8] It is this illusion "which the spectator encourages in himself and supports by a voluntary contribution on his own part, because he knows that it is at all times in his power to see the thing as it really is."[9]

Why is this response of illusion the proper one to the drama? Because of the nature of the drama, which is an imitation of reality: of its "objects, actions, or passions, under a *semblance* of reality."[10] To say the drama is an imitation of reality is to imply it is not a copy of it. For a copy must be an exact resemblance of what it copies, whereas an imitation signifies a difference between the imitation and the object imitated. The mind recognizes this crucial distinction between a copy and an imitation, hence, it never deceives itself into taking imitation for reality. Instead it attends to the implied difference in order to foster the response of poetic illusion. And once illusion, required by the imitative nature of the drama, is dominant, the spectator has no need whatever for the two unities because they are unnecessary to sustain the illusion.[11] The two unities, therefore, have

[8] *Biographia Literaria*, ed. J. Shawcross (2 vols., Oxford, 1907), II, 6.

[9] Raysor, *op. cit.*, I, 178. See also *ibid.*, II, 55. Cf: "The mind of the spectator, or the reader, therefore, is not to be deceived into any idea of reality, as the French critics absurdly suppose; neither, on the other hand, is it to retain a perfect consciousness of the falsehood of the presentation. There is a state of mind between the two, which may be properly called illusion, in which the comparative powers of the mind are completely suspended; as in a dream, the judgment is neither beguiled, nor conscious of the fraud, but remains passive." (*Ibid.*, II, 258). For Coleridge on dreams and poetic illusion, see also his notes on *The Tempest*, Raysor, *op. cit.*, I, 116.

[10] *Ibid.*, I, 177 (italics in original).

[11] My exposition is based on the following: one of Coleridge's lectures of

no defensible status; and Shakespeare cannot be said to violate them or the principles on which they are supposedly based.

Coleridge also rejects another version of the traditional assessment: that Shakespeare was a wild genius—a *lusus naturae*. Here he appeals to a new conception of form or unity that he acknowledges he derived from A. W. Schlegel.[12] To accuse Shakespeare of supposed irregularities and extravagances, he says, is like arraigning the eagle because it lacks the dimensions of the swan. Shakespeare cannot be judged by particular rules that were practiced by other dramatists. He has his own rule, just as he has his own unity, even though in neither case does he follow "the rules" or "the unities." Shakespeare's dramas, like all works of genius, have an order or unity:

> No work of true genius dare want its appropriate form; neither indeed is there any danger of this. As it must not, so neither can it, be lawless! For it is even this that constitutes it genius—the power of acting creatively under laws of its own origination.[13]

The charge that Shakespeare is irregular, then, rests on another principle which, like that of the three unities being necessary to drama, is false, namely, the principle that all form (or unity, order, rule, law—these are almost synonyms for Coleridge) is mechanic. Some form, Coleridge, reiterating Schlegel, claims, is not mechanic:

> The form is mechanic when on any given material we impress a pre-determined form, not necessarily arising out of the properties of the material, as when to a mass of wet clay we give whatever shape we wish it to retain when hardened. The organic form, on the other hand, is innate; it shapes as it develops itself from within, and the fullness of its development is one and the same with the perfection of its outward form. Such is the life, such the form. Nature, the prime genial artist, inexhaustible in diverse powers, is equally inexhaustible in forms. Each exterior is the physiognomy of the being within, its true image reflected and thrown out from the concave mirror. And even such is the ap-

---

1811–12, as reported by Collier (Raysor, *op. cit.*, II, 46); his notes for a lecture on dramatic illusion, c. 1808 (*ibid.*, I, 176–80); and a newspaper report of a lecture given by Coleridge, 1818 (*ibid.*, II, 258).

[12] *Ibid.*, I, 197–98. [13] *Ibid.*

> propriate excellence of her chosen poet, of our own Shakespeare, himself a nature humanized, a genial understanding directing self-consciously a power and an implicit wisdom deeper than consciousness.[14]

Shakespeare's dramas are imitations of the organic forms of nature. How, then, can he truly be called wild and irregular? He cannot: his plays possess the same unity as nature. The greatness of Shakespeare, to indulge in a Coleridgeanism, inheres in his being true to nature and in his being truly natural.

Before proceeding to Coleridge's further clarification and confirmation of the commensurability of Shakespeare's judgment and genius, we must ask certain important questions that arise from his refutation of the traditional censure of Shakespeare.

If Coleridge's refutation is to stand, then the doctrines upon which it depends must be true as well as consistent with each other. The first of these doctrines about which there is some question is that of the unities in Greek drama. Is Coleridge right in his analysis of them? Can they be explained as artificial inconveniences that arose from the constant presence of the chorus on the stage? Many students of ancient drama, for example Nietzsche, would object to this explanation. But what is most surprising in Coleridge's account is his "mechanic" approach (to borrow his term) to the construction of that drama. Surely it deserved from him the same quality of insight that he offers for the understanding of Shakespearean drama.

Second, Coleridge assumes that the drama has an essence, that is, a set of necessary and sufficient properties, that can be formulated in a true, real definition of drama. This, too, is debatable. But I skip over this question to raise a subordinate one: Is Coleridge correct in his doctrine that the drama is essentially an imitation of reality whose main purpose is to beget poetic illusion? He seems to relate imitation and illusion in such a way that imitation without poetic illusion is a contradiction and poetic illusion without imitation is impossible. But surely the doctrine of poetic illusion can be defended on grounds other than imitation; and imitation can be joined with responses other

[14] *Ibid.*, I, 198.

than illusion. My question, then, is this: Does Coleridge prove that dramatic imitation entails poetic illusion? It seems to me he does not.

Third, and most important because consistency is at stake, Coleridge affirms that Shakespeare's regularity or unity is like that of nature's: it is true to what is basic in nature, and it is itself one manifestation of nature's unity. This doctrine implies a metaphysical theory about nature that is certainly disputable. It also implies that Shakespeare is a metaphysical poet, not in the sense of a John Donne but in the sense of a poet who dramatizes ultimate characteristics of reality. Now, this doctrine that Shakespeare is true to nature and truly natural, i.e., that Shakespeare's dramas are imitations and ideal manifestations of nature, cannot easily be said to induce poetic illusion. Nor does Coleridge, in his metaphysical argument for Shakespeare's unity and regularity, think so. His emphasis is just the reverse: Shakespeare is great because of his truth, and ultimately we respond to his dramas as we respond properly to truth, not by a kind of illusion but by a straightforward conviction and belief in them.

And we are back to Johnson. For does not Coleridge, like Johnson, imply as his fundamental view about Shakespeare that he is great because his dramas are true, and that this truth only is worthy of our belief? The issue between Johnson and Coleridge on disbelief and make-believe, consequently, is superficial and involves the characters and events of the dramas. Basically they agree, their major difference being the relatively minor one of what is truth-to-nature. Thus, insofar as Coleridge's clarification and justification of his claim that Shakespeare's judgment is commensurate with his genius rest upon these doctrines about the drama, and insofar as these doctrines are open to question or inconsistent with each other, his clarification and justification of his claim are inadequate, which I believe they are.

But Coleridge, in his evaluation of Shakespeare, also offers a confirmation and, through it, a further clarification of his claim of commensurability. His confirmation consists of an evaluation of the plays as a whole and as individual dramas. Throughout the discussion of the plays his constant concern is with the congruence of Shakespeare's judgment and genius not only in characterization but in the whole play. Hence I find no support in the fragments for the common objection that Coleridge reduces the plays to the portrayal of character. On the contrary, his critical interests range from characterization to metaphysical insight, and include language, unity of feeling, thematic development, and plot in Shakespeare's dramas. Indeed, his penetrating remark—"Shakespeare shewed great judgment in his first scenes; they contained the germ of the ruling passion which was to be developed hereafter"[15]—is sufficient to refute this objection. In the analysis of each play Coleridge emphasizes those aspects that exhibit Shakespeare's exquisite judgment. And in many of his analyses he reinforces his claim with arguments against certain counterclaims that Shakespeare often lacks judgment.[16]

What, now, are the excellences of Shakespeare's dramas: those products of his judgment equal to his genius? Shakespeare is a dramatic poet. Hence, his general excellences must inhere in his command of poetry and drama in their organic relationship. The requisites of great poetry, Coleridge specifies, are deep feeling, exquisite sense of beauty, objectivity, sympathy, love of nature, fancy, imagination, and profundity. Shakespeare, he insists, satisfies all of them.[17] The requisites of great drama are language, passion, and character, each realized with the highest degree of good sense, talent, sensibility, imagination and, although less important, fancy, and a quick sense of beauty. Shakespeare also satisfies these.[18] Coleridge exhibits these criteria in the dramas of Shakespeare. Consider to begin with, his assessment of Shakespeare's characters. They are all, from the heroes to the clowns,

> ideal realities. They are not the things themselves, so much as abstracts of the things, which a great mind takes into itself, and

[15] *Ibid.*, II, 230.

[16] An excellent example is Coleridge's reply to Pope's charge of bombast regarding two lines of *The Tempest*. He dissolves the charge by an appeal to the context and appropriateness of their utterance. Coleridge's discussion is in Collier's report of one of Coleridge's 1811–12 lectures (Raysor, *op. cit.*, II, 138–40).

[17] See Coleridge's notes on Shakespeare's poetry, Raysor, *op. cit.*, I, 187–90.

[18] See Coleridge's notes for a lecture on dramatic illusion, *ibid.*, I, 182–83.

> there naturalizes them to its own conception. Take Dogberry: are no important truths there conveyed, no admirable lessons taught, and no valuable allusions made to reigning follies, which the poet saw must for ever reign? He is not the creature of the day, to disappear with the day, but the representative and abstract of truth which must ever be true, and of humour which must ever be humorous.[19]

Later, Coleridge adds to his evaluation:

> The truth is, Shakespeare's characters are all *genera* intensely individualized; the results of meditation, of which observation supplied the drapery and the colors necessary to combine them with each other. He had virtually surveyed all the great component powers and impulses of human nature,—had seen that their different combinations and subordinations were in fact the individualizers of men, and showed how their harmony was produced by reciprocal disproportions of excess or deficiency. The language in which these truths are expressed was not drawn from any set fashion, but from the profoundest depths of his moral being, and is therefore for all ages.[20]

Closely tied to Shakespeare's characterization is his psychological insight:

> Shakespeare has this advantage over all other dramatists—that he has availed himself of his psychological genius to develope all the minutiae of the human heart: shewing us the thing that, to common observers, he seems solely intent upon, he makes visible what we should not otherwise have seen. . . .[21]

Also related to Shakespeare's ability to create characters is his understanding of how different people talk in various circumstances. Coleridge discusses this excellence in the essay, "Method in Thought" (1818), and in his other observations on Shakespeare's wit and puns where Shakespeare's judgment had been severely attacked. The essay is of particular importance to us because it contains part of Coleridge's evaluation of *Hamlet*.

By "The Science of Method" Coleridge means the study of the

[19] *Ibid.*, II, 125. See also *ibid.*, II, 29.

[20] *Ibid.*, I, 122–23.

[21] *Ibid.*, II, 98.

logic of spontaneous, ordinary talk. In real life there are great differences between the talk or conversation of the uneducated as against the educated, which are disclosed not in information about matters of fact or in qualities of elegant language but in the ways ideas are put together. The uneduated live in, hence talk of, a world of things and events related, if at all, only by space and time. The educated, on the other hand, live in, hence talk of, a world of things and events related causally; they see connections, and their talk inevitably shows that they do. Now, one of Shakespeare's excellences is the manner in which he dramatizes these laws and truths of the science of method. Coleridge illustrates this excellence by contrasting two extremely opposed types: the talk of Mrs. Quickly to Falstaff (*Henry IV, Part II*, II, 1) and the talk of Hamlet to Horatio about his aborted trip to England. Mrs. Quickly sees no connections, Hamlet too many in the way he generalizes on each of the events he narrates.

Shakespeare's wit Coleridge describes as one of combinations of images rather than of words. Here, too, Shakespeare is excellent:

> The wit of Shakespeare is, as it were, like the flourishing of a man's stick, when he is walking, in the full flow of animal spirits: it is a sort of exuberance of hilarity which disburdens, and it resembles a conductor, to distribute a portion of our gladness to the surrounding air. While, however, it disburdens, it leaves behind what is weightiest and most important, and what most contributes to some direct aim and purpose.[22]

The puns Coleridge acknowledges but not the correctness of the objections to them. Here again Coleridge's main appeal is to real life: "Is there not a tendency in the human mind, when suffering under some great affliction, to associate everything around it with the obtrusive feeling, to connect and absorb all into the predominant sensation?"[23] But punning is not only true to life; when it is congruous with the feeling of a particular dramatic scene, it may also function as "one of the most effectual intensives of passion."[24]

Other excellences Coleridge mentions are Shakespeare's unity of

[22] *Ibid.*, II, 91. [23] *Ibid.*, II, 231. [24] *Ibid.*, I, 136.

feeling which "pervades the whole of his plays";[25] his characteristics of "expectation in preference to surprize"; "signal adherence to the great law of nature that opposites tend to attract and temper each other"; "independence of the interest on the plot . . . or on *the story* as the groundwork of the plot"; "the interfusion of the lyrical, of that which in its very essence is poetical"; and that "Shakespeare's characters are like those in life, to be *inferred* by the reader, not *told to him.*" "Of this excellence I know no other instance"; Coleridge, echoing Morgann, adds this to his assessment of the last characteristic.[26]

So much for Coleridge's survey of Shakespeare's general excellences as a dramatist. Before raising questions about this part of his evaluation we should consider at least his evaluation of one of the plays. Since our main concern is *Hamlet,* let us turn to Coleridge on the evaluation of it.

Is Shakespeare's judgment equal to his genius in *Hamlet?* Is *Hamlet* a great play? In 1819, Coleridge wrote:

> *Hamlet* was the play, or rather Hamlet himself was the character in the intuition and exposition of which I first made my turn for philosophical criticism, and especially for insight into the genius of Shakespeare. . . .[27]

His assigned date for his "turn," 1798, has been questioned by scholars, but not his initial interest in *Hamlet* among the plays of Shakespeare.

If we take all the extant items by or about Coleridge on *Hamlet,* it can be seen, I think, that the emphasis is on the character of the hero and Coleridge's explanation of him. But it is also clear that Coleridge constantly joins explanation with evaluation as he discusses Shakespeare's creation of the hero's character. Coleridge also engages in description and exegesis in his criticism of the play. Indeed, his whole criticism of *Hamlet* includes description, exegesis, explanation, and evaluation. They constantly interweave; nevertheless, in my opinion, Coleridge is primarily concerned with a correct evaluation of the play,

[25] *Ibid.,* II, 216.
[26] *Ibid.,* I, 199–201 (italics in original).
[27] *Ibid.,* I, 16–17.

consequently, he mostly employs his descriptions, exegeses, and even explanations to enhance Shakespeare's excellence as a dramatist.

Among the descriptions in his criticism of *Hamlet* are his reports on some of the qualities of particular characters or scenes; for example, the familiar language of the opening scene, "the armour, the dead silence, the watchfulness that first interrupts it . . ."; the presence of the word "again" in line 21 of the first scene; the unobtrusive introduction of Hamlet in the second scene; Polonius' respectability to all but Hamlet; Hamlet's idealism, ratiocinative meditativeness, and courage; the epic quality of the Player's Speech; the not-so-noble qualities of Laertes—and so on.

Among the exegeses, Coleridge offers, among others, glosses on Hamlet's opening pun; his "fishmonger" epithet to Polonius; and his talk of the devil in Hamlet's second soliloquy.

The explanations include those of Ophelia, Claudius, Polonius, Laertes and, of course, the world-famous one of Hamlet. Shakespeare, Coleridge says,

> never wrote any thing without design. . . . [In Hamlet] he intended to pourtray a person, in whose view the external world, and all its incidents and objects, were comparatively dim, and of no interest in themselves, and which began to interest only, when they were reflected in the mirror of his mind.[28]

Coleridge repeats this theme, with variations, in all his analyses of Hamlet.[29]

[28] *Ibid.*, II, 150.

[29] Here are two of the variations:

"Hamlet's character is the prevalence of the abstracting and generalizing habit over the practical. He does not want courage, skill, will, or opportunity; but every incident sets him thinking . . ." (*Table Talk*, 1827).

"Shakespeare's mode of conceiving characters out of his own intellectual and moral faculties, by conceiving any one intellectual or moral faculty in morbid excess and then placing himself, thus mutilated and diseased, under given circumstances. . . . In Hamlet I conceive him to have wished to exemplify the moral necessity of a due balance between our attention to outward objects and our meditation on inward thoughts—a due balance between the real and the imaginary world. In Hamlet this balance does not exist—his thoughts, images, and fancy [being] far more vivid than his perceptions, and his very perceptions instantly passing thro' the medium of his contemplations, and acquiring as they

In his explanation of Hamlet, Coleridge relates his hypothesis to a general theory of human behavior and its moral implications which, he says, he shares with Shakespeare. He also enlarges upon his explanation by relating it to the crucial events of the play, the most famous being the sparing of the King at prayer which for him, as it has been for many, is pure rationalization on Hamlet's part.

But what is most striking in the fragments on *Hamlet* is the pervasiveness of evaluation, the persistence of the theme that Shakespeare's judgment is equal to his genius. Coleridge scarcely enters upon any description, exegesis, or explanation without immediately relating it to dramatic excellence as further proof of commensurability in Shakespeare. In *Hamlet*, the first scene, the "germ" of all that follows, is Shakespeare's greatest first scene; in it his judgment and genius are uncompromisingly displayed. The language is the easy, familiar one of common life:

> It is the language of *sensation* among men who feared no charge of effeminacy for feeling what they felt no want of resolution to bear. Yet the armour, the dead silence, the watchfulness that first interrupts it, the welcome relief of guard, the cold, the broken expressions as of a man's compelled attention to bodily feelings allowed no man,—all excellently accord with and prepare for the after gradual rise into tragedy. . . .[30]

The information needed by the audience is also excellently dramatized:

> Just as much as was precisely necessary: how gradual first, and with the uncertainty appertaining to a question—
>
> What, has *this thing* appeared *again* to-night.
>
> Even the word "again" has its *credibilizing* effect.[31]

The opening also dramatizes well what we know to be true about attested human encounters with ghosts, especially the accompanying external chills and internal anxieties.

---

pass a form and color not naturally their own. Hence great, enormous, intellectual activity, and a consequent proportionate aversion to real action, with all its symptoms and accompanying qualities." (Raysor, *op. cit.*, I, 34; editor's brackets).

[30] Raysor, *op. cit.*, I, 18 (italics in original).

[31] *Ibid.* (italics in original).

> It has been with all of them as with Francisco on his guard —alone, in the depth and silence of the night—" 'twas bitter cold and they were sick at heart"—and "not a mouse stirring." The attention to minute sounds,—naturally associated with the recollection of minute objects, and the more familiar and trifling, the more impressive from the unusualness of their producing any impression at all—gives a philosophic pertinency to this last image, but it has likewise its dramatic use and purpose, for its commonness in ordinary conversation tends to produce the sense of *reality*, and at once hides the poet and yet approximates the reader or spectator to the state in which the highest poetry will appear, and in its component parts, tho' not in whole composition, really is the language of nature.[32]

Other excellences Coleridge touches upon (we must always remember we have mostly fragments, not complete essays) are the initial presentations of Hamlet and Laertes in the second scene: that of Hamlet because it shows "how judicious that Hamlet should not have to take up the leavings of exhaustion,"[33] and that of Laertes because it shows "Shakespeare's art in introducing a most important but still subordinate character first."[34] The third scene Coleridge singles out as an example of Shakespeare's excellence of the interfusion of the lyrical with the dramatic. The Ghost is also praised, especially Shakespeare's ability to make him dramatically credible:

> How admirable, too, is the judgment of the poet! Hamlet's own disordered fancy has not conjured up the spirit of his father; it has been seen by others: he is prepared by them to witness its re-appearance, and when he does see it, Hamlet is not brought forward as having long brooded on the subject.[35]

Coleridge adds in a later note: "The admirable judgement and yet confidence in his own marvellous powers in introducing the ghost twice, each rising in solemnity and awfulness before its third appearance to Hamlet himself."[36] Even Hume, Coleridge concludes, could not but believe dramatically in *this* ghost!

Coleridge praises both the Player's Speech and "The Murder of

[32] *Ibid.*, I, 38–39 (italics in original).
[33] *Ibid.*, I, 19.
[34] *Ibid.*, I, 20.
[35] *Ibid.*, II, 150–51.
[36] *Ibid.*, I, 35.

Gonzago," as manifestations of Shakespeare's judgment. In the first, there is a genuine epic style and not, as Dryden and others had said, a mere burlesque upon it; in the second, we have a playlet in rhyme. Both differ from the rest of *Hamlet* because Shakespeare had to distinguish between them and the play: "But what if Shakespeare had made the language truly dramatic? Where would have been the contrast between *Hamlet* and the play of *Hamlet*?"[37] He praises also Hamlet's dialogue with the players as "one and among the happiest [instances] of Shakespeare's power of diversifying the scene while he is carrying on the plot."[38]

Coleridge, thus, praises Shakespeare's language, exhibition of passion, characterization, and poetry in *Hamlet*. But his greatest concern is with Shakespeare's excellence in his creation of the hero. For in Hamlet Shakespeare epitomizes his greatness, his commensurability of judgment and genius. Recollect Shakespeare's design, which is to create a character in whom the due balance between the real and the imaginary is destroyed. How does Shakespeare do it? By giving to his hero a set of qualities that exemplifies truly and dramatically such a person. Hamlet's opening line is already the clue to his character which Shakespeare successively unfolds; his pun expresses not only his contempt for Claudius but also "what is highly characteristic of superfluous activity of mind, a sort of playing with a thread or watch chain or snuff box."[39] In his next speech Hamlet expresses his

> aversion to externals, the betrayed habit of brooding over the world within him, and the prodigality of beautiful words, which are, as it were, the half embodyings of thoughts, that make them more than thoughts, give them an outness, a reality *sui generis*, and yet retain their correspondence and shadowy approach to the images and movements within.[40]

The first soliloquy, with its *taedium vitae*, caused by his "exhaustion of bodily feeling from perpetual exertion of mind,"[41] crystallizes his character. The character of Hamlet is then reinforced in the scene after his meeting with Horatio, who tells him of the Ghost, by Hamlet's "running into long reasonings [while waiting for the

[37] *Ibid.*, I, 37.
[38] *Ibid.*, I, 27 (editor's brackets).
[39] *Ibid.*, I, 35.
[40] *Ibid.*
[41] *Ibid.*

ghost], carrying off the impatience and uneasy feelings of expectation by running away from the *particular* in [to] the *general*."[42] And just before Hamlet's encounter with the Ghost, there is his wassail speech in which his idealism and meditativeness express themselves.

> A double purpose is here answered, which demonstrates the exquisite judgment of Shakespeare. By thus entangling the attention of the audience in the nice distinctions and parenthetical sentences of Hamlet, he takes them completely by surprize on the appearance of the Ghost, which comes upon them in all the suddenness of its visionary character.[43]

The aftermath of Hamlet's interview with the Ghost is finely drawn; in Hamlet's "instant and over violent resolve [we see] how he wastes his efforts of resolving the energies of action."[44]

Hamlet's second and fourth soliloquies Coleridge praises, too, because they express so well Hamlet's sense of inadequacy and, through them, Shakespeare's consistency of character delineation. The refusal to kill the King is exactly right:

> He [Shakespeare] saw at once how consistent it was with the character of Hamlet, that after still resolving, and still deferring, still determining to execute, and still postponing execution, he should finally, in the infirmity of his disposition, give himself up to his destiny, and hopelessly place himself in the power, and at the mercy of his enemies.[45]

Even toward the end of the play, Hamlet remains in words all resolution but in action all words. Coleridge sums up his assessment of Shakespeare's creation of Hamlet:

> Anything finer than this conception, and working out of a great character, is merely impossible. Shakespeare wished to impress upon us the truth, that action is the chief end of existence—that no faculties of intellect, however brilliant, can be considered valuable, or indeed otherwise than as misfortunes, if they withdraw us from, or render us repugnant to action, and lead us to think and think of doing, until the time has elapsed when we

[42] *Ibid.*, I, 36 (italics in original; editor's brackets).
[43] *Ibid.*, II, 225. [44] *Ibid.*, I, 36. [45] *Ibid.*, II, 154.

> can do anything effectually. In enforcing this moral truth, Shakespeare has shown the fulness and force of his powers: all that is amiable and excellent in nature is combined in Hamlet, with the exception of one quality. He is a man living in meditation, called upon to act by every motive human and divine, but the great object of his life is defeated by continually resolving to do, yet doing nothing but resolve.[46]

Coleridge's goal in his evaluative criticism of Shakespeare's dramas, including *Hamlet*, is to substantiate his thesis that Shakespeare's judgment and genius are one; that his plays in form and content are organically united, as form and content are in nature; consequently, that his greatness as a dramatist is complete—there is nothing at fault in his plays.

To realize this objective he first refutes that criticism which denies his thesis; in doing so, as we have seen, he formulates and defends a number of principles that he subsequently employs as criteria of greatness in drama. The two basic criteria, I have argued, are poetic illusion and metaphysical truth. Each is open to question and both together are inconsistent.

His second move is to substantiate his thesis in positive terms, by means of a confirmation of it in the plays. The confirmation introduces certain new principles or criteria of greatness in drama that he also defends, clarifies, and exhibits in general as well as in particular terms in the plays.

There are many of these new principles but the ones that Coleridge develops at length are those of characterization, language, profundity, and movement of the plot. He takes for granted, as well he might, some of his criteria, such as deep feeling, fancy, imagination, passion, objectivity, and love of nature, since he clarifies, defends, and applies them in his other writings, notably *Biographia Literaria* and, so far as Shakespeare is concerned, in his analysis and evaluation of *Venus and Adonis*. His confirmation of the greatness of the dramas, especially of *Hamlet*, relies heavily upon those principles or criteria he develops at length; consequently, we can confine ourselves to them. *Hamlet*, then, is a great play at least because of its characterization, language,

[46] *Ibid.*, II, 154–55.

plot, and profundity. In each of these Shakespeare exhibits an exquisite judgment equal to his genius as a dramatist.

Greatness in characterization, Coleridge says, is the creation of ideal realities, i.e., genera intensely individualized. He clarifies this and shows how Shakespeare's characters, especially Hamlet, satisfy this criterion. Now, there are many problems here, all of which have arisen in the history of *Hamlet* and Shakespearean criticism: Does Coleridge's concept of an "ideal reality" make sense? That is, Are there, in real life or in the drama, concrete universals? What about Pope's and Johnson's views on this matter? Or, more importantly, why are great characters ideal realities? Coleridge's answer turns on one of his two basic criteria, the importance of truth in art: great characterization in drama is the creation of characters who are true to what is ultimate in real-life persons. My point is borne out, I think, in Coleridge's particular evaluation of Hamlet, who is a great character because he is true to that ideal reality or genus of human behavior that Shakespeare represents. Much is debatable here: Coleridge's criterion of great characterization, his specific analysis of the sort of ideal reality Hamlet represents, and his particular explanation of Hamlet.

Coleridge's appeal to profundity is open to the same questions as his appeal to characterization, for it, too, must rest on the criterion of truth. I do not wish to challenge Coleridge on any of the questions, What is profundity? Is Shakespeare profound? and What has profundity to do with dramatic greatness? but only to point out at this stage how his argument for Shakespeare's greatness keeps returning to one of the principles of his refutation of the early critics of Shakespeare.

Even the appeal to language turns mostly on the criterion of truth. Shakespeare's dramas are great because of the language; and the language, whether it is wit, fancy, puns, or ordinary prose, is "the language of nature."[47] It is true to life. Recollect Coleridge's assessment of the language in the first scene of *Hamlet:* it is a great use of language because it imitates the language of real life in similar situations. So, too, with the puns, or *almost:* they are right, they show Shakespeare's judgment because they also imitate situations in real life where punning is the natural expression of a particular emotion.

[47] *Ibid.*, II, 217.

I say *almost* because Coleridge also seems to defend the puns on grounds other than the imitation of real life. Puns are justifiable, provided they are congruous with the feeling of a particular scene, because they intensify the passion and thereby move the action of the drama. What, now, is the appeal here? To real life or to something different from real life? Will it resolve my difficulty to say that everything that moves dramatically does so because it, too, is true to, or an imitation of, real-life movement?

Let us see. Coleridge praises the deftness with which Shakespeare prepares his audience in the first scene of *Hamlet;* the introductions of Laertes and Hamlet in the second scene; the contrast between the Player's Speech or the playlet and the rest of *Hamlet;* and the fusion of the lyrical with the dramatic. The appeal here is to aesthetic criteria that do not obviously relate to real life at all. In the way, say, that the language of Francisco and Barnardo is like the language of real men in similar situations, hence praiseworthy, is the introduction of Laertes to be praised because it, too, is an imitation of real life? Do we live in a world in which important but subordinate people are introduced first?

And look now at the Ghost. He, too, is praised by Coleridge, as a marvel of judgment in harmony with genius. Why? Surely not because in its objectivity and dignity it is like a real ghost, but simply because Shakespeare makes him dramatically convincing. If the greatness of the creation of the Ghost depends on his credibility, is this credibility a matter of truth to reality or of what Coleridge calls poetic illusion?

So we are back to our comments on the consistency of Coleridge's two ultimate criteria: truth and belief as against imitation and illusion. It seems to me that throughout his confirmation of Shakespeare's greatness, there is this vacillation (or perhaps confusion) between a dramatic greatness based on truth and a consequent belief in it and a dramatic greatness based on imitation and an adventitiously recommended illusion in regard to it. Every argument Coleridge offers for his thesis of commensurability, hence of Shakespeare's uncompromised greatness, returns to one or the other of his basic criteria or principles: that illusion is basic or that belief is basic. Perhaps Coleridge reconciles this conflict, but I have not been able to determine that he does.

Does Coleridge, then, realize his aim? Does he prove that Shakespeare is great, that his judgment is equal to his genius? If my exposition and analysis have been correct, he does not. What he succeeds in doing instead is to state certain principles as criteria of greatness in drama, give arguments for them, and apply them by exhibiting them in the plays. But the principles are not self-evident and, hence, are debatable. The arguments are based on these principles and are, therefore, also challengeable. Above all, the arguments are inconsistent. Nevertheless, the application or exhibition of the principles, as in the case of Johnson's, is magnificent in its fulness and concreteness. Indeed, it is difficult to imagine a better defense, once Coleridge's new principles are accepted and the traditional ones repudiated. His apologia stands in evaluative criticism as a model of the application of reformulated traditional and formulated new principles to the dramas of Shakespeare. Yet, it cannot be truly said that he has won his brilliant case. But, then, was it ever lost? In the end, I wonder if Coleridge did not himself realize the futility of argument about Shakespeare's greatness when he wrote, as a manuscript note on *Hamlet:*

> O heaven! words are wasted to those that feel and to those who do not feel the exquisite judgement of Shakespeare.[48]

2

Tolstoy's essay, "Shakespeare and the Drama" (1906),[49] is, as far as I know, the most vehement denunciation of Shakespeare ever written. Because it represents a complete contrast to all the evaluations that have been considered, it is worth detailed examination.

Tolstoy's thesis is brutally simple: Shakespeare is a mediocre dramatist. With one exception, Shakespeare satisfies none of the requisite criteria of good drama. The most striking feature of Tolstoy's

[48] *Ibid.*, I, 18.

[49] Leo Tolstoy, "Shakespeare and the Drama," reprinted in *Recollections and Essays,* trans. Aylmer Maude (Oxford: World Classics, 1937). All page references are to this edition.

attack is that he argues his case against Shakespeare by accepting completely the same general criteria of good poetic drama that traditional admirers and idolators had employed in their arguments for his greatness: true-to-life characterization, finely-wrought exhibition of passion, an appropriate and poetic use of language, and profundity of theme. Tolstoy does not challenge these criteria in rejecting Shakespeare's greatness; he simply denies that Shakespeare realizes them, and he offers a confirmation of his denial through an analysis of some of the plays, especially *King Lear*.

But he does more: he states further criteria of good drama and good art in general, which he defends, and then shows that Shakespeare does not satisfy these criteria either. Having proved the mediocrity of Shakespeare, his remaining problem is to explain and evaluate the reasons for his reputation as a great dramatist. In his role of prosecutor Tolstoy condemns more than Shakespeare by bringing to trial the social forces that produced him as well as his unwarranted, hence evil, reputation of greatness.

Tolstoy does not wear his robe as prosecutor lightly. He tells us at the very beginning of the essay about his long bouts of conscience regarding Shakespeare, especially Shakespeare's great reputation, and about his own persistent disappointment in the plays. Seeking aesthetic pleasure, he received instead repulsion, weariness, and bewilderment. He read the plays many times, in several languages, including the original, but always with the same result, except that this time, at seventy-five years old and preparing his essay, the feeling of bewilderment has passed, for now he knows why he feels this repulsion and weariness. The essay is the product of his enlightenment.

King Lear is almost universally praised by critics, so it is a good example with which to start in order to demonstrate Shakespeare's mediocrity as a dramatist. Tolstoy gives a running commentary on the plot, characters, language, and theme of the play. From the beginning, with Gloucester's vulgarity of speech, which is completely inappropriate in so noble a person, to the end, with Lear's entreaty to undo one of his buttons, there is a succession of vulgar repartee; witless attempts at wit; dull jokes; obscure and bombastic metaphors, similes, and images; inconsistent characters and scenes; unnatural relations;

improbable happenings; incredible motives; and confused sequences of events. Exaggeration is the pervasive tone of the play; character, language, plot, and exhibition of emotion are violated. The one saving grace is the genuine quality of some of the feelings, for example, Lear's curse upon Goneril, but even here Shakespeare ruins it by his inflated writing.

It is interesting to compare Tolstoy with Lamb on what Lamb (along with many others) regards as one of the great scenes of the play. It is scene 2 of Act III, where Lear, Kent, and the Fool are on the heath during the storm. Lamb says of this scene:

> The greatness of Lear is . . . in intellectual [dimension]: the explosions of his passion are terrible as a volcano: they are storms turning up and disclosing to the bottom that sea, his mind, with all its vast riches. It is his mind which is laid bare . . . ; while we read it [the play], we see not Lear, but we are Lear,—we are in his mind, we are sustained by a grandeur which baffles the malice of daughters and storms; in the aberrations of his reason, we discover a mighty irregular power of reasoning, immethodized from the ordinary purposes of life, but exerting its powers, as the wind blows where it listeth, at will upon the corruptions and abuses of mankind.[50]

And here is Tolstoy:

> Lear walks about the heath and utters words intended to express despair: he wishes the winds to blow so hard that they (the winds) should crack their cheeks, and that the rain should drench everything, and that the lightning should singe his white head and thunder strike the earth flat and destroy all the germs "that make ingrateful man!" The fool keeps uttering yet more senseless words. Kent enters. Lear says that for some reason all criminals shall be discovered and exposed in this storm. Kent, still not recognized by Lear, persuades Lear to take shelter in a hovel. The fool thereupon utters a prophecy unrelated to the situation and they all go off.[51]

[50] Charles Lamb, "On the Tragedies of Shakespeare, Considered with Reference to their Fitness for Stage Representation" (1811); reprinted in *English Critical Essays: Nineteenth Century*, ed. E. D. Jones (Oxford: World Classics, 1956), p. 95.

[51] Tolstoy, *op. cit.*, p. 321.

Lamb's reading of this scene (or, perhaps, of the whole symbolic motif in *King Lear*) is not at issue here; what is of concern is the disagreement on the power of that scene. The grandeur of the poetry as seen by Lamb dissolves into unnatural bombastic speech for Tolstoy. It is this dissolution that is typical of much of Tolstoy's commentary; where others find the very peaks of poetry, Tolstoy (who claims to understand and love poetry as much as anyone) discovers only a desecration of language.

What is true of *King Lear* for Tolstoy holds for all the plays. The traditional claim that Shakespeare is great because of his ability to create characters who are individuals, various, consistent, and true-to-life is false. Shakespeare's characters are all alike: they are inconsistent, not true-to-life, unnatural, both in speech and action, and not individuals. Indeed, they are not *characters* at all for they lack the essential quality of character: "individuality of language—that each person should speak in a way suitable to his own character."[52] Only Falstaff is a real character since "he alone speaks in a way proper to himself . . . because he talks just that Shakespearian language, filled with jests that lack humour and unamusing puns, which while unnatural to all Shakespeare's other characters is quite in harmony with the boastful, distorted, perverted character of the drunken Falstaff."[53] Nor is Shakespeare's language great. Throughout the plays, the language is as it is in *King Lear:* debased, inflated, obscure, witless, unnaturally metaphorical, and completely out of keeping with the characters uttering it. So, too, with Shakespeare's exhibition of passion, that is, his ability to make us feel as well as see (Dryden) or his power over our passions (Pope). The exhibition is always spoiled by the expression. The plots, too, are bad, for they are incredible, confused, superfluous in their incidents, untrue-to-life, and poorly constructed. Finally, Shakespeare is not profound. First, Tolstoy rejects profundity as a criterion of great drama unless it is artistically integrated with the characters and plot; then he rejects the idea that Shakespeare is profound by identifying Shakespeare's message with a thoroughly immoral and superficial philosophy of life.

[52] *Ibid.*, p. 338.

[53] *Ibid.*, p. 349.

Tolstoy then argues that Shakespeare not only fails to meet the criteria for which he is praised but that he does not even satisfy certain elementary criteria of good drama. Consider, again, Shakespeare's tragedies. Tolstoy agrees with Shakespeare's admirers that

> the conditions of every tragedy are that the persons who appear should, as a result of their own characters, actions, and the natural movement of events, be brought into conditions in which, finding themselves in opposition to the world around them, they should struggle with it and in that struggle display their inherent qualities.[54]

In *King Lear*, as well as in the other tragedies, although the characters struggle against the external world, "the struggle does not result from a natural course of events and from their own characters, but is quite arbitrarily arranged by the author. . . ."[55] Lear's resignation, his relations with his three daughters, Gloucester's relation to his two sons, and Lear's failure to recognize his follower, Kent, are completely unnatural—hence, one necessary condition of tragedy is violated.

Shakespeare violates another necessary feature of drama, that a drama should produce illusion in the reader or spectator: "that what the persons represented are living through and experiencing is being lived through and experienced by himself."[56] Everything in Shakespeare's plays is so exaggerated, so lacking in any proper proportion, that it is quite impossible for us to share in the experiences depicted in them.

But worst of all is the fact that Shakespeare destroys the basic conditions of art altogether. Here Tolstoy employs certain criteria of "true" as against "counterfeit" art which he had argued for in *What Is Art?* (1898). He denies that Shakespeare meets these and, hence, that Shakespeare's dramas possess the essential properties of works of art. Nothing, Tolstoy claims, can be a work of art without four qualities: (1) a content that is important for humanity; (2) an external beauty or craftmanship, which in the drama is equivalent to individuality of character, a "natural" and "touching" plot, a correct

[54] *Ibid.*, pp. 335–36. [55] *Ibid.*, p. 336. [56] *Ibid.*, p. 354.

exhibition of feelings, and a sense of proportion; (3) sincerity, i.e., "the author should himself vividly feel what he expresses;"[57] and (4) religion, by which Tolstoy does not mean a didactic representation of any religious dogma, "but the expression of a definite view of life corresponding to the highest religious understanding of a given period."[58] No one, Tolstoy adds to this last criterion, can write true drama unless he "has something to say to men—something highly important for them—about man's relation to God, to the universe, to all that is infinite and unending."[59]

Shakespeare satisfies none of these criteria: The content of the plays

> is the lowest, most vulgar view of life which regards the external elevation of the great ones of the earth as a genuine superiority; despises the crowd, that is to say, the working classes; and repudiates not only religious, but even any humanitarian, efforts directed towards the alteration of the existing order of society.[60]

Craftmanship is lacking "except in his handling of scenes in which a movement of feelings is expressed."[61] And there is no sincerity: "One sees in all of them [the plays] an intentional artificiality; it is obvious that he is not in earnest but is playing with words."[62]

One aspect of Tolstoy's indictment relates immediately to *Hamlet*. He points out that Shakespeare's greatness of characterization is usually associated with Lear, Cordelia, Othello, Desdemona, Falstaff, and Hamlet. With each of these characters, Shakespeare does not invent the character but borrows it from a previous story. With the exception of Falstaff, Tolstoy affirms, Shakespeare, in borrowing these characters, ruins them by his tricks of exaggeration and unnaturalness. Hamlet he singles out as the best example of Shakespeare's artistic destruction of an early, plausible character:

> In the legend Hamlet's personality is quite intelligible. . . . But Shakespeare, by putting into Hamlet's mouth speeches he wished to publish, and making him perform actions needed to

[57] *Ibid.*, pp. 363–64. [58] *Ibid.*, p. 376. [59] *Ibid.*
[60] *Ibid.*, p. 364. [61] *Ibid.* [62] *Ibid.*

> secure effective scenes, destroys all that forms Hamlet's character in the legend. Throughout the whole tragedy Hamlet does not do what he might wish to do, but what is needed for the author's plans. . . . There is no possibility of finding any explanation of Hamlet's actions and speeches, and therefore no possibility of attributing any character to him.[63]

Although critics realize that Hamlet is not a plausible character, Tolstoy sarcastically adds, they continue to write treatises on Shakespeare's profundity in creating a character with no character; it is high time to exclaim that the prince is really naked.

Shakespeare's dramas, thus, are mediocre, yet his reputation is great. How can this be explained? First, there are the "external" causes. These have to do with the historical facts that Shakespeare's fame started in Germany under the sponsorship of Goethe; that Goethe turned to Shakespeare as a contrasting model in the struggle against the hegemony of French classical drama in Germany; and that Goethe's admiration of Shakespeare's dramaturgy was soon generalized into the apotheosis of Shakespeare's theory of life and drama by German aestheticians and dramatists. Like wildfire, Shakespeare's fame spread to England, then to the rest of Europe, and finally to America. But the far more important cause for Shakespeare's fame, "the internal," is that his dramas and their philosophy of life coincided with the growth of secularism and its predominant concern for the human rather than religious problems of man, a growth which is inherently evil and immoral, that has continued to our own time. Indeed, it is so enormous that it has enabled Shakespeare's reputation to spread to "epidemic" proportions. One cannot even argue reasonably about Shakespeare's mediocrity because the whole world has come to accept the empty and immoral outlook of Shakespeare. It is therefore imperative to destroy the grounds of his reputation by dispelling this "epidemic suggestion." The fate of books depends on the understanding of those who read them, Tolstoy pleads, and our human fate is at stake so long as we encourage and prolong this contemporary disease of secularism of which Shakespeare's dramas and reputation are corruptive symptoms.

[63] *Ibid.*, pp. 350–51.

What can one reply to so thoroughgoing, fundamental, and far-reaching a criticism? Are Tolstoy's criteria, including the moral and religious ones, incorrect? Is his exhibition of Shakespeare's lack of characterization, poetry, credible passion, and profundity inadequate? Has he perhaps missed something that is *the* clue to Shakespeare's greatness? Or does he prove that Shakespeare's dramas are mediocre?

There are two replies worth noting because they, too, sharpen the issues that Tolstoy raises. The first, "Lear, Tolstoy and the Fool,"[64] by George Orwell, is a brilliant psychoanalytic explanation of Tolstoy's attack. Orwell first observes Tolstoy's misrepresentations of the plays; his contradictions, for example, Tolstoy's statements that Shakespeare is insincere in the way he plays with words and earnest in the way he allows his characters to serve as mouthpieces for his ideas; and Tolstoy's total deafness to the verbal music of the dramas. Even so, Orwell says, there is no good argument against Tolstoy: "Properly speaking one cannot *answer* Tolstoy's attack. The interesting question is: why did he make it?"[65] Orwell suggests that Tolstoy made it and singled out Lear to do so because of his unconscious identification with Lear, especially in their similar unsuccessful acts of renunciation. More particularly, it is Tolstoy's unconscious irritation at Lear's apparent lack of motivation in the renunciation of his realm that makes Tolstoy incapable of comprehending the theme or moral of the play which is:

> "Give away your lands if you want to, but don't expect to gain happiness by doing so. Probably you won't gain happiness. If you live for others, you must live *for others,* and not as a roundabout way of getting an advantage for yourself."[66]

Furthermore, Tolstoy is psychologically incapable of grasping that which is pervasive in *King Lear* and Shakespeare's dramas as a whole: Shakespeare's humanism, his love of this life as against his hope in a next.

[64] George Orwell, "Lear, Tolstoy and the Fool" (1947), reprinted in *Selected Essays* (Harmondsworth, 1957). All page references are to this edition.

[65] Orwell, *op. cit.*, p. 105 (italics in original).

[66] *Ibid.*, p. 114 (italics in original).

> In Tolstoy's impatience with the Fool one gets a glimpse of his deeper quarrel with Shakespeare. He objects, with some justification, to the raggedness of Shakespeare's plays, the irrelevancies, the incredible plots, the exaggerated language: but what at bottom he probably most dislikes is a sort of exuberance, a tendency to take—not so much a pleasure as simply an interest in the actual process of life.[67]

Tolstoy's main objection to Shakespeare, his disdain of Shakespeare's humanism, Orwell suggests, springs from Tolstoy's "spiritual bullying," that is, his attempt (late in life) to convert all artistic expression and all the natural differences in experience to the one activity that he thought would bring mankind their salvation.

Orwell's is one sort of reply. He challenges some of Tolstoy's criteria, especially the primacy of the religious function of art; and he suggests that at least one aspect of Shakespeare's greatness is in his themes as they are supported by and artistically integrated with his command of poetry, a poetry that escapes Tolstoy.

G. Wilson Knight, in "Tolstoy's Attack on Shakespeare,"[68] welcomes Tolstoy's essay because it justly calls into question the nineteenth century overemphasis on Shakespeare's realism, especially on the characterization. If Shakespeare is judged by realistic standards which, he says, are applicable only to the novel, Tolstoy's attack stands. But, Knight counters, Shakespeare's is a *poetic* drama, not a realistic one. It is the symbolism, or what he calls the "spatial" rather than the "temporal" core, that is central. In his praise of Shakespeare's "movement of feeling," Tolstoy had a glimpse of this but lost it because of the impact on him of the critics of Shakespeare who concentrated on the characters in their commendation. To answer Tolstoy as well as to understand Shakespearean drama is to accept Shakespeare's poetic vision of the world:

> To understand Shakespeare, one must make this original acceptance: to believe, first, in people who speak poetry; thence in

[67] *Ibid.*, p. 109.

[68] G. Wilson Knight, "Tolstoy's Attack on Shakespeare," English Association Pamphlet, 1934; reprinted in *The Wheel of Fire*. All page references are to this reprint in the Meridian edition, 1957.

human actions which subserve a poetic purpose; and, finally, in strange effects in nature which harmonize with the persons and their acts; the whole building a massive statement which, if accepted in its entirety, induces a profound experience in the reader or spectator.[69]

In effect, Knight challenges a basic criterion of poetic drama which both Tolstoy and Shakespeare's admirers share: that character and plot are primary in drama. As we have already seen (chap. iii), according to Knight, Shakespeare's dramas are basically "spatial realities" or "sets of correspondences," in which plot and character are subordinate and are to be understood only as aspects of the spatial realities of the dramas. The movement of feeling is central; it constitutes Shakespeare's greatness.

Are these two replies adequate? Is Orwell's appeal to the theme and the verbal music or Knight's insistence on the primacy of symbolism sufficient to refute Tolstoy? Orwell does not think so; although Knight does, his refutation requires the acceptance of a theory of Shakespearean drama that is itself extremely doubtful.

Only this seems clear: that Tolstoy does not prove his case. The premises of his argument, their justification, and their confirmation in the plays of Shakespeare are as debatable as those of his opponents. Each of his criteria, whether shared by Shakespeare's admirers or not, is open to question. Thus, what Tolstoy does with the criteria of characterization, exhibition of passion, appropriate and poetic use of language, plot, and theme is to subsume them under his second-order criteria of naturalness and exactitude so that the criteria he shares become quite different from the interpretations given them by Shakespeare's admirers. It is extremely important to understand this subsumption because, while it looks as if Tolstoy accepts, for example, the criterion of true-to-life characterization, or exhibition of passion, as conceived by Shakespeare's admirers, he really does not, since his is a conception of "true-to-life" very different from theirs. Again, Tolstoy and traditional admirers accept profundity of theme (if integrated with the other elements) as a criterion of great drama; but Tolstoy means by "profundity" something quite different from what,

[69] Knight, *op. cit.*, p. 284.

say, Johnson or Coleridge means by it. Thus, when Tolstoy rejects Shakespeare's greatness in characterization, exhibition of passion, or profundity of theme, in effect, he also rejects the specific criteria of these general criteria that are accepted and employed by Shakespeare's admirers. Consequently, by way of a reply to Tolstoy, we may properly ask him for a justification of his formulations of these general criteria: for example, Why is great characterization the creation of characters who act and speak *exactly* like people in real life?

We can challenge Tolstoy not only on the criteria he shares with Shakespeare's admirers, but also on his own: illusion, craftmanship, content, sincerity, and religion. Does he justify them and his formulations of them? For example, is he right on the necessity of sincerity in art? Is he even right on the meaning of "sincerity"?

Another possibility in meeting Tolstoy's argument for Shakespeare's failure as a dramatist is to accept his particular criteria and then ask whether or not Shakespeare satisfies them? Are Shakespeare's characters unnatural, their motivations incredible, his plots improbable, his themes immoral, and his language inflated and debased? Are these criticisms more relevant to Shakespeare than they are, say, to *Oedipus Rex* or *Anna Karenina?* One need only remember Anna on the way to her suicide and compare her to Lear on the heath.

To question Tolstoy is not to refute him. Shakespeare may still be a mediocrity. But Tolstoy, it seems to me, offers not a shred of evidence or good argument to support his case. Everything he claims, from his necessary and sufficient properties of a "true" work of art to Shakespeare's inflated and debased language, is completely open to fundamental debate. Yet, even so, what can one say to the author of *Anna Karenina* and *War and Peace*, who rejects as poetry,

> Blow winds, and crack your cheeks,

because it is unnatural?

In the last two chapters I have surveyed a few of the major evaluations of the dramas of Shakespeare. Evaluation, it is clear, comprises a number of activities, among them, praising, condemning, defending, exhibiting, and revaluating. These involve, in different ways, the formulation of new principles, the reformulation or refutation of traditional principles, the justification of these principles, and the clarification and application of them to the dramas of Shakespeare. This preoccupation with principles is equivalent to a concern with the good-making properties of drama as an art or with the criteria of artistic merit in the drama; it ranges, as we have seen, from a consideration of necessary and sufficient criteria of greatness in dramatic art to those criteria which have nothing to do with artistic merit. Criteria as diverse as the three unities, decorum, propriety, originality, restriction on metaphor, well-constructed or regular plots, appropriateness of language, true-to-life characterization, metaphysical, moral, or religious truth, power over our passions, subtle exhibition of passion, ability to create and sustain illusion, naturalness, and the harmony of form and content have all been put forth in one way or another as essential or contributing properties of great drama. Involved in this use of criteria are certain assumptions or even explicit theories about the relation between certain criteria and dramatic greatness. The whole question of the relation between the criteria of evaluation and a poetics of drama or an aesthetics of art is at stake here: Does any evaluation of Shakespeare's dramas imply or presuppose a poetics or an aesthetics: a theory of the nature of drama and art or of great drama and great art?

I have raised other questions as well. Is evaluation true or false? Each of the major assessments I have considered purports to be true. Yet they cannot all be true. Are any of them? If none is true or false, what, then, are they? Are they or, at any rate, some of them invocations rather than true or false statements? Dryden seems to suggest that some are invocations, at least in his particular evaluation of York's speech in *Richard II*. Or are they all, as some philosophers contend, mere verbal ejaculations? What, then, is the logical status of an evaluation in literary criticism?

Further, Can criticism either prove or refute affirmations or denials of dramatic or artistic greatness, shades of ordinariness, or downright mediocrity? Involved in this question is, first, What are the criteria of adequacy of evaluative argument? and second, Is evaluation argument at all?

Thus far—in these two chapters especially—I have only surveyed these problems in critical evaluation, which are among the recognized basic ones in the philosophy of criticism. Later I shall attempt solutions of them.

PART TWO

XII THE ISSUES

THE CRITICISM of *Hamlet* is a paradigm. What can be said about its aims, doctrines, procedures, disagreements, issues, and assumptions is applicable to the criticism of other works of art. Its history, voluminousness, multiplicity, and residual problems are similar to those of much extant criticism in literature, painting, sculpture, architecture, and music. One need only recollect, for example, the history of the criticism of the *Odyssey*, the "Mona Lisa," the "Laocoon," the Parthenon, or *Don Giovanni*, or imagine the possibilities latent in the development of the criticism of any work of art, ancient or modern.

Although I am convinced that whatever of philosophical importance can be said about the criticism of *Hamlet* is applicable to any criticism, I cannot prove it since to do so would be to expound (in the lengthy manner of this *Hamlet* survey) all the criticisms of all works of art. For how else could one show that there is no criticism that differs fundamentally from that of *Hamlet?* There may very well be certain bodies of criticism that are sufficiently dissimilar to warrant a new and radically different treatment of problems. Consequently, I must narrow my thesis. Rather than claim that what is true of the aims, doctrines, procedures, issues, and assumptions of the criticism of *Hamlet* is true of the aims, doctrines, procedures, issues, and assumptions of *any* criticism (which I believe but cannot prove), I shall say that what is true about *Hamlet* criticism is true at least about some of the whole of criticism. This is a limited claim but almost as important as my larger one because even it implies certain doctrines about criticism that demand recognition and accommodation in any large-scale theory of the nature of criticism, such as many critics and philosophers have been wont to produce.

Furthermore, the correct answer to What is criticism? must include any conclusions we derive from our survey; and correct answers to certain philosophical questions, whether traditional or new, that arise in criticism must incorporate whatever correct answers there may be to those philosophical questions that emerge in an examination of *Hamlet* criticism. Any denial of my limited claim is equivalent to the thesis that the entire criticism of *Hamlet* is not really criticism. Such a view is not only patently absurd; but, more important, it rests upon a redefinition of "criticism" that constitutes a gross rejection of the linguistic and logical criteria for the correct employment of the concept of criticism.

To consider our survey in its entirety: What are the significant characteristics of the criticism of *Hamlet?* The most obvious one, I think, is its multiplicity—of procedure, doctrine, and disagreement.

To begin with, recollect the various procedures or activities, the various jobs or tasks that critics engage in. As our survey shows, these include description, interpretation, explanation, comparison, evaluation, and poetics or aesthetics.

Each of these activities has its own range. Among the descriptions are those of the characters, plot, dialogue, versification, images, metaphors, theme, symbolism, rituals, theatrical effects (e.g., cannon shot), and the sources and environment of the play. These descriptions may be individual or general: for example, descriptions of Hamlet's or Clausius' traits, or a description of the pervasive traits of all the characters.

The interpretations and explanations range from explanations of one item—for example, the imagery in relation to the whole play—to explanations of the whole play; often the explanations function as "readings" of the play in which "the meaning" of the play is made explicit in terms of what is "central" in it.

Comparisons include those of characters, images, scenes, symbols, source materials, and the like: for example, Hamlet compared with Laertes; Claudius' language in contrast to Hamlet's; or Hamlet compared with, say, Brutus in *Julius Caesar*, where the comparison is between elements of two works.

Evaluations extend from arguments for *Hamlet*'s and Shakespeare's greatness to arguments for their pervasive mediocrity. Involved here, as we have seen, are praising, condemning, defending, judging, and revaluating, as well as the procedures of formulating and reformulating the criteria of greatness in drama as an art and the application of them to *Hamlet* and Shakespeare.

Poetics and aesthetics in *Hamlet* criticism include theories of the nature or essence of poetic drama, tragedy, and artistic truth, and of the best way to comprehend and talk about *Hamlet* as a work of art.

The specific doctrines, theses, or claims of the various critics of *Hamlet* are as multifarious as the procedures, and their range is as great as that of the procedures. There are views on the characters, images, themes, and episodes; on why the characters, plot, language, or themes are as they are in the play, for example, why Hamlet delays or why he treats Ophelia as he does; on the meaning of the play; on its greatness or lack of it; on the essence of drama, artistic response, tragedy, and truth in art; and on the origins and impact of the sources, textual or ideational, of *Hamlet*.

The procedures and doctrines show the multiple character of *Hamlet* criticism. But it is the area of disagreement among the critics of the play that brings out most forcibly this multiplicity as an undeniable feature of *Hamlet* criticism. To begin with, there are all the disagreements we have encountered in the critics over certain descriptions of elements in the play. There are the vehement quarrels over the dominant as well as the less significant traits of Hamlet; these quarrels are repeated in the competing descriptions of Ophelia, Gertrude, Claudius, Horatio, Laertes, Fortinbras, Polonius, and the Ghost. Critics argue not only about the characters but about the description and meaning of the images, similes, and metaphors in the play, for example, Clemen on the "native hue of resolution." There are also arguments about the themes; sequences of the plot; the meanings of difficult and key words; and certain bits of staging, entrances, and punctuation. Then there are the debates on purely historical matters, such as the sources of Shakespeare's *Hamlet* and the exact relationship between the Ur-*Hamlet*, the First and Second Quartos, and the First Folio; the nature of Elizabethan optimism and pessimism; Elizabethan notions of tragedy and passion and their dramatic functions; and the composition of Shakespeare's audience, its influence upon the writing of *Hamlet*, and the dramatic devices or conventions at Shakespeare's disposal when he was writing *Hamlet*. There are even crucial disagreements about single words: whether or not they occur in the authentic Shakespearean text.

Besides these disagreements over purported matters of fact, the critics argue about the role or function of character, imagery, symbolism, plot, and the sources of *Hamlet*. They even disagree about the relevance of scholarship to dramatic criticism.

Disagreement is also rife in critical interpretation and explanation. Indeed, this is the area of the most violent disagreement. From Hanmer to the present day, critics have disputed each other in their offerings of the "correct" interpretation, explanation, or reading of *Hamlet*.

They disagree, too, about the correct categories of interpretation and explanation. Some say that character is central, others that plot, and still others that imagery, poetry, symbolism, or theme is central. Whole "schools" of criticism are erected on these categorial sites, and critics refer to themselves, but usually to their opponents, by various labels, like "Imagist," "Symbolist," "Historicist," or "Psychologist."

There are also disagreements among the evaluations of *Hamlet*. Some argue that it is a masterpiece; others, that it is not without glaring defects; and a few, that it is an artistic failure. Critics also praise or condemn certain aspects as against others, for example, they praise the characterization of Hamlet but condemn that of Laertes. They also disagree about the true principles or criteria of greatness in drama, their correct formulations, and their specific applications.

Finally, there are vast disagreements among the critics about correct answers to questions of poetics and aesthetics. More particularly, they oppose each other on the nature of characterization; the unity of action; the nature and function of tragedy; the relation between drama and life; whether *Hamlet* is organically unified or a mere assemblage of intense episodes; and how best to understand *Hamlet:* as myth and ritual, imagery, symbolism, or character and plot.

Here, then, are the issues of *Hamlet* criticism, as they arise from an inquiry into its aims, procedures, doctrines, and disagreements:

(1) Is Hamlet mad? Recollect the divergent answers from "Hamlet is insane," to "Hamlet is only feigning madness," with all the in-between views that he is less than mad but more than feigning, that he is troubled, hysterical, neurotic, or sorely distracted. Every critic who discusses this question believes that a true answer is forthcoming and that one of his tasks is to provide it.

(2) Is Hamlet callous? Is he cruel? Is he cynical? Is he malcontent? Is he ambitious? Is he idealistic? Is he noble (ideal)? Is he obscene? Is he brutal? Here, too, different critics give unequivocal affirmative or negative answers. Some deny that he is cruel, obscene, or brutal. Others ignore these qualities, and stress others, such as his noble nature. Still others affirm his cruelty, obscenity, and callousness, but go on to insist on the predominance of certain contrary traits. What, then, do these questions, as the critics raise and discuss them, come to? In each case, it seems that there are two different questions: (a) Is Hamlet *ever* cruel, noble, or obscene? and (b) Is Hamlet *predominantly* cruel, noble, or obscene?

(3) Is Hamlet melancholic? Here consider merely Bradley and Lily Campbell. Both give affirmative replies, yet disagree with each other. For Bradley, Hamlet is melancholic, but in Bradley's sense of "being disposed to obsession with the feeling or mood of the moment." For Miss Campbell, Hamlet is melancholic, but not in Bradley's, the contemporary, or even the Elizabethan sense of melancholy as a natural humor; Hamlet's is a melancholy adust. This agreement on Hamlet's melancholy and yet disagreement over its

exact nature show how the question, Is Hamlet melancholic? needs to be refined and expanded upon before we can even understand any true or false answer. Of course, even after this clarification, the question, Is Hamlet melancholic in either sense or in some other sense? remains.

(4) Is Hamlet an ideal hero (with no defect) of a revenge or romantic tragedy (of intrigue, blood, and fate)? Are his undeniable self-reproaches really self-exhortations and, finally, exculpation? Stoll answers these questions with an unequivocal yes, and Wilson, with an unequivocal no. Yet both agree that these are factual questions to which true answers can be given.

(5) Does Hamlet vacillate? Does he rationalize in his doubting of the Ghost or in his sparing of the King at prayer? Does he, therefore, deceive himself? Is he psychologically infirm? Why does he delay, if we assume that he does? Here, too, critics are divided in their answers; each answer is regarded by the individual critic as a true one if he has given it and a false one if offered by other critics with whom he disagrees.

(6) Is Hamlet a slave of passion? Is he a victim of excessive intellect? Is he a scapegoat? Is he a Baroque hero? I bring these questions together because they seem to be similar in that they are about the classification of Hamlet as a *type*-hero. Miss Campbell, Coleridge, Fergusson, and Schücking, who respectively give affirmative replies to these four pivotal questions, regard their replies as true answers to what they take to be factual questions about Hamlet? But if these answers can be true, does the truth of one of them exclude the truth of the others? Can Hamlet, for example, be both a slave of passion and a scapegoat (in the myth and ritual sense)?

(7) Does Hamlet say in Shakespeare's *Hamlet* (I, 2, 129): "O, that this too too sullied flesh would melt"? Wilson answers affirmatively, giving arguments based on bibliographical and dramatic evidence to support his reply. Other critics agree with him but reject his particular arguments. Still others reject his reply, claiming that "solid" not "sullied" is the correct word in that line. On this issue, a clean-cut yes or no seems possible: Did Shakespeare write in his authentic manuscript (if there is one) "sullied" or not?

(8) Does Hamlet overhear Polonius and Claudius plotting in II,

2, 158? That is, does Hamlet have an entrance on the inner stage at that moment of the play? Does Hamlet plan the dumb-show? Does Claudius see it? Does Hamlet say in his "Speech on Man" (II, 2, 309–10): "how like an angel in apprehension" or "in action, how like an angel" or neither? Is the pointing of Hamlet's first soliloquy light or declamatory? These questions, like (7), seem to be factual ones to which true answers are forthcoming or have already been given.

(9) What are the meanings of "son," "coil," "nature," "fishmonger," "miching mallecho," "angel," and "action" in their dramatic contexts in *Hamlet?* Are their meanings equivalent to Elizabethan usages? These questions look like (7) and (8), but are they?

(10) Which, if any, is authentic: the First Quarto, the Second Quarto, or the First Folio, of *Hamlet?* What is the exact nature of the relationship between the Ur-*Hamlet*, Quarto 1, Quarto 2, and Folio 1? Is Shakespeare's *Hamlet* of 1604–5 an adaptation of a play on Hamlet by Thomas Kyd? These are straightforward, historical, scholarly questions. Are they factual, yielding true answers?

(11) Is Hamlet a symbol of death? Knight says he is, many others say he is not. Is this a factual issue?

(12) Is Hamlet's emotion in excess of the facts of the play? Recollect the different answers of Eliot, Wilson, or Fergusson on this issue. What is Hamlet's emotion? What are the facts in *Hamlet?* Can we decide clearly on Eliot's question until we know what is meant by the "facts" of *Hamlet?*

(13) Has Hamlet's mystery a heart? Wilson says it has not; almost everyone else says it has, adding that unless it has—unless Hamlet can be adequately explained—*Hamlet* fails as a work of art. It seems clear that either Hamlet's mystery has a heart or it has not. Yet can this issue be settled in any true or false fashion? What is an adequate explanation of Hamlet? How does "adequate explanation" function here, in relation to a fictional character?

(14) Is Ophelia honest, weak, in love with Hamlet? Is Hamlet in love with her? Bradley says she is honest, not weak, and that she loves Hamlet. Others disagree, claiming that she is weak, dishonest, in fact, a decoy, and that she never loves Hamlet. Lamb says that their relation is one of supererogatory love. But Bradley has his doubts, at

least about Hamlet, and confesses that he is unable to arrive at a solution. Well, now, is it a factual problem, whether they love each other during the course of the drama? Does the solution turn on the meaning of "love"? Or, the meaning of "love" having been rendered unambiguous in the discussion of this issue, is it simply the textual or dramatic evidence that precludes a clear solution?

(15) Is Gertrude an adulteress? Is she privy to the murder of King Hamlet? Critics give yes or no answers. But, like Hamlet's melancholy, Gertrude's adultery has an Elizabethan as well as an exclusively modern sense. So we must ask, Is she an adulteress only in her incestuous marriage to a brother of a deceased husband or was she also the mistress of Claudius while her first husband lived? There is little historical doubt about her adultery in the Elizabethan, incestuous sense. But is the textual evidence clear that she was Claudius' mistress before she became his wife? One wants to say: Either she was his mistress or she was not; and so a clear answer seems possible here, too. Then, why all the residual doubt?

(16) Is Claudius a usurper? Is he a hypocrite? These, too, are ambiguous questions, although unambiguous answers to them can be given once the ambiguities of "usurper" and "hypocrite" are resolved. Each of these questions is at least two separate ones: one about the Elizabethan uses of the terms; the other about later uses which, of course, relate to but are not identical with the Elizabethan. Is Claudius a usurper and a hypocrite—as the Elizabethans understood them? Is Claudius a usurper and a hypocrite—as we understand them? In both forms of the question what is at stake is not any exact definition of terms, but whether certain established criteria for the Elizabethan or later (or both) uses of these terms are applicable to Claudius?

(17) Is *Hamlet* a study in the passion of grief? Is it a myth-ritual celebration of the mystery of human life? Is it a revenge tragedy with an ideal, epical hero? Is it a psychological study of a vacillating hero? Is it a dramatization of the conflict between optimism and pessimism as these doctrines were understood in the Elizabethan age? Is it a symbolization of the theme of life versus death? Is it a palimpsest of popular bits of melancholy, malcontentism, and

exciting heroic episodes? Is it a metaphorical rendition of the rottenness of the world? I bring these questions together because they seem to converge on the one issue of what is central in *Hamlet*. Each of these separate questions has its affirmative answer that purports to be the true one about *Hamlet*, its meaning, and about its central fact of character, plot, imagery, symbolism, theme, or pattern.

(18) Why is Hamlet tragic? Is he the only tragic figure in the play? Has he a tragic flaw? What is Shakespearean or Elizabethan tragedy? What is tragedy? Compare the answers proposed by Bradley, Wilson, Alexander, Lily Campbell, Schücking, Stoll, Fergusson, and others. All of these questions are conceived of by their discussants as factual ones to which true answers can be given. Are they?

(19) Is *Hamlet* a representation of life? Is it true? Is it to be comprehended as a representation of life? Jones is vociferous in his affirmation; Stoll, equally vociferous in his denial; Wilson, somewhere in-between these extremes. What kinds of questions are these? Do they, too, yield true answers?

(20) What defines *Hamlet* as a poetic drama? This leads immediately to the question, What is the essence of poetic drama? Here, too, critics as different from each other as Knight, Bradley, Coleridge, and Stoll give as their individual replies definitions that function in their work as purportedly true answers.

(21) How can we best understand *Hamlet* as a work of dramatic art? Contrast, for example: any of our historical critics; Trilling's enlargement of the historical approach; Wilson's modification of it; Miss Spurgeon's concentration on the imagery; Clemen on the organic structure of imagery, plot, and characterization; Bradley and Jones on the psychological emphasis; and Knight and Fergusson on symbolic interpretation. Do all of them argue about an issue that can be solved in any true or false fashion?

(22) Is scholarship a necessary condition for the criticism and understanding of *Hamlet?* Or is it an intrinsic part of the criticism and comprehension of the play? Or is it completely irrelevant? What sort of issue is this? Does it have a true solution?

(23) Is *Hamlet* a great work of dramatic art? Think of the conflicting answers given by the critics of *Hamlet* since the beginnings

of *Hamlet* criticism. Is this question, and its corollary, What is dramatic or artistic greatness? factual?

(24) What is the primary aim, task, or function of criticism? Each critic states or implies his answer in his particular essay on *Hamlet*. Many of these differ. Is there a true or correct answer to this question?

There are other issues in *Hamlet* criticism: about the characters in *Hamlet* and characterization in drama; about certain episodes in the play and plot in drama—and more. But my list, I think, suffices as a summary of the main issues of *Hamlet* criticism. This list should serve us well in the attempt to unravel some of the troublesome threads of controversy in *Hamlet* criticism. If I can clarify these issues and secure resolutions even of some of them, we shall, I think, go a long, long way toward the solution of problems in the philosophy of criticism.

I have been discussing the various doctrines, procedures, disagreements, and issues of *Hamlet* criticism. There is another element in this whole corpus that I can now state. It is the basic assumption of *Hamlet* criticism and, ironically, the only aspect of it about which there is almost total agreement. This basic assumption, implicit in all the critics that have been considered, is that all the questions and answers of criticism, all its procedures, doctrines, disagreements, and issues, are factual ones. In their utterance and argument, whether in their descriptions, interpretations, explanations, evaluations, or poetics and aesthetics—that is, in their writings on: the characters of *Hamlet* or the nature of characterization in drama; the images of *Hamlet* or the nature of imagery; the plot of *Hamlet* or the nature of plot; the theme of *Hamlet* or the nature of theme in drama; the symbols of *Hamlet* or the nature of symbolism in drama; what is central in *Hamlet* or what is central in poetic drama; the tragic in *Hamlet* or the nature of tragedy; the greatness of *Hamlet* or what is greatness in drama; the comprehension of *Hamlet* or the nature of dramatic response; the text of *Hamlet;* and the dramatic and ideational sources of *Hamlet*—in all these the critics of *Hamlet* assume that their utterance and argument are true (or false) in relation to an objectively existing set of facts in *Hamlet* or the world. They agree that there is the real *Hamlet*, however they conceive of that reality; that there are historical facts, some of which are the dramatic and ideational sources of *Hamlet;* and that tragedy, drama, aesthetic comprehension or response, and dramatic and artistic greatness or merit are also facts in the world which are (ideally) definable in terms of their essences. The aim of the critic, thus, is presumed to be the making of true statements about the nature of *Hamlet,* its influences, its correct conception, its tragic character, its greatness, and its relation to life and the world.

Are *all* the utterances and arguments of the critics of *Hamlet* true (or false) statements about facts: in *Hamlet,* in history, or in the world? Are description, interpretation, explanation, evaluation, poetics, or aesthetics procedures that report truly (or falsely) on objectively existing facts? Or, if I may formulate my question technically: Are the utterances of the critics of *Hamlet* of the same type, namely, a discourse or use of language the only function of which is to make true-false, factual statements? My thesis, which I shall try to clarify and confirm in subsequent chapters, is that this assumption—of the *logical univocity* of the language of *Hamlet* criticism—is false; that the realization that it is false is basic to any understanding and solution of the major issues and disagreements of *Hamlet* criticism; and insofar as *Hamlet* criticism reflects the whole of criticism, that this realization is fundamental to the comprehension and solution of the major problems of criticism and the philosophy of criticism.

However successful I may be in the confirmation of my thesis about the logic of *Hamlet* criticism, one conclusion about *Hamlet* (and any theory about all of) criticism can be stated now: that criticism is many things, not just one. That is, it is more than one procedure, or set of doctrines, or tissue of disagreements. Its multiple character is guaranteed at least by its range: from description to interpretation, explanation, evaluation, poetics, and aesthetics. Even at this stage of our inquiry, consequently, we can say (truly) that criticism, as practiced by the critics of *Hamlet,* is a combination of and a choice among many different activities. Hence, criticism is not merely evaluation, interpretation, explanation, or elucidation, as some philosophers and many critics—in their unfortunate moments of monism—are wont to claim.

To conclude: A philosophical examination of our survey of *Hamlet* criticism reveals the undeniable multiple linguistic character of this criticism as well as its pervasive assumption that this linguistic multiplicity is reducible to a logical univocity. This assumption, I believe, is false. Its falsity can already be detected in the ostensible multiple character of the language of *Hamlet* criticism which itself reflects the logically multiple character of its discourse.

XIII PHILOSOPHY AND CRITICISM

THIS IS a study in the philosophy of criticism, not an essay in criticism. The aim thus far has been to survey and systematize in a preliminary way the reigning issues of *Hamlet* criticism. Nowhere, I believe, has there been any attempt to set forth my own answers to the many problems suggested by *Hamlet* or posed by its critics. Occasionally, objections or questions have been ventured in order to further a particular argument of a critic, but there has been no conscious effort to state Hamlet's traits, the meaning of *Hamlet*, the essence of poetic drama or tragedy, the correct aesthetic response to *Hamlet*, the artistic merits of the play, or answers to any of the other questions of our survey.

There is a conception of philosophy and philosophy of criticism, traditional among many critics and philosophers, according to which philosophy in general and philosophy of criticism in particular unite in their pursuit of the answers to certain basic questions and, in this specific area of *Hamlet* criticism, in their attempt at a definitive solution of the critics' questions about *Hamlet*. Philosophy in this context is conceived of as a thorough investigation of these problems that eventually leads to a definitive solution of them. Thus, the function of the philosopher of the criticism of *Hamlet* is to provide the ultimate essay *in* the criticism of *Hamlet;* this he is to attain by techniques and arguments that the ordinary critic omits or lacks. Through the clarification and correct definition of relevant basic terms, the discovery and formulation of certain essences, and the justification of absolute standards of evaluation, the philosophy of *Hamlet* criticism aims at a final solution of the major problems concerning *Hamlet:* Is Hamlet mad, melancholy, excessively intellectual? What does the play really mean? Why is it a tragedy? How can we best respond to the play as a work of art? Why is it great? And so on. Thus, on this view, ours being a study in the philosophy of (*Hamlet*) criticism, the task is neatly set: to solve the problems of *Hamlet* through philosophy.

This conception of philosophy and of philosophy in relation to criticism is no doubt a noble one, commanding respect. After all—such is the popular notion of philosophy—who else if not the philosopher is able to settle these ultimate issues? And there are few among the philosophers who can easily refuse such an accolade, especially when the darling in distress is as seductive a drama as *Hamlet.* Yet literate philosophers also know that there have been many Quixotes among the dons of criticism, and that the windmills of controversy are still turning, even for the errant philosophical critics. Hence, before the philosopher proceeds to the rescue, he should (with all due modesty of course) reject the enticing lance and take up instead less formidable albeit more delicate instruments. There will undoubtedly be less tumult, but the hits may be more accurate.

Whether the philosopher essays the grand critique or not, *before* he accepts or repudiates his assigned or self-appointed role of the custodian of ultimate truth and, in regard to *Hamlet,* of the definitive solutions of its problems, he has a different job to perform, one which, although also a custodian's, is extremely menial since no one else wants it. This job is the salutary one of simply trying to elucidate the problems: to become as clear as possible on the nature of the issues the critics raise and argue about.

How does the criticism of *Hamlet* appear to philosophy as elucidation? Criticism, whatever else it is, is a professional, sophisticated form of discourse. One problem, certainly initial if not basic, is to elucidate this discourse: its many subjects and predicates (or terms) and its many functions.

What complicates this task of the elucidation of the language of criticism, including *Hamlet* criticism, is that this language already incorporates a particular conception of language, one that is derived from and sponsored by the history of philosophy. Both criticism and much traditional philosophy (which is also a professional, sophisticated use of language) are tied to a particular conception of language: of its nature, and of its relations to thought and reality. All the critics of *Hamlet* whom I have considered share in this traditional philosophical conception of language.

What is this traditional conception of language that is embodied in criticism and that criticism shares with much traditional philosophy?

From Plato to Russell, and even later, among certain contemporary philosophers, there persists a set of doctrines about language that is expounded or accepted by almost all the great philosophers, so much so that it can be and rightly is called "the classical theory of language." According to this theory, language consists of individual words and their combinations in sentences. Each word, if it is a word and not merely a shape or noise, is a name of an entity. The meaning of the word is the entity, of whatever kind, for which the word stands. Meaning, therefore, is a relational fact between language and reality, such that to ask for or to give the meaning of any word is to ask for or to give what that word designates. Nouns, proper names, adjectives, and verbs are all construed as names of things, people, qualities, properties, actions, or ideas. Language consists of terms that correspond to the entities or different kinds of objects that are their meanings. Sentences, as combinations of names, serve primarily (for some philosophers, exclusively) to make true (or false) statements about the different entities of the world.

Language also relates to thought, the expression of thought, and to philosophy. This relationship is stated by another doctrine of the tradition: There can be no intelligible, correct thought or expression of it unless we know the essence of the entity about which we are thinking, writing, or speaking, and are able to formulate that knowledge in a true, real definition of its nature.

Plato's *Euthyphro* provides an excellent example of this doctrine.

In this dialogue Plato, through Socrates' questioning of Euthyphro, implies that no one can say meaningfully and truly of an act that it is impious, for example, unless he knows the nature or essence of piety (and impiety) and can give a real definition of it.

The *Euthyphro* is the model of the whole classical tradition. For according to this tradition, there can be no intelligible, true thought or expression (of this thought) about anything without prior knowledge of the nature of that thing. The main assignment of philosophy, then, on this view, is clear: to guarantee our thought and expression of it by means of the determination of true, real definitions of the objects (meanings) of our thought and its expression. Philosophy, thus, is construed, at least in major part, as the disciplined attempt to insure the correspondence between language, thought, and reality.

Of course there are variations, emendations, and modifications of, and even crucial specific objections to, the classical theory among traditional philosophers (e.g., Berkeley's denial that general words are names of entities). Adverbs and prepositions are embarassing difficulties in the tradition from Plato's *Sophist* on; Aristotle singles out prayers and wishes as utterances that are neither true nor false; many distinguish between factual and normative utterances, although this distinction is usually marked as one between two sorts of facts about both of which true or false statements are made; and, recently logical positivists in philosophy and I. A. Richards in literary criticism have challenged the traditional dichotomy of true-false utterance by introducing a third type, the emotive or cognitively meaningless, of which C. L. Stevenson's "persuasive definitions" are a variant. Consequently, the doctrines that all words are names, that all uses of language are identical with the making of true or false statements, and that all true statements are about entities have been questioned by philosophers (and some critics) from Plato to Russell. But the basic doctrines that language, if it is to function correctly, must correspond to the real world, and that meaning is a relational fact between words and the objects they stand for remain intact until the advent of the later Wittgenstein and others working along the same lines.

Now, whatever the complete account of the classical correspondence theory of language in the history of philosophy may be (I have tried only to provide as much of a sketch as seems appropriate here) it is true, I think, that this theory is fundamental in the criticism of *Hamlet.*

As a use of language, this criticism from its beginnings to the present adheres to the central doctrines of the classical theory. As magnificently aware of the language of *Hamlet* as the critics of *Hamlet* are, they are almost totally unperceptive of their primary instrument of criticism—their own language. What they say about *Hamlet* is said in a language whose assumptions and doctrines—about the nature of language, its relations to thought and the expression of thought, and its relation to *Hamlet,* the historical environment of *Hamlet,* and especially to tragedy, aesthetic response, poetic drama, and artistic greatness—they do not grasp, let alone question. Thus, it may be that many of their problems about *Hamlet* arise not from difficulties in the play but from their own working assumptions about their language—its terms and functions—which derive from the classical philosophical tradition.

Let me be more specific. The critics of *Hamlet* presuppose that their language—not *Hamlet*'s!—consists of words and sentences, where the words are names and the sentences, combinations of them. That is, they assume that the subjects and the predicates—the nouns, proper names, adjectives, or verbs—they employ in their writings are all names of entities (or properties) of some sort: characters, events, qualities, ideas, etc. They assume that their terms are meaningful in relation to the entities these terms refer to or designate; and that all their utterances are true or false, that is, that these utterances state facts which can be ascertained in *Hamlet,* its historical environment, or in the complexes of artistic greatness, tragedy, and true comprehension of poetic drama. In other words, they assume, as their language and employment of it reveal, that there are certain facts or entities or complexes which are drama, comprehension, tragedy, and artistic greatness; that these facts (entities, complexes) possess real essences; and that—this, too, ties them with the classical view—it is a philosophical assignment, whether critics or philosophers persevere in it or not, to ascertain these essences and to formulate them in real definitions in order to guarantee the intelligibility and truth of their statements about the properties of drama, tragedy, or greatness in *Hamlet* or anywhere else. Thus, in their conception of the nature and uses of language, and in their views about the relations between language and thought and between language and reality, in their views about the meaning of terms, and the necessity of fixing essences for adequate discourse, the critics of *Hamlet* are in agreement with traditional philosophers on a particular philosophy of language.

Is the classical theory of language correct? More particularly, is this theory as it is embodied in *Hamlet* criticism, as a particular employment of language, correct? Are the terms of this criticism, its subjects and predicates, names of entities of one sort or another—from "Hamlet" as the proper name of the hero of the play to "great" or "tragic" as names of other qualities the play shares with similar qualities elsewhere in the world? Do all the major terms of this criticism name, refer to, designate, or denote objective entities that are the meanings of these terms and that possess essential, defining, or necessary and sufficient properties which can be fixed in a real definition of them? Are all the terms of this criticism used to describe properties?

Are all the sentences of *Hamlet* criticism combinations of terms that are employed only to make statements, i.e., true or false utterances about objective entities and their essential natures?

Finally, is *Hamlet* criticism correct in its assumption, derived from and shared by much traditional philosophy: that the very intelligibility of its language—its terms and their combinations—rests on the existence and knowledge of certain essences that correspond and give meaning to its language?

Recent philosophy of language, especially that of the later Wittgenstein, challenges every doctrine of the classical theory: on the nature of language, its uses, its meaning, its relation to thought and the expression of thought in writing and speech, its relation to reality, and the assignment to philosophy of the determination and formulation of essences in the world in order to insure intelligibility of discourse.

If we examine the way in which language works, we shall find, I think, that language is not at all what the classical theory claims it to be. Language consists of words and their combinations; but not all words function as names. Instead of being like a corresponding picture or mirror of the world, language is like an enormous toolbox, filled with the most diversified assortment of tools, practically no one of which resembles those things in the world that it might be applied to—no more, say, than a shovel must resemble the hole it digs in order to dig it. Moreover, words and sentences by themselves, i.e., independently of our employment of them, do not refer to or name anything. It is only in the context of our employment of them that some words are used to name, others to describe or classify, and still others to ascribe, prescribe, emote, persuade, etc.

Sentences, too, can be employed to do many different things not all of which are to make true or false statements or even, in addition, to emote or persuade, as the positivists have it. John Austin contrasts the descriptive use of sentences, e.g., "I like X," and the emotive, e.g., "Hurrah for X!," with, say, "I apologize," which is neither. "I apologize," said, for example, after I push you inadvertently, describes or narrates nothing; yet it is a perfectly good indicative, declarative sentence—a very traditional model of a true or false sentence. Austin uncovers a number of these verbs which, in their first person singular, present indicative use, are not descriptive and do not give rise to true or false statements at all. "I bet," "I swear," "I promise," and "I do" are examples. As utterances they do not report on what I am doing, they do it. "I promise" promises, it does not report on or describe a promise. Because of their distinguishing characteristics and functions, Austin calls these verbs, in their first person singular, present indicative use, "performatory." They are irreducible to the descriptive, emotive, or persuasive use of language. Other philosophers point out further uses of language; e.g., the ethical, as exemplified by "You ought to do X," which functions to advise and guide rather than to describe, emote, or persuade.[1] Language, thus, has many uses, many different tasks assigned it; these cannot be reduced to one or two uses.

Meaning, too, is reconstrued. Instead of tying it to object reference,

[1] See John Austin, "Other Minds," *Proceedings of the Aristotelian Society*, Suppl. Vol. XX (1946); R. M. Hare, *The Language of Morals* (Oxford, 1952); and H. L. A. Hart, "The Ascription of Responsibility and Rights," reprinted in A. Flew (ed.), *Logic and Language*, 1st ser. (Oxford, 1951).

it is regarded, at least in its primary sense of "the meaning of an expression 'X'," as the rules, regulations, and conventions governing the use of an expression. To understand the meaning of an expression, then, is not to become acquainted with the object for which it stands, but to learn and be able to apply the criteria for its correct use. Meaning, thus, is not a relation or relational fact at all.

The classical doctrines that all words are names, all sentences are statements about entities, all utterances are true or false or even true, false, or cognitively meaningless, and all meaning is reference, are false. Hence the classical conceptions of language and meaning and the doctrine that language corresponds to reality, are false. What about the doctrines of the classical tradition concerning language, thought and its expression in writing and speech, and the consequent role of philosophy?

Does the very intelligibility or correct employment of language rest on the existence and knowledge of certain essences in the world that correspond to and give meaning to language? That is, can we talk adequately about anything in the world without knowing its nature or without assuming that it has a nature, an essence, a set of necessary and sufficient properties, or a set of defining properties, where these terms are synonyms?

Is it a proper, feasible philosophical assignment or function to guarantee this talk by the determination of these essences that correspond to our talk of certain things and by the formulation of these essences in real, true definitions?

Classical philosophy of language and its particular embodiment in *Hamlet* criticism imply affirmative answers to these two questions about language. These answers also sponsor the perennial quest for "theories" in philosophy and the arts: for true, real definitions of different kinds of essences. In *Hamlet* criticism, these answers may be the logical roots of the theories or purportedly true, real definitions of the essences of drama, aesthetic response, tragedy, and greatness, as these essences are exemplified in *Hamlet* and elsewhere.

Do we need theories or real definitions of essences of various kinds of entities in order to talk about these entities, which theories it is the philosopher's primary task to provide? Or, more rigorously: Is it a necessary condition of the correct, intelligible use of language that its terms have corresponding essences? Or more particularly in regard to *Hamlet* criticism: Do we need to know or to assume that there is an essence of tragedy, artistic greatness, centrality, drama, characterization, imagery, plot, melancholy, or aesthetic response to be able to talk meaningfully and correctly about the tragedy, greatness, drama, characterization, etc., of *Hamlet?* The critics of *Hamlet,* I think mainly because of their adherence to the classical philosophical theory of language, give or imply affirmative answers in the way they use language and especially in their statements of issues.

Recent philosophy of language, inspired by Wittgenstein and others, challenges these doctrines and, by implication, the specific application of them in the criticism of *Hamlet.* The refutation is not directed against the reality of essences, hence, is not, as some opponents of this new approach claim, a countermetaphysical theory. Nor is the refutation an appeal to the lack of testability and agreement among the theories on the exact defining properties of these essences. The refutation rests on logic: on the elucidation of the functions of the terms of our language in relation to the conditions under which they function.

If we examine how our language actually works, that is, if we describe the various uses of our terms in relation to their conditions or criteria of use, we shall find terms whose intelligible, correct employment of them does not entail or presuppose any corresponding essence.

No one makes this as clear as Ludwig Wittgenstein, in his *Philosophical Investigations* (1953).[2] Much of this book is concerned with problems of language and philosophy of language. Wittgenstein introduces a number of different examples of language-games; whereupon he raises the traditional crucial question:

> You talk about all sorts of language-games, but have nowhere said what the essence of a language-game, and hence of language, is: what is common to all these activities, and what makes them into language or parts of language. . . .

[2] Ludwig Wittgenstein, *Philosophical Investigations,* trans. G. E. M. Anscombe (Oxford, 1953).

> And this is true.—Instead of producing something common to all that we call language, I am saying that these phenomena have no one thing in common which makes us use the same word for all,—but that they are *related* to one another in many different ways. And it is because of this relationship, or these relationships, that we call them all "language." I will try to explain this.
>
> Consider for example the proceedings that we call "games." I mean board-games, card-games, ball-games, Olympic games, and so on. What is common to them all?—Don't say: "There *must* be something common, or they would not be called 'games' "—but *look and see* whether there is anything common to all.—For if you look at them you will not see something that is common to *all*, but similarities, relationships, and a whole series of them at that.[3]

Card games are like board games in some respects but not in others. Not all games are amusing, nor is there always winning and losing or competition. Some games resemble others in certain respects—that is all. What we find, then, are no necessary and sufficient properties, only "a complicated network of similarities overlapping and criss-crossing";[4] so that we can say of games that they form a family with family resemblances but no common trait.

If one asks, "What is a game?" we pick out sample games, describe these, and add: "These and similar things are called 'games'." This is all we need say, indeed, all anyone knows, about games. Knowing what a game is, therefore, is not knowing a real definition or "theory" of game, but being able to recognize and explain games, and to decide among imaginary and new examples which would or would not be called "games."

"Game," thus, is a term in our language the employment or use of which in perfectly intelligible, correct talk about games in no way entails or presupposes a set of necessary and sufficient properties that all games have in common and that gives meaning to the term. "Game" does not depend upon an essence for its use; hence, it is simply an error in the logical description of language to maintain that

[3] Wittgenstein, *op. cit.*, p. 31e (italics in original).

[4] *Ibid.*, p. 32e.

all terms depend for their intelligible employment upon their corresponding essences.

How does Wittgenstein's argument apply to *Hamlet* criticism? Are there terms in this criticism whose intelligible use does not entail or presuppose a corresponding essence? What about the terms "tragedy," "comprehension," "greatness," and "poetic drama"? Is it a closed matter or also one for "looking and seeing" whether these terms require essences and real definitions of them—"theories"—in order to render intelligible their correct use in the criticism of *Hamlet?* Perhaps the overriding assumption of the critics that there must be these essences that correspond and give significance to their key terms is as erroneous as the assumption that there must be an essence corresponding to the term "game" if our use of it is to be intelligible. Moreover, perhaps "tragedy" and "great" do not function in the way that terms like "melancholy," "madness," or "adultery" do. It may even be true of certain terms in *Hamlet* criticism that it is a necessary condition of their intelligible, correct use that they *cannot* have corresponding essences, that their very uses preclude sets of necessary and sufficient conditions under which they function; hence, that theories or statements of such sets of conditions foreclose on the uses themselves, thereby violating their logic altogether. I shall discuss this possibility when we come to the elucidation of the concept of tragedy. At any rate, it is certainly worth our while to examine closely the logical characteristics of the terms of *Hamlet* criticism instead of remaining complacent in the thought that they all play the same role, under the same basic condition of a corresponding essence or exhaustive set of conditions or properties that guarantees their correct employment, in making true or false statements.

This brings us to the last doctrine of the classical tradition: the assigned task of philosophy to ascertain the essences that correspond to our terms, thence, to state these essences in real, true definitions.

If the goal of the assignment represents a distortion of the actual function of language, it is patently not a proper one. But whether or not it is proper, fruitful, or even feasible, the assignment is tantamount to the elucidation of language anyway. For to state the essence that corresponds to a particular term is, willy-nilly, to say how that term functions in our language. One cannot talk, for example, about imagery without at the same time talking about "imagery"—the term, its functions, and the conditions under which it functions. So the philosopher, whether he wishes it or not, likes it or not, must describe the uses of terms in language. The alternative is to say nothing; hence, to give up *doing* philosophy.

In doing philosophy, Wittgenstein suggests: Do not ask for the nature of X, or for the meaning of its purportedly corresponding term, "X"; ask instead for the use of "X," how "X" functions in the language, and the actual conditions under which it functions.

In an inquiry into the nature and problems of criticism, and *Hamlet* criticism in particular, the philosopher's primary assignment should be the logical elucidation of the language of criticism: of its many key terms, its many different sorts of utterance, and its various conditions of use, where none of these aspects of language may be understood by the users, that is, the critics themselves. Thus, rather than try once more to prove, for example, that *Hamlet* is great, or that Hamlet is mad, the philosopher's first sights should be aimed at different but equally important targets: the careful logical description of the extremely rich language and linguistic functions of the criticism of *Hamlet*, and the general or specific misconceptions of this language as these are used by the critics, and exhibited in their disagreements and issues.

Fundamental in *Hamlet* criticism is its assumption that its language is logically univocal; that its multiplicity of procedures, arguments, and issues involves one set of similarly functioning terms and one set of similar uses of language, namely, the making of true or false statements about facts.

In this chapter I have traced the roots of this assumption of logical univocity to the classical theory of language, a theory that comprises a set of doctrines about the nature, meaning, and uses of language, and about the relations among language, reality, thought, and philosophy. I pointed out that this whole set of doctrines has been challenged and refuted by recent philosophy. The upshot of the refutation of the classical theory is that language, as it actually operates, is not logically univocal but has many uses and many different kinds of conditions for its uses.

I have clarified the contrasting notions of language as logically univocal and language as logically multiple, but I have not showed that the pervasive assumption of *Hamlet* criticism, that *its* language is logically univocal, is false. I shall now try to do this, and in some detail, employing throughout the arguments and ideas advanced or suggested by recent philosophy of language. Of course, in showing that this assumption is false, I shall also attempt to exhibit the full range of the logical multiplicity of *Hamlet* criticism as well as the significance of that range to the understanding and solution of the problems of *Hamlet* criticism.

XIV DESCRIPTION

IN *Hamlet,* as in any work of art, there is a certain grouping of elements, their characteristics, and the relations among them. The exact nature of these constituents is a matter of perennial dispute. So are the questions, Which is the central constituent? Which are the important ones? and Which are the less important ones? For many critics of *Hamlet,* it is Hamlet and his vacillation which are the controlling element and characteristic. To others, the central element and its characteristic are the plot of revenge, or the imagery of rottenness, or the theme of death. Some critics emphasize juxtaposition or episodic intensification as the pervasive relation among the elements. Others insist upon the organic nature of the various elements and their characteristics.

The hierarchy of the elements, characteristics, and relations remains a matter of persistent critical argument. But if we waive, at any rate for the moment, the problem of the proper hierarchy of constituents in *Hamlet* and postpone discussion of the question, What is most important in the play? can we find anything in *Hamlet* about which there can be no doubt or about which if there are doubts and debate, these can be resolved by a direct appeal to the various elements, characteristics, and relations of the play?

Our immediate question, then, is What are the *données* in *Hamlet?*

that is, What, if anything, is given in the play that criticism can or does state in its writings about the play? It is proper and fruitful to begin with this question in the attempt to elucidate the major issues of *Hamlet* criticism.

Among the elements, distinguishable if not in all instances separable from each other, are the various characters, their traits, speech, and actions; the dialogue, soliloquies, versification, prose, and language; and the plot, with its individual episodes. In *Hamlet*, that there are Hamlet, Horatio, Laertes, Gertrude, etc., that they say certain things to others or themselves, that they do or have done to them certain things, and that certain events occur before and after other events, no one denies.

How incredibly trivial, one wants to say; criticism is surely *other* than that. I want to reply that much of what the critics say is exactly like these undeniable remarks and, most important, far from trivial, in the only sense that counts here, namely, the enlightenment their remarks afford readers in their common search for clarification and understanding of the play.

Let us now try to establish this claim that there are statements about what is given, hence cannot be denied, in *Hamlet* that are not trivial.

Consider, to begin with, Bradley's criticism of *Hamlet*. As a critic, he explains, evaluates, and theorizes. But he also describes: he reports on some of the constituents in *Hamlet*. He does this sometimes with, sometimes without, an accompanying explanation. In either case, his descriptions are logically independent of his explanations. Bradley, for example, tells us that Hamlet delays; he also proposes an answer to *why* he delays. The truth (or falsity) of Bradley's claim that Hamlet delays depends not at all on the purported truth (or falsity) of Bradley's explanation that Hamlet delays because he is melancholy.

Hamlet is one constituent character in *Hamlet*. Well, now, what does Bradley say about him that is not trivial in the way that saying that Hamlet is in *Hamlet* is trivial? Bradley, in his full discussion of the play, tells us a great deal about Hamlet. He tells us that before his father's death, Hamlet was athletic, joyful, fearless, idealistic, open, adoring of his parents, and in love with Ophelia. He points out that some of these traits, for example, his interest in athletics (especially fencing), his openness (which cost him his life), and his love for his father, he retains throughout the play. Bradley reminds us of Hamlet's alertness and intellectual perceptiveness, and reveals that Hamlet was disposed to nervous instability, sudden changes of mood and, because of his moral sensitivity, was vulnerable to shock.

The shock occurs in response to Gertrude's indecent remarriage; Hamlet becomes depressed, sick of life. This *taedium vitae,* even after his encounter with the Ghost, stays with him, manifesting itself in his vacillation, incessant dissection of his task, sudden bursts of energy, and forgetfulness of his duty. His final trait, toward the end of the play, after the aborted trip to England, is one of resignation: it is no matter, nothing matters.

There is more, even about Hamlet, that Bradley describes. I leave out Bradley's emphasis on Hamlet's melancholy and rationalization, especially in Hamlet's sparing of the King at prayer and his doubting of the Ghost, because it functions as an explanation of data (e.g., why he spares the King) and not as a description of them (e.g., that he spares the King). We may question Bradley's insistence on melancholy as Hamlet's pervasive trait or even on rationalization as a trait, but we cannot question Hamlet's heart-sickness, openness, and adulation of his father, among other qualities, that Bradley describes or reports upon.

We know a great deal about Hamlet. One reason we do, I am suggesting, is that Bradley tells us about him, by pointing out some of his characteristics, including his dispositional, as they are presented in the play. Consequently, however we may explain Hamlet, there are certain data or *données* that cannot be denied: that Hamlet is athletic, fearless, vulnerable, dilatory, adoring of his father, depressed, as well as—here, too, Bradley helps us with his descriptions—brutal, callous, obscene, sarcastic, fond of quibbles, and given to repetitions of words. Do what we wish with these, put them in any hierarchy we please, none can be rejected as aspects of Hamlet's character; and no explanation of Hamlet, in its emphasis upon one of these aspects, can deny the presence of the others. Even as it stands here, Bradley's description of the attributes of Hamlet is sufficient to refute many critical descriptions and explanations: for example, that Hamlet is shy, retiring, a young Werther; or that Hamlet fails to act because he is fearful, too pure, or excessively intellectual.

Thus, there are facts, *données*, or data in *Hamlet*. These can be and are described. The descriptions of them are important because they point out the many facets or qualities of the elements, for example, of Hamlet himself. They remind us, and should remind other critics too, of what we neglect, sometimes at the very peril of our understanding of the play. Recollect, for example, Wilson Knight's reading of Claudius in the prayer scene: Who, he asks, is closer to heaven in that scene, Claudius or Hamlet? But Bradley's report is a reminder that Claudius' prayer for pardon for his first murder, sincere or not, follows immediately upon his final arrangement for the second murder, that of Hamlet; hence, his report is sufficient to blow Knight's question and implied answer to the moon. Bradley's narration here of the sequence of events is a superb example of the non-triviality of descriptive statement in criticism: in effect, Bradley warns all critics that Claudius' prayer, with another contemplated murder in his heart, is not "the fine flower of a human soul in anguish" (Knight).

If works of art are like tulips, Dr. Johnson is probably right about the poet numbering the streaks. But it is different with the critic. To number at least some of the streaks, to enumerate some of the facts, is basic. For the adequacy of explanation and evaluation rests upon it; erroneous descriptions of certain constituents in *Hamlet* imperil the explanations and evaluations based on them.

Thus: To say What is in *Hamlet?* as against Why it is in *Hamlet?* or How we can best explain its role in *Hamlet?* is one important job of criticism. The critic can tell us something about the play that is not trivial, yet is as undeniable as the statement that Hamlet is in *Hamlet.*

Bradley describes also some of the other characters. He informs us, for example, that Ophelia is honest, not weak, in love with Hamlet, unselfish, and obedient to her father; that Gertrude is sensual, shallow, an adulteress, and not privy to the murder of her first husband; that Claudius is courteous, adroit, and dignified. Here, too, Bradley's descriptions, although parts of his explanations of the behavior of these characters, function as true (or false) statements of their traits, and they remind us of what is given of them in the play. Thus, to say, for example, of Ophelia that she is dishonest, is to make a simple error of fact; for on the normal criteria of "honesty," her actions are honest.

Bradley's is no isolated case of criticism as description. There are, among the other critics of *Hamlet,* similar illuminating statements about undeniable elements, characteristics, and relations in the play: about its characters, dialogue, and plot. Here are some examples: Fergusson points out—reminds us of, if we have read carefully but not as effectively as he—the various rituals in the play, the cannon shot, the multiple plot, the various analogies of the action and, especially, the role and qualities of Fortinbras. It is a fact, for example, that Fortinbras is mentioned at the beginning of the play as a threat to Denmark, appears briefly in IV, 4, and completes the action as the future monarch of Denmark. Why this role? What is his place in the play? Fergusson gives an explanation (as do others); but quite independently of it, his description is important because it focuses attention on these facts about Fortinbras.

Stoll points out that Hamlet's self-reproaches end with resolutions. He explains this as exculpation leading to heroic revenge. Dubious though the explanation is or is said to be, it is enlightening to be told that Hamlet does finish his self-reproaches with self-exhortations, make of them what we will.

Miss Spurgeon enumerates and characterizes the images of *Hamlet* in her criticism of the play: "blister," "sick soul," "mildew'd ear," "blasting," "vicious mole," "probed wound," "purgation." Rottenness, she discloses, is the tenor of the imagery. She, too, goes on to explain the play, including the tragic element, in terms of the imagery. Yet one can reject the explanation and retain her description of the imagery. Who would dare charge that her *findings* are trivial?

Clemen also reveals certain of the qualities of the images in *Hamlet.* He points out the contrasting imagery of Hamlet and Claudius: Hamlet's keen, penetrating images, drawn from trades, callings, everyday objects, and games, as against Claudius' conventional ones. He notes the parallels between the imagery and the plot, especially their common tenor of infection and disease. He also discerns that certain images are introduced early in the play and are repeated later, thereby locating in the play what he calls "clusters" of images. Once again, Clemen's descriptions of the images and their relations to the plot enlighten us since these descriptions function logically independently of his explanation that the imagery in *Hamlet* derives mainly from the incest and murder of the plot.

Spencer also describes certain features of *Hamlet*. He reminds us that Hamlet constantly invokes the distinction between appearance and reality; and he reminds us of Hamlet's tendency toward generalization, especially in the shift from the "I" of the first two major soliloquies to the "we" of the third. To be sure, Spencer explains these traits, along with other aspects of the play, as expressions of the conflict between optimism and pessimism in the Elizabethan age. But, once more, we need not accept the explanation in order to find the description illuminating.

Finally, Coleridge also describes in his criticism of *Hamlet*, even though, as we have seen, his main concern is with evaluation. Throughout the fragments there are descriptions of the characters, language, and plot. Probably his best example, in fact one of the great examples of descriptive criticism anywhere, is his analysis of the first scene. Remember his report on some of the dramatic elements: the easy language of common life, the armor, the dead silence, the watchfulness that first interrupts it, the welcome relief of guard, the cold, the uncertainty appertaining to a question,

> What, has this thing appeared again tonight?,

where even the word "again" has its credibilizing effect. In his description Coleridge achieves a marvel of pointed reading such that one can never read or see that first scene again except through his eyes, leveled as they are on its dramatic facts.

There are other examples of description in the criticism of *Hamlet*. Indeed, every critic begins with his own set of true (or false) reports on the dramatic items of the play as these items have to do with the characters, language, or plot. Criticism of *Hamlet,* thus, entails description—reports on or reminders of some of the elements, characteristics, and relations in *Hamlet*—that constitutes a body of true (or false), verifiable statements about what is given, and which, hence, are undeniable.

Are there in the criticism of *Hamlet* descriptions other than those of the characters, plot, and language in the play? Consider the range of this criticism as it includes writings on the sources of Shakespeare's *Hamlet:* its textual, dramatic, theatrical, and intellectual sources—what we may call its threshold—as well as on the authentic text of Shakespeare's *Hamlet* itself. As our survey shows, *Hamlet* criticism encompasses all sorts of statements about the relation between the authentic Shakespearean *Hamlet* and the First and Second Quartos, the First Folio, the lost Ur-*Hamlet*, *The Spanish Tragedy*, and other Elizabethan dramas; about the dramatic devices employed by Shakespeare; about his audience; about Elizabethan views of man, tragedy, passion, ghosts, and politics; and about the exact text of Shakespeare's authentic *Hamlet.*

Much of this criticism is employed by its proponents to explain *Hamlet* or certain aspects of it. Spencer's use of the Elizabethan intellectual conflict, Wilson's use of Elizabethan demonology, Miss Campbell's use of Elizabethan doctrines of the humors, passions, and function of tragedy, and Schücking's use of Elizabethan dramatic devices are examples of purported historical facts being employed in the framing of hypotheses to explain certain data in *Hamlet.*

But my concern, for the moment, is not with the use of this historical material. I am asking instead if these critics also make descriptive statements in their historical, explanatory criticism of *Hamlet:* Do they make true (or false) reports on the causal environment or threshold materials of Shakespeare's *Hamlet* as well as on the authentic text itself? Are their reports enlightening? Are they true (or false) independently of the purported truth (or falsity) of the explanations of which they are parts? Do these statements resemble the descriptive ones of Bradley, Fergusson, Coleridge, etc.?

It seems to me that many of the statements of the critics of *Hamlet* about its authentic text and its intellectual and dramatic environment are also descriptions, that is, true (or false) reports on various items in and surrounding *Hamlet*.

Here, too, examples are called for to support this claim about the compass of description in criticism. Consider, first, Spencer. His main self-appointed task, of course, is to explain the play; in doing so he details two sets of doctrines, optimism and pessimism, that prevailed in the age of Elizabeth and that Shakespeare dramatized in *Hamlet*. He also contends that these sets of doctrines, especially the conflict between them, were pervasive in Shakespeare's time. Now, much of this is open to question, especially, his conception of a neat Elizabethan Weltanschauung, and his explanation of *Hamlet*. But there is much in his criticism that is not questionable, namely, the detailed exposition—description—of the various philosophical doctrines about man and his place in the world which were propounded by orthodox Christian theology and the attacks upon this theology. Here Spencer, as an historical critic, makes true (or false) statements about these doctrines. Because he presents his corroborative evidence in the form of certain Renaissance authors, widely read in Elizabethan England, his critical descriptive reports on Elizabethan optimism and pessimism, construed according to his intention as historical utterances, are not only verifiable but verified as well. Consequently, whatever of his criticism we may wish to challenge, we still learn much from it about the intellectual milieu of Shakespeare's *Hamlet*.

What is true of Spencer also holds for Lily Campbell. Here, too, one must separate her explanation of *Hamlet* and her claim that tragedies were *exempla* to Shakespeare from her well-established historical, critical descriptions of Elizabethan theories of the humors, especially the distinction between melancholy and melancholy adust; of the Elizabethan conception of the function of tragedy; and the Elizabethan view of the moral role of consolation in grief. If we accept historical criticism as at least one part of criticism, then her extremely enlightening reports on certain aspects of Elizabethan thought stand by themselves as true (or false), verifiable, and, in her case, as true and verified statements about items in the milieu of Shakespeare's *Hamlet*.

Wilson's is a consummate example of descriptive criticism. His descriptions cover the characters, language, and plot of *Hamlet;* certain aspects of its intellectual environment; and the actual wording, staging, and punctuation of the text of the play. Just here we can skip over his own set of reports on some of the data in *Hamlet* (e.g., the characters), since they resemble others already noted. But consider, to begin with, Wilson's findings on the Elizabethan views regarding ghosts and spirits. Quite independently of the purported truth (or falsity) of his explanation of the attitudes of Marcellus, Horatio, and Hamlet toward the Ghost as variations on Elizabethan demonology, these historical findings are true (or false), verifiable and, in his case, verified by his references to various exponents of Catholic, Protestant, and skeptical doctrines. As a critic of *Hamlet* he tells us important historical truths about Elizabethan demonology.

He also offers a report on the nature and history of the text of *Hamlet* from the Ur-*Hamlet* to the First Folio. One great problem in *Hamlet* criticism, we remember, is to determine the relation between the lost Ur-*Hamlet, The Spanish Tragedy,* the First and Second Quartos, the First Folio, and *Der bestrafte Brudermord.* There are many competing descriptions of that relationship and as many competing explanations of the similarities and dissimilarities among these texts. Robertson, Stoll, Schücking, Greg, Chambers, Alice Walker, Duthie, Bowers, Wilson, V. K. Whitaker, and others, give accounts of parts or the whole of the history of *Hamlet* from its lost version to the German one. They attempt to decide tentatively or dogmatically which, if any, is the authentic Shakespearean *Hamlet.* Only one thing is certain about this relationship: that there is one and only one set of objectively existing facts about its history from its modern dramatic inception to its German version. This set may be simple or complex, but it exists in exactly the same sense as any other set of historical events and their relations. As far as criticism is concerned, there can be one and only one true description of the relation between the lost *Hamlet,* its Quarto and Folio versions, its German rendition, and any authentic, authoritative, and definitive Shakespearean *Hamlet.*

Wilson's description of that relationship, especially of the Second

Quarto and Shakespeare's authoritative *Hamlet*, like other descriptions, is either true or false, as a whole or in its parts. It is also verifiable; but, unfortunately, verifiable only in principle and not in fact, since there is not enough evidence to verify it.

The descriptive criticism of the history and relations of the versions of *Hamlet* is like the descriptive criticism of data in *Hamlet* or in *Hamlet*'s immediate environment in that both consist of true (or false) and verifiable statements about objectively existing items. The difference between them is that the latter criticism is verifiable in fact, i.e., actually verified as true (or refuted as false) whereas the former is verifiable only in principle, since the evidence for this descriptive criticism of the history and relations among the different versions of *Hamlet* is not sufficient to establish its truth or falsity. Consequently, the doubts about the history of *Hamlet* in relation to the authoritative text, although they are resolvable, are so only in principle, not in fact, because of the paucity of available evidence.

This distinction between verifiable and verified descriptions in criticism also clarifies another facet of Wilson as a descriptive critic: his specific reports on the authentic Shakespearean text of *Hamlet*. Wilson describes certain textual items in *Hamlet* in his claims, for example, that Hamlet refers to his sullied, not solid, sallied, or assaulted, flesh, in his first soliloquy; that he overhears Polonius and Claudius plotting in II, 2, 158; that Claudius does not see the dumb-show; and that, in his speech on man, Hamlet compares man to an angel in apprehension, not to an angel in action. These, and there are many more, are reports, or textual critical statements, on the wording, staging, and punctuation of Shakespeare's *Hamlet*.

Here, too, Wilson's statements are true or false, and they are verifiable in principle. But they are not verified in fact because, once more, we simply do not have enough evidence to determine or verify what Shakespeare's wording, staging, and punctuation were in these cases. Wilson's claims are true or false in relation to the textual facts; the difficulty is that we do not know these facts; hence, although his claims are true or false, the arguments for them are at best plausible or implausible. That is, in Shakespeare's authoritative, definitive *Hamlet*—if there is one—Hamlet either says "sullied" or he does not. The descriptive claim that he does is either true or false and verifiable; but since we do not know what that text is, we do not know if "sullied" is the right word or not.

Our elucidation of the nature, variety, and functions of descriptions in *Hamlet* criticism can now be applied to some of the issues of that criticism. Issues (1), (2), (3), (5), (7), (8), (9), (10), (14), (15), and (16) are descriptive, either as wholes or in some of their parts. Elucidation of them discloses logical features similar to those already brought out in our examination of description in *Hamlet* criticism. It also reveals other logical features that must be acknowledged in any attempt at their solution.

(1) Is Hamlet mad? (I remind the reader that my aim is not to offer answers that compete with the critics' to the various questions of *Hamlet* criticism but to try to clarify the questions and the kinds of answers that are forthcoming.)

Recollect the various views and disagreements of the critics about Hamlet's madness. In the ones surveyed, the point at issue is not the meaning or criteria of "madness." (There are critics, mostly doctors or cranks, who do not know better, and literary critics, who should know better, who do make the meaning of "madness" the point at issue, so that they interpret the question as: Does Hamlet satisfy the true criteria of real madness? Their answers, however, function logically as stipulated redefinitions and not as real, true definitions of "madness.") Nor is the problem the lack of evidence, which is ample: Hamlet's "antic disposition," his behavior in the cellarage, nunnery, and graveyard scenes; his apology to Laertes, his "sore distraction," and Ophelia's account of the episode in his closet.

The point at issue—as our critics argue about this madness—is whether Hamlet satisfies the recognized, everyday criteria of madness. The critics disagree on *this* point. Some claim that he satisfies all of them; others, none; still others, some of them.

Solution of this issue, whether Hamlet embodies any, none, or some of the ordinary criteria of madness, depends upon our recognition that these criteria, logically speaking, are multiple and not clearly or exactly marked off from the criteria of sanity (including feigned madness). Once this logical feature of the term "madness" in its everyday (versus medical or legal) usage is acknowledged, one can say truly that Hamlet does satisfy some of these criteria. Eliot's remark, for example, that Hamlet's madness is "less than madness but more than feigned" serves as a true description of that aspect of Hamlet as a character in *Hamlet*. The criteria of madness, multiple and unbounded in any exact manner as they are, allow for a true (or false) solution to the question, Is Hamlet mad? But they do not allow for a solution to the problem of how mad or how sane he is, that is, the logical character of the criteria of madness does not allow us to make any statement about Hamlet's exact state. We can no more settle the question about how mad Hamlet is than we can determine how much money makes one wealthy, although we know very well who are rich and who are poor. All we can say of Hamlet is that he is not quite as mad as Lear on the heath or quite as sane as Laertes in Paris. Hence, it is *vagueness*, not Shakespeare or our language, that precludes an absolute yes or no answer to Is Hamlet mad? Hamlet's madness is a borderline case of it, for he satisfies some but not all the ordinary criteria of madness. This logical fact must be accepted in the solution of the problem of his madness.

(2) Is Hamlet cruel, obscene, brutal, idealistic, callous, cynical, or ambitious? In the sense of Is Hamlet *ever* any of these? the answers are also true (or false), verifiable, and indeed verified by textual data. With regard to these questions critics raise no problems about the criteria of cruelty, obscenity, etc.; they ask instead whether established common criteria for the correct use of these terms apply to Hamlet.

In the sense of Is Hamlet *predominantly* any of these? the answers, like all answers to What is Hamlet's most important trait? are explanatory, not descriptive, and will be considered as such in our next chapter.

(3) Is Hamlet melancholic? Critical discussion and disagreement here converge on the criteria for "melancholy," and not on whether Hamlet satisfies them or on the substantiating textual evidence. There are at least three different sets of criteria for "melancholy" which are operative in critical disputes over this question: the Elizabethan criteria of natural melancholy, the Elizabethan criteria of melancholy

adust, and the modern criteria of melancholy as a disposition toward or a state of mind characterized by depression, moodiness, and *taedium vitae*.

Thus, as critics present and answer the question, it functions elliptically for three different questions: Is Hamlet melancholic in one or another of the two Elizabethan senses or in the modern sense? "Melancholy," consequently, is an *ambiguous* term; hence, no clear answer is forthcoming until the critic first specifies which sense or set of criteria he is employing in his question. Once these senses are specified, the answer, for example, that Hamlet is melancholy in the Elizabethan sense of a preponderance of this natural humor can be classified as a descriptively true and verified answer, since Hamlet gives us the evidence in his second soliloquy and in his opening remarks to Rosencrantz and Guildenstern (II, 2). That he is melancholy in our modern sense, that is, depressed or prone to depression, is also a true and verified answer, the evidence that supports the first answer being similar to that which supports this one since, after all, the Elizabethan and modern senses of "melancholy" join at least on the criterion of depression. But that Hamlet is a melancholy adust is not a descriptively true answer; it is rather an explanation of his behavior by means of an hypothesis which is garnered from Elizabethan medical doctrines. Nor is Bradley's view that Hamlet is predominantly melancholic in the Elizabethan and modern sense of being disposed to brooding and depression a descriptive claim; it, too, is an explanation of his behavior in the play.

(5) Does Hamlet vacillate? Does he rationalize or deceive himself? Why does he delay? Is he infirm? These are different sorts of questions that critics lump together. Only one, Does Hamlet vacillate? is descriptive; the others are explanatory. The question, Does he vacillate or delay? is clearly answerable, by Hamlet himself. Indeed, the dramatic evidence is so overwhelming in the text that few critics deny it, only its significance as, for example, Stoll, in his attempt to reconcile it with epical heroism; and the few critics who do reject it, for example, G. B. Harrison, shift the question from whether Hamlet satisfies normal criteria of "delay" to one about the criteria themselves, with the result that they reject our everyday criteria in favor of a

redefinition of "delay" which renders delay remote from what most of us and the critics consider it to be.

(7) and (8) I have already attempted an elucidation of questions on the wording, staging, and punctuation in *Hamlet* in the discussion of Wilson as a descriptive critic.

(9) These questions on the meanings of "son," "coil," "nature," "fishmonger," "miching mallecho," "angel," and "action" (and others), in their particular contexts in *Hamlet*, are partly descriptive, partly aesthetic and explanatory. True (or false) descriptions can be given of some of their non-Shakespearean, Elizabethan usages, at least of those that are extant. Wilson's claim, for example, that angels to Elizabethans are discarnate spirits, hence essentially non-physical, is a true (or false) statement about one aspect of Elizabethan theology. Further, true (or false) reports can be given on some of Shakespeare's usages of them as they are similar to or different from other Elizabethan usages. Knight's statement, for example, that Shakespeare's angels, quite independently of Elizabethan theology, are regularly depicted as physically active, is a true (or false) one. Thus, exegetical statements or exegeses in *Hamlet* criticism are true (or false), verifiable, and verified (or refuted) descriptions of Elizabethan, including Shakespearean, words and their meanings.

But are these exegetical statements on the meaning or meanings of a word in a particular poetic and dramatic context true (or false) and verifiable in principle as well as in fact? Exegeses of particular words in their poetic and dramatic contexts are *readings;* they are attempts to relate a particular word (or phrase) and its meaning or meanings to the dramatic situation of which it is an integral part. Inevitably they introduce aesthetic and explanatory or interpretive criteria, i.e., a hypothesis about what fits or seems aesthetically right in a particular context.

In *Hamlet* (II, 2, 174), Hamlet in answer to Polonius'

Do you know me, my lord?,

replies,

Excellent well, you are a fishmonger.

Some critics point out extant Elizabethan equivalents of "fishmonger" as "bawd," "fleshmonger," or "seller of women's chastity"; others point out classical references, for example, Ovid's story in which Neptune changes his beloved, a girl sold by her father to a man, into fisherman in order to prevent her being recognized. These usages are then applied to "fishmonger" in *Hamlet*. But Coleridge reads the word in its whole sentence as "You are sent to *fish* out the secret;" Polonius, thus, is a catcher, not a seller, of fish. The whole context, of "fishmonger," "god- (or "good)-kissing carrion," "daughter," and "conception," is amenable to different interpretations. Whether Polonius is (to Hamlet) a male bawd, a panderer, a seller of fish (taken literally), or one who tries to fish out Hamlet's secret is not a descriptive issue, in the way that the problem of extant Elizabethan and Shakespearean usage may be. The decision on the meaning or meanings of "fishmonger" in this context is aesthetic, controlled, of course, by explanatory hypotheses which are formulated with the help of Elizabethan and Shakespearean usages. In other words, " 'Fishmonger' means such and such in this dramatic context" is not a true (or false) descriptive report on a particular meaning but a reading of a word that is assessed by aesthetic plus linguistic criteria. What is the case with "fishmonger"—that its usages are describable but that its meaning (or meanings) in a particular dramatic context is at best interpretable or explicable in terms of a proposed reading—holds for all exegeses of words in their dramatic contexts in the criticism of *Hamlet*. Consequently, whether Hamlet conceives of angels as physically active or as purely discarnate spirits is not a wholy descriptive problem. The context—Elizabethan and other usages in Shakespeare aside—yields both Knight's and Wilson's readings, although neither is a true (or false) report on *the* meaning.

(10) I have already discussed the logical status of statements about the history and relations of the various texts of *Hamlet* in our review of Wilson as a descriptive critic.

(14) Statements about Ophelia's traits are also true (or false), verifiable, and actually verified by the text. What is obscure in this issue is the nature of the love relation between Hamlet and Ophelia. Is the statement, "Hamlet and Ophelia love each other in the play," a true (or false) one? It certainly appears to be: either they love each other or they do not. Critics, however, disagree. It is significant that

they do not argue about the meaning or criteria of "love." Nor is it vagueness that makes it hard to decide whether their love is a border-line case. The difficulty lies in the evidence itself; not in its paucity, but in its *unclarity*. It is the dramatic data, rather than ambiguity, vagueness, or dearth of evidence, that render a solution difficult if not impossible. Shakespeare's dramatization of their love is not clear; for the dramatization satisfies some established criteria of "love," but it also satisfies as many criteria of "indifference," especially in Hamlet. Perhaps the truth about their relationship is that it is not clear whether they love each other or not. From an aesthetic point of view, this lack of clarity may be a fault; one's evaluation depends on what significance is attached to this particular obscurity, because it is as plausible to argue that it enriches the play as that it renders the play defective. But these aesthetic or evaluative considerations are, in any case, not relevant to description.

(15) Is Gertrude privy to her first husband's murder? Is she an adulteress? The answer to the first is that there is no textual evidence that she is and crucial evidence that she is not, namely, her reply to Hamlet in the bedroom scene. The answer to the second is less easy because, as was noted before, the question is ambiguous. It seems clear that she is an adulteress in the Elizabethan incestuous sense. But is it obvious that she was Claudius' mistress before she became his wife? Critics divide sharply on this issue; all agree, however, that a definite yes or no answer is forthcoming. Yet all the evidence—(direct) King Hamlet's "that adulterate beast," said of Claudius; (indirect) King Hamlet's talk of "seduce," "my most seeming-virtuous queen," and "shameful lust"; Hamlet's talk of a mother whored; and Horatio's summary "of carnal, bloody and unnatural acts"—is compatible with Gertrude's incest (in the Elizabethan sense) rather than with her infidelity while her first husband lived.

This issue of Gertrude's adultery is like that of Hamlet's love for Ophelia during the action of the play. It is not the ambiguity of "adultery," or the fact that adultery is vague, which of course it is not, or that there is a lack of evidence; rather it is the unclarity of the evidence that is the source of difficulty in the solution of the problem. Gertrude, one wants to say, was either faithful or unfaithful to her first husband while he lived; but all we can say that is a true description of her as she appears in *Hamlet* is that it is not clear which she was.

(16) Is Claudius a usurper? Is he a hypocrite? Since the Elizabethan senses of these, although they include more than the modern senses, especially the Elizabethan conception of the hypocrite, are still very close to ours, and since the criteria for these terms are clear as the critics discuss the issues, both questions are descriptive ones to which true, verified answers can be given. That Claudius holds a throne which is rightly Hamlet's, and that Claudius pretends to be what he is not are both true of him and the play, and are verified by its textual data.

To sum up: There are descriptions in the criticism of *Hamlet*. As reports on or reminders of items in or connected with *Hamlet*, they are informative and enlightening. They illuminate the play's characters, language, and plot; its textual variants and history; and its intellectual, dramatic, and linguistic sources. These descriptions are basic in *Hamlet* criticism since explanation and evaluation depend on them. Although they are true or false, verifiable, and logically independent of explanation and evaluation, they function mostly in certain explanatory and evaluative contexts that determine which possibilities of descriptive criticism shall be articulated by the individual critic. Further, although they are true or false, there are difficulties in the determination of their truth or falsity because of the lack of requisite evidence, unclarity of data, ambiguity of terms, and certain phenomena of vagueness. Finally, as statements, some of them are singular statements of fact, for example, "Hamlet loves his father"; some are statements about dispositions, for example, "Hamlet was vulnerable to shock"; some are comparative, for example, "The First Quarto is a shortened version of the Second Quarto"; and some are summary or general statements, for example, "The tenor of the imagery in *Hamlet* is rottenness."

XV EXPLANATION

PREDOMINANT in the criticism of *Hamlet* is the explanation of the play. From the beginnings of this criticism to the present, its practitioners have concerned themselves with the explanation either of some of the attributed or acknowledged puzzling parts of the play (e.g., Hamlet's delay), or of the whole play. Their language fluctuates but their problem remains the same. Thus, they talk of the understanding, true interpretation, correct reading, and meaning of, or of what is central, primary, or most important in, *Hamlet* (all or some of it); yet explanation persists as the common denominator of their utterances. Such, at any rate, is the thesis I shall now try to clarify and support: that an elucidation of the uses and the conditions of use of the concepts of true understanding, true interpretation, correct reading, what is central, and the meaning, as these concepts are applied to *Hamlet*, reveals their identical roles as explanation. Hence, to give an interpretation, a reading, the meaning of part or the whole of *Hamlet*, or to state what is most important in *Hamlet* or in the understanding of *Hamlet*, is to give an explanation of it. My thesis, consequently, contradicts that which is shared by some critics of *Hamlet* and some philosophers of criticism according to which interpretation of *Hamlet*, as a work of dramatic art, is logically distinct from explanation. I have already suggested, in discussions of Knight and Fergusson, that their conceptions of interpretation imply that it is really explanation. I shall try to reinforce this suggestion and, further, to show that certain contemporary philosophical attempts to distinguish interpretation from explanation are not correct descriptions of the actual logical functioning of critical interpretations or readings but are only salvage procedures for rescuing these from cognitive oblivion. In effect, then, I shall reverse the theme of the preceding three chapters: the ostensible multiplicity of utterance about the correct reading, interpretation, meaning, understanding, and explanation of some or all of *Hamlet* does not embody a multiplicity of functions, but only the one function of explanation.

How do the critics of *Hamlet* employ—not How do they sometimes *say* they employ—these terms: "explanation," "understanding," "interpretation," "meaning," "central," and "reading," in their criticism of the play? Our survey, I shall now try to show, supports the logical identification of these terms with explanation. Consider, once more, Bradley and his use of these terms. Bradley engages in much explanation in his criticism of *Hamlet.* He explains Hamlet's delay, the central fact (for Bradley) of his character. He explains his doubt of the Ghost, his sparing of the King at prayer, Hamlet's irritability, sudden bursts of energy, incessant dissection of his task, and other data. How does Bradley do this? By stating various contending classical hypotheses—"theories" he calls them—of the delay, testing them in relation to the text, rejecting them because they presuppose false hypotheses or distort crucial data; and then by stating, clarifying, and defending his own hypothesis that he also tests and confirms. Bradley proposes as the true hypothesis one that he borrows from psychology: that Hamlet, disposed to melancholy, becomes a full-blown melancholic upon the indecent remarriage of his mother, and that this state of mind makes it impossible for him to prosecute his appointed task. In effect, Bradley explains Hamlet's delay by subsuming it under a general psychological law about the behavior of melancholically inclined, morally vulnerable persons in a state of shock. He also employs this hypothesis to explain certain other data related to the delay as effects of Hamlet's melancholy.

The confirmation of his hypothesis occupies a major part of Bradley's reading or interpretation and of his understanding of the meaning of *Hamlet.* But the meaning of the play is larger than Hamlet's melancholy, for the meaning includes his tragedy as well, which Bradley also explains by employing as a hypothesis what he takes to be a true statement about the tragic fact in the world: the self-waste of good in its struggle with evil.

Thus, for Bradley, the explanation of Hamlet, who is the primary element in *Hamlet,* is a clarification of his melancholy and tragedy, where the clarification consists of the application of certain (true, for Bradley) generalizations or hypotheses to Hamlet's character, struggle, and defeat.

Bradley's reading, explanation, or understanding of *Hamlet* as essentially a story of a melancholic and tragic figure is challengeable. His purportedly descriptive statement that Hamlet is the primary element in the play is open to question: as a description, since it functions instead as a hypothesis; and as a hypothesis, since other hypotheses about what is central in *Hamlet* are possible and have been put forth by critics. His hypothesis about the nature of tragedy and of Hamlet's tragic quality has been challenged. His emphases upon character and its psychological analysis have been rejected, hence his categories of explanation, psychological and metaphysical, are debatable. Even his specific application of the psychological hypothesis, that Hamlet delays, spares the King at prayer, doubts the Ghost, etc., because he is melancholy, has been challenged (most interestingly) by critics who accept his emphases upon character and psychological analysis, on his ground that it, too, distorts the data, especially the doubt and the sparing. For Bradley, these data are explained as rationalizations. His critics deny this and give other reasons and explanations for them; thus they reject the hypothesis from which their being instances of rationalization are derived. The dispute between Bradley and his critics brings out the extremely important logical fact that explanation (reading, meaning, interpretation, understanding, the primary datum) of *Hamlet* can be challenged in many different ways: By rejecting a hypothesis and its particular application to undeniable data; by converting a purported description of a primary datum into a hypothesis about *a* datum and then rejecting the hypothesis; by rejecting a general hypothesis (e.g., about human behavior) as true or a specific application of it (e.g., that Hamlet is melancholic) as relevant; or by denying that the specific hypothesis in its application covers all the data without distortion.

Ernest Jones as a critic of *Hamlet* also explains. His explanation is identical with his Freudian interpretation. In his explanation he also states the meaning of the play, what is central in it, and the correct understanding of it. For him, too, Hamlet's delay is central; the correct explanation of it explains everything else in the play as well as the psychological sources of Shakespeare's creation. We recollect from our survey that Jones applies to the delay a particular psychoanalytic hypothesis, which he affirms to be true about real life: that Hamlet cannot avenge his father because of the complicated form of his oedipal complex. Like Bradley, Jones explains the delay by subsuming it under an established (for him) general hypothesis about human behavior. His explanation, enlarged upon in his reading of the play, is also challengeable: in its assertions that there is such a thing as the oedipal complex or, if there is, that Hamlet is dominated by it; in its assumption that psychology or psychoanalysis is relevant to *Hamlet;* in its hypothesis (which Jones also takes to be a datum) that Hamlet's delay is primary; and in that part of his confirmation or reading of the play according to which Hamlet, although he professes love for his father, really hates him and wishes him out of the way, an implication that by itself reduces to absurdity Jones's explanation, because it distorts an undeniable datum.

Knight also explains, his denial notwithstanding. Indeed, he explains the whole play. All his talk about "the true interpretation" of *Hamlet,* as he employs this concept, is equivalent to the formulation and confirmation of a grand hypothesis about what is central in *Hamlet,* hence what should control our true reading of it. His grand hypothesis is this: Shakespearean poetic drama is essentially thematic (symbolic, spatial, metaphorical); and the theme of *Hamlet* is life versus death, health versus disease, good versus evil. This hypothesis is regarded by him as true about Shakespeare's dramas in general and *Hamlet* in particular. The application of this hypothesis, which is his confirmation of it, serves also as his reading, interpretation, and exfoliation of the meaning of the play. What distinguishes Knight from Bradley and Jones, therefore, is not that he interprets and they explain, but that his explanation is based upon a hypothesis that is derived from a theory (i.e., a purportedly true, real definition) of poetic drama whereas theirs is based upon hypotheses that are derived from theories of human behavior. Much is challengeable in Knight's explanation: his theory of poetic drama; his hypothesis that theme, specifically the theme of life versus death, is central in *Hamlet* and, more particularly, that Hamlet is primarily a symbol of death; and his reading of the play according to which Hamlet is evil and Claudius is good, which represents a blatant distortion of the ostensible qualities of both.

Eliot also explains. For him, Hamlet's feeling toward a guilty mother is the basic emotion as well as the primary *donnée* in the play. This emotion, Eliot contends, cannot be reconciled with the rest of the play or even with all of Hamlet. But Eliot's statement that Hamlet's emotion is basic is not a true (or false) description of what is given; it is a hypothesis about what is central. As such, it is as challengeable as any other hypothesis. Think, for instance, of Dover Wilson's counter-hypothesis (also set forth, incorrectly, I believe, as a description) that Hamlet's feeling toward his mother, primary or not, is toward an incestuous and not merely a guilty mother.

All the historical critics explain. Indeed, criticism *is* explanation for them. *Hamlet* can be correctly understood, a true reading of it given, and its real meaning or significance grasped, only by means of hypotheses that are derived from general (and true) hypotheses about the Elizabethan age. Their categories of explanation are historical ones about the ideas and dramaturgy of that age. Thus, all their hypotheses about *Hamlet* depend for their cogent applicability upon true statements or hypotheses about, and even large-scale explanations of, historical facts. The historical critics, therefore, are also challengeable not only on the relevance of their method or category of explanation (the historical) but on the truth or probability of their general hypotheses. As we have already seen in our survey, one can ask of the historical explanation of *Hamlet* whether, for example, its assumption (general hypothesis) that there was so tidy an Elizabethan Weltanschauung as, for example, the historian's Elizabethan World Picture is true. If this assumption can be proved to be true or not, is it relevant to an explanation of *Hamlet?*

For Robertson, our first historical critic, *Hamlet* is an adaptation of a double play by Kyd, who laid down the action which was so popular with audiences that Shakespeare could not change it in his transmutation. But Robertson's thesis is not a descriptive statement about data in *Hamlet*. Rather it is a hypothesis about data in *Hamlet*, some given, for example, Hamlet's pessimism, some hypothetical, for example, Kyd's plot. What is central in *Hamlet* is a mixture of Kyd's plot and Shakespeare's contributions of pessimism and transfiguration of the characters. Robertson confirms this hypothesis mostly by the evidence of the verbal parallels between Kyd's *Spanish Tragedy* and the First Quarto of *Hamlet*. But since this evidence has been discredited by Duthie, who explains the parallels as a reporter's patchwork when his memory of performances of what became the Second Quarto of *Hamlet*, failed him, Robertson's hypothesis is seriously impugned, if not altogether defeated. Of course, Robertson can also be challenged, as he has been, on his general methodological assumption that *Hamlet* is explicable by its dramatic sources.

Stoll offers a full-fledged reading or interpretation as well as the meaning and understanding of *Hamlet* in his explanation that *Hamlet* is a revenge tragedy. How descriptively true (or false) this seems as a statement about the data of the play! Yet it is also, I believe, a hypothesis which functions as part of his whole explanation. He begins with a (to him) true historical statement about Senecan revenge tragedy and its popularization by Kyd in the English Renaissance: revenge tragedy is characterized by blood, intrigue, fate, and a hero who remains ideal (with no defect) in achieving his revenge. Then he postulates or hypothesizes that *Hamlet* is in this Senecan-Kyd tradition: Shakespeare rewrote Kyd's (lost) *Hamlet*, kept the delay as a necessary ingredient of the tradition, and slurred it over. Stoll applies these hypotheses and the principle that criticism of *Hamlet* should explain it in terms of its age to the play in a confirmation reading of them. He appeals to the allusions and critical responses to the play up to the late eighteenth century as well as to the data of the play as his confirming evidence. Every datum of the play, he claims, supports his specific hypothesis that *Hamlet* is a revenge tragedy. Stoll's reading, hypotheses, and historical category of explanation are also questionable, so is, especially, his explanation of Hamlet's delay and self-reproaches as manifestations of a heroic, rather than as symptoms of a faltering, avenger—an explanation rejected by other critics because it distorts the delay and related data.

Schücking explains *Hamlet* as a fusion of two plays by Kyd, with the hero of one, *The Spanish Tragedy,* and the plot of the other, the (lost) *Hamlet;* and he explains it by means of his general hypothesis about the nature of dramatic devices and conventions in Elizabethan drama plus his specific hypothesis about *Hamlet* as a reworking of an old play. His hypotheses about Elizabethan devices and conventions, especially the dramatic use of them, their relevancy to *Hamlet,* and his particular confirmation are all challengeable.

Spencer explains *Hamlet* as the dramatization inside the hero's consciousness of the Elizabethan conflict between optimism and pessimism. His reading of the play, his understanding of it, and his statement of its meaning add up to his total explanation. The explanation (or the reading or the statement of the meaning) of *Hamlet* is based upon general doctrines about philosophical ideas and their dramatization in the Elizabethan age as these dramatized ideas apply to that or any other age regarding the problem of the nature of man. His explanation, as a whole, or in its parts, is also challengeable.

Miss Campbell explains *Hamlet* as a study in the passion of grief. Her reading details her explanation in such a manner that the characters, their similarities and contrasts, and the action reflect the theme of passion, and Hamlet, Fortinbras, Laertes, and Ophelia, the particular passion of grief. She, too, formulates, then employs, certain hypotheses about matters of the English Renaissance, especially its views of tragedy, passion, and consolation in grief. Her use of these hypotheses enables her to derive from them her specific hypothesis about *Hamlet*: that it is a study in the passion of grief designed to show that men can avoid ruin by divine retribution through a proper balance of passion and reason. Here, too, her general hypotheses about Elizabethan views of tragedy, passion, and consolation are questionable; her category of explanation, that the ideas of an age are primary in the explanation of a work of art of that age, is challengeable; her specific hypothesis about *Hamlet,* that it is a study in the passion of grief, is debatable; and her reading, especially of Hamlet's grief, constitutes a distortion of the data that relate to his grief.

For Fergusson, *Hamlet* is a series of analogues, a multiple plot, on the major *donnée,* the theme of the attempt to find and destroy the hidden imposthume that threatens Denmark. It is Denmark's plight, not Hamlet's, thus, that is central. Hamlet is but chief agonist and reflector in this plight. But Fergusson's reading also involves a hypothesis about, not a descriptive report on, what is central in *Hamlet.* As a hypothesis, it derives from the well-known view which originated in Greek antiquity that drama is essentially myth and ritual, a celebration of the mystery of human life. This general hypothesis relates not only to Fergusson's specific hypothesis about *Hamlet* but also to his category of explanation: Explanations of any tragic drama from Aeschylus to Shakespeare are to be based upon its religious, mythical, and ritual sources. This explanation, from the general hypotheses to the particular readings of parts of *Hamlet,* is questionable, and some of it, objectionable, because it also distorts data in the play.

Miss Spurgeon explains *Hamlet* in terms of its predominant imagery, as a tragedy of the inevitable natural condition of man, which is his infection and decay. Here, too, we find a general hypothesis about imagery as basic in poetic drama, a specific one about *Hamlet,* a category of explanation, and a reading of *Hamlet,* each of which is challengeable.

Clemen also explains the imagery of *Hamlet.* But he does so on the assumption that the imagery is only one contributing element in the whole play. He explains the imagery by relating it to the plot and the characters. He formulates no hypothesis about the whole play, its meaning, or the correct understanding of it, only a hypothesis about the images: that they function dramatically to forebode sequences of the plot, to reinforce them, to reveal character traits, and to create some of the atmosphere or tone of the play. He applies this hypothesis to the images in *Hamlet* and confirms it in his readings of them. Of course, his explanation is derived from a general principle about poetic drama: that it is an organic unity of many elements including the imagery. His explanation is also based upon the hypothesis that, although the imagery of *Hamlet* is not primary, what is primary about its imagery is the tenor of ulcerousness as this tenor affects and is affected by the plot. Thus, one could concur on the tenor and still disagree on its dramatic impact or the organic character of *Hamlet* and poetic drama. What Clemen does, then, as a critic of *Hamlet*, is to describe the pervasive quality of the imagery, then, to explain the imagery by showing how it works dramatically in relation to the whole play. Showing how it works is giving an explanation that involves hypotheses and their confirmations, even though this showing involves no reading or interpretation of, or statement about what is primary or most important in, the play.

Finally, Wilson also explains. He formulates hypotheses about the texts of *Hamlet* and the authoritative Shakespearean text. He formulates hypotheses about Elizabethan usages of certain words, doctrines about ghosts and spirits, political ideas, and dramatic devices and practices. Much of his criticism is easily convertible into historical description and explanation of Elizabethan thought and drama. Many of these established (for him) hypotheses are employed in his major set task of explaining what happens in *Hamlet*. He presents certain data, for example, the different attitudes toward the Ghost; the cellarage scene; Hamlet's doubt of the Ghost, talk of ambition, usurpation, and incest, treatment of Ophelia, and hysterical episodes; the dumb-show; Claudius' blenching only at the playlet and not at the dumb-show; the invisibility of the Ghost to Gertrude in the bedroom scene, etc. In each case, he explains by introducing a hypothesis that is garnered from Elizabethan history, projected Shakespearean intentions, or the purported authentic text of *Hamlet*. He then employs that hypothesis to clarify the particular datum and to tie it causally to preceding and succeeding events. The aim of explanation, as well as being a part of it, is to provide a running account of what is going on in *Hamlet* that is coherent, sound, and dramatically satisfying. The realization of this aim requires much application of particular hypotheses, for example, that Claudius does not see the dumb-show, and general hypotheses, for example, that Elizabethans believed that angels are essentially discarnate spirits, as well as many particular confirmations or readings of particular episodes. Although Wilson offers a large-scale explanation of the textual variants of *Hamlet* and a grand hypothesis on the authoritative text, namely, his edition of the play, he offers no large-scale explanation or reading of *Hamlet* and even disclaims any explanation of its hero, any plucking out of the heart of Hamlet's mystery.

Wilson's textual, exegetical, and dramatic explanations, large and small, have also been challenged. His specific hypothesis about the authenticity of the Second Quarto rather than the First Folio, his confirmation of that hypothesis, his readings of words according to their Elizabethan rather than uniquely Shakespearean usage, his specific hypotheses about certain words, bits of staging, and punctuations, and his hypothesis that Hamlet is intended by Shakespeare to be a mystery without a heart to it, are all challengeable and have given rise to much argument in criticism.

All the critics of our survey explain in their essays on *Hamlet*. They present general or specific hypotheses and their confirmations: about the text of *Hamlet;* the intellectual and dramatic influences on Shakespeare's authoritative *Hamlet,* whether it is the Second Quarto, the First Folio, or some eclectic combination; and the dramatic data of the play itself. Their explanations, I have tried to show through an précis of our survey, include interpretations, readings, exfoliations of meanings, and understandings of, as well as claims about what is central, primary, or most important in, part or the whole of the play.

What is true of explanation in our survey holds for explanation in *Hamlet* criticism from Hanmer to the present: all the talk of true interpretation, correct reading, what is primary, true understanding, and the meaning, as they apply to *Hamlet,* is explanation. I shall not try to support this claim since it involves detailed examination of every critic in the corpus of *Hamlet* criticism. Instead I assume that our survey is a fair sample and that the role of explanation in it is typical of explanation in *Hamlet* criticism.

Now, if we generalize from this survey, can we state certain characteristics that these explanations of the data in *Hamlet* share, such that a precise elucidation of their logical functioning can be given?

What is immediately striking about explanation in the criticism of *Hamlet* is its parallel with evaluation. In both, there are formulations of principles, their applications, and the confirmations of them. They differ mainly in that explanation aims at true clarification; evaluation, at true assessment. Whether the latter is possible, I shall reserve for the next chapter. Whether true clarification of part or the whole of *Hamlet* is possible, I shall try to determine after an elucidation of critical explanation.

In his explanation of *Hamlet*, the critic begins with his true (or false) descriptions of some of the data in the play. He then asks of these data *why* they are what (he says) they are or *how* they relate to each other? In answering these questions, he introduces a hypothesis that he derives from another, more general, hypothesis about human nature, certain metaphysical facts (e.g., the tragic fact in the world), historical facts, or the nature of poetic drama. This hypothesis—psychological, metaphysical, historical, or aesthetic, in any one of their great variety—is conceived of by him as a *true* statement about objective facts in human life, history, or poetic drama.

It is in the derivation of his specific hypothesis about *Hamlet* that the critic ties his explanation to a poetics, in particular, to a category of explanation according to which *Hamlet* can and should be best explained by psychology, metaphysics, history, or aesthetics. It is also at this juncture that criticism and critical "schools" join because the critic, in his statement of his general hypothesis (about life, history, or poetic drama), implies an answer to How can we best explain (understand, read) a work of dramatic art like *Hamlet?* Criticism as explanation, at least so far as *Hamlet* criticism is concerned, thus, does seem to function in dependence upon a theory about which category or combination of categories of explanation is most effective in a resultant clarification of the play. The critic, in his explanation of *Hamlet*, hence, implies or states explicitly an answer to What is the best way (through psychology, metaphysics, history, or aesthetics:

through character analysis, the nature of tragedy, intellectual or dramatic historical facts, myth and ritual, imagery, theme, symbolism, or organic unity, etc.) to explain it? as well as an answer to From what general metaphysical, psychological, historical, or aesthetic hypothesis or hypotheses shall one derive a particular hypothesis about *Hamlet?*

He then introduces his specific hypothesis about *Hamlet* in order to answer Why these data? or How do they relate? But in answering these questions he may, as many critics do, introduce a further hypothesis about a purported datum or the primacy of a particular datum. Bradley's and Jones's insistence upon the primary character of Hamlet's delay; Eliot's, on the primacy of Hamlet's emotion toward a guilty mother; and Knight's, on the theme of life versus death as central, are cases in point, where the data themselves are attributed ones, hypothesized by the critic. That Hamlet delays is given in the play, but that his delay is central or even that Hamlet is central is not; that Hamlet suffers is given in the play, but that his suffering is his central trait and that this trait is most important in the play are not given. What is central, primary, most important, or what is *the* theme of *Hamlet* is not a datum but a hypothesis, which the critic defends by further hypotheses: from a specific hypothesis about *Hamlet* to a general one about drama. Consequently, what supremely complicates this aspect of explanation is that the critic in saying why or how things are in *Hamlet* has already identified real data that can be described with hypothetical ones that cannot be described at all.

After introducing his hypothesis about *Hamlet,* the critic confirms it by a more or less detailed reading of one or other aspect of *Hamlet* or of the whole play.

His whole explanation of part or the whole of *Hamlet*—his category or particular method of explanation, his general hypothesis, his specific hypothesis, his description of data, and his confirmation—is offered as true, testable, and complete, that is, his explanation purports to be based upon true principles, to give true reasons for or correct causes of the data (some or all of it) in *Hamlet,* and to cover its data without distortion.

If we are to comprehend why there is such vast and perennial disagreement over competing explanations (readings, statements of meanings, etc.) of *Hamlet,* we must perceive the range of this disagreement as it encompasses debates and disputes about the categories or methods of explanation of *Hamlet;* the general hypotheses about human nature, tragedy, assorted historical facts, and the nature of drama; the relevancy of these categories and general hypotheses to *Hamlet;* the specific hypotheses about parts or the whole of *Hamlet;* the hypothetical as against the given data; and the adequacy of the hypotheses to cover all the data, attributed or undeniable, without distortion. It is simply a fact about critical explanations of *Hamlet* that critics may and do disagree with one another about each of these parts of explanation. Hence, a critic's explanation, reading, understanding, or interpretation of *Hamlet,* his statement of its meaning or of what is central in it may be challenged on any of the levels of explanation: from his category (for example, that *Hamlet* should be explained historically) to his reading of a particular passage (for example, that Hamlet spares the King at prayer out of hardness of heart, not weakness). An ideal explanation of *Hamlet,* therefore, would be one whose statement of method or category of explanation is true; whose general historical, psychological, metaphysical, or dramatic claim is either true or highly probable; whose specific hypothesis about *Hamlet,* some or all of it, is confirmable; and whose confirmation is complete in the sense that it covers all the relevant data without distortion of them.

Can this ideal explanation be realized? Some of the general hypotheses about psychological and historical matters can be established as highly probable; many of the specific hypotheses can be shown to be clear, consistent, and complete in their coverage of the relevant data of the play. But it is difficult to see just how a metaphysical statement about tragedy or the nature of man, or an aesthetic statement about the nature of drama can be established as true. It is equally difficult to understand how one could substantiate a particular method or category of explanation as *the* true or best one. There is nothing logically self-evident or metaphysically or empirically true that could establish the claim that psychology, metaphysics, intellectual or dramatic history, myth and ritual, imagery, symbolism, poetry, organic unity, or any other category, is the correct and best one with which to approach and explain *Hamlet*. There is also the further difficulty that many of the statements about the data are not true (or false) but are themselves hypotheses requiring confirmation and justification.

Because of these difficulties, the ideal explanation cannot be attained. Differences, debates, or disagreements are always possible both with regard to the particular category or method of explanation (i.e., the point of view from which the general and specific hypotheses proceed) as well as to what is primary, central, or most important in the whole of *Hamlet* or even in one or other of its parts. Thus, both *what* is to be explained and *how* it is to be explained are constant sources of dispute in the explanatory criticism of *Hamlet*, especially when the particular *what* itself is hypothetical and is derived as primary in the play from the *how* or category of explanation.

There is no true, best, correct, or right explanation, reading, interpretation, or understanding of *Hamlet*, nor can there be as long as debate and doubt are possible on the categories of explanation and on what is primary in the play. Rather, critical interpretations, understandings, statements of meaning, and readings of some or all of *Hamlet* are more or less adequate explanations of some of the describable data of the play. These explanations can only be adjudicated in vague terms as to their adequacy but not in precise terms as to their truth or falsity. Certain minimum criteria, I think, can be stated for their adequacy, although these are not equivalent to the unrealizable criteria of the ideal explanation propounded by the critics of *Hamlet* who set as one of their goals the true explanation of the play. These minimum criteria are: a clear statement or employment of the method or category of explanation adopted by the critic so that we, his readers, know exactly from what point of view he is explaining *Hamlet;* employment of general hypotheses that are relevant to the explanation, empirically verifiable, and already confirmed as highly probable by others or confirmed as such by him in his explanation; a formulation of a specific hypothesis about *Hamlet* that covers the data to be explained without distorting them; and, vaguest of all, a quality of coherence in his whole explanation.

These criteria, I believe, are realizable. Moreover, they are the criteria that readers of the critics (though not the critics as readers of each other) apply to the many different, competing explanations, once the quest for the ideal explanation is repudiated. Judged in terms of these minimum criteria, all the readings, interpretations, understandings, and statements of meanings of *Hamlet* satisfy them more or less. Some fail to meet the first criterion; others employ unempirical or insufficiently confirmed general hypotheses about human nature, history, or drama; still others do not cover all the data relevant to the particular explanation; but most flounder on the hard data they explain by distorting them. Our survey reveals that the distortion of the very data the critic sets out to explain is the dominant failure. One need only think, for example, of Miss Campbell on Hamlet's grief, Bradley on Hamlet's sparing of the King at prayer, Knight on the King at prayer, Jones on Hamlet's feeling for his father, or Stoll on Hamlet's soliloquies, especially the self-reproaches. Finally, many of them—dare I say all?—leave some of their readers with the gnawing feeling that a more coherent account or explanation is possible, one perhaps that does not exaggerate character, plot, theme, imagery, or Hamlet; or perhaps one that places more emphasis than is usual upon some particular aspect of the play, for example, the wonderful variety of experience in *Hamlet* that Dr. Johnson observed but that most of his successors seem to have forgotten.

Critical interpretations, readings, understandings, exfoliations of meanings of, and statements about what is primary, central, or most important in, *Hamlet* are all explanatory. This much I hope I have shown through our survey and by the elucidation of the logical functioning of these concepts. All of them involve the formulation, employment, and confirmation of hypotheses about data; they give reasons for or causes of these data; they provide answers to how these data relate to each other and why they are as they are in the play; and, even though none of them is true or definitive, all of them are more or less adequate in their realization of the minimum criteria for explanation of *Hamlet*.

My description of the logical functioning of interpretations differs from that of certain other philosophers. Consequently, I must now set forth this counterdescription and try to reply to it. The best exposition of it, in my opinion, is in C. L. Stevenson's essay, "Interpretation and Evaluation in Aesthetics" (1950).[1] Basic in his conception of interpretations in criticism is that they do not serve as explanations. Analysis of their role in criticism reveals that they function as resolutions or recommendations on how to respond to, rather than as explanations of, one or more aspects of a work of art.

Stevenson does not discuss any of the critical interpretations of *Hamlet*. But I assume from the examples he offers and the generalization he allows from them that, on his view, the critical remark, "*Hamlet* is a study in the passion of grief," is a typical example.

What, now, would Stevenson say about this remark as it functions in the criticism of the play? On the basis of what he says about similar interpretations, he would say, I think, that: it expresses the critic's (Lily Campbell's) decision to respond to *Hamlet* as a study in the passion of grief; it guides the critic's readers to respond to *Hamlet* as the critic does; it is a result of a careful survey of the possibilities of response to *Hamlet;* it has been arrived at causally, but not inductively or deductively, by much knowledge of relevant matters of fact, for example, about Elizabethan drama and thought; it represents a decision on what is the *proper* response to *Hamlet;* and, most important, it has the same meaning as: "*Hamlet* appears a study in the passion of grief under proper conditions of response," where "proper" means "is to be cultivated" or "should be cultivated" and does not mean "descriptively or scientifically correct." And since "proper" includes in its meaning "is to be cultivated in a certain way," the critical interpretation, "*Hamlet* is a study in the passion of grief," has the same meaning as: "*Hamlet* appears a study in the passion of grief under conditions of response to *Hamlet* that are to be (should be) cultivated by those who care about the play." Critical interpretation, then, for Stevenson, is irreducibly normative, quasi-imperative, and not explanatory at all.

I do not think that I have sacrificed any of the subtleties of

[1] C. L. Stevenson, "Interpretation and Evaluation in Aesthetics," in M. Black (ed.), *Philosophical Analysis* (Ithaca, 1950), pp. 341–83.

Stevenson's analysis by converting it into a purportedly true elucidation of interpretations in *Hamlet* criticism; for the philosophical problem of interpretations turns on which description (if either) is the true one of the logical functioning of interpretations in criticism: Do interpretations function as explanations or as decisions and recommendations in a quasi-imperative, normative sense?

I have already presented my case for interpretations as explanations. It remains, therefore, to reply to Stevenson's view or, at any rate, the view that I have attributed to him.

I agree with him that critical interpretations do express decisions or resolutions on possibilities of response, and that they recommend proper responses. But—and I rest my reply on this single, crucial objection—decisions, resolutions, and recommendations are secondary or accompanying uses that derive from and depend upon the primary use of interpretations as explanations. As derivative, they function exactly like their counterparts in science. The critic decides among possibilities and guides his readers in their responses. But then so does the scientist. And both do so on the assumption that their explanations are proper in the sense of "correct: founded on true or highly probable hypotheses and supported by available evidence." "*Hamlet* is a study in the passion of grief," when said by a critic, expresses a decision on his part and promotes or changes responses on our part, but only because the critic and we, if we accept the interpretation, assume that it summarizes a true or adequate account of the play. The remark is no more normative and quasi-imperative than any other similar scientific, explanatory remark, which also expresses a decision, recommends, and attempts to change our responses, all on the assumption that it is true or adequate and functions in a social context where truth is valued and commands respect.

Stevenson, thus, does not give a true account of critical interpretations. They do not function, except incidentally, as quasi-imperatives. His statement of the identity of the meaning of an interpretive remark with a quasi-imperative one—according to which, if I may improvise on a pattern of analysis that Stevenson advocates, "*Hamlet* is a study in the passion of grief" has the same meaning as "I see *Hamlet* as a study in the passion of grief; do so likewise!"—is itself a proposed use. It is a decision and recommendation on his, the philosopher's, part to read interpretations in criticism as quasi-imperatives.

Of course, there is something to be said for this view: Let us read each critical interpretation (explanation, reading, statement of the meaning, or understanding) of *Hamlet* as an invitation by the critic to respond to the play in the way that he proposes in his interpretation. Like the director of a production of *Hamlet,* the critic rehearses with his readers the various possible ways of viewing the play, then invites them to see it his way, just as the director offers his way of recreating the play in performance to the actors: "See it my way; it is not the only or best way, but it is *a* way."

This recommendation to read critical interpretations as rehearsals and performances and not as true or false statements must nevertheless submit to criteria of adequacy. Even though there is no such thing as the true or the best production or performance of *Hamlet,* there are better and worse ones. Think of the recent productions of *Hamlet:* the effeminate Hamlet of Leslie Howard, the all-action Hamlet of Jean-Louis Barrault, the lyrical Hamlet of John Gielgud, and the Wagnerian Hamlet of Laurence Olivier. Each of these also stands or falls more or less in relation to its realization of the criteria of adequacy. Thus, even if interpretations are read as invitations, in the sense of rehearsals and performances, they are still based upon reasons: we are not merely invited to see the play in a particular way, we are so invited because the invitation is purportedly a just one, i.e., it is assumed to be by the producer or the critic—or by both together as in the classic case of Granville-Barker—as adequate a one as can be secured.

We may now return to our issues and attempt clarification of those that are explanatory. Issues (2), (4), (5), (6), (9), (10), (11), (12), (13), (17), and (21) are, I believe, explanatory, in part or as a whole. I have presented my main point about these issues, that they are not factual, yielding true or false answers as the descriptive issues do, but explanatory, to which more or less adequate answers can be given. Hence, I can afford to be brief in the little I have to add to the clarification of these issues. (Once again I remind the reader that the philosopher's task, as I construe it here, is to clarify the possibilities of solutions to these issues, not to offer answers that compete with the critics'.)

(2) Is Hamlet predominantly callous, cruel, cynical, malcontent, ambitious, obscene, brutal, idealistic, noble, pure, melancholy, or anything else similar to these? Each of these questions, taken separately, turns on the question, What is central, primary, or most important in Hamlet? Consequently, it can be answered only by a specific hypothesis about Hamlet's traits. The adequacy of this hypothesis rests upon a confirmed general hypothesis about human nature as well as upon its coverage of the data regarding Hamlet in the play. Most of these specific hypotheses, for example, that Hamlet is predominantly cruel, callous, cynical, malcontent, ambitious, obscene, or brutal, are inadequate because they omit or distort some of Hamlet's attributes. (They are not inadequate because they involve ambiguous or vague terms.) That Hamlet is predominantly idealistic, noble, pure, or melancholy (which, as hypotheses, involve no problems of ambiguity or vagueness either, at least as our critics dispute them), is more adequate than less. That Hamlet is more melancholy than cruel covers more data in the play than that he is more cruel than melancholy. Nevertheless, many readers of *Hamlet* and, of course, critics who oppose any of these hypotheses feel that none of these hypotheses quite squares with Hamlet's traits either. What, then, is the correct answer to What is central in Hamlet? There is no true answer and none that is completely adequate, that is, none that covers all of Hamlet's ostensible attributes without distortion. Some are more adequate than others. They leave us less unhappy than the others for something more on "the meaning of Hamlet."

(4) Is *Hamlet* a revenge tragedy in which the hero remains ideal? Are Hamlet's self-reproaches self-exhortations, hence, exculpation? What sort of dispute is this between Stoll who gives an affirmative and Wilson who gives a negative reply? Both are wrong, I think, in their assumption that self-exhortation or exculpation is or is not a datum in the play. Whether or not Hamlet exhorts and exculpates himself in his self-reproaches is a hypothesis about the self-reproaches in relation to the other data of Hamlet and the play. Their dispute

over which hypothesis about Hamlet covers most adequately his self-reproaches is explanatory. Stoll's hypothesis fails for Wilson because it does not relate the self-reproaches to Hamlet's and others' sickness at heart and Hamlet's sense of frustration and infirmity; Wilson's objection and counterhypothesis fail for Stoll because they do not relate these very same data of the heart-sickness and Hamlet's frustration to the epical aspects of the tradition of revenge tragedy in which the first datum, along with that of something amiss in Denmark, is part of the intrigue, and the second, part of the momentous action. Their dispute, therefore, is over a large-scale hypothesis and explanation; it is not over whether one of the data of Hamlet is or is not his infirmity. "Self-exhortation," "exculpation," and "infirmity" function as explanatory, not as descriptive, terms in their disagreement. The seemingly descriptive question, Are Hamlet's self-reproaches self-exhortations, hence, exculpation? is not, therefore, descriptive or factual, yielding a true (or false) answer. Instead it functions as an explanatory question and, as such, as part of a larger explanatory problem: Is Stoll's hypothesis about *Hamlet* and its hero adequate? Is it clear, founded on confirmed historical hypotheses? Does it cover all the data, for example, Hamlet's

> I do not know
> Why yet I live to say "This thing's to do,"
> Sith I have cause, and will, and strength, and means,
> To do't . . . [IV, 4, 43–46],

without distortion of them? and, most important, Does it leave us, readers as well as critics, with the feeling that nothing is missing, that *Hamlet* is a typical revenge tragedy?

(5) Does Hamlet rationalize, deceive himself? Why does he delay? The latter—and examples like it can be multiplied: Why does he treat Ophelia as he does? Why does he assume the "antic disposition"? etc.—is clearly explanatory. I can only repeat: Any proffered answer, whatever it may be, is not a true (or false) answer that corresponds to a particular datum or set of data in the play, not even to Hamlet's reference to his melancholy (II, 2, 605); the answer is a hypothesis that is adequate, more or less, where this

hypothesis is presented as part of a larger hypothesis about Hamlet and his role in the play.

Does he rationalize? Does he deceive himself? Both questions are explanatory, not descriptive. They are questions about the adequacy of a hypothesis that purports to explain especially the two data of Hamlet's sparing of the King at prayer and his doubt of the Ghost. Moreover, just as Does Hamlet delay? differs from Why does he delay? in that the first functions descriptively and the second, explanatorily; so Does Hamlet delay? differs from Does Hamlet deceive himself or rationalize? even though the latter question looks similar to the former. For it is not a true (or false) report on the *data* of the play that Hamlet rationalizes; at best, it is a more or less adequate hypothesis about and explanation of his delay or instance of it. How utterly futile it is, then, for critics to argue about this issue (Does Hamlet rationalize or deceive himself?) as if there were some datum or data in the play which can decide it one way or the other.

(6) Is Hamlet a slave of passion, a victim of excessive intellect, a scapegoat, a Baroque hero, or anything similar? These, too, taken individually, are not questions to which a true (or false) answer is forthcoming. Each is an explanatory question which involves a hypothesis about Hamlet in relation to the play, that is more or less adequate in its clarity, assumptions, and coverage of the data of the play.

(9) I have nothing to add to the explanatory character of particular exegeses offered in our discussion of the descriptive and explanatory aspects of exegeses in (9) of the previous chapter.

(10) The explanatory aspects of textual problems were also discussed in the previous chapter. I wish only to supplement what was said there, by way of clarification and not of a particular solution. Claims about Shakespeare's authentic text of *Hamlet*, the transmission of the manuscript, the exact relationship between the various texts of *Hamlet*, and Shakespeare's *Hamlet* as an adaptation of a double-play by Kyd are clearly explanatory in their concern for hypotheses and confirmations of them in relation to the available evidence. Because of the lack of evidence or data that are required and because of

the complexity of the evidence or available data, each of the major explanations and its specific hypothesis about the history of the textual variants of *Hamlet* is at best more rather than less adequate.

(11) Is Hamlet a symbol of death? It should be clear by now, if my view of interpretation as explanation is correct, that this, too, is not a descriptive question as Knight asks it. Nor is his affirmative answer true (or false). Rather his answer is a proposed reading or explanation of Hamlet, that is supported by a specific hypothesis about him which is derived from a larger hypothesis about the play as a dramatization of the conflict between life and death. It, too, is more or less adequate and, I think (to repeat), almost woefully inadequate because of the distortion of the data regarding Hamlet and his struggle with Claudius.

(12) Is Hamlet's emotion in excess of the facts of the play? This is also in part an explanatory issue as Eliot and Wilson debate it in their answers to the question. Eliot's answer is a complex hypothesis: that Hamlet's emotion is his primary trait, that it is central in a play which is for the most part unrelated to that emotion, and that the emotion is that of a son toward a guilty mother. Wilson challenges the whole hypothesis by repudiating the last part of it: it is inadequate, according to Wilson, because it does not account for an incestuous and not merely a guilty mother. Even so, a particular datum is not at stake; what is being disputed is Eliot's hypotheses, joined into one, about ostensible and attributed data. Wilson's is but one challenge. Eliot's explanation remains vulnerable in each part of his grand hypothesis.

(13) Has Hamlet's mystery a heart? What sort of question is this? What sort of answers can be given to it? As Wilson raises it, the question is metaphorical for the questions, Is any one of Hamlet's traits primary? and Can a single hypothesis cover them all? His rejection of a heart to Hamlet's mystery is, I think, a negative reply to both non-metaphorical questions. It is also a meta-explanatory answer to a meta-explanatory question, hence, not simply an answer in competition with others to an explanatory question. For his question, Has Hamlet's mystery a heart? is tantamount to the question, What *sort* of answers can be given to: What is Hamlet's primary trait? and

Which hypothesis covers all his traits? His denial that Hamlet's mystery has a heart is equivalent to a denial that a true explanation of Hamlet is forthcoming. Critics, therefore, do Wilson logical injustice when they identify his meta-explanatory answers to his meta-explanatory questions with competing answers to explanatory questions about Hamlet. Wilson cannot be refuted on his negative answers to his questions (Has Hamlet's mystery a heart?, that is, What is Hamlet's primary trait? and Which hypothesis covers all his traits?) by another explanation of Hamlet, only by a demonstration that a true explanation is forthcoming. In the language of contemporary formal logic, we may say that Wilson's metaphorical question and answer are second-order ones about first-order questions and answers regarding Hamlet's central trait and unity of character. For Wilson, therefore, to claim that there is nothing central in Hamlet or that he is not a unified character (i.e., a character whose total traits can be subsumed under one psychological type) is to claim neither that Hamlet is unintelligible nor that his answers are also competing explanations of Hamlet.

(17) Is *Hamlet* a study in the passion of grief? Is it a myth and ritual celebration of the mystery of human life? Is it a revenge tragedy? Is it a psychological study of a disturbed hero? Is it a dramatization of the Elizabethan conflict between optimism and pessimism? Is it a palimpsest of popular bits of melancholy, malcontentism, and revenge? Is it a metaphorical rendition of the natural condition of man? Is it *any* of the univocal things that the critics claim it is? Elucidation of these questions and their affirmative or negative answers epitomizes what I have tried to say about interpretation and explanation in *Hamlet* criticism. None of these questions is solely about facts or data in *Hamlet;* none yields a true (or false) answer. None of the answers affords the true meaning or even a true meaning; none gives the correct understanding or even a correct understanding; none possesses the true reading or even a true reading—of some or all of *Hamlet.* Instead, each of the answers to the questions is an explanation that involves a particular category or method of explanation, a general hypothesis, a specific hypothesis about *Hamlet* and

what is primary in it, and a confirmation of that specific hypothesis; at most, each answer is more or less adequate in terms of its realization of the minimum criteria of explanation.

(21) How can we best understand *Hamlet* as a work of dramatic art? This question and the many answers to it provided by historical, anti-historical, aesthetic, psychological, and other types of critics, involve evaluative, poetic, and explanatory issues: roughly, issues concerning the meanings of "best," "drama," and "understanding." The only part of this question that can be clarified at this stage concerns understanding: Whatever can be cogently said in answer to (21) must take into account that to provide an understanding of *Hamlet* is the same as explaining it, and that explaining it is not offering true (or false) statements about facts. Hence, "best understanding of *Hamlet*," whatever it does mean, cannot be identified with "true explanation of *Hamlet*." I shall return to this question.

In this chapter, I have tried to show that critical interpretations, readings, understandings, or statements of the meaning, of some or all of *Hamlet*, as the employments of these bring out, are explanatory. I have also tried to show that, although they are alike in their critical functions, they are nevertheless different from descriptions in criticism. This last attempt is more important than the first because it relates to the main theme of the previous four chapters about the logical multiplicity of *Hamlet* criticism. My major claim in this chapter, thus, is that questions like Does Hamlet delay? and the answers to it function differently from questions like Does Hamlet rationalize? and the answers to it. The first are descriptive, the second, explanatory. If this is correct, then solutions of many problems in the criticism of *Hamlet* rest on an understanding and acknowledgement of this distinction between these two kinds of critical questions and answers.

XVI EVALUATION

EVALUATION is neither a necessary nor a sufficient procedure in the criticism of *Hamlet*. The history of that criticism, as even our limited survey shows, includes much criticism which has nothing whatever to do with evaluation. Contrary claims, that all criticism of *Hamlet* comprises or is identical with evaluation, rest respectively on the confusion of evaluation with an act of choice (i.e., confusing "X is good" with "X is worth criticizing"), or on an honorific redefinition of "criticism" that represents a distortion of the actual functions of critical procedures.

Evaluation is *a* procedure of *Hamlet* criticism. One philosophical task is to elucidate it: to set forth its various forms; to describe what it does and what it tries to do; and to determine whether it succeeds or can succeed in what it tries to do.

Part of this task is already done. Some of the acknowledged major examples of evaluations of Shakespeare's dramas, including *Hamlet*, are presented in chaps. x and xi on "The Major Tradition." There, the evaluative procedures, doctrines, disagreements, and issues of at least five representative critics, Dryden, Pope, Johnson, Coleridge, and Tolstoy, are detailed. The major assumption—the basic agreement—of Shakespearean evaluative criticism, that critical evaluation is an employment of language which makes true (or false) statements about the essential properties of greatness in drama and the realization or absence of them in the dramas of Shakespeare, is stated as well as challenged in chap. xii on "The Issues." What remains, therefore, is to examine this assumption that evaluation of Shakespeare's dramas is true (or false) statement about certain properties and their embodiment in the plays; and to determine the success or failure of evaluation as *true* assessment of Shakespeare's dramas or, more particularly, to attempt a clarification of the issue (23): Is *Hamlet* a great work of dramatic art?

It will serve us well, once again, to begin with a systematic summary of our survey, especially the evaluations made by Dryden, Pope, Johnson, Coleridge, and Tolstoy. What, then, do they do when they evaluate the dramas of Shakespeare in their entirety, individual plays, or certain aspects of one or other of the plays? As our examples show, they do many things: they praise, condemn, defend, extenuate, exhibit, judge, and revaluate.

Do these evaluative activities reduce to one? They do not. Johnson, for example, as judge, weighing evidence and deciding on principles, makes a verdict; but not all evaluation begins or ends with a verdict. Pope exhibits Shakespeare's excellences; he does not—as exhibitor—make a verdict. Coleridge challenges traditional verdicts and attempts a revaluation. Is revaluation the making of a judgment? Is revaluation closer perhaps to jurisprudence? What about extenuating Shakespeare's faults? This is neither praising nor judging, but closer to ascribing; and in Pope's case, of changing the attribution of blame from Shakespeare to his audience. Of course, there are similarities among these activities, but I find no truth and little point in certain contemporary philosophical accounts that assimilate all these evaluative procedures to one, which is then construed as the paradigm case. It is simply a false description of the logical behavior of critical evaluations to say that *all* of them recommend, guide our choices, grade, persuade, judge, counsel, or emote.[1]

Our examples also reveal that critical evaluation is argument. At

[1] See e.g., Hare, *The Language of Morals*, chap. viii; J. O. Urmson, "On Grading," *Mind*, LIX (1950); Stevenson, "Interpretation and Evaluation in Aesthetics"; M. Macdonald, "Some Distinctive Features of Arguments Used in Criticism of the Arts," *Proceedings of the Aristotelian Society*, Suppl. Vol. XXIII; and A. J. Ayer, *Language, Truth and Logic* (New York, 1936), chap. vi.

times, especially when they praise, our representative critics merely exclaim or compose inspired metaphors. But mostly they argue; their arguments are based upon principles and are attempts to determine what Johnson aptly calls "the merit of composition" of Shakespeare's dramas. As argument, this evaluation involves formulation of new and reformulation or employment of traditional principles or criteria of merit, as well as their clarification, justification, and application to the plays. Among these principles or criteria are: the three unities, decorum, propriety, regularity, comprehensibility, originality, metaphysical or moral truth, true-to-life characterization, individuality, variety, and consistency of character, power of evocation, subtlety of exhibition of passion, ability to create and sustain illusion, and organic integration of the various characters, language, plot, and theme. Each of these, or a collection of some of them, is put forth by one critic or another as a necessary or sufficient property, or as a member or members of a disjunctive set of sufficient properties, of great or good drama that Shakespeare's dramas satisfy or do not. Thus, each critic, in arguing his case for Shakespeare's merits or lack of them, does so on the basis of reasons, where these reasons involve certain principles or criteria and the realization of them in the dramas of Shakespeare. Each critic says or implies that his is the true assessment of Shakespeare's merits (or demerits), that his are the true reasons (principles, criteria), and that his is the correct argument for the assessment.

Critical evaluation, thus, contains what we may call an "evaluative utterance" and reasons that are given in support of this utterance. Examples of evaluative utterances in Shakespearean criticism are: "Shakespeare's dramas are good," "They are mediocre," "In them, the neglect of the unities of time and place is not a fault," "His dramas are vulgar and obscene, but these defects were forced upon him by his audience," "The characterization in Shakespeare is superb," "His dramas are partly good, partly bad," and "His dramas are flawless, uncompromisingly great, masterpieces."

The critic, then, in making an evaluation, gives or implies a reason (or reasons) that supports his praise, condemnation, extenuation, defense, exhibition, judgment, or revaluation. His central problem is to validate this relation between his utterance and his reason (or reasons); it is not, as many recent philosophers, especially the logical positivists, have wrongly claimed, to verify his evaluative utterances, i.e., to ascertain or locate the referents of his evaluative predicates. What is involved in this giving of reasons as support for critical evaluative utterances? How, for example, does the critic validate his praise, defense, judgment, etc., of Shakespeare's dramas?

What is involved here, I think, are certain applications of criteria of dramatic merit, the clarification of these criteria, and the justification of them.

The first, the application of criteria, is the giving of reasons in direct support of the utterance; for example, "Shakespeare's dramas are great because they have P," where "P" denotes some criterion like "being true to nature." The application may be general, as it is in Dryden and Pope, or it may be concrete, as it is in Johnson, Tolstoy and, especially, Coleridge. But in either case, the critic supports his evaluative utterance by showing that the dramas possess or do not possess the property (or properties) that makes them great.

The critic, in giving a reason as support for his evaluative utterance, also clarifies his criterion (or criteria). Much evaluative criticism has to do with this clarification. Sometimes, in Coleridge, for instance, the clarification ends in a real definition of the criterion. At other times, in Johnson, for instance, clarification proceeds through examples: Johnson does not define "just representations of general nature," he gives examples of them in Shakespeare's dramas and counterexamples in the dramas of others.

The most troublesome feature of evaluative criticism, however, is not in the application of criteria, their clarification, or even their consistency, since inadequacies here can be easily remedied, but in the justification of the criteria. Every evaluative critic of Shakespeare's dramas commits himself to "P is a great-making property of drama," when he says "Shakespeare's dramas are great because they have P" or "Shakespeare's dramas are not great because they do not have P." His commitment immediately raises the perennial question, "But what has P to do with dramatic greatness?"

This question is a request for a reason for a reason; as such, it implies that a reason can be given in support of a particular criterion, i.e., "P," of dramatic greatness. Yet among our five representative critics, neither Dryden nor Pope offers such a reason for his criterion or criteria. Pope says that among the excellences of the dramas of Shakespeare are originality; individuality, variety, and consistency of character; moving and subtle exhibition of passion; and profundity. But he never raises, let alone answers, the question, What have these qualities to do with dramatic excellence? Dryden thinks that the dramas are great when we feel as well as see what is being depicted. He does not identify dramatic greatness with this quality, but he suggests that it is a great-making property of drama that is present in some of Shakespeare's dramas. In spite of the fact that they do not ask it, both Pope's and Dryden's criteria and their employment of them seem to invite the question, What have these criteria to do with dramatic greatness? Johnson, Coleridge, and Tolstoy, on the other hand, ask and answer, What have their criteria of dramatic merit to do with dramatic greatness? Johnson and Coleridge in particular offer reasons for their reasons in support of their claims that Shakespeare's dramas are great; they attempt to justify their criteria of dramatic greatness as well as to show that Shakespeare's dramas realize them. Johnson claims that Shakespeares's dramas are great because they are just representations of general nature (they have P), and that P pleases us since we repose only on the stability of truth. Thus, he praises Shakespeare's dramas ("They are great"), gives a reason in support of his praise ("Because they are just representations of general nature"), and implies a further reason in support of the first one ("Just representations of general nature satisfy our desire for truth"). Coleridge, or at least in part, also claims that Shakespeare's dramas are great because they are true to nature, and defends his criterion by the further reason that truth to nature produces metaphysical insight.

Johnson and Coleridge exemplify best among our representative evaluative critics the two traditional ways that critics attempt to justify their reasons for their critical praise: (1) to state that the reason given, "Because Shakespeare's dramas have P," implies that P is a necessary or a sufficient property or a member of a disjunctive set of sufficient properties of dramatic greatness; or (2) that P causes Q (e.g., pleasure in truth or metaphysical insight), and that Q is a necessary or a sufficient property or a member of a disjunctive set of sufficient properties of dramatic greatness.

Are there necessary or sufficient properties of dramatic greatness? All five of our representative evaluative critics affirm that there are. But none of them succeeds in showing that there are. For neither their "P"s (e.g., "just representations of general nature" or "truth to nature") nor their "Q"s (e.g., "pleasure in truth" or "metaphysical insight") are established by them as such properties. Nor have their "P"s and "Q"s withstood the challenge of other critics who substitute and argue for different criteria as necessary or sufficient properties of dramatic greatness. Nor do these critics fare any better than our representative ones since their sets of properties have also been challenged and rejected by still other critics. Indeed, the history of dramatic criticism, including criticism of the plays of Shakespeare, is in great part a history of unresolved disagreement over the necessary and sufficient properties of dramatic greatness. If there are such properties, then, we must nevertheless admit that no one has ever stated satisfactorily what they are. There is no property that has been shown on any ground whatever, empirical, conceptual, or metaphysical, to be a necessary or a sufficient property or a member of a disjunctive set of sufficient properties of dramatic greatness; hence, there exists no reason in support of the praise of Shakespeare's dramas that can be said to be a good reason on the ground that it states an established necessary or sufficient property of dramatic greatness.

Can there be these necessary or sufficient properties of dramatic greatness that evaluative critics of Shakespeare's dramas presuppose in their purported justification of their reasons for their praise (or condemnation) of Shakespeare's dramas?

Suppose there can be. Then dramatic greatness itself is a property, albeit a complex one, composed of an exhaustive set of necessary and sufficient, or essential, properties; and the term, "dramatic greatness," or its adverbial derivative, "dramatically great," is a name of this complex property.

Now, if "dramatically great" is the name of a complex property, this term functions grammatically as a predicate that critics employ to describe the property of dramatic greatness. "Shakespeare's dramas are great," then, is a referring *cum* descriptive utterance about the property of dramatic greatness in his dramas. It follows from this that *praising* (or *condemning*) Shakespeare's dramas is really describing them: what begins in critical evaluation as an attempt at a justification of a reason for a reason in support of praise (or condemnation) ends in the elimination of the activity of praising (or condemning) altogether.

Praising (or condemning) Shakespeare's dramas is not identical with describing them. The term, "dramatically great," when used by critics to praise, and the term, "dramatically mediocre," when used by critics to condemn, do not function as descriptive predicates. The assumption, pervasive in evaluative criticism, that there are necessary or sufficient properties, or members of a disjunctive set of sufficient properties, of dramatic greatness, the particular statements of which serve as major premises of deductive evaluative argument and as justifications of evaluative criteria entails that evaluative criticism does not praise (or condemn) but describes. Because this assumption makes impossible the critical procedure of praising (or condemning) the dramas of Shakespeare, it must be repudiated.

The doctrine that critical evaluation of Shakespeare's dramas is true assessment implies that dramatic greatness (or mediocrity) is a property. But dramatic greatness (or mediocrity) cannot be a property without destroying evaluation altogether. Critical evaluation of Shakespeare's dramas, consequently, is not, and, more important, cannot be, true (or false) deductive argument for the merits (or demerits) of these dramas; nor can it be true (or false) empirical statement about their merits (or demerits). The traditional ideal of Shakespearean evaluative criticism, namely, the determination of the merits of Shakespeare's dramas on the basis of principles, has not been and cannot be realized. The persistent failure to provide true assessments of the dramas cannot be remedied; instead the ideal must be relinquished.

If reasons in support of praise (or condemnation) are not and cannot be justified by the further reason that these reasons are about necessary, sufficient, or members of a disjunctive set of sufficient properties of dramatic greatness, what, then, does validate these reasons? Are any of them good reasons; for example, reasons that support the praise of Shakespeare's dramas?

To answer this question, we must reject the pervasive doctrine of Shakespearean evaluative criticism that a good reason in support of praise is one for which a further reason can be given. We must ask instead whether for *every* reason of the form, "Because they have P," offered in support of "Shakespeare's dramas are great," the traditional question, "But what has P to do with dramatic greatness?" is legitimate and forthcoming?

It seems to me, as I read critical evaluation of Shakespeare's dramas, that at least some of the reasons offered in support of the praise of the dramas are good reasons, hence validate the praise, not because further reasons for them can be given, but simply because they employ certain criteria—certain "P"s—about which the question, "But what have these to do with dramatic greatness?" cannot be intelligibly asked since no answer to it can be given.

In both Pope and Coleridge, for example, there are praise utterances about Shakespeare's dramas that are supported by reasons which are different from those reasons (e.g., "Because they are just representations of general nature" or "Because they are true to nature") about which the question, "But what have these to do with dramatic greatness?" is appropriate and legitimate, and which lead to the attempt—unsuccessful, I hope I have shown—to justify these reasons in terms of necessary or sufficient properties of great drama. Pope praises Shakespeare's dramas and offers as a reason for his praise that the characters in them are individuals, various, and consistent, even in their language; he neither proposes nor implies a further reason in justification of his reason for praise. Coleridge, too, praises the dramas: one reason he gives in support of his praise of *Hamlet*, specifically, Hamlet's use of puns, is that these puns intensify the depicted passions, hence move the action of the drama. To be sure, Coleridge imposes on this reason an attempted justification of it by his principle of poetic illusion. But his reason can stand alone; it requires no justification.

Pope's appeal to character delineation and Coleridge's, to the dramatic function of language are prime examples of reasons in evaluative criticism of Shakespeare's dramas that are good reasons, not because they are justified by further reasons, but because they state properties of a work of dramatic art which, although neither necessary nor sufficient properties of dramatic greatness (or even of drama), are such that one cannot sensibly ask, "What have they to do with dramatic greatness?"

There are other examples of good reasons in Shakespearean evaluative criticism. A superb one is Coleridge's persistent employment of the criterion of unity which, unfortunately and quite unnecessarily, he tries to defend by the further and false metaphysical principle of organic form in nature. "Shakespeare's dramas are great because in them character, plot, theme, and language work together to form an integrated whole" stands alone. Once the reason is clarified and applied with particularity to the dramas, it needs no justification. For what further reason for the reason, "Because they are unified," could be offered in support of the praise of Shakespeare's dramas?

One test of a good reason in evaluative criticism, then, is that it employs a criterion of dramatic greatness which is unchallengeable. Other tests are (the already mentioned) clarity, concrete application, and consistency.

Is the criterion of unchallengeability—that for some employments of criteria of dramatic greatness the question, "What have these criteria to do with dramatic greatness?" cannot be asked because it cannot be answered—a necessary or a sufficient criterion or a member of a disjunctive set of sufficient criteria of good reasons in evaluative criticism? I do not know if it is necessary or sufficient. But it is *a* criterion whether it is necessary or sufficient or neither. Like unity, which can be a criterion of dramatic greatness without being a necessary or a sufficient property of dramatic greatness, unchallengeability can also serve as a criterion of good evaluative reasons without being a necessary or sufficient property of good evaluative reasons.

At least some critical evaluations are or can be validated; that is, some evaluative utterances can be supported by good reasons: by criteria or principles the employment of which cannot sensibly be questioned. If this contention is correct, it refutes two opposing views: the traditional one, shared by the evaluative critics of Shakespeare and many philosophers, that *all* critical evaluative utterances can be supported by reasons which can be defended by further reasons about necessary or sufficient properties of dramatic greatness; as well as the contemporary view that *no* critical evaluative utterance can be supported by good reasons. This latter doctrine, initiated by logical positivism, is held, in one way or another, by C. L. Stevenson, for whom reasons do not support critical evaluative utterances but function instead either to guide our evaluative decisions or as parts of persuasive definitions, a relevant example of which definition would be: "*Hamlet* is dramatically great because it has P and P *is* greatness in drama"; by M. Macdonald, for whom reasons do not support critical evaluative verdicts but serve to convey, present, or show the verdicts, in the manner in which an actor interprets his role or a counsel creates his case; and by A. Isenberg, for whom reasons do not support critical judgments but serve instead as linguistic directions for experiencing the work of art as the critic does, the meanings of which directions the reader completes in confrontation with the work.[2] Both the traditional and the contemporary views are in error on the logical role of reasons in critical evaluation.

That some evaluative utterances are supported by good—unchallengeable—reasons, however, does not validate all critical evaluation. Much of it, particularly of the dramas of Shakespeare, remains open to crucial debate, because it involves the persistent application of certain criteria of dramatic greatness that are not unchallengeable and for which unchallengeable reasons cannot be given. That is to say, although it does not make sense to ask of the criteria of unity, individuality, consistency, and variety of character, or subtlety of exhibition of passion, "But what have these to do with dramatic greatness?" it does make sense to ask this question of the criteria of the three unities, propriety, metaphysical or moral truth, true-to-life characterization, evocative power, and the creation of poetic illusion, among others, employed by the critics of Shakespeare.

[2] Stevenson, *op. cit.*; Macdonald, *op. cit.*; and A. Isenberg, "Critical Communication," *The Philosophical Review*, LVIII, No. 4 (1949), 330–44.

Because these latter criteria are challengeable, the contemporary doctrine, that all reasons function in evaluations not as supports for evaluative utterances but as invitations to experience the work as the critic does, can perhaps come into play. Should this happen, however, it cannot be said to be a true philosophical description of critical evaluation but, at most, a philosophical recommendation to salvage much of this evaluation by an arbitrary if attractive transformation of all of this evaluation from argument into art.

How, now, does my elucidation of the critical evaluations of Shakespeare's dramas apply to issue (23): Is *Hamlet* a great work of dramatic art? First, this issue is not and cannot be a factual one that yields a true (or false) answer. "*Hamlet* is a great drama" and "*Hamlet* is a great drama because it has P," whatever "P" may be, are not deductively valid conclusions from true premises about the necessary or sufficient properties of dramatic greatness and the instantiation of these properties in *Hamlet*. Nor are the utterances empirically true (or false) statements about necessary or sufficient properties of dramatic greatness in *Hamlet*.

Rather, "*Hamlet* is a great drama" is an evaluative utterance that praises; and "*Hamlet* is a great drama because it has P" is an expression of praise that is joined by a reason in support of the praise. This reason is a good reason if it employs a clear and empirical criterion that cannot intelligibly be challenged.

"*Hamlet* is great" and "*Hamlet* is great because it has P" are not true (or false) statements. Dramatic greatness is not a property because if it were praising (or condemning) *Hamlet* would be describing *Hamlet*. How, then, can the perennial critical disagreement about whether *Hamlet* is great be resolved by a true answer? *It cannot.* There is nothing in this disagreement—no self-evident intuition, metaphysical essence, or empirical property—about which an answer could be true (or false).

"*Hamlet* is a great drama" or "Hamlet is a great character," therefore, does not function in *Hamlet* criticism like "*Hamlet* is a revenge tragedy" or "Hamlet is melancholy." "Great" is not a term that critics use to describe or to explain, but primarily to praise;

"*Hamlet* is a great drama" is not a sentence that critics employ to state a fact, it, too, functions primarily to praise. It is their assumption of the logical univocity of language that prevents the critics from recognizing that praising is not reducible to describing. As a result, they miss the importance of this fact in the understanding of critical disputation. No critic can resolve the issue of *Hamlet*'s greatness as a drama or of Hamlet's greatness as a character as long as he construes this issue as either descriptive, like Hamlet's melancholy, or explanatory, like *Hamlet* considered as a revenge tragedy.

That the question, Is *Hamlet* a great drama? does not and cannot yield a true (or false) answer must not be interpreted as a "relativistic" solution to the historically important problem of the standards of critical evaluation. For "relativism," as well as "absolutism," "objectivism," "subjectivism," and "impressionism," vehemently opposed to each other though they are, agree completely on the central thesis: that critical evaluations are true (or false) descriptive reports on the merits or demerits of works of art or on our responses to them. I have tried to show that this thesis misrepresents the role of evaluation in criticism.

Nor must the philosophical thesis that "Is *Hamlet* a great drama?" cannot yield a true (or false) answer, be interpreted as meaning that "*Hamlet* is a great drama" is an expression of feeling, a persuasive definition, or an invitation to experience *Hamlet* in the way proposed by the critic.

"Is *Hamlet* a great drama?" although it cannot be answered truly (or falsely), can be answered, like explanatory questions in *Hamlet* criticism (e.g., "Is *Hamlet* a revenge tragedy?"), more or less adequately, except that adequacy in evaluation centers on criteria of merit rather than, as it does in explanation, on hypotheses.

What, then, is a more rather than less adequate answer to Is *Hamlet* a great drama? Whether the critic praises, condemns, judges, or revaluates *Hamlet*, he employs certain criteria in the reasons he gives or implies. These criteria or reasons, first, should be clear or clarified by the critic. They need not be defined. Perhaps some cannot be defined. (What is the definition of "profundity"?) But at least their specific meanings should be made clear by the critic, either explicitly or by examples. On this point, Johnson's "just representations of general nature" is a more adequate criterion than, say, Pope's "original," because Johnson's is rendered clear by examples and Pope's is not clarified at all.

Second, the critic's criteria should be empirical. If, say, the critic gives as a reason for his praise of *Hamlet* that it is true to nature, then he owes us not only a clarification of "true to nature" but some grounding of his term in the ordinary world, so that we, his readers, can verify the term for ourselves. It is no good praising *Hamlet* because it is true to nature and not say what "true to nature" is supposed to describe or not show that the term actually describes something. Coleridge, I believe, comes off badly here because his criterion, "truth to nature," is not empirically ascertainable.

Third, the critic's criteria, when they are employed as a set, should be consistent. It will not do to praise *Hamlet* because it is true to nature and, consequently, induces belief, and, in the same evaluation, to praise it because it is an imitation of nature and, consequently, induces poetic illusion. Something has gone wrong and the critic—in this case, once more, Coleridge—owes us at least a clarification of this apparent inconsistency between belief and the suspension of it.

Fourth, some of the critic's criteria should be unchallengeable: they should relate to the characters, language, and plot of the play—the individuality, variety, and consistency of the characters; the freshness, appropriateness, and poetic qualities, for example, the musical, of the language; and the relevancy and consistency of the episodes in the plot, all working together toward an harmonious drama. Coleridge on the relation between Hamlet and his language, both in dialogue and soliloquies; on the purely dramatic effects of the language of the first scene in relation to the plot; on the introductions of Hamlet and Laertes; on the entrances of the Ghost; on the interfusion of the lyrical with the dramatic; on the qualities of the wit as it moves the action; and on the Player's Speech and the playlet as epical contrasts to the rest of the play—in all these Coleridge gives us brilliant examples of the application of unchallengeable or purely aesthetic criteria to *Hamlet*. Dryden's use of the criterion of the unity of manner and matter of expression in his evaluation of York's speech in

Richard II is another example. Perhaps any *specific application* of an unchallengeable criterion is challengeable. That is, consistency of character, for example, is not open to question as a criterion of evaluation of Shakespeare's dramas; but that Hamlet is consistent may be open to debate. Nevertheless, the critic does his evaluative job when he states and applies unchallengeable criteria of evaluation, however we may disagree with his specific interpretations of them. We may, for example, challenge Coleridge's particular rendition of Hamlet's consistency of character, but we cannot, I think, question Coleridge on consistency of character as a criterion (although not a necessary or sufficient one) of greatness in characterization.

So far as the challengeable criteria are concerned, those having to do with truth, morality, and the emotional effects of drama, the critic, in his almost inevitable employment of them, should also set them out clearly, consistently, and, most important, completely, by articulating their implications, especially for the evaluations of other dramas or works of art. For example, if he employs the criterion of truth in order to assess *Hamlet*, he should tell us—or else we shall do it for him—what is implied by such a criterion. So, too, with any moral criterion. Tolstoy denounces *Hamlet*, along with the other plays of Shakespeare, giving as one of his reasons for doing so that *Hamlet* is immoral; this, for him, means that *Hamlet* is not religiously humanitarian. If *Hamlet* is artistically bad because it is immoral, in Tolstoy's sense, then almost all drama is artistically bad. Now, there is nothing true (or false) in this implication that almost all drama is artistically bad but, for those who disagree, the implication suffices to make them question its premise of the criterion of morality. Thus, at least one test of the adequacy of a challengeable criterion of evaluation is how much it costs and whether we are willing to pay that price. If the acceptance of a criterion for the critical evaluation of *Hamlet* or any other drama or work of art calls for the repudiation of almost all drama or art, it may be an adequate criterion for the assessment of some things, such as Tolstoy's community of universal brotherhood or Plato's Utopia, but it seems hardly adequate for the assessment of dramas as works of art.

Fifth, whatever criteria the critic employs, he should clarify not only their implications but the criteria themselves in the work of art. If he praises *Hamlet* or the whole of Shakespeare's dramas and gives as a reason for doing so that they possess a certain criterion or set of criteria, he should enlarge fully upon their presence in *Hamlet* or all the plays of Shakespeare. Johnson, Coleridge, and Tolstoy, because they apply in great detail their respective criteria of greatness in drama to *Hamlet* or the whole of Shakespeare's dramas fulfil one important criterion of adequacy of critical evaluations. We may reject their particular criteria of evaluation or their particular applications of them, but we must at least recognize that they give us more than generalities as they unfold them in rich and welcome detail. Tolstoy, for example, is more adequate than Dryden in the condemnation of Shakespeare's language: Dryden says Shakespeare is sometimes bombastic but provides no examples; Tolstoy says he is always bombastic and gives many examples. Whatever we may think of these examples or however we may pity Tolstoy for what we regard as his lack of understanding of poetry in drama, at least we must admit that he offers examples, consequently, that he renders specific what he considers to be an undeniable element of mediocrity in Shakespeare's dramas.

Here, then, are five different tests or criteria for the adequacy of evaluative criticism. We cannot, I think, rank these criteria of adequacy so that particular critics can be graded. For we cannot say which criterion of adequacy in the employment of evaluative criteria is most important or which is more important than another. Once the question of the truth (or falsity) of evaluations is repudiated, as it must be, the reader can choose for himself his favorite evaluative critic, giving as the reason for his choice any of these criteria of adequacy: that his favorite critic has clear evaluative criteria, employs primarily aesthetic ones, or applies all his evaluative criteria with great particularity, so that his assessment, whether challengeable or not, is coherent, hence, makes possible another, new response to *Hamlet* or the whole of Shakespeare's plays. Few today regard Johnson's or Coleridge's (or Morgann's, or Schlegel's, etc.) evaluations as defensible; yet readers of Shakespeare's dramas and of his critics keep returning to these critics, not because they speak truly about

Shakespeare's merits, but because they speak clearly, empirically, and, for the most part, richly about the aesthetic, psychological, and moral criteria exemplified in the dramas. Their evaluations, because they speak in such a voice, constitute permanent orientations toward the dramas of Shakespeare.

XVII POETICS

THE CRITICS of *Hamlet* describe, explain, or evaluate the play. Their descriptions, explanations, and evaluations vary within themselves, but they differ logically only among each other. As we have seen, they function differently—they do different critical jobs. Hence, they are irreducible. Of course, they interrelate not only in a single critical essay, short or long but also, sometimes, in a single paragraph or even sentence of criticism. Nevertheless, because they play different roles, they must be kept distinct if they are to be correctly elucidated.

The critics of *Hamlet* also engage in poetics. That is, some of them theorize, in their critical essays on *Hamlet,* on the nature of poetic drama, tragedy, and the relation between drama and real life. To be sure, many employ these concepts of drama, tragedy, representation, or related concepts without definition; but some also attempt definitions, especially of "tragedy" and "poetic drama," which are put forth as real definitions or true statements of the essence of tragedy or poetic drama.

In this chapter, I shall discuss poetics as one aspect of *Hamlet* criticism. The previous examination of description, explanation, and evaluation—if my basic thesis, that they are logically multiple, is correct—should put us on our guard against the assimilation of poetics by any of the other procedures of criticism. Poetics, because of its variety and range in *Hamlet* criticism, may also possess certain logical characteristics that distinguish it from description, explanation, and evaluation. Indeed, my main point in this chapter will be that poetics in *Hamlet* criticism, and elsewhere, is logically distinct from the other procedures of criticism. The recognition of this difference is basic to an understanding and a solution of at least some of the issues in *Hamlet* criticism.

What is poetics? Traditionally, it is the determination of the fundamental principles of one or other of the arts or species of them. What is the nature of literature, painting, sculpture, music, architecture, drama, dance or, latterly, the motion picture? What is poetry, drama, or tragedy? These are among the questions traditionally associated with poetics. To each question, a poetics is a purportedly true answer in the form of a theory of the essential, defining, or necessary and sufficient, properties of the art in question.

In *Hamlet* criticism, poetics has traditionally centered on attempts to state the defining properties of poetic drama and of tragedy, although some of this criticism has also essayed real definitions of characterization, poetry, imagery, ritual, and symbolism.

Poetics, of course, enters *Hamlet* criticism in ways other than these attempts at real, true definition. Some critics, especially the historical, describe and explain the dramaturgy of the Elizabethan age. This, although part of the criticism of *Hamlet*, is not the same as poetics: Stoll, Miss Campbell, Schücking, Spencer, Fergusson, and others state the Elizabethan or Shakespearean theories of drama and tragedy; their statements, as such, are not statements of their own poetics. They may have such a poetics or their historical approach may imply or presuppose a poetics but these are not equivalent to their historical criticism.

Further, some, perhaps all, critics employ certain categories of explanation or certain criteria of evaluation in the criticism of *Hamlet*. This employment may imply or presuppose theories of drama or tragedy or of great drama or great tragedy. But this employment is not the same as explicit essays in theory or real definition.

Eventually this whole question, whether all criticism implies or presupposes a poetics (as well as an aesthetics, i.e., a general theory of art) must be considered. It will facilitate the understanding of the role of poetics and the philosophical issues involved in poetics, however, if I begin instead with some of the particular discussions of the tragic in *Hamlet*. Can a critic say why *Hamlet* is tragic without stating, implying, or presupposing a theory of tragedy? Is there a theory (a poetics, a true statement) of the nature of tragedy? Can there be such a theory? Need there be such a theory in order to guarantee, to render intelligible, critical talk about *Hamlet* as a tragedy or Hamlet as tragic? These shall be the focal questions as we turn to the poetics of tragedy in *Hamlet* criticism.

Once more Bradley is an excellent starting point. We remember from our survey that he asks, Why is Hamlet tragic? and Why is Hamlet the only tragic figure in the play? and that his answers are derived from his answers to the more general questions, What is Shakespearean tragedy? and What is tragedy? Hamlet alone is tragic in the play because only he "rises to the tragic level."

For Bradley, both general questions function as factual questions that can be answered truly (or falsely). Indeed, his answer to What is Shakespearean tragedy? is determined in part by his answer to What is tragedy? Because his answer to What is tragedy? constitutes a poetics or theory of tragedy, poetics is involved in his statement of the nature of Shakespearean tragedy as well as, of course, in his reasons for Hamlet being the only tragic figure in *Hamlet*.

He begins his analysis of Shakespearean tragedy by limiting it to a class of four members: *Hamlet*, *Othello*, *King Lear*, and *Macbeth*. They are the "mature" and "pure" Shakespearean tragedies. The others are either "pure" but "immature," i.e., *Romeo and Juliet;* or tragic histories, for example, *Julius Caesar;* or not really tragic at all, in spite of early classifications of them as tragedies, for example, *Troilus and Cressida*. Bradley's question about Shakespearean tragedy, thus, reduces to the more restricted one: What do the four major tragedies have in common?

His answer, briefly, is this: Each is predominantly the story of one man of a high estate. The story concerns his exceptional and unexpected suffering and calamity that lead to and include his death. His fall and death reverberate upon the welfare of his nation. His suffering and calamity contrast with a previous glory and happiness. This suffering and calamity are also the chief source of our tragic emotions, especially pity.

Further, the hero s fall does not merely happen and is not imposed upon him by non-human forces. Rather, it results from human actions, including his own, that are products of his character and for which he is at least in part responsible.

Other elements are present in the story, among them, abnormal conditions of mind, supernatural intervention, or accidental events. But these are not essential to the tragedy, for they neither originate, compel, nor dominate the causal chain that leads to the catastrophe. They are all subordinate to deeds issuing from character.

The action of these tragedies is a conflict not of an undivided soul against an external force but of a divided soul struggling in part against itself.

The hero is not only responsible for his fall but has, as one cause of his fall, a fatal flaw, his fundamental tragic trait. In each of the heroes, there is a marked one-sidedness, "a fatal tendency to identify the whole being with one interest, object, passion, or habit of mind."[1] But he is also touched by greatness (human excellence), even in his flaw. His fall involves the destruction of that greatness, which moves us not only to pity but to the other tragic emotions of terror, awe, and admiration.

This destruction or self-waste of greatness is the center of the tragedy. The hero, morally good or not, when he falls, epitomizes the tragic fact in the world, which is the irretrievable loss of value, spirit, or greatness. Thus, Shakespeare's dramatic universe of the tragedies is one in which, although there is an ultimate power that is akin to good and alien from evil, good is destroyed and wasted in its struggle with and extirpation of evil. We may experience reconciliation to or even exultation in this self-waste of good, especially when we feel that the hero has never been greater than he is at the moment of death, but we are still left with the sense of the painful mystery of this ultimate,

[1] Bradley, *Shakespearean Tragedy*, p. 20.

undeniable, and unrationalizable fact that something good has been destroyed.

Tragedy, thus, for Bradley, is the inexplicable self-waste of spirit in the conflict of spiritual forces in the world. This is the essence of all tragedy not only of Shakespearean. Bradley makes this explicit in his essay, "Hegel's Theory of Tragedy": "Tragedy portrays a self-division and self-waste of spirit, or a division of spirit involving conflict and waste."[2]

Shakespearean tragedy is tragic and Hamlet is a tragic figure, then, because they satisfy this essential criterion of tragedy.

What, now, is the relation between the essence of tragedy—the self-waste of spirit in the conflict of spiritual forces, with which there is tragedy, and without which there is not tragedy—and the other properties or characteristics that Bradley enumerates in Shakespearean tragedy: a story predominantly of a man of high estate, his exceptional and unexpected suffering and fall, the social reverberations at his fall, the contrast between his previous happiness and fall, his fatal flaw, his moral responsibility, the conflict between the evil that begets disaster and the good that destroys the evil, the death of the hero, and our tragic feelings of pity, fear, terror, awe, admiration, or exultation?

Some of these (to Bradley) are necessary to all tragedy, for example, the hero's moral responsibility, flaw, great suffering, and fall, the collision and conflict of spiritual forces, and the tragic effect.

Others (to Bradley) are constituent properties of Shakespeare's tragedies (as well as other tragedies) but not necessary to all tragedy, for example, the death of the hero, evil as the source of tragedy, and the social reverberations at the fall of the hero.

What, then, according to Bradley, is the relation between the essential properties of tragedy and the properties of Shakespearean tragedy? One wishes he were clearer than he is on this important question. In line with his remarks on the difference between the essence and species of tragedy in the essay on Hegel, I suggest that the relation for him is this: Those properties of Shakespearean tragedy

[2] Bradley, "Hegel's Theory of Tragedy," *Oxford Lectures on Poetry*, p. 86.

that are necessary (but not necessary and sufficient, i.e., essential) to all tragedy are aspects of, or entail the property of, the self-waste of spirit in the conflict between spiritual forces; the other characteristics of Shakespearean tragedy Bradley lists are contributory to, but not necessary or sufficient for, tragedy. Thus, Hamlet's stature, flaw, moral responsibility, exceptional suffering, and fall are aspects of or entail the essential self-waste; whereas Hamlet's death, the evil generated by Claudius' murder of King Hamlet, and the restitution of order by Fortinbras are constituent, contributory characteristics of, but neither necessary nor sufficient to, *Hamlet* as a tragedy.

Is Bradley correct in his views on the nature of tragedy, the nature of Shakespearean tragedy, why Hamlet is tragic, and why he is the only tragic figure in *Hamlet?*

Lily Campbell is certainly one critic of our survey who thinks Bradley is not correct. She rejects his theory of tragedy, his account of Shakespearean tragedy, and his reasons for Hamlet being a tragic figure. All three, she claims, are false; in their place she substitutes her own, purportedly true, views of the nature of tragedy in general and Shakespearean tragedy in particular.

She initiates her attack on Bradley as well as the exposition of her counterviews by challenging his attribution of a subordinate character to the three factors of abnormal conditions of mind, the supernatural, and the accidental in Shakespearean tragedy. Far from being subordinate, they (especially the first) are essential parts of the moral pattern of Shakespearean tragedies. The abnormal conditions of mind, for example, Hamlet's melancholy, Lear's madness, Macbeth's hallucinations, and Othello's epilepsy, "are landmarks on the inevitable progress to doom."[3] They are among the effects of unchecked passion in the struggle between passion and reason, as such, they are also manifestations of sin for which their perpetrators are justly punished by a retributive God.

What are subordinate for Bradley, then, are among the primary or defining properties of Shakespearean tragedy for Miss Campbell. Each of the major four that Bradley discusses she reconstrues as a

[3] Campbell, *Shakespeare's Tragic Heroes*, Appendix A, p. 249.

study in passion. In it, the central figure suffers because his particular passion has not been checked by reason and falls deservedly because this vice or sin of unchecked passion, for which he is to blame, is divinely punished.

The central figure is a tragic hero when his sin is a venial one in which passion remains unchecked by reason. But he is a "hero-villain," not a tragic hero, when his sin is a mortal one in which passion perverts the will and reason directs this perverted will. Bradley's identification of Hamlet and Macbeth as tragic heroes, therefore, is erroneous; what they share is not greatness and its self-waste but slavery to passion.

The function of Shakespearean tragedy is to teach morals in a lively, pleasing manner; specifically, how men are to avoid sin and its just, divine punishment by a proper balance of passion and reason. Shakespearean tragedy, thus, is religious, and Bradley is again wrong in proclaiming it secular.

Shakespearean tragedy, like all other tragedy, presents evil. But it also explains it, especially the tragic fact which is the change from happiness to misery, "the permanent and essential material of tragedy."[4] The Elizabethan and Shakespearean explanation (she says nothing about other tragedies) is the religious one of divine justice for human folly. Hence, Bradley, once more, is wrong: there is no mystery, painful or not, about tragedy. It is an explicable fact in an ordered universe.

There are serious issues between Bradley and Miss Campbell on the nature of tragedy, the nature of Shakespearean tragedy, and what makes *Hamlet* tragic. But I shall postpone discussion of them until I have reviewed or surveyed other doctrines about the nature of tragedy and the tragic in *Hamlet* which enlarge upon and sharpen these issues.

First, let me review briefly some of the views in our survey about *Hamlet* as a tragedy. For Stoll, *Hamlet* is a revenge tragedy, characterized by blood, intrigue, and fate, in which the momentous deed of revenge, as part of the Senecan, epical tradition, comes at the

[4] *Ibid.*, p. 15.

end. Its hero, Hamlet, is the Avenger: noble, ideal, and without a tragic (or other) flaw. He is heroically tragic because he dies young, at the moment of his triumph, with much blood on his hands. Neither his tragedy nor the tragic element in *Hamlet*, in which the central fact is the hero's achievement of the revenge, has anything to do with a self-waste of spirit or a just punishment for the sin of sloth. Both Bradley and Miss Campbell, therefore, are in error in their claims about what makes *Hamlet* and its hero tragic. Since *Hamlet* is a test case of Shakespearean tragedy, as well as of tragedy altogether, they are also wrong in their respective theories; Shakespearean tragedies are neither painful mysteries nor moral *exempla*.

Schücking also stresses the role of the passions in Elizabethan tragedy, including *Hamlet*. But these tragedies, he insists, served neither as moral *exempla*, helping to check the passions, nor as real-life imitations, inviting purgation of them. Rather the aim of Elizabethan tragedy was to arouse the passions. Hence, the climax of each of the tragedies was its exhibition of unrestrained passion. This aim and its realization were aspects of the early Baroque in art, which was characterized by great energy, plenitude of power, exuberance, and heightened contrasts. The arousal of the passions, the aim of Elizabethan tragedy, explains also the Elizabethan tragic hero. For this arousal required a sensational or impressive figure, who outstripped ideal or real-life representation in his intensity, eccentricities, extravagances, and self-exaltation. *Hamlet* and Hamlet are instances of these salient features of the early Baroque in tragedy.

For Fergusson, *Hamlet* is a tragedy in the myth and ritual tradition in which the mystery of the cycle from birth, through maturation and death, to rebirth is celebrated. The progress of the play is its tragic rhythm or action from pollution to health, achieved through suffering and death. Hamlet, the tragic hero, is the appointed witness and scapegoat victim in this purgatorial progress. Yet *Hamlet* is tragic not because of Hamlet, but because of the whole situation, which is the attempt to find and destroy the hidden imposthume that is destroying Denmark. Rituals, invocations, and scourgings are present as part of the celebration. Even the form of the ancient myth and ritual pattern is exemplified in *Hamlet:* prologue, agons, climax, peripety, recognition, pathos, and epiphany.

For Miss Spurgeon, *Hamlet* is tragic because it exemplifies, through its imagery of rottenness, the natural condition of man, his physical corruptibility, which itself is tragic.

Dover Wilson, unlike the others of our survey, does not define "tragedy" in his discussion of the tragic elements in *Hamlet.* Instead he employs certain traditional (more or less) Aristotelian criteria of dramatic tragedy: sympathy for the hero; the moral responsibility of the hero; his greatness; his fall as it is caused by affliction or weakness; and the responses in the spectator of astonishment and awe at human endurance. *Hamlet* is "the tragedy of a genius caught fast in the toils of circumstance and unable to fling free."[5] Hamlet is tragic, not because he is weak, but because of his burden:

> So great is Hamlet's moral stature, so tough is his nerve, that the back does *not* break. But he is crippled, and the arm which should perform the Ghost's command is paralysed. Thus he continues to support the burden, but is unable to discharge it. That, in a sentence, is "the tragical history of Hamlet, Prince of Denmark."[6]

Peter Alexander, in *Hamlet: Father and Son,* also answers the question, Why is *Hamlet* tragic? His answer is based upon a poetics of tragedy that differs radically from traditional theories and, for that reason, is worth detailing here, as I turn from this survey of the views of the critics I have already discussed to some other views on *Hamlet* as a tragedy.

Alexander first formulates, then rejects as false, what he calls the "orthodox" interpretation of the tragic in *Hamlet* and the whole theory upon which that interpretation rests.

According to this orthodox interpretation, *Hamlet* is a tragedy of a man who could not make up his mind. As such, it is a clear case of the traditional conception of tragedy in which *hamartia* (the tragic flaw of the hero) is primary and the main cause of his suffering and fall.

On this view, *hamartia* is a necessary property or condition of tragedy. It not only induces the hero's fall; it also explains and justifies the fall, thus effecting in the spectator a rational acceptance of

[5] Wilson, *What Happens in "Hamlet,"* p. 39.

[6] *Ibid.*, p. 50 (italics in original).

the hero's just and deserved fate. *Catharsis* is the rational acceptance of the hero's fate.

This orthodox view of *Hamlet* and tragedy as primarily *hamartia* claims support from many sources, among them, Hamlet's famous speech on the battlements (I, 4, 13–38), Aristotle's and Bradley's theories of tragedy, and the Greek tragedies. Alexander denies that these sources support the orthodox theory, contending that they serve instead as evidence for his own anti-orthodox explanation of *Hamlet* and poetics of tragedy.

I have already presented Alexander's argument against the orthodox reading of Hamlet's speech in the discussion of his objections to Lily Campbell's reading of it as the key to Hamlet's tragedy. We recall that Alexander points out that Hamlet on the battlements is simply "commenting on a fault in his countrymen that draws on them the censure of the world, and so soils their reputation that their virtues lose all colour and commendation."[7] To read these lines as an explicit or even implicit statement of *hamartia,* then, is to make Hamlet a prophet about himself since, in their context, they are uttered before he could be aware of any dereliction of duty; it is also to make the tragic flaw absurdly large in that the flaw would be present everywhere from "Nature's livery to Fortune's star."

Next, what about Aristotle? Does he, the acknowledged founder of the doctrine of *hamartia,* proclaim it necessary to tragedy? He does not, Alexander says. It is true, of course, that in the *Poetics* Aristotle states that *hamartia* is necessary because without it the spectator would experience revulsion, not *catharsis,* at the hero's fall. But elsewhere, in his poem on his friend, Hermeias, Aristotle's lines,

> Virtue toilsome to mortal race,
> Fairest prize in life,

pay tribute to Hermeias' death by torture without in any way finding a fault in him in order to render the tragedy less odious. In effect, Aristotle here glorifies Hermeias' virtue; he does not chastise him for a flaw or mistake that causes and consummates in a catastrophe.

[7] Alexander, *Hamlet: Father and Son,* p. 40.

The great tragedies of Greece also exemplify this heroic ideal of virtue shining through suffering and calamity. It is therefore incorrect to view them, in the traditional way, as manifestations of divine retribution for human transgression. To make *hamartia* central in, say, *Oedipus at Colonus* is to reduce the play to a piece of nonsense. Like Aristotle, Sophocles glorifies the virtues; in *Oedipus at Colonus,* he celebrates and commemorates the hero's greatness achieved through terrible suffering.

Bradley, too, has been mistaken as an exponent of *hamartia,* even by himself! For, in spite of his ostensible emphasis upon the tragic flaw, Bradley also turns the flaw into virtue by making it the source of the hero's greatness.

Tragedy, then, does not dramatize the faults but the virtues of men. *Arete,* not *hamartia,* is central. Tragedy includes the requisite suffering and calamity, but these need not be created and sustained by human frailty or wickedness. Loyalty, honor, and duty can also effect suffering and catastrophe. *Hamartia,* thus, is not a necessary feature of tragedy and was never meant to be in Aristotle, Bradley, or the Greek tragedies.

Moreover, *catharsis,* as Aristotle understood it, is not a rational acceptance of the fall of the tragic hero through his flaw. *Catharsis* is reconciliation or redemption, that is, an active mastery over the painful aspects of life. Only the glorification of human virtues can render intelligible this experience of *catharsis. Catharsis* as active mastery over the painful is already implicit in Aristotle's *Poetics,* especially in his reply to Plato's attack on tragedy. There Aristotle argues, in effect, that tragedy strengthens rather than weakens man's moral stature. It is also implicit in Bradley's remarks on reconciliation as a part of our response to tragedy. Its best formulation, however, is in Wordsworth and Keats, although they describe the same experience in different words.

Tragedy, for Alexander, thus, is the celebration of the virtues of men—their glory, achieved through affliction and calamity—which produces in its spectators an intense mastery over life's pain:

> What consumes or sweeps away the disagreeables is not some nice calculation arrived at by weighing the hero's fate against the

> faults and mistakes that are inseparable from mortality but the sense of something in mortals that has risen superior to their condition.[8]

In his tragedies Shakespeare glorifies *arete*. To regard *hamartia* as central, which the orthodox view does, is to reduce the tragedies of Shakespeare to mere cautionary tales that would have lost their appeal long ago. *Hamlet*, rather than being a tragedy of a man who could not make up his mind,

> is a kind of consecration of the common elements of man's moral life. Shakespeare introduces the common man in Hamlet not for what we are apt to think of as his "commonness" but for this strange power however you care to name it that he possesses—we have used *arete*, or virtue, or we might have borrowed from Henry James "the individual vision of decency."[9]

More particularly, Hamlet, the tragic hero of the play, consecrates the unity of the virtues represented by the two Hamlets, father and son: "the instinctive wisdom of antiquity and her heroic passions" and "the meditative wisdom of later ages."[10] In the tribulations and final fall of Hamlet, Shakespeare glorifies Hamlet's specific excellence: how to remain humane without loss of toughness.

G. B. Harrison, in *Shakespeare's Tragedies* (1951), also analyzes the tragedies of Shakespeare, including *Hamlet*, by first proposing his (purportedly true) theory of tragedy: "If we are to arrive ultimately at any conclusion or general idea of the quintessence . . . of Shakespearean tragedy, we must first try to define our terms."[11] He defines "Shakespearean," then "tragedy."

So far as "tragedy" is concerned, Aristotle's definition, he says, is still the best. Like Aristotle, we should begin the analysis of tragedy with the concept of dramatic action. Dramatic action has three aspects: actors, a stage, and spectators. Hence, no conception of tragedy is complete without an adequate place for the role of the spectator. "Indeed, Aristotle in his famous definition of tragedy shows that true tragedy only exists when it produces in the spectators a definite emotional reaction, which he calls *catharsis* or purging."[12]

[8] *Ibid.*, pp. 88–89. [9] *Ibid.*, p. 183. [10] *Ibid.*, p. 184.
[11] Harrison, *Shakespeare's Tragedies*, p. 10. [12] *Ibid.*, p. 16.

What, now, is *catharsis?* Harrison, claiming that he is following Aristotle's meaning, says it is a release: "a visible surrender of the emotions." In order to be indulged in fully, this release requires the public character of the theater performance. When this condition is satisfied, *catharsis* (as release)

> leaves the feelings so utterly stirred and drained that one's whole emotional state and balance are for an appreciable time completely changed. . . . The experience is exalting and cleansing, exactly expressed by Aristotle's word "catharsis"—"purgation."[13]

Purgation, thus, for Harrison, is a defining property of tragedy. But not all so-called tragedies effect this purgation. Harrison meets this difficulty not by rejecting them as tragedies but by distinguishing among tragedies those that purge from those that merely end unhappily. The first he calls "deep tragedy," the second, "tragedy."

A deep tragedy is *"a play which when adequately acted before a suitable audience can produce a complete cleansing of the emotions."*[14] One test of a tragedy's being deep is that it evokes the response, "Oh, the pity of it all!" Further defining conditions of a deep tragedy are its means of purgation which include: a profound sense of morality, the expression of the pathos in human suffering, craftsmanship, selection, compression, and inevitability of the action.

In Shakespearean drama, only *King Lear* and *Othello* are deeply tragic. *Macbeth* is not. Nor is *Hamlet* because it

> lacks two of the qualities necessary to produce deep tragedy: a sense of universal morality and inevitability; for Hamlet's death is not the predictable result of error or of mortal frailty but of the chance of combat.[15]

Hamlet is essentially a drama of revenge, which is tragic only because it ends unhappily. But, Harrison adds:

> though not deep tragedy of the kind which utterly purges the emotions, *Hamlet* remains the most fascinating and interesting play in the English language, probably in all drama. . . .[16]

H. B. Charlton, in *Shakespearian Tragedy* (1948), also answers the question, Why is Hamlet tragic? His answer rests not on a theory of

[13] *Ibid.*, p. 17.
[14] *Ibid.*, p. 21 (italics in original).
[15] *Ibid.*, p. 273.
[16] *Ibid.*, p. 110.

tragedy or even of Shakespearean tragedy, which he denies are possible, but on a doctrine of inevitability as basic in tragedy.

Tragedy ends in the death of the hero. But, to be tragic, his death must appear inevitable, deriving, as it were, from some ultimate fact of necessity in the universe. In the Greek tragedies, this ultimate fact is Nemesis. In Shakespeare's, where Fate had already lost its vital hold on Elizabethan imagination, necessity or inevitability is centered in the laws governing human nature. Hence, Shakespeare's tragic drama

> finds its *ultima ratio*, its spring of inevitability, in the interplay of man and the world, in which the subtle though elusive link of psychological cause and effect gives to events sufficient appearance of a cosmic order.[17]

Mere inevitability, however, Charlton implies, is not enough; it must be joined with a greatness in the hero so that his fall holds our sympathy, and it must be integrated with the total inevitability of the action in the particular drama. The inevitable death of a weak person is not tragic; nor is the inevitable death of a hero tragic if his death is imposed upon him by forces that are not integrated in his own nature. What Charlton does, then, is to modify his criterion of inevitability by restricting the range of application of the criterion to a *certain kind* of inevitability, namely, an inevitability that involves great deeds which issue from character. Consequently, his criterion functions for him as an evaluative as well as a descriptive criterion of tragedy. This dual use of inevitability is most obviously present in his discussion of Shakespeare's early tragedies: *Richard III*, *Richard II*, *Romeo and Juliet*, and *Julius Caesar*. They are not really tragic, he argues, because they lack one or other aspect of his qualified criterion of inevitability: Richard III is defeated by God not himself; Richard II is too weak to retain our sympathy; Romeo and Juliet are destroyed by Fate; and neither Julius Caesar nor Brutus is inevitably doomed.

Hamlet, therefore, is the first of the dramas in which Shakespeare realizes the "tragic idea"—an inevitable death that matters. Hamlet is presented as an admirable person whose failure and death do matter, hence, who retains our sympathy, and whose doom proceeds inevitably from his own nature. Why is Hamlet tragic? Because, great and fine

[17] H. B. Charlton, *Shakespearian Tragedy* (Cambridge, 1948), p. 12.

as he is, he fails and dies necessarily. Hamlet, by nature, is incapable of meeting his task. It is not his moral idealism, sensitivity, or reflectiveness that destroys him, but something more fundamental: the way he thinks about things. His mind

> is fired by a temperamental emotionalism and guided by an easily excited imagination. The emotion thrusts one factor of the thinker's experience into especial prominence, and the imagination freely builds a speculative universe in which this prominence is a fundamental pillar.[18]

Hamlet, thus, distorts his world. He mistakes the abstract world, constructed and projected by his emotions and imagination, for the real world in which he must act. Given this propensity toward intellectual distortion, his failure to kill Claudius until it is too late and his death are thus inevitable.

E. M. W. Tillyard relates tragedy to Shakespearean drama in two books, *Shakespeare's Last Plays* (1938) and *Shakespeare's Problem Plays* (1950). He distinguishes between three types of tragedies: suffering, sacrifice, and regeneration. The first involves the suffering of a strong, or of a momentarily strong, character, who is not greatly responsible for his plight and protests against it as he reflects upon it and its place in the universe. *The Duchess of Malfi* is an example. The second, that of sacrificial purgation, is rooted in religion. It has for its characters a god, a victim, a killer, and an audience, and for its aim the riddance of a taint on the social organism. The third

> has to do with renewal consequent on destruction. It occurs when there is an enlightenment and through this the assurance of a new state of being. This kind penetrates deep into our nature because it expresses not merely the tragedy of abnormal suffering but a fundamental tragic fact of all human life: namely that a good state cannot stay such but must be changed, even partially destroyed, if a succeeding good is to be engendered.[19]

For Tillyard, "those tragedies which we feel most centrally tragic contain, with other tragic conceptions, this third one."[20]

[18] *Ibid.*, p. 93.
[19] E. M. W. Tillyard, *Shakespeare's Problem Plays* (London, 1950), p. 14.
[20] *Ibid.*

In his earlier work, *Shakespeare's Last Plays,* Tillyard characterizes this third type as the tragedy of reconciliation, meaning by it, the tragedy of spiritual renewal or reconstruction after disintegration. It symbolizes the cycle of life from birth to destruction that leads to re-creation. One great example of this third type of tragedy is Aeschylus' *Oresteia,* in which the complete tragic pattern from destruction to renewal is recorded. Shakespeare's *King Lear* and *Othello* are other examples.

Hamlet, however, is not an example of the centrally tragic. It is primarily a tragedy of the first type, with elements of the purgatorial as well. But it contains no reconciliation: no revelation, reversal of direction, renewal, or enlightenment. Unlike Othello or Lear, Hamlet undergoes no spiritual change. His speech defying augury (V, 2, 217–22) is crucial here; Tillyard, following Bradley, reads it as an expression of quietism rather than of religious enlightenment. Hamlet remains unregenerated; hence, the play is not tragic in the third and fullest sense.

But not only is *Hamlet* not tragic in the fullest sense; even in the other senses, the tragic is not the central quality of the play. Basic in the play are the themes of the effect of Gertrude's remarriage on Hamlet and the call to revenge; the first, especially Hamlet's awakening to Gertrude's guilt, is the more fundamental one. The coherence and structure of the play inhere in the coexistence of the two themes as Hamlet responds to them. Indeed, the greatness of the play has little to do with the tragic but with the richness and variety of presented experience. "*Hamlet* is best understood as a play . . . presenting the utmost variety of human experience in the largest possible cosmic setting."[21] Thus, it is more accurate to classify *Hamlet* as a problem play than as a tragedy:

> When sheer explication, or abundance of things presented, takes first place, then we leave the realm of tragedy for that of the problem play. Here it is the problems themselves, their richness, their interest, and their diversity, and not their solution or significant arrangement that come first.[22]

[21] *Ibid.,* p. 28.

[22] *Ibid.,* p. 31.

Hamlet is not fully tragic. Nor is the tragic central in it. Tillyard has one further relevant claim. He defends the view that Shakespeare's last plays, *Cymbeline, The Winter's Tale,* and *The Tempest,* are tragic in the third sense. For one element in each play is the regenerative phase of the tragic pattern; *The Winter's Tale* even exhibits the whole cycle. This tragic component of regeneration is joined, more or less successfully, he concludes, with the non-tragic themes of romance in each of these last plays.

There are many more critics who state why *Hamlet* or Hamlet is tragic and formulate theories of tragedy in order to do so.[23] And there are as many critics and philosophers who in their statements of the nature of tragedy imply answers to why *Hamlet* and Hamlet are tragic.[24] But they need not be considered here since our examples adequately represent the major issues of poetics in *Hamlet* criticism.

These representative critics raise the issues: Why is, or what makes, *Hamlet* or Hamlet tragic? What is Shakespearean tragedy? What is the nature of tragedy? Can one say why *Hamlet* or Hamlet is tragic without stating, implying, or presupposing a theory of tragedy? Each of the representative critics asks and answers the first question; each considers his answer a true statement about *a* or *the* tragic property in *Hamlet* and some other answers, false statements about this property. Further, although some of these critics raise doubts about the kind of

[23] Besides the classical discussions of Lessing, the Schlegels, Goethe, Hegel, Schopenhauer, and Nietzsche, there are, among others, these recent discussions of the tragic in *Hamlet:* John Lawlor, *The Tragic Sense in Shakespeare* (London, 1960); Joseph, *Conscience and the King;* Cunningham, *Woe or Wonder;* William Rosen, *Shakespeare and the Craft of Tragedy* (Cambridge, 1960); Brents Stirling, *Unity in Shakespearian Tragedy* (New York, 1956); Robert Speaight, *Nature in Shakespearian Tragedy* (London, 1955); John Vyvyan, *The Shakespearean Ethic* (London, 1959); Willard Farnham, *The Medieval Heritage of Elizabethan Tragedy* (Oxford, 1956); and H. D. F. Kitto, *Form and Meaning in Drama* (London, 1956).

[24] Besides Aristotle, Lessing, Goethe, the Schlegels, Hegel, Nietzsche, and Schopenhauer, there are, among the recent writers on the nature of tragedy: J. W. Krutch, *The Modern Temper* (New York, 1929); F. L. Lucas, *Tragedy* (revised ed.; London, 1957); D. D. Raphael, *The Paradox of Tragedy* (Bloomington, 1960); and T. R. Henn, *The Harvest of Tragedy* (London, 1956).

tragedy *Hamlet* is, for example, Harrison on whether it is "deep" tragedy and Tillyard on whether it is "centrally" tragic, no one of them asks, *Is Hamlet* or Hamlet tragic? Tillyard comes closest to asking this question when he challenges the primacy of the tragic in the play. In the sense in which one could not ask, "Is *Hamlet* really a drama?" without violating the meaning of "drama," could one ask, without violating the meaning of "tragedy," "Is *Hamlet* really tragic?" Much that concerns the logic of "tragedy" turns on the right answer to this question.

What is immediately striking about our critics' answers to the first question is the diversity of the reasons. And what diversity! Thus: Bradley says that *Hamlet* is tragic because its hero, noble in station and virtue, suffers, falls, and dies; that he is partly responsible for his fate as it proceeds from his character, flaw, and inner conflict; and his death involves the destruction, hence waste, of spiritual value which, as we witness this spectacle, induces in us pity, admiration, exultation, and awe at the inexplicable mystery of this waste of good. Miss Campbell counters that *Hamlet* is tragic because it presents the evil exemplified in the sin or vice of unchecked passion, especially in the hero's sin of sloth, and it rationalizes this evil as the just, divine punishment of the hero's fall. Stoll says that *Hamlet* is tragic because Hamlet dies young, with much blood on his hands, but with his task heroically accomplished. For Schücking, *Hamlet* was tragic because it aroused Elizabethans to a high emotional pitch by means of its greater-than-life, impressive hero. (Whether *Hamlet* is still tragic because of its ability to arouse us, Schücking does not say.) Fergusson claims that *Hamlet* is tragic because it celebrates the perennial mystery of human life, with its hero reflecting this mystery as the necessary scapegoat. For Wilson, *Hamlet* is tragic because its hero, great as he is, is unable to discharge his inordinate burden. Alexander considers *Hamlet* tragic because it celebrates, through the hero, human excellence or *arete*, achieved through terrible affliction; by means of this celebration, it effects in us a *catharsis*—active mastery over pain. Charlton says that *Hamlet* is tragic because its worthy hero dies necessarily. Miss Spurgeon finds that *Hamlet* is tragic because it depicts the tragic natural human condition of physical corruptibility. For Harrison, *Hamlet* is tragic because it ends unhappily. Finally, for Tillyard, *Hamlet* is tragic (although not "centrally") partly because its hero suffers, protests against, reflects upon, stoically accepts, and remains not greatly responsible for, his suffering; and partly because Hamlet is a victim in a sacrificial purgation.

In giving a reason for the tragic in *Hamlet,* that is, in saying why *Hamlet* or Hamlet is tragic, the critic states or implies that a certain property or certain properties of the tragic are exemplified in *Hamlet.* These properties serve as criteria for the particular critic's use of the concept of tragedy.

Consider some of these properties: a hero, dramatic conflict, and emotional response; or, more particularly, a noble hero, his flaw or flawless nature, his greatness, his terrible suffering, his fall, deserved or undeserved, his responsibility or lack of responsibility for his plight, the inevitability or contingency of his fall and death, the waste of good, the struggle between good and evil, *arete,* and *catharsis* as purgation, mastery over the painful, redemption, or exultation. However difficult it may be to comprehend some of these properties—those that are not empirical—at least one thing is clear about them: that *Hamlet* as a tragedy cannot possess all of them since some are inconsistent with each other. For example, *Hamlet* cannot be tragic because its hero has a tragic flaw as well as an ideal (flawless) nature, nor can Hamlet be both responsible and not responsible for his plight. Consequently, whatever else can be claimed for these properties, it cannot consistently be said that they are all necessary to tragedy.

Our representative critics disagree on the need for a theory in order to give a reason for *Hamlet*'s being a tragedy. Some, Wilson and Charlton, for instance, do not support their reasons by a theory. But most do. For them, to say that or why *Hamlet* is tragic is to presuppose or imply a theory of tragedy. Their assumption that criticism cannot say that or why *Hamlet* or any drama is a tragedy without an explicit or implicit theory of tragedy is shared by all the great philosophical theories of tragedy from Aristotle, through Lessing, Goethe, Schiller, the Schlegels, Hegel, Schopenhauer, Nietzsche, and Bradley, to J. W. Krutch, U. Ellis-Fermor, F. L. Lucas, and S. K. Langer, among others.[25] All these critics and philosophers concur on the doctrines that "tragedy" denotes a class of works of art; that this class is distinguishable from all other classes; that the members of this class—i.e., all tragedies—possess certain properties that are common and peculiar to these member-tragedies, by virtue of which properties they are tragic; hence, that these properties are necessary and sufficient, essential, or defining ones of tragedy; that a true statement or real definition of the essence of tragedy is forthcoming; and that without such a true statement of the nature of tragedy, critical discourse about particular tragedies cannot be shown to be either intelligible or true; consequently, that one task of philosophical criticism is to provide such a true theory.

Is there, then, a true theory, a poetics, of tragedy? Do any of our representative critics or any of the traditional philosophers provide a true statement of the exhaustive set of necessary and sufficient properties of all tragedies, their common, essential nature, by virtue of which all of them, including *Hamlet*, are tragic? Does any philosophical formula cover all tragedies, Greek, Elizabethan, French, and modern, without leaving out any of them or any of their tragic properties?

The fundamental disagreements on the nature of tragedy even among our representative critics seriously call into question the possibility of arriving at such a true theory. To be sure, they are unanimous on the defining properties of a hero, his suffering and calamity; dramatic conflict involving important values; and the tragic effect. But there is little agreement on the specific requisite attributes of the hero, the cause of his suffering, and the particular response of the ideal spectator. And there is no agreement on what is essential in tragedy. For Bradley, the essence of tragedy is the self-waste of value in the conflict of spiritual forces that ultimately leaves us with a sense of wonder at the inexplicable mystery of unresolved pain in the world. For Miss Campbell, it is the presentation and explanation of evil that leave us rationally satisfied with our ordered universe. For

[25] The new references are: Una Ellis-Fermor, *The Frontiers of Drama* (London, 1948); and S. K. Langer, *Feeling and Form* (New York, 1953).

Alexander, it is the glorification of human virtue as it produces in us an active mastery over life's pain. For Fergusson, it is the celebration of the cycle of life from birth, through death, to renewal. For Miss Spurgeon, it is the natural condition of physical corruptibility. For Harrison, when tragedy is "deep," its essence is a suffering that cleanses. Finally, for Tillyard, when tragedy is "centrally" tragic, the essence of it is regeneration.

Do any of these formulas cover all tragedies and all tragic properties of all tragedies? Each critic claims or implies that his theory does and that the other theories do not; which is one reason why he puts forward a new theory. But every critic who proffers a purportedly true theory of the nature of tragedy is immediately countered by other critics who reject his theory as false or inadequate. Bradley, for example, claims that spiritual waste is the essence of all tragedies. But Miss Campbell, Stoll, Schücking, Fergusson, Miss Spurgeon, Harrison, Charlton, and Tillyard disagree with Bradley, some contending that Bradley's theory does not even cover the tragic in *Hamlet!*

Our representative critics also disagree about the necessary properties of tragedy. Do all tragedies have a hero? Do all tragic heroes possess the tragic flaw? Are all tragic heroes responsible for their fates? Do all of them suffer terribly, fall, and die? Are all touched by greatness? Do all get their just deserts? Do all tragedies commemorate human excellence? Do all end unhappily? Do all stir us deeply or at all? Are all inevitable in their action? Are there conflict and collision in all? Do all induce *catharsis* in any of its numerous senses: redemption, active mastery over pain, purgation, etc.? Do all produce any other uniform effect in their spectators? For each critic who answers affirmatively any of these questions, there is another critic who offers a negative reply. Basic disagreement is rife over both the essential as well as the purely necessary properties of tragedy.

Can this disagreement be resolved? Is there anything that can establish the truth of any theory of tragedy? Perhaps, as most critics think, the disagreement can be resolved by further probing and research.

Two possibilities suggest themselves: dramatic tragedies and the human condition. But neither of these yields a true theory of tragedy. Further research into the whole extant corpus of dramatic tragedies and the resultant probing of their shared properties reveal no essences. What do *Oedipus Rex, Oedipus at Colonus, Medea, Hamlet, Phèdre, Hedda Gabler, The Weavers,* and *The Three Sisters*[26]—to mention but a few tragedies—have in common by virtue of which they are tragic and distinguishable from other works of art? Perhaps they have some similarities but no set of necessary and sufficient properties. Further examination of the human situation will not furnish us with a theory of tragedy either because there is no tragic fact in the world about which a theory of tragedy could be true or which could corroborate such a theory. There may be spiritual waste, loss of greatness, suffering, struggle, defeat, *arete*, regeneration, explicable or inexplicable evil, and *catharsis*. But that any of these, or a collection of them, is tragic cannot be determined by any investigation, past, present, or future.

There is no established true theory of tragedy, offered by the critics of *Hamlet*, other critics, or philosophers, that states the requisite set of essential properties of all tragedies. Further research and probing, no matter how exhaustive or deep, cannot resolve the disagreements among the theories of tragedy or remedy their failure to provide a true, real definition of tragedy. However, the reason that there cannot be a true theory is logical, not factual. For underlying every theory of tragedy, every purportedly true statement of the essence of tragedy, is the assumption that tragedy has a set of necessary and sufficient properties; this assumption is equivalent to the doctrine that the concept of tragedy or the term, "tragedy," or their adjectival derivatives, have a set of necessary and sufficient conditions for their correct, intelligible use. This doctrine is false. That it is false is revealed by the logical behavior of the concept of tragedy, whose use shows that it does not and cannot have a set of essential conditions of employment. All theories of tragedy, thus, misconceive their basic concept: they attempt a definition of a concept whose very employment requires that it have no defining conditions.

[26] F. L. Lucas writes of *The Three Sisters:* "There is, for me, no more really tragic ending in all drama" (*op. cit.*, p. 74).

It is the disagreements over the necessary and sufficient properties of tragedy among the critics of *Hamlet* which furnish the clue to the logical behavior of the concept of tragedy and the consequent impossibility of a theory or poetics of tragedy. Because these disagreements, unlike others in *Hamlet* criticism, are not primarily over the application of accepted criteria, however multiple or fluctuating, for the correct use of certain concepts but over the very criteria themselves. What is central in the disagreements among the theories of tragedy are the debates over which criteria shall determine the correct use of the concept of tragedy. The critics do not dispute, for example, the criteria of "adultery" or "madness" when they argue about whether Gertrude was an adulteress or whether Hamlet was mad; they dispute whether certain criteria apply or do not. But it is precisely the dispute over the criteria of "tragedy" that characterizes their arguments when they attempt a true theory in order to answer Why is *Hamlet* or Hamlet tragic?

The concept of tragedy, thus, is *perennially debatable*. The employment of the concept, especially by the critics in their disputes over the nature of tragedy, reveals that "tragedy" is a term whose every criterion of use is always open to fundamental question, challenge, rejection, and replacement. That the concept of tragedy or the term "tragedy" or their adjectival derivatives are perennially debatable is their most important logical characteristic as they function in *Hamlet* criticism and in all other attempts to state the nature of tragedy. Now, because the concept of tragedy is subject to perennial debate, it *cannot* (logically) have a set of necessary and sufficient conditions of its use. Hence, any theory, poetics, or real definition of tragedy, which must involve a statement of the necessary and sufficient conditions of the employment of the concept of tragedy constitutes a violation of the logic of that concept: One cannot state the essential conditions for the correct use of a concept whose very use precludes such a set of conditions.

"Tragedy" is not definable in the requisite theoretical sense of a true statement of the necessary and sufficient properties of all tragedies because all the purportedly requisite properties are challengeable, emendable, and corrigible. But "tragedy" is not definable (in the theory sense of true, real definition) for another reason, namely, that its use must allow for the ever present possibility of *new* conditions. Think of the history of the concept of tragedy. It is simply a historical fact that the concept, as we know and use it, has continuously accommodated new cases of tragedy and, more important, the new properties of these new cases. Thus, a second logical feature of the concept of tragedy is its *perennial flexibility;* that is, its being applicable to conditions that are unlike those that govern the extant use of the concept. "Tragedy," as its historical employment reveals, has been and still is, employed to talk about past or present tragedies; but it is also part of the task assigned the term to be applicable to future tragedies as well which may differ from the past and present ones as much as the present ones (at any particular time) differ from the past ones. To state the necessary and sufficient conditions for the correct use of the concept of tragedy, then, once again, is to foreclose upon the use of the concept which is, at least in part, to accommodate itself to these new conditions.

Elucidation of the concept of tragedy reveals that a theory of tragedy is not only factually difficult but logically impossible. An important consequence for the philosophy of language follows. Wittgenstein showed that it is a condition of our intelligible, correct employment of language that some of its terms do not, hence need not, have corresponding essences that guarantee their meanings. The elucidation of the concept of tragedy enables us to go beyond his rejection of the assumption that there are or must be essences to affirm that it is a condition of our intelligible, correct use of language that at least one of its terms cannot have a corresponding essence; for "tragedy" is a term whose use entails that there cannot be an exhaustive set of necessary and sufficient conditions for its use. Wittgenstein asks and answers negatively, Does the use of every term, for example, "game," depend upon a set of defining conditions? I am asking and also answering negatively, Can the use of every term, for example, "tragedy," depend upon such a set? It is logically impossible—i.e., a violation of its employment and rules of employment—for "tragedy" to perform the tasks it has been and is designated to perform and at the same time for "tragedy" to depend upon a set of necessary and sufficient conditions.

"Tragedy" is a perennially debatable and flexible term that critics (and others) use to describe or evaluate certain dramas, other works of art, and certain human situations. There are many criteria that govern its correct use; but none, I have argued, that are or can be necessary or sufficient.

Every theory of tragedy—every statement of its essential properties—is not and cannot be a true, real definition of tragedy. Instead, it expresses an honorific redefinition of "tragedy" that restricts the use of the term to a selection from its multiple criteria. Whether "tragedy" is defined as a descriptive or as an evaluative term (for example, Bradley's "pure, mature tragedies," Harrison's "deep tragedies," or Tillyard's "centrally tragic"), the definition represents a selection of, an emphasis upon, and an argument for, some of the many criteria of "tragedy."

It is this selection, emphasis, and argument, rather than the logically vain attempt at real, true definition of what is unamenable to such definition, that give point and value to all the theories of tragedy; for each serves as a recommendation to concentrate upon certain preferred criteria or properties of tragedy that are neglected, distorted, or omitted by other critics. If we attend to these criteria or properties instead of to the unsuccessful essays in essentialist definitions, we can learn much from the individual theories, especially about what to look for in tragedies and how to look at them.

The answer to What is tragedy? then, is not a statement of what all tragedies have in common, of their necessary and sufficient properties. The answer consists primarily in offering undeniable examples, paradigm cases. "*Oedipus Rex* and dramas like it are tragedies" is an adequate answer. *Oedipus Rex*—let us call it A—has certain properties: a hero, terrible suffering, reversal of fortune, reconciliation, momentous action, etc. Let us call these properties, 1, 2, 3, 4, and 5. Now, "dramas like *Oedipus Rex*" refers to dramas B–N that contain properties 1–5; or properties 1–3 but not 4 and 5; or properties 2–5 plus new properties 6–8. Thus, dramas B–N, roughly the history of dramatic tragedies, are tragedies because they have properties, 1–5, 1–3, or 2–5, plus 6 and 7; and so on. They are not tragedies because they have properties 1–5 that are the necessary and sufficient ones of all tragedies. Drama N + 1 (e.g., *Death of a Salesman*), is a tragedy, then, not because it contains a set of essential properties, but because it is like the recognized tragedies A–N in some respects, although it differs from them in others. Knowing what tragedy is, finally, is not knowing a true theory of tragedy, but being able to cite indisputable examples and to decide on the basis of similarities and dissimilarities what else is to count as a tragedy.

Does criticism need a theory of tragedy in order to give intelligible reasons for *Hamlet*'s being tragic? Must it know the essence of tragedy or assume that tragedy has an essence in order to say cogently that or why *Hamlet* or Hamlet is tragic? If criticism requires such a theory then, because there is not and cannot be this theory, discourse about the tragic in *Hamlet* (or in any other work of art) is not intelligible. But this discourse is intelligible, hence, its intelligibility must depend upon something other than a theory. On what, then, do the reasons depend? The critic says, for example, "*Hamlet* is tragic," and gives a reason, "Because it has P," where "P" denotes a property of tragedy. (None of our representative critics ask, "Is *Hamlet* tragic?" Past critics, such as Voltaire, asked this question and denied that *Hamlet* is tragic because it violates decorum, the three unities, and the form of ancient as well as modern (French) tragedy. But Dryden's attack on the French theorists and Johnson's arguments against Voltaire, which were based upon traditional as well as new criteria of "tragedy," established *Hamlet* as one of the paradigms of tragedy. Their arguments against and victory over the French and Voltaire point up once again the perennial debatability and flexibility of the concept of tragedy.) The critic's reason, "Because *Hamlet* has P," is intelligible, has a use, not because "P" is necessary or sufficient for tragedy, but because "P" is a member of an open set of acknowledged (yet debatable) traditional properties or argued-for new properties of the tragic. "*Hamlet* is tragic because its hero, noble in virtue and station, suffers, falls, and dies; is partly responsible for his fate as it proceeds from his character, flaw, and inner conflict; and whose death involves the destruction, hence waste, of spiritual value which, as we witness the spectacle, induces in us pity, admiration, exultation, and awe at the inexplicable mystery of this waste of good" (Bradley) is an intelligible utterance because it employs certain criteria of "tragedy" that derive from the Greek tragedies which, after all, constitute the home base of the concept, and from Bradley's own recommendations and arguments for other, new criteria that were suggested to him by Hegel. "*Hamlet* is tragic because it celebrates the virtues of men" (Alexander) employs an entirely new (i.e., newly-formulated) criterion, that is fully argued-for and that achieves intelligibility because of the open character of the concept of tragedy.

I began this chapter by asking whether, as many critics claim, criticism of *Hamlet* requires a poetics of tragedy in order to give meaning or intelligibility to its reasons for *Hamlet*'s being a tragedy. I have argued that there is no true poetics of tragedy, that there cannot be such a poetics, and that there need not be in order to guarantee the cogency of the reasons. I have also argued that poetics, unlike description, explanation, and evaluation, is an illegitimate procedure of criticism in that it tries to define what is indefinable, to state the necessary and sufficient conditions of the functioning of a concept whose very functioning shows that it has and can have no such conditions. What is tragedy? consequently does not function like Does Hamlet delay? Why does Hamlet delay? or Is *Hamlet* a great drama? in *Hamlet* criticism. Why is *Hamlet* or Hamlet tragic? also differs from the descriptive, explanatory, and evaluative questions of *Hamlet* criticism in that it involves not only debates over the clarification and application of established criteria, whether clear, ambiguous, or vague, but often debates over the very criteria themselves. Further, Is Hamlet the only tragic figure in *Hamlet?* that is, Is Claudius also tragic? cannot be answered as Bradley answers it. For Is Claudius tragic? is not equivalent to Does Claudius satisfy all the requisite essential criteria of the tragic hero? Rather it is equivalent to: Does Claudius satisfy any of the traditional (yet debatable) or newly argued-for criteria of the tragic hero? It is certainly within the compass of the concept of tragedy to allow for cogent argument for the tragic stature not only of Claudius and Hamlet but, if one wishes to follow Schopenhauer for example, of all the characters as they exemplify the sheer suffering of mere existence. There is nothing true or false about "Claudius is tragic." It, too, represents a decision, based on argument for new criteria of the tragic, to extend the concept of the tragic to cover the properties, thence the character, of Claudius.

What about the nature of Shakespearean tragedy as our critics discuss it? Although critics divide sharply on whether they require a theory of tragedy in order to state the defining features of Shakespearean tragedy, it should be clear by now—if my argument against a theory of tragedy is correct—that critical discourse about these features of Shakespearean tragedy is intelligible without such a theory. Instead of beginning with the questions, What makes these tragedies tragic? or Are they tragic? one simply starts with the correct assumption that Shakespearean tragedies are among the indisputable members of the open class of tragedies and form a subclass which have their own set of properties that unite them as well as distinguish them from other tragedies. In effect, one draws a boundary around the concept of tragedy, namely, "Shakespearean" and asks, What characterizes this particular subclass? Each of the theories of Shakespearean tragedies then serves as a statement of the defining features of this subclass of tragedies. In our survey, Bradley's is one such statement; Miss Campbell's, another. Their basic disagreement is not over the presence of the abnormal conditions of mind, the supernatural, and the accidental in Shakespearean tragedy, but over the importance of these in relation to the other features. Even so, theirs is not a factual quarrel that can be settled by a common datum or set of data in the four major tragedies; it involves a disagreement over an explanation of some of the data in the four tragedies, consequently it can be adjudicated only in terms of which hypothesis, Bradley's or Miss Campbell's, is more rather than less adequate in explaining the data of the plays. Perhaps, as Kenneth Muir acutely argues, both are in error in their assumption that even the major four are alike in any important way. In *Shakespeare and the Tragic Pattern* (1958), Muir writes:

"There is no such thing as Shakespearian Tragedy: there are only Shakespearian tragedies."[27] All generalizations about Shakespearean tragedies and all attempts to distinguish among them the "pure" as against the "impure," the "major" as against the "minor," fail because they exaggerate their resemblances and obscure their differences. The English and Roman historical tragedies, *Titus Andronicus, Romeo and Juliet*, the major four, that is, *Hamlet, Othello, King Lear*, and *Macbeth, Coriolanus, Antony and Cleopatra*, and *Julius Caesar* are all tragedies; the assumption, prevalent among critics, that some are not rests on the false thesis that they deviate from the essence of the major four. But the major four, Muir argues, differ as much from each other as the others do among themselves or in relation to the major four. Thus there are many conceptions of the tragic in the tragedies of Shakespeare:

> the medieval idea of the man in high estate brought to his ruin by the workings of fate; the Senecan idea that calamity was inescapable and that man must endure; the idea that the essential function of tragedy was to warn people against pride, ambition, and other vices; the Marlovian idea of man brought to his ruin by excess; and underlying all the Christian idea that misery is often God's punishment for sin, the punishment falling on the innocent as well as the guilty.[28]

The twelve Shakespearean tragedies, consequently, according to Muir, have no properties in common. If they share any one quality, it is the aesthetic quality of *all* great art, the intensity noted by Keats in his maxim:

> The excellence of every art is its intensity, capable of making all disagreeables evaporate, from their being in close relationship with Beauty and Truth.

So much for issue (18): Why is *Hamlet* tragic? What is tragedy? and What is Shakespearean tragedy? My claim about poetics, that it

[27] Kenneth Muir, *Shakespeare and the Tragic Pattern*, Annual Shakespeare Lecture of the British Academy, 1958, p. 146.
[28] *Ibid.*, p. 153.

comprises debates over and recommendations of criteria and not true, real definitions of essences, is relevant to the clarification of issues (19), (20), and (21) as well.

(19) Is *Hamlet* a representation of life? Is it true? Is it to be comprehended as a representation of life? Jones answers these questions affirmatively; Stoll, negatively; Wilson, somewhere in-between. But none of their replies is correct because the questions, although they look (grammatically) like factual ones, function normatively—indeed, elliptically for: *Should Hamlet* be comprehended as a representation of life, hence as true (or false)? The answer to *this* question is neither true nor false; it is a decision and recommendation, which one can accept or reject in accordance with the role one assigns to drama (and art) in one's economy of values.

(20) What defines *Hamlet* as a poetic drama? What is the essence of poetic drama? Is *Hamlet*, as a poetic drama, basically character and plot, symbolism, imagery, myth and ritual, or poetry? It should be clear by now that these questions are bogus, in spite of the heated argument they inspire among contemporary critics. *Hamlet* is essentially none of these: not essentially character and plot, or imagery, or poetry, etc.—nor is any other poetic drama—for the simple but conclusive reason that, like tragedy, poetic drama has no essence, no exhaustive set of necessary and sufficient properties. Of course, it has properties: characters, plot, dialogue, imagery, myth and ritual, symbolism, and poetry. Some, for example, characters, plot, and poetry, are necessary; some, for example, myth and ritual or symbolism, are contingent; none is sufficient; and no collection of them is necessary and sufficient. All the theories of the essence of *Hamlet* as poetic drama—in our survey, Bradley's, Knight's, Fergusson's, and Miss Spurgeon's theories—are at best stipulated, honorific redefinitions of "poetic drama," i.e., recommendations of certain properties rather than others, not true, real definitions of poetic drama at all. Like theories of tragedy, theories of poetic drama serve as much-needed reminders of what we should look for in poetic drama and how we should look at it. The contemporary doctrine that Shakespearean drama is essentially poetry, not character and plot, a doctrine stated not only by Knight, but by L. C. Knights, especially in his well-

known essay, "How Many Children Had Lady Macbeth?"[29] and by D. A. Traversi,[30] among others, is no refutation of Bradley's view of Shakespearean drama; indeed, it plays a more important role than an attempt at refutation, because, in effect, it says: In an age in which character analysis has run riot in the criticism of Shakespearean drama, let us return to the poetry of the dramas. The most effective instrument for initiating and promoting this desiderated shift is the employment of the definitional form: to provide a "persuasive definition" of "poetic drama," which the critics of Bradley have done.

(21) How can we best understand *Hamlet* as a work of dramatic art? Once again, there is no true (or false) answer to this question. To be sure, there are more and less adequate explanations of *Hamlet;* but even a relatively adequate explanation, vague as this is, is not equivalent to the best way to comprehend *Hamlet.* Evaluative, poetic, and aesthetic, as well as explanatory, issues are involved in this question. Every answer ultimately turns on a particular theory of art, an aesthetics. And every theory of art, like every poetics, is neither true nor false, but an honorific redefinition of "art." Consequently, every purportedly true answer to (21) functions instead as a recommendation as to how we, the readers of *Hamlet,* should respond to and comprehend *Hamlet.* Our concern, consequently, should be with the reasons for and the implications of the recommendation, not with its non-existent truth (or falsity).

[29] L. C. Knights, "How Many Children Had Lady Macbeth?," *Explorations* (London, 1951).

[30] Traversi, *An Approach to Shakespeare.*

XVII SUMMARY AND CONCLUSION

IN THIS book I have assumed that the criticism of *Hamlet* is a test case of criticism and that the primary task of philosophy in relation to criticism is to elucidate the various procedures, doctrines, disagreements, and issues of criticism. I have attempted such an elucidation, the net result of which has been to establish the logical multiplicity of *Hamlet* criticism, and, consequently, the falsity of the assumption, pervasive in this criticism, that all its discourse is true or false statement. The critics of *Hamlet* mostly describe, explain, evaluate, or theorize. These four procedures, I have tried to show, are irreducible. Only one, description, is true or false statement, the others are not. That much of the criticism of *Hamlet* is not true or false, hence that many of its disagreements and issues do not yield true or false solutions, is central in the clarification of the reigning problems in *Hamlet* criticism.

My basic claim about the logical multiplicity of *Hamlet* criticism can also be stated with regard to the questions raised by this criticism. The critics of *Hamlet*, we have seen, ask four major types of questions: (1) Does Hamlet delay? Is Hamlet mad? Is Hamlet melancholy? Does Hamlet love Ophelia throughout the play? Does Hamlet say "sullied" in the first line of his first soliloquy? Does Claudius see the dumb-show? Is Gertrude an adulteress? (2) Why does Hamlet delay? Does Hamlet deceive himself? Is Hamlet ideal? What is central or most important in *Hamlet?* Is Hamlet predominantly melancholic? Is there a heart to Hamlet's mystery? Is Hamlet a slave of passion? (3) Is *Hamlet* a great play? Why is it great? (4) Why is *Hamlet* or Hamlet tragic? Is Claudius tragic? What is the nature of tragedy? What is the essence of poetic drama? Is *Hamlet* a true representation of life? How can we best understand *Hamlet?* These four kinds of questions, I have argued, are not of the same type, namely, questions to which true or false answers can be given. There are true or false answers, however difficult it is to determine them, to questions of (1), but not of (2), (3), or (4).

Descriptions in *Hamlet* criticism are true or false statements about *Hamlet:* about its intellectual, dramatic, or social environment; or about its textual history. They are important, not trivial, mainly because they report upon, hence remind us of, the undeniable data of the play or its environment: i.e., the traits of the characters; the sequences of the plot; the qualities of the language; or the various facets of the Elizabethan age.

Explanations in *Hamlet* criticism, although they purport to be true statements about the meaning of *Hamlet* or correct conceptions of *Hamlet,* are at best more or less adequate in terms of the clarity, relevance, and completeness of particular hypotheses about *Hamlet.*

Evaluations in *Hamlet* criticism, which also purport to be true assessments of the play, are not true or false statements about the properties of artistic greatness or the presence or absence of them in *Hamlet;* evaluations are mostly praise or condemnation of the play that are supported by good, that is, unchallengeable, reasons or that are joined by reasons for which further reasons are required but are not provided.

Poetics in *Hamlet* criticism are attempts at true, real definitions of essences that do not exist, need not exist, and, in the case of tragedy, cannot exist. They are logically vain attempts to define the indefinable. Although logically illegitimate, these definitions are, nevertheless, invaluable because they incorporate debates over and recommendations of criteria that function as guides in the enrichment of our understanding of art.

I have also tried to show that interpretation is not the autonomous procedure that some critics claim it is but is the same as explanation; that the meaning of a work of art or of what is central in a work of art are not descriptive but explanatory concepts; that evaluation is often argument, and that good evaluative argument is neither deductive nor inductive argument but simply the employment of unchallengeable criteria in support of praise or condemnation; that dramatic (or artistic) greatness is not a property; that praising and condemning are not describing; and, finally, that criticism need not state, imply, or presuppose a true poetics of drama or tragedy or an aesthetics of art in order to render intelligible or to justify its utterances about *Hamlet*.

Two issues remain: (22) What is the role of scholarship in the criticism of *Hamlet?* Is knowledge of Elizabethan ideas, dramatic devices, political events, and vocabulary a necessary or a sufficient condition of the criticism of *Hamlet?* Is it an intrinsic part of that criticism? Or is it irrelevant? (25) What is the primary aim, task, or function of the criticism of *Hamlet?* Is it to explain *Hamlet*, for example, by probing the meaning of or by stating just what happens in the play? Or is it to evaluate the play?

Neither, we can now see, is a yes or no issue that can be settled by an appeal to the defining properties of criticism. For criticism itself, as this whole survey of *Hamlet* criticism reveals, has no such set of properties. The multiplicity of procedure, doctrine, and disagreement of this criticism incorporates a multiplicity of properties, none of which is necessary and sufficient. Criticism of *Hamlet* includes many things; any claim about what is primary or relevant or necessary or sufficient in criticism, consequently, is not a true (or false) statement about its nature, but an expression of a preference on the part of the particular critic that he converts into an honorific redefinition of "criticism." Criticism has no primary aim, task, or function, except the second-order or general goal of facilitating and enriching the understanding of a work of art. A critic may choose, for example, to evaluate *Hamlet*. For him, scholarship may be at most a necessary condition for his evaluation; that is, he tries to make as sure as he can that the play he is to evaluate is the authentic Shakespearean *Hamlet*. Another critic may choose to explain *Hamlet* in purely Elizabethan terms. For him, scholarship is an integral part of his explanation (criticism). Any specific answer to (22) depends at least in part upon one's answer to (25). Thus, the important thing is to realize that any particular answers to (22) and (25) are not true (or false) statements about the nature of criticism and scholarship but are expressions of preference by an individual critic about criticism and the role of scholarship in it.

BIBLIOGRAPHY

ONLY books cited in the text or notes, or books that relate to the issues in the text, are listed here. Articles from periodicals referred to in the text or notes are not listed here, since the full facts of their publications are given in the notes. Readers who wish to probe further may consult: A. A. Raven, *A Hamlet Bibliography and Reference Guide, 1877–1935* (Chicago: University of Chicago Press, 1936), which enumerates 2,167 items; Clifford Leech, "Studies in *Hamlet*, 1901–1955," *Shakespeare Survey*, IX (Cambridge: Cambridge University Press, 1956); E. K. Chambers, *William Shakespeare: A Study of Facts and Problems* (2 vols.; Oxford: Clarendon Press, 1930); or the readings listed in a good standard textbook, such as G. B. Harrison, *Shakespeare: Major Plays and the Sonnets* (New York: Harcourt, Brace, 1948). D. Nichol Smith's anthology, *Shakespeare Criticism* (Oxford: World Classics, 1916) and Anne Bradby's anthology, *Shakespeare Criticism 1919–35* (Oxford: World Classics, 1936) contain selections from many of the major critics of Shakespeare's dramas from Ben Jonson to E. E. Stoll.

ABRAMS, M. H. *The Mirror and the Lamp: Romantic Theory and the Critical Tradition.* New York: Oxford University Press, 1953.

ADAMS, JOSEPH QUINCY. *Hamlet.* Boston: Houghton Mifflin, 1929.

Joseph Quincy Adams Memorial Studies. Washington: Folger Library Publications, 1948.

ALEXANDER, PETER. *Hamlet: Father and Son.* Oxford: Clarendon Press, 1955.

ANDERSON, RUTH. *Elizabethan Psychology and Shakespeare's Plays.* Iowa City: University Press, 1927.

ARISTOTLE. *The Poetics.* Translated by S. H. BUTCHER. London: Macmillan, 1911.

BIBLIOGRAPHY

Aspects of Shakespeare. Oxford: Clarendon Press, 1933.

AYER, A. J. *Language, Truth and Logic*. New York: Oxford University Press, 1936.

BABCOCK, R. W. *The Genesis of Shakespeare Idolatry, 1766–1799*. Chapel Hill: University of North Carolina Press, 1931.

BEARDSLEY, MONROE C. *Aesthetics: Problems in the Philosophy of Criticism*. New York: Harcourt, Brace, 1958.

Der Bestrafte Brudermord. 1710. Translated as *Fratricide Punished* and reprinted in COHN, ALBERT. *Shakespeare in Germany*. London and Berlin: Ascher, 1865.

BETHELL, S. L. *Shakespeare and the Popular Dramatic Tradition*. London: Staples Press, 1944.

BOWERS, FREDSON. *On Editing Shakespeare and the Elizabethan Dramatists*. Philadelphia: University of Pennsylvania Press, 1955.

———. *Textual and Literary Criticism*. Cambridge: Cambridge University Press, 1959.

BRADBROOK, M. C. *Themes and Conventions of Elizabethan Tragedy*. Cambridge: Cambridge University Press, 1957.

BRADLEY, A. C. *Oxford Lectures on Poetry*. London: Macmillan, 1909.

———. *Shakespearean Tragedy*. London: Macmillan, 1904; 2d ed. 1924.

BRANDES, GEORG. *William Shakespeare*. Translated by W. ARCHER, M. MORISON, and D. WHITE. New York: Macmillan, 1931.

BRIDGES, ROBERT. *The Influence of the Audience on Shakespeare's Drama*. London: Oxford University Press, 1907.

BUSH, GEOFFREY. *Shakespeare and the Natural Condition*. Cambridge, Mass.: Harvard University Press, 1956.

CAMPBELL, LILY B. *Shakespeare's Tragic Heroes: Slaves of Passion*. Cambridge: Cambridge University Press, 1930. Reprinted, New York: Barnes and Noble, 1952.

CAMPBELL, O. J. *Shakespeare's Satire*. New York: Oxford University Press, 1943.

CHAMBERS, E. K. *Shakespeare: A Survey*. London: Sidgwick & Jackson, 1925.

———. *The Elizabethan Stage*. 4 vols. Oxford: Clarendon Press, 1923.

CHARLTON, H. B. *Shakespearian Tragedy*. Cambridge: Cambridge University Press, 1948.

CLEMEN, W. H. *The Development of Shakespeare's Imagery*. London: Methuen, 1951.

COLERIDGE, S. T. *Biographia Literaria*, ed. J. SHAWCROSS. 2 vols. Oxford: Oxford University Press, 1907.

———. *Table Talk*, 1827, ed. H. N. COLERIDGE. London: John Murray, 1835.

———. *Coleridge's Shakespearean Criticism*, ed. T. RAYSOR. 2 vols. Cambridge, Mass.: Harvard University Press, 1930. Reprinted, with minor omissions, in Everyman's Library, Nos. 162 and 183. London: J. M. Dent, 1960.

———. *Coleridge's Writings on Shakespeare*, ed. T. HAWKES. New York: G. P. Putnam's Sons, 1959.

CONKLIN, P. S. *A History of Hamlet Criticism: 1601–1821*. London: Routledge and Kegan Paul, 1957.

CRAIG, HARDIN. *The Enchanted Glass: The Elizabethan Mind in Literature*. New York: Oxford University Press, 1936.

CRANE, MILTON. *Shakespeare's Prose*. Chicago: University of Chicago Press, 1951.

CROCE, BENEDETTO. *Ariosto, Shakespeare and Corneille*. Translated by DOUGLAS AINSLIE. London: George Allen & Unwin, 1920.

CUNNINGHAM, J. V. *Woe or Wonder: The Emotional Effect of Shakespearean Tragedy*. Denver: University of Denver Press, 1951.

DE QUINCEY, THOMAS. "Shakespeare," *Encyclopaedia Britannica*, (7th ed.). Reprinted in part in SMITH, D. NICHOL. *Shakespeare Criticism*.

DOWDEN, EDWARD. *Shakspere: A Critical Study of His Mind and Art*. London: Kegan Paul, Trench, Trubner, 1875.

DRAPER, J. W. *The Hamlet of Shakespeare's Audience*. Durham: Duke University Press, 1938.

DRYDEN, JOHN. *Essays of John Dryden*, ed. W. P. KER. 2 vols. Oxford: Clarendon Press, 1926.

DUTHIE, G. I. *Shakespeare*. London: Hutchinson's University Library, 1951.

———. *The "Bad" Quarto of Hamlet*. Cambridge: Cambridge University Press, 1941.

ELIOT, T. S. *Selected Essays*. London: Faber and Faber, 1932.

ELLIOTT, G. R. *Scourge and Minister: A Study of Hamlet as a Tragedy of Revengefulness and Justice*. Durham: University of North Carolina Press, 1951.

ELLIS-FERMOR, UNA. *The Frontiers of Drama*. London: Methuen, 1945.

English Studies Today, ed. G. A. BONNARD. 2d ser. Bern: Francke Verlag, 1961.

EVANS, B. I. *The Language of Shakespeare's Plays*. Bloomington: Indiana University Press, 1952.

FARNHAM, WILLARD. *The Medieval Heritage of Elizabethan Tragedy*. Oxford: Blackwell, 1956.

FERGUSSON, FRANCIS. *The Idea of a Theater*. Princeton: Princeton University Press, 1949.

GARDNER, HELEN. *The Business of Criticism*. Oxford: Clarendon Press, 1959.

GOETHE, JOHANN WOLFGANG VON. *Wilhelm Meister's Apprenticeship*. Translated by THOMAS CARLYLE. New York: Collier, 1917.

GOLLANCZ, ISRAEL. *The Sources of Hamlet, With an Essay on the Legend*. London: Oxford University Press, 1926.

GRANVILLE-BARKER, HARLEY. *Prefaces to Shakespeare.* 3d ser. London: Sidgwick and Jackson, 1937.

GREENE, ROBERT. *Complete Works,* ed. A. B. GROSART. 15 vols. London: Hazell, Watson and Viney, 1881–86.

GREG, W. W. *The Editorial Problem in Shakespeare: A Survey of the Foundations of the Text.* Oxford: Clarendon Press, 1942.

HANMER, THOMAS. *Some Remarks on the Tragedy of Hamlet.* 1736.

HARBAGE, ALFRED. *As They Liked It.* New York: Macmillan, 1947.

———. *Shakespeare's Audience.* New York: Columbia University Press, 1942.

HARE, R. M. *The Language of Morals.* Oxford: Clarendon Press, 1952.

HARRISON, G. B. *Shakespeare's Tragedies.* London: Routledge and Kegan Paul, 1951.

HARRISON, JANE. *Ancient Art and Ritual.* New York: Henry Holt, 1913.

———. *Themis.* Cambridge: Cambridge University Press, 1912.

HAZLITT, WILLIAM. *Characters of Shakespeare's Plays.* 1817. Reprinted, Oxford: World Classics, 1916.

HEGEL, GEORG WILHELM FRIEDRICH. *The Philosophy of Fine Art.* Translated by F. P. B. OSMASTON. 4 vols. London: G. Bell and Sons, 1920.

HENN, T. R. *The Harvest of Tragedy.* London: Methuen, 1956.

Henslowe's Diary, ed. W. W. GREG. 2 vols. London: A. H. Bullen, 1904–8.

Henslowe's Papers, ed. W. W. GREG. London: A. H. Bullen, 1907.

JAMES, D. G. *The Dream of Learning: An Essay on the Advancement of Learning; Hamlet and King Lear.* Oxford: Clarendon Press, 1951.

JOHNSON, SAMUEL. *Johnson on Shakespeare,* ed. WALTER RALEIGH. Oxford: Oxford University Press, 1908.

———. *Lives of the English Poets.* 1779–81. Reprinted in 2 vols. Oxford: World Classics, 1906.

JONES, ERNEST. *Hamlet and Oedipus.* New York: W. W. Norton, 1949.

JOSEPH, BERTRAM. *Conscience and the King: A Study of Hamlet.* London: Chatto and Windus, 1953.

KAMES, *Lord* (HENRY HOME). *Elements of Criticism.* 1762.

KITTO, H. D. F. *Form and Meaning in Drama.* London: Methuen, 1956.

KNIGHT, G. WILSON. *The Imperial Theme.* London: Oxford University Press, 1931.

———. *The Wheel of Fire.* London: Oxford University Press, 1930; 5th ed. revised. New York: Meridian Books, 1957.

KNIGHTS, L. C. *An Approach to Hamlet.* Stanford: Stanford University Press, 1961.

———. *Explorations.* London: Chatto and Windus, 1946.

KRUTCH, JOSEPH WOOD. *The Modern Temper.* New York: Harcourt, Brace, 1929.

KYD, THOMAS. *Works,* ed. F. S. BOAS. Oxford: Clarendon Press, 1901.

LAMB, CHARLES. "On the Tragedies of Shakespeare, Considered with Reference to their Fitness for Stage Representation." 1811. Reprinted in JONES, E. D. (ed.). *English Critical Essays: Nineteenth Century.* Oxford: World Classics, 1956.

LANGER, S. K. *Feeling and Form.* New York: Scribner's Sons, 1953.

LAWLOR, JOHN. *The Tragic Sense in Shakespeare.* London: Chatto and Windus, 1960.

LEECH, CLIFFORD. *Shakespeare's Tragedies and Other Studies in Seventeenth Century Drama.* London: Chatto and Windus, 1950.

LESSING, GOTTHOLD EPHRAIM. *Hamburgische Dramaturgie.* 1767–69.

LEVIN, HARRY. *The Question of Hamlet.* New York: Oxford University Press, 1959.

LEWIS, C. M. *The Genesis of Hamlet.* New York: Henry Holt, 1907.

Logic and Language, ed. A. FLEW. 1st and 2d ser. Oxford: Blackwell, 1951 and 1953.

LOVEJOY, ARTHUR. *The Great Chain of Being: A Study of the History of an Idea.* Cambridge, Mass.: Harvard University Press, 1936.

LUCAS, F. L. *Tragedy.* revised ed. London: The Hogarth Press, 1957.

MADARIAGA, Salvador de. *On Hamlet.* London: Hollis and Carter, 1948.

MORGANN, MAURICE. "An Essay on the Dramatic Character of Sir John Falstaff." 1777. Reprinted in SMITH, D. NICHOL, *Eighteenth Century Essays on Shakespeare.* Glasgow: MacLehose, 1903.

MUIR, KENNETH. *Shakespeare and the Tragic Pattern.* London: Oxford University Press, 1958.

MURRAY, GILBERT. *The Classical Tradition in Poetry.* Cambridge, Mass.: Harvard University Press, 1927.

MURRY, JOHN MIDDLETON. *Shakespeare.* New York: Harcourt, Brace, 1936.

NASHE, THOMAS. *Works,* ed. R. B. MCKERROW. 5 vols. London: A. H. Bullen, 1904–10.

NIETZSCHE, FRIEDRICH. *The Birth of Tragedy.* Translated by FRANCIS GOLFFING, together with *The Genealogy of Morals.* New York: Doubleday, 1956.

ORWELL, GEORGE. *Selected Essays.* Harmondsworth: Penguin Books, 1957.

OSBORNE, HAROLD. *Aesthetics and Criticism.* New York: Philosophical Library, 1955.

PANOFSKY, ERWIN. *The Life and Art of Albrecht Dürer.* 1 vol. ed. Princeton: Princeton University Press, 1955.

Philosophical Analysis, ed. MAX BLACK. Ithaca: Cornell University Press, 1950.

POLLARD, A. W. *Shakespeare's Fight with the Pirates and the Problems of the Transmission of his Text.* 2d ed., revised. Cambridge: Cambridge University Press, 1920.

POPE, ALEXANDER. *The Works of Alexander Pope*, ed. W. ELWIN and W. J. COURTHOPE. 10 vols. London: John Murray, 1871–89.

QUILLER-COUCH, *Sir* A. T. *Shakespeare's Workmanship*. London: Benn, 1908.

RALEIGH, WALTER. *Shakespeare*. London: Macmillan, 1907.

RALLI, A. *A History of Shakespearean Criticism*. 2 vols. Oxford: Oxford University Press, 1932.

RAPHAEL, D. D. *The Paradox of Tragedy*. Bloomington: Indiana University Press, 1960.

RICHARDSON, WILLIAM. *A Philosophical Analysis and Illustration of some of Shakespeare's Remarkable Characters*. 1774.

ROBERTSON, J. M. *The Problem of "Hamlet."* London: George Allen and Unwin, 1919.

———. *"Hamlet" Once More*. London: R. Cobden-Sanderson, 1923.

ROSEN, WILLIAM. *Shakespeare and the Craft of Tragedy*. Cambridge, Mass.: Harvard University Press, 1960.

RYLANDS, GEORGE. *Words and Poetry*. New York: Payson and Clarke, 1928.

RYMER, THOMAS. *A Short View of Tragedy*. 1693; *The Tragedies of the Last Age Considered*. 1678. Both reprinted in ZIMANSKY, CURT A. (ed.). *Critical Works*. New Haven: Yale University Press, 1956.

SCHILLER, FRIEDRICH. *Essays Aesthetical and Philosophical*. London: Bohn's Standard Library, 1916.

SCHLEGEL, A. W. *A Course of Lectures on Dramatic Art and Literature*. Translated by JOHN BLACK and A. J. W. MORRISON. London: H. G. Bohn, 1846.

SCHLEGEL, FRIEDRICH. *Lectures on the History of Literature, Ancient and Modern*. Translated by J. LOCKHART. 2 vols. Edinburgh: W. Blackwood, 1818.

SCHOPENHAUER, ARTHUR. *The World as Will and Idea*. Translated by R. B. HALDANE and J. KEMP. Reprinted, New York: Doubleday, 1961.

SCHÜCKING, LEVIN LUDWIG. *Character Problems in Shakespeare's Plays*. Translated into English. London: George Harrap, 1922.

———. *The Baroque Character of the Elizabethan Tragic Hero*. London: Oxford University Press, 1938.

———. *The Meaning of "Hamlet."* Translated by G. RAWSON. Oxford: Oxford University Press, 1937.

———. *Shakespeare und der Tragödienstil seiner Zeit*. Bern: A. Franke, 1947.

SHAKESPEARE, WILLIAM. *Hamlet*. First Quarto, 1603, in collotype facsimile. London: Shakespeare Association, 1951.

———. *Hamlet*. Second Quarto, 1604–5, in collotype facsimile. London: Shakespeare Association, 1940.

———. *Hamlet: A New Variorum Edition of Shakespeare:* ed. H. H. FURNESS. 2 vols. (Vols. III, IV). Philadelphia: Lippincott, 1877.

SMITH, D. NICHOL. *Shakespeare in the Eighteenth Century*. Oxford: Clarendon Press, 1928.

SPEAIGHT, ROBERT. *Nature in Shakespearian Tragedy*. London: Hollis and Carter, 1955.

SPENCER, HAZELTON. *The Art and Life of William Shakespeare*. New York: Harcourt, Brace, 1940.

SPENCER, THEODORE. *Shakespeare and the Nature of Man*. 2d ed. New York: Macmillan, 1949.

SPURGEON, CAROLINE F. E. *Shakespeare's Imagery and What It Tells Us*. Cambridge: Cambridge University Press, 1935. Reprinted, Boston: Beacon Press, 1958.

STEWART, J. I. M. *Character and Motive in Shakespeare*. London: Longmans, Green, 1949.

STIRLING, BRENTS. *Unity in Shakespearian Tragedy*. New York: Columbia University Press, 1956.

STOLL, E. E. *Art and Artifice in Shakespeare: A Study in Dramatic Contrast and Illusion*. Cambridge: Cambridge University Press, 1933.

———. *Hamlet: An Historical and Comparative Study* ("Research Publications of the University of Minnesota," Vol. VIII, No. 5, September, 1919).

———. *Hamlet the Man*. The English Association, Pamphlet No. 91, 1935.

SWINBURNE, A. C. *A Study of Shakespeare*. London: Chatto and Windus, 1880.

TILLYARD, E. M. W. *Shakespeare's Last Plays*. London: Chatto and Windus, 1958.

———. *Shakespeare's Problem Plays*. London: Chatto and Windus, 1957.

———. *The Elizabethan World Picture*. London: Chatto and Windus, 1943.

TOLSTOY, LEO. *Recollections and Essays*. Translated by AYLMER MAUDE. Oxford: World Classics, 1937.

TRAVERSI, D. A. *An Approach to Shakespeare*. 2d ed., revised and enlarged. New York: Doubleday, 1956.

TRILLING, LIONEL. *The Liberal Imagination*. New York: The Viking Press, 1950.

VIVAS, ELISEO. *Creation and Discovery*. New York: The Noonday Press, 1955.

VOLTAIRE. *The Letters Concerning the English Nation*. 1733. Ed. CHARLES WHIBLEY. London: P. Davies, 1926.

———. *Appel à toutes les nations de l'Europe*. 1761; *Lettre à l'Académie française*. 1776. Reprinted in *Oeuvres complètes*, ed. L. MOLAND. 52 vols. Paris: Garniers frères, 1877–85.

VYVYAN, JOHN. *The Shakespearean Ethic*. London: Chatto and Windus, 1959.

WALDOCK, A. J. A. *Hamlet: A Study in Critical Method*. Cambridge: Cambridge University Press, 1931.

WALKER, ALICE. *Textual Problems of the First Folio*. Cambridge: Cambridge University Press, 1953.

WALKER, ROY. *The Time is out of Joint: A Study of Hamlet.* London: Andrew Dakers, 1948.

WELLEK, RENÉ. *A History of Modern Criticism.* Vols. I–II. London: Jonathan Cape, 1955.

——— and AUSTIN WARREN. *Theory of Literature.* New York: Harcourt, Brace, 1942.

WERDER, KARL. *The Heart of Hamlet's Mystery.* Translated by E. WILDER. New York: G. P. Putnam's Sons, 1907.

WHITAKER, VIRGIL K. *Shakespeare's Use of Learning: An Inquiry into the Growth of his Mind and Art.* San Marino: The Huntington Library, 1953.

WHITER, WALTER. *A Specimen of a Commentary on Shakespeare.* 1794.

WILSON, JOHN DOVER. (ed.). *Hamlet.* Cambridge: Cambridge University Press, 1934.

———. *The Manuscript of Shakespeare's "Hamlet" and the Problems of its Transmission.* 2 vols. Cambridge: Cambridge University Press, 1934.

———. *What Happens in "Hamlet."* Cambridge: Cambridge University Press, 1935.

WITTGENSTEIN, LUDWIG. *Philosophical Investigations.* Translated by G. E. M. ANSCOMBE. Oxford: Blackwell, 1953.

INDEX